An
Unreasonable
Woman

An Unreasonable Woman

A True Story of Shrimpers, Politicos, Polluters, and the Fight for Seadrift, Texas

Diane Wilson

Foreword by
Kenny Ausubel

CHELSEA GREEN PUBLISHING COMPANY
WHITE RIVER JUNCTION, VERMONT

Editor: John Barstow
Managing Editor: Marcy Brant
Copy Editor: Robin Catalano
Proofreader: Eric Raetz
Designer: Peter Holm, Sterling Hill Productions
Design Assistant: Daria Hoak, Sterling Hill Productions

Printed in the United States on 100 percent pcw recycled paper.
First printing, July 2005
10 9 8 7 6 5 4 3 2 1

Recycled Paper
Chelsea Green sees publishing as a tool for cultural change and ecological stewardship. We strive to align our book manufacturing practices with our editorial mission, and to reduce the impact of our business enterprise on the environment. We print our books and catalogs on chlorine-free recycled paper, using soy-based inks, whenever possible. Chelsea Green is a member of the Green Press Initiative (www.greenpressinitiative.org), a nonprofit coalition of publishers, manufacturers, and authors working to protect the world's endangered forests and conserve natural resources.
   An Unreasonable Woman was printed at Maple-Vail on Ecobook 100 Natural, a 100 percent post-consumer waste recycled, old growth forest-free paper supplied by New Leaf.

Library of Congress Cataloging-in-Publication Data
Wilson, Diane, 1948-
An unreasonable woman : a true story of shrimpers, politicos, polluters, and
the fight for Seadrift, Texas / Diane Wilson.
    p. cm.
ISBN 1-931498-88-1
1. Wilson, Diane, 1948- 2. Shrimpers (Persons)—United States—Biography.
3. Chemical plants—Waste disposal—Environmental aspects—Texas—Seadrift.
4. Environmental protection—Texas—Seadrift—Citizen participation. 5.
Environmentalism—Texas—Seadrift. I. Title.
SH20.W55A3 2005
639'.58'092—dc22

                                   2005009894

Chelsea Green Publishing Company
P.O. Box 428
White River Junction, VT 05001
(800) 639-4099
www.chelseagreen.com

For Wayne, Molly, and Kenny
And the sweet, sweet water underneath my skiff

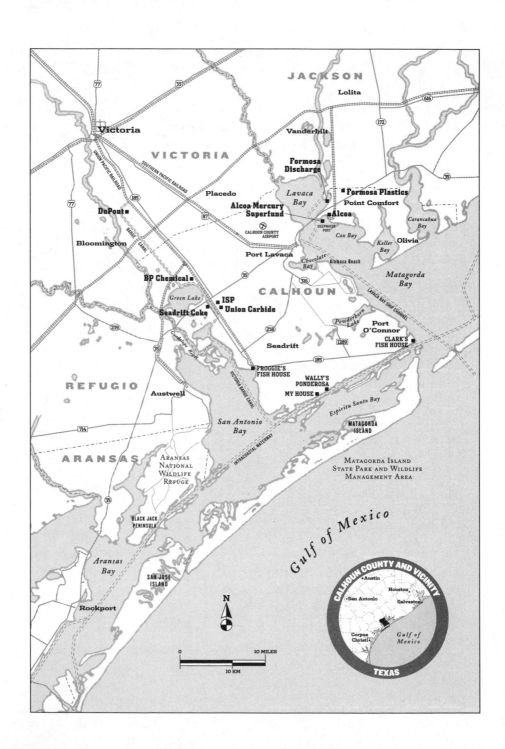

JACKSON

Lolita

Vanderbilt

VICTORIA

Victoria

UNION PACIFIC RAILROAD

SOUTHERN PACIFIC RAILROAD

Placedo

DuPont

Bloomington

BARGE CANAL

Formosa
Discharge

Lavaca
Bay

Formosa Plastics
Point Comfort

Alcoa Mercury
Superfund

Alcoa

CALHOUN COUNTY
AIRPORT

DEEPWATER
PORT

Cox Bay

Carancahua
Bay

Keller
Bay

Olivia

Port Lavaca

Chocolate
Bay

Alamosa Beach

Matagorda
Bay

LAVACA BAY SHIP CHANNEL

BP Chemical

Green Lake

ISP
Union Carbide

Seadrift Coke

CALHOUN

Powderhorn
Lake

Port
O'Connor

CLARK'S
FISH HOUSE

Guadalupe River

Seadrift

REFUGIO

Austwell

VICTORIA BARGE CANAL

FROGGIE'S
FISH HOUSE

WALLY'S
PONDEROSA
MY HOUSE

Espiritu Santo Bay

San Antonio
Bay

MATAGORDA
ISLAND

ARANSAS

Aransas
NATIONAL
WILDLIFE
REFUGE

INTRACOASTAL WATERWAY

MATAGORDA ISLAND
STATE PARK AND WILDLIFE
MANAGEMENT AREA

BLACK JACK
PENINSULA

Gulf of Mexico

Aransas
Bay

SAN JOSE
ISLAND

N

Rockport

0   10 MILES

10 KM

CALHOUN COUNTY AND VICINITY

Austin
Houston
San Antonio
Galveston

Corpus
Christi

Gulf of
Mexico

TEXAS

Contents

Foreword   9
Prologue: Sabotage   15

Part One

  1 Dirty Secrets Revealed   31
  2 A Shrimping Career Rehashed   45
  3 An Outlaw and a Letter   60
  4 Adversaries Approach   70
  5 Of Fishermen and Politicos   81
  6 Knocked Clean out of the Ring   91
  7 Negotiating with the Enemy   102
  8 The Press Arrives to Liars and Fools   113
  9 Texas Water Commission Files   124

Part Two

10 Dirty Facts Revealed   135
11 A Dream Is a Dream Come True   149
12 Losses, Gains, and Petitions   156
13 Money, Money, Money   166
14 The Informant   179
15 Battle Lines Are Drawn   193
16 Union Carbide Blows; the Fed Arrives   204
17 We Strike at the Heart of Formosa   218
18 Beauty Queens, Banquets, and Spies   225
19 Raining on the Chairman's Parade   232
20 A Hydrochloric Cloud; a Worker Talks   245
21 Kickbacks Paid; Internal Memos Conveyed   255
22 A Bay under Siege; an Activist Born   266
23 Hunger Strike   276

24 I Strike at the Gates of Hell   287
25 Death Threats and Deals   299
26 Pain and Defeat   313
27 A Woman Enters the Sea   324

Part Three

28 Island of Fire and Solidarity   333
29 A Radicalized Woman   347
30 The Vietnamese Connection   356
31 The Sinking of the *SeaBee*   367
32 Sanchez Comes Home   374
33 Victory, Redemption, and Loss   384

Epilogue   387
Acknowledgments   390

Foreword

When the first-draft manuscript of *An Unreasonable Woman* arrived in the mail from Diane Wilson, I had already resolved, sight unseen, to option her story for development into a dramatic film. Her larger-than-life heroine's journey had all the makings of an electrifying Hollywood thriller. Visions of *Erin Brockovich*, *Silkwood*, *China Syndrome*, and *The Perfect Storm* danced before my eyes. It would be hard to make up a more dramatic and colorful mythic tale of archetypal heroism than Diane's true story of her epic battle to stop the massive pollution of her beloved Texas Gulf Coast by Formosa Plastics and other giant chemical corporations.

All of us, worldwide, now contain industrial chemicals in our bodies unknown to our grandparents. A *National Geographic* advertisement by the American Plastics Council in 2000 celebrated plastic as the "sixth basic food group." In fact, Americans now ingest an average of 5.8 milligrams a day of DEHP, a phthalate plasticizer used in everything from food wrappings to children's toys, medical devices, and ubiquitous PVC products. DEHP is an endocrine disrupter, a gender bender whose adverse health effects are evident at parts per *trillion*. Such estrogen-mimicking chemicals are associated with early puberty in girls, some as young as one year old. In infants and children, they produce measurable neurological deficits and changes in temperament, including laughing and smiling less, feeling more fearful, and becoming agitated under stress. As Dr. Theo Colborn has said, these chemicals can change the very character of human societies.

The Texas Gulf Coast is one of the richest and most diverse ecosystems in the world. The region's biggest manufacturer of PVC (polyvinyl chloride) is Formosa Plastics, a multi-billion-dollar global octopus that has systematically been plasticizing Lavaca Bay. PVC is one of the most toxic and noxious substances in the organochlorine family of chlorine-based industrial poisons. The international treaty on persistent organic pollutants recently banned these chemicals, and members of the European Union are phasing out their use. It's easy to see how Formosa got its reputation as a poster child for villainous corporations. This leader of Taiwan's petrochemical industry had environmental practices and safety violations so appalling that twenty thousand Taiwanese came out under threat of police violence to protest its proposed new $8 billion complex. That's how Formosa ended up in Texas.

Texas and Louisiana regularly vie for which can lead the nation as the most toxic state, and Texas was willing to give Formosa $200 million in subsidies to retain a shot at the title. When Formosa announced its plans for a $1.3 billion expansion of a plant making the raw materials for PVC, it got the customary red-carpet treatment and chamber-of-commerce confetti parade for creating jobs in an economically depressed region.

All that changed when Diane learned of an EPA report that rated Diane's little Calhoun County (population fifteen thousand) as the most toxic in the nation. Diane wondered if that might help explain the mass dolphin die-offs and alligators floating belly up on her beloved Lavaca Bay. And why the commercial fishing was dying off as well. She decided to ask some questions, and started holding meetings.

With only a high school education (and a dislike of chemistry) Diane taught herself to file successful legal briefs and decipher mountains of scientific and technical EPA records. Her knowledge of Formosa became so intimate that the company's own lawyers routinely called her for information about their operation. After exhausting all other means, she resorted to nonviolent civil disobedience and direct action, ultimately leading her to a daring and likely fatal showdown on Lavaca Bay.

I knew Diane's story because she had spoken at the 1997 annual Bioneers Conference, which I founded. We were doing a special program that year on water, from the myriad environmental threats against water to the hopeful raft of solutions that bioneers—biological pioneers working with nature to heal nature—were applying to cleaning up, conserving, and protecting the world's imperiled waters.

Following talks by an impressive array of accomplished scientists and social innovators, Diane began to speak. She exuded authenticity and sincerity. She described how, as a mother of five and former head of the PTA, she came to challenge some of the largest and most powerful chemical corporations in the world. Growing up, Diane said, the bay was like her grandmother; she spent endless hours in private conversation with her. She took the destruction of the bay very personally. Call it family values.

Once Diane started turning over some political rocks, just about everyone in the tiny company town, who depended on the chemical plants for their livelihood, warned her to back off. She did not. Along the way she realized that when a system is so profoundly corrupt, sometimes upholding the law means breaking the law. The rest is history, or, in this case, her story.

Diane recounted her jaw-dropping tale in the plainspoken eloquence of South Texas. The audience was transfixed. She received a standing ovation. Being unnaturally shy, she practically ran off the stage.

A year later I tried to reach Diane to invite her back to speak at Bioneers, but she seemed to have fallen off the map. Then, two years later, I got a call from her out of the blue. I immediately invited her back to Bioneers, but soon discovered her reason for calling: she had written a book and wanted to know if I would mind looking at it. Like many writers, she was bashful and self-deprecating. Of course I wanted to see the book! I felt as if I were already watching the movie.

It had been an exceedingly long day by the time I plunked down to leaf through Diane's manuscript. It was heavy, weighing in at over seven hundred pages, usually not a good sign. I figured I'd scan the first chapter or two and then call it a night.

Finally I looked up. Many hours had passed. To say the book was a page-turner is an understatement. The story was octaves richer than I could have imagined, filigreed with eye-popping characters and a gemstone narrative.

What I had not anticipated was Diane's dazzling writing. It evokes the magic realism of Gabriel García Márquez, replete with dreams and prophecies. It is richly marbled with the hardcore *realpolitik* of corporate skulduggery, power politics, and the grievous personal betrayals that can turn so bitter in a small, familial community. The numbing contrast between her generational connection to the breathtaking natural beauty of the Texas Gulf and its hideous ravaging by industrial corporations and their political handmaidens conjures powerful visual and visceral resonances.

As a profoundly shy child, Diane filled her solitude with a fertile

inner life that included voracious reading. It shows. Her vivid, idio-
syncratic prose and perfect pitch dialogue resides somewhere between
Alice Walker and William Faulkner. She tosses off metaphors and
imagery like a dog shaking off water in a thunderstorm.

I got up the next morning and played hooky to finish the book. It
never let up. A literary voice like Diane's surfaces only a few precious
times in a generation. I'm sure she did not believe me when I called to
tell her that.

When Diane returned in 2001 to speak at Bioneers, the gathering had
grown to well over two thousand people. Backstage, she was mightily
anxious. I assured her that all she needed to do was be herself and tell
her story as if she were sitting with friends around the kitchen table.
She braced herself, walked onstage, and turned it into a kitchen table.
The audience was rapt, enveloped in deep communion with this
uniquely brave, soulful, and unstoppable woman.

In closing, she read one of her favorites quotes, from George
Bernard Shaw: "A reasonable woman adapts to the world. An unreasonable woman makes the world adapt to her." She looked up, reached
out her arms, and grinned. "So I'm telling all you women out there to
be unreasonable!"

The hall literally shook from the standing ovation. In seismic
California, you never know. In this case, it was raucous, stomping
applause, but it felt like an earthquake.

Several days later, Diane called me back at home. She was bursting
with excitement. Through the rest of the conference, she couldn't walk
ten feet without streams of women coming up to her, tears running
down their cheeks, saying, "Thank you for saying that!" She didn't
know exactly what it meant, but she knew some kind of vision was
unfolding before her eyes.

I pulled my partner and wife Nina Simons onto the call. Nina, who
has co-produced Bioneers with me since its inception, has always
advocated for strong women's voices at the annual conference. Perhaps
as a result, about half the audience are women, an anomaly among
environmental and scientific conclaves. As Diane repeated her story, I
could see the goose bumps rising on Nina's skin.

The result was that Nina hosted a retreat of carefully chosen women
from the Bioneers network. Loosely called Unreasonable Women for

the Earth, the mission was straightforward: collectively imagine a movement capable of catalyzing women's greater participation in taking a stand on behalf of the Earth and people. Survey after survey shows that the huge majority of women worldwide are ardently in favor of environmental protection. Yet for whatever reasons, there has been a historical disconnect between the environmental and women's movements. What if women around the world could mobilize around environmental restoration? What if women could come together and show real leadership with the force of half the world's people?

The retreat was a powerful experience—or so I'm told, since obviously I was not there. One immediate outcome was the birth of Code Pink: Women for Peace (www.codepink4peace.org), cofounded by Jodie Evans, an independent change-maker, and Medea Benjamin, cofounder of Global Exchange.

A month after the retreat, Diane announced her next action to the group: a hunger strike to protest Dow Chemical's refusal to take responsibility for the tragedy of Bhopal, which sickened and killed many thousands of people when a chemical plant exploded. Spontaneously the group organized to support her, sending a relay team of women from around the country to join her, while also organizing protests and media events at Dow factories across the nation. Dow's local PR representative was flummoxed at finding a daisy chain of women from out of town anchored with Diane on a daily basis. It was practically the first time anyone had come to support her over her many years of often dangerous civil disobedience.

I believe that Diane's shared vision is just getting going. Her current mission is to launch a national zero-discharge campaign. Twenty years ago, the federal Clean Water Act mandated use of technologies that contain pollution in a closed industrial loop at the source. The technology is state-of-the-shelf: it's here now. While up-front capital costs can be higher, it gives businesses subsequent cost savings as well as providing obvious environmental virtues. It has long been in use in regions such as the Middle East, where clean water is at a premium. And by the way, soybean and other vegetable oils make perfectly viable substitutes for PVC, phthalates, and plastics. The future of chemistry is green, as we learn how to model how nature does it harmlessly.

Of all the problems we face, transforming the chemical metabolism is perhaps the most doable in the near term. That is perhaps Diane's highest purpose in writing *An Unreasonable Woman*. There is no good reason—legal, technical, economic, or ethical—that industry should be emitting any toxic pollution into the environment, our bodies, and our children's bodies. Diane's own son Crockett is autistic—a condition that could have resulted from the widespread toxic contamination his mother has been struggling to stop. Yes, it gets that personal. None of us is immune, and even gated communities offer no protection against the havoc caused by the pervasive, universal poisoning of the web of life.

Diane likes to say that she is "nobody particular." If she could do what she's done, then anyone can. It's an inspiring message, and it's true. Whatever our own path may be, each of us can rise to the occasion and act. Diane's vision, courage, persistence, and absolute commitment are a beacon to us all. She speaks to our highest aspirations, and hopefully we will rise to meet her challenge.

Diane's astounding journey shows just how great a difference one individual can make. She likes to quote Henry David Thoreau, grandfather of American civil disobedience, who on his deathbed said that his only regret was that he was "too well behaved." Sometimes, as Diane puts it, it takes being outrageous, being "unreasonable." After all, look where reason has gotten us.

You are now holding this book in your hands because of the vision and commitment of Margo Baldwin and Chelsea Green. What every writer hopes for in a publisher is an impassioned champion who truly "gets it." Margo called back just a few days after receiving the manuscript. She, too, had been unable to put the book down. She was roaring to bring it into the world, which is a gift to us all.

Diane could hardly believe that her book was going to be published. In fact, her skeptical ninety-something-year-old mother had promised Diane she would stand on her head if it ever got into print.

I don't know whether Momma is standing on her head right now. But I do imagine that Diane's grandmother—Lavaca Bay—is rolling with swells a head higher and whitecaps a shade brighter. Her granddaughter is as unreasonable as she is, and did not forsake her.

KENNY AUSUBEL
Santa Fe, New Mexico
May 2005

Sabotage

Most shrimpers will admit they go to sea as much for the silence as for the catching of shrimp. At least in the beginning they do. The shrimping was incidental and wasn't what they were really on the water for. If they were lucky they remembered, but if not then they never escaped what years of toiling with nets and poverty and bad weather could exact on a fisherman. So a fisherman's original reason could switch like babies switched in a hospital. Then ten years down the road, a fisherman could suddenly look up and say, "Who the hell is this baby and what is he doing with me?" And the sea that had been the liquid part of his life and had given him balance and purpose and had whispered in his ear who he really, really was, was suddenly nothing more than a backbreaking job.

So I kept my boat, the *SeaBee*, as quiet and as uncluttered as possible. Only nobody was happy about my shrimping alone, and particularly Momma, who said the water was a gravedigger and they were gonna find me drowned out there one fine day. Just see if they didn't.

She told my daddy, Billy Bones, a dozen times a day, "Go talk to that son of yours and make him give her a job on land. That job at the fish house!"

Billy Bones said it was a waste of time. He rarely saw Froggie anymore and the only times he did was to watch him through the kitchen window, carrying one of his shrimp nets out of the barn and into the back end of Froggie's truck.

"That boy would take my underwear if I didn't have 'em on," Daddy said.

Billy Bones had quit the bay. *Officially*, so his nets were fair game. He had walked off his shrimp boat on the very day he had forgotten to tighten a bolt and all the oil in his engine had drained out and ruined a brand new engine. He was seventy-three years old and said he would never set foot on a boat again. He was too old and too stupid. And Daddy never did. But still he pined like a man in the desert dying for want of something. Only he was too stubborn to admit it. Still, whenever I said where I had went shrimping, his eyes would flare like coal in the wind. "That's a good place," he'd say. "I've spent the night out there, nearly right on top of that spot."

Sometimes when I wanted to shrimp someplace new, I'd get Daddy to draw a map of the area. A cut into Spirit Center Bay. The lay of Panther Point Reef. I'd stick my finger on the paper and he'd slap it away, saying, "Leave it alone. I'm doin' it. I ain't that old yet."

So as resolutely as Daddy quit the bay, I worked alone. I left in the dark and came home to the kids by evening. It was the spring run on brownie shrimp, and for several months there was a time and a pound limit. As long as the net was picked up by two o'clock, the game wardens didn't care what time a boat got to the docks. It just mattered to the fish house. No fish house wanted to stay open for hours, waiting on a few straggling boats. Still, I was usually the last boat in. After their last drag, most captains hauled their nets on board, and while their deckhand culled the catch, they headed for the docks. I didn't. I sat in the middle of the bay (the only boat for miles) and culled the catch in silence. Then I iced down the shrimp and washed off the deck, and after hanging the net in the air with a block and whip line, I steered for the docks.

The truth was I was happiest on the bay and loved that it never changed, even when I left. The water had the same smell and the same sounds that I remembered, and it no more changed than the blood in my veins changed. I didn't need to be told that I had went off and danced wildly, then come back tired and weary and lay down hard at her feet. She was the one thing that didn't quit when everything else fled like a fire was driving them.

Every evening and most mornings I took the *SeaBee* through three rituals. I pulled off the engine hatch and squatted over the engine (one boot on the deck and the other on the head of the diesel) and checked the oil gauge and the day tank's water level. Then I squeezed down between the hatch and the engine and crawled to the stern of the boat and poked at the stuffing box. If there were only a couple of drips of water where the shaft made its way to the outside of the boat, then that was good. There was nothing a shrimper obsessed over more than a loose stuffing box where the sea rushed in and a boat sank beneath him.

The *SeaBee* was forty-two foot long, ten years old (not old in boat years), and had one of the tightest keels in the harbor. She never leaked and rarely needed the automatic pump that was as critical to a shrimper as the single white mast light that identified a shrimp boat as a shrimp boat when coming down a channel at night next to a mountain-sized barge.

The day I stepped on the railing the boat groaned. The wind was high in the rigging and flipped my hair and shirt collar, so I went inside the cabin and took an old yellow slicker off a nail. Then I put both the thermoses of coffee on the catchall. I never hooked up the radio. It was gone—swiped off the boat when some hoodlums made a run on all the boats at the docks.

Then I let down the net and threw the ropes off the bow and stern and headed out of the harbor. Even though I had been off the boat for a while, it took only seconds to remember how a boat felt and sounded when she hit deep water. I didn't need a depth meter to tell me where I was. It was pitch black and I knew already.

The sky was half cleared in front with fast-moving clouds, and the moon was sinking. Behind me the town was black, except for the yellow harbor lights. I hadn't pulled the cabin door shut, so the wind came from the back door and it came in through the front windows I had propped open with sticks, and there it met on my front slicker. I stood with both hands on the wheel, feet spread to take the roll of the sea. I never bothered to sit in the captain's chair. The chair had swiveled once, but didn't any more. I never used it unless I was in the middle of a drag, and then I would prop my boots on the cabin wall and stare out to sea.

Now and then I glanced down at the lighted compass that floated in its own little water world, bobbing due south with a little east in it. The compass was bolted too. Everything I didn't want on the cabin floor was bolted. The stainless steel thermoses just rolled. I had given up on glass ones long ago.

I didn't have a map, but I knew where I was going: due south, across the intercoastal canal, then into the middle of San Antonio Bay for an early morning drag. In the fall, when the shrimp season was legally longer and time didn't play such a huge role, I could go farther into the bay or into another bay entirely. The spring run narrowed the options. If money was to be made at all that day, the first drag was the most critical. Shrimping usually went downhill from there.

Generally shrimp settled at night, but by early morning they were either lying in bunches somewhere beneath the surface of the water or were scattered like buckshot across the bay. The scattered trend made shrimping a bore, but the captain would have a fairly good idea of what he would catch for the day, and a deckhand would have a field day. A shrimper scratching for scattered shrimp just needed to put in some dragging time, and he didn't need to check his try net every fifteen minutes to see what in the heck he was catching because he knew *exactly* what he was catching. So his deckhand lay around half a day, sleeping on a homemade icebox and eating up all the groceries.

When shrimp bunched and offered the captain the possibility of a large catch, the situation changed radically. The shrimper got excited. The deckhand got excited. Then they both jumped all over the back deck and the captain lied up a storm on the radio, saying things like he wasn't catchin' a cryin' thing or he was thinking about taking his boat and headin' for the house. That lie was so common that every shrimper who heard it knew it for the lie it was and picked up his net and headed straight for the one lying.

The games on the radio were partly the reason why Baby quit shrimping. Games and the competition. Baby didn't want to be in a race with nobody. Baby wanted shrimping the way it was when he was still in his momma's belly and maybe that little bit of time afterwards; that summer long long ago when he worked with his uncle and his daddy and there had been a possibility of finding a spot on the bay that hadn't been drug twice, and he didn't have to spend half his time checking the water to make sure it wasn't some other shrimper's mud trail he was dragging through.

I don't know when it started changing. I just know it changed. Shrimpers quit believing there was a bay that hadn't been drug or a reef or a mud flat that hadn't been searched. The day the shrimpers realized that, they started figuring a means to overcome that loss. A bigger engine. A bigger net. Double the propeller. Then an hour or two less sleep. And in their rush to overtake their loss, they tried hard to avoid the dead dolphins and the buzzards that flew at the water's edge. Then when the red tide and the brown tide and the green tide came and their nets came up empty, the shrimpers simply threw them over again. There was nothing else to do. They were fishermen. They couldn't quit. But if one did, he never fully recovered. He was a dead man walking.

I was no different. I couldn't imagine a time when southern Gulf water didn't fill it. At times it pained me, the water with its grand-daddy wave and its great-granddaddy wave. They weren't dead. None of them. They were just back there. Back there. I could almost sling my head in that direction.

If I didn't know who I was, I sure knew where I came from. A direction from rather than a description of, which, I suppose, was the reason why every time the water dipped me and the *SeaBee* and rolled us in the warm salty night I was closer to home than I had ever been, and it was the closest thing to dreaming while being awake that I had ever known.

So I listened to the water and watched the compass, and those two led me and the *SeaBee* crazy into the night. It was intoxicating. I was drunk on as addictive a thing as was ever poured from a bottle. I sang to myself, *The sea, the sea, the crazy old black sea.*

A tiny light fastened on one of the hundreds of beacons on the intercoastal canal flashed red every seven seconds and seemed a hundred miles away. It wasn't. It was only an illusion and was the reason I put the beacon's light hard off the starboard side. Twenty degrees more to the west and I could sink the *SeaBee* on a two-foot-wide piling sticking straight up beneath the surface of the water. The piling was only one of a hundred wrecks strewn across San Antonio Bay, and this bay wasn't special. Every bay had wrecks. Old sunken boats. Abandoned gas wells. Pitched over and left behind oil field equipment. Submerged pilings that once marked a path for something everybody forgot the reason for. Airplanes that went down twenty years ago.

Shrimpers learned the wrecks one by one, and they either learned them the easy way or they learned them the hard way. When I first started shrimping and had the fate of the boat in my hands, I would scribble in pencil on the cabin wall the locations of wrecks I had got the night before from my daddy. My brother, Sanchez, got his from loran readings he took of each and every wreck and wrote them in black ink in a spiral notebook.

The alternative to not knowing where the wrecks were wasn't good.

Because there was no sadder fool on the bay than a captain who either ran over a wreck with his boat or caught one in his net. Then every shrimper who saw it happen or heard it over the radio just shook his head and privately said to himself, or to his deckhand if he was nearby, "I could've told him where it was." Of course, no shrimper asked because nothing aggravated an *independent* shrimper more than another shrimper volunteering information. The shrimper told would walk the back deck of his shrimp boat all evening long, thinking, *Am I stupid? Does he say I am stupid?*

So I held the wheel firm and redirected the bow time and time again, pulling it back south with a little east, pulling it back to starboard side. Then when the *SeaBee* went hard into the waves, I took the spray full in the face. The water ran off my face and into my shirt, and where it dried it left white lines of salt. I could have seasoned a gumbo with all the salt I had on me.

When the seas got really rough, I tightened the slicker around me and yanked the hood over my head. In the yellow slicker with the hood over my head and a coffee cup somewhere near, I was totally and singularly alone and complete. I was maybe mildewed, but I was Buddha in the rain with the snake over me.

It was only when the beacon light got closer and I knew I was entering the channel that I yanked off the hood and glanced down at the depth meter. Eighteen feet. Twenty. Twenty-two. Twenty-five. Twenty-eight. Thirty. I was in the middle of the channel. And the *SeaBee* sat down like an old woman with bad shoes and needing a chair. I slowed her down, edged across the channel, then over a spoil dump. Then with the night fumbling at more and more clouds and the east slowly clearing, I opened the throttle and headed the *SeaBee* into open water.

There was no mark, no scarred reef to show the way. Just something done time and time again, and anything more—a spotlight turned on over the cabin window or a deckhand talking in my ear—would have thrown me into instant confusion. I simply focused on the water I knew better at night than I knew my own home by daylight.

What happened next, I could have escaped. There are choices. I didn't have to read Bill Bailey's paper. I could have canceled that first and second meeting in town. But this is all hindsight. I had the *SeaBee* in forty-five minutes' worth of open water, and behind her the east was cleared and only here and there a glob of cloud cooled its heels. To the west the sky was a rolling boil, and when I reached the middle of the bay I knew why. I just wondered when the wind was gonna shift.

There are some captains who see bad weather coming and head straight for the docks. Sometimes it is an excuse to go in, and sometimes it is wisdom standing on thirty years of dealing with the weather and the water. But if a man wanted to gamble on his boat and on a black sky, then he had to come up with the one constant in the whole equation, and that was unpredictability. Because the sky could blow up black and stiff, then shrink down to a flat wave, or the storm could miss the part of the bay the fleet was in and hit another bay and sink a boat or two.

Then other times a storm was innocent enough. It would blow and rain and maybe throw a hatch cover over or pitch an icebox into the water. Then I either tied up to a gas well or I got into a wide-open area of the bay, put over the net, shut the door, then drank coffee and drug until the storm was over.

Today I wasn't sure, so I pulled the throttle to shut her down and I walked out on the back deck and watched the west rise up in front of me. I couldn't smell the wind shift, so I still had time to put over the net and drag through the storm. Securing my non-escape, I walked into the cabin and gave the *SeaBee* a little throttle and put the bow into the wind. Then I slipped a rope to hold the wheel and I walked back to the stern and threw the net over. The sack and chaffing gear slipped past my boots and over the stern and I watched it feed out, and when a bit of webbing twisted I put my boot on it and slowed it down.

A rush of water roared through the net like a thousand wildly rustling leaves, and pulled it tight. Then the net yanked on the shrimp doors and stopped. The lazy line floated on the outside of the net from sack to shrimp door. A pile of tickler chain bolted at both ends to the two separate shrimp doors lay in a clump on the back deck, and I kicked it over with my boot.

I glanced across the bay, and a black skyline rose like bad dough on a dough board. It climbed high and black and stiff so that the white sand cliffs off the game refuge punched out stark and white. The full end of the bay was spilt ink, and I knew this storm wasn't going to miss. I smelt it coming—green and brand-new—and I knew the wind shift wasn't far behind. I went back to the cabin, flipped off the rope, and shoved the throttle. The shrimp doors lifted off the back deck and came up three or four feet and stopped. They were suspended by two thin, baby-finger-wide cables, and hardly swayed as the *SeaBee* ran across the water. Later, after the wind picked up, it would be different and could, in a heartbeat, deal out a hip-crunching blow or toss a shrimper into the bay as lightly as ash flicked from a cigarette. A five-hundred-pound sledgehammer couldn't do more damage.

I gave the *SeaBee* more throttle and the doors cleared the deck, and then, after I tied the wheel off, I walked to the winch outside the cabin door and slowly turned the handle. The doors slipped in one smooth rush into the water and vanished, while the cables peeled out from the metal drum and through a block hanging from the rigging, then vanished into the water with the doors.

When the double twine on the cable that marked the length showed, I turned the handle back and walked to the deck and grabbed a twenty-pound metal hook tied by a short rope onto the *SeaBee*'s iron-works and put it in the middle of the deck. Then I walked back to the cabin and slowed the *SeaBee* into a dead still. What I did next was the only time I ever *ran* on the *SeaBee* and the only time I *really* needed a deckhand and was the closet I ever came to a fatal accident: I shifted the *SeaBee* into reverse and ran out of the cabin and grabbed the cable that was slowly winding back onto the deck and put the hook around the cable, then I ran back to the cabin and shoved the gear from reverse to forward and hit the throttle almost at the same time. Then I stood with my back to the wheel and looked out the cabin door as the cable straightened out, considerably lower on the deck with the hook around it, and slowly began to widen as the shrimp doors caught the rush of water and spread the net. I stayed at the wheel, watching the net spread and making sure it stayed out of the boat's wheel wash, then I put the *SeaBee* into a slow turn.

I steered the boat in one slow, woman-rounded turn after another, one turn flowing into the next and the next and each one a little farther on down the bay. Sometimes I drug across the bay or down one side of a reef or through a twisted pass into another bay, but *always* the trick (and it was a trick—part skill and part just a knack for the thing) was to hold the wheel and the stern of the boat and the cable and the net in one long sustained ballet-type maneuver. So in the rain with the cabin door closed and a slicker over my head, I did that. I stayed with my back hard against the wheel to keep the boat in its turn and not undone by the wind, and watched the rain pound the door. When the storm blew over I would put over the try net, but now I didn't.

I was fifteen minutes into the drag when I felt something had gone wrong. Did I hit something? I got out of my chair and looked out the side window. The water rushed past the bow where her nose was in the wind, so the *SeaBee* still moved. She just moved *different.*

I slung open the cabin door and looked outside. *Waves were sweeping over the deck!* A squall wouldn't put the *SeaBee* that far into the water.

I couldn't think what was wrong, so I tied off the wheel, knowing it wouldn't hold in the wind, and walked out into the rain to the stern of the boat. The sea was inches from the deck! Normally it was two or three feet. The *SeaBee* was taking on water!

The wind slapped at my face and slung my slicker almost off one arm. I turned and walked back to the engine hatch and jerked it up. Instead of seeing the diesel engine and straight to the bottom of the boat, I saw water. No plywood where I crawled around the engine, no wooden ribs. Still, it didn't register. The *SeaBee* was full of water? I didn't remember hitting anything. No jerk. No automatic pump running, constant and loud enough to signal a problem with the hull. I ran over to the side of the boat and looked for the bilge hole where the water would discharge if the water pump was working. No water. Not a trickle. There was nothing but a boat filling up with water and sinking.

I yanked harder on the hatch cover and the wind grabbed it and pitched it against the icebox. I ignored it. I ignored the cables that slipped behind the boat and the bow of the boat that drifted in the wind. The rain was hitting the deck hard and filling it to the railing, and when the *SeaBee* rolled into a wave the water poured over the side. I ignored that too. I looked only at the engine with the water slowly rising around it. I didn't know how long I had. Would the engine stay running, and if so, how long before it sucked in the salt water that was filling the stern and triggered a compression shock that would bend rods and snap head bolts? But if I shut off the engine, would it start again? And with no engine, there was no way of getting the net and doors back on board and the boat to the dock, and would almost certainly guarantee a sinking.

I ran back to the cabin, turned the boat downwind and set it on idle, then slid past the grinding engine and crawled into the water towards the stern of the boat. I forced myself to crouch underneath the deck, my head scraping the boards, while my hands and knees felt for the ribs in the boat. I could smell diesel fumes and the heat off the engine, and I reached with my hands, feeling underwater for the plywood. The plywood was floating a few inches from the bottom, and when I pressed it with my knees and hands, it sank. It was one thing to work on a boat on the water, but an entirely different thing to have it around your face and mouth.

I had no idea what to do besides find the leak. If I had hit a wreck and tore a hole in the hull, then nothing would keep the *SeaBee* from sinking. I had *no* idea why the bilge pump wasn't working either, but that wasn't a priority so I didn't glance towards the bow and the boat battery. I just hoped it wasn't underwater and most of the damage was towards the stern. I inched my way back, rushing water on my hands, and suddenly felt sick. Maybe I should stop and puke? *No, no, keep going!* So I kept crawling, moving farther to the stern, my hands groping for the rush of cool water that would tell me, *finally*, that *this* is where the hole is. *This* is why the *SeaBee* is sinking. I sat on my heels with the water around my waist, and a dead bleached crab went by, its feelers stiff from engine heat. Everything in the bilge floated. Pits of wood. An old coffee can I used to clean out the scuffords. Oil rags bobbed up and down and twisted around my arm like dead squid.

My thinking was wild. What pocket of air would I have if the *SeaBee* went down? Would I have *none*? Would the *SeaBee* go down fast or would she go slow? Maybe I'd twist and wrestle with the water and my black hair would turn white in the seconds before I drowned. I knew a hundred tales of near-drowned fishermen, and almost all had white hair to show for it. I felt my insides suck back from the thought.

Then a thought climbed high in my head: *The stuffing box. The stuffing box.* I didn't hear the rain hitting the deck or the diesel engine pounding in my ear. There was another monkey on my head, and it clambered far worse the closer I got to the stern of the boat. But the stuffing box made no sense. Sure, a stuffing box and the shaft that ran through it and outside of the boat could leak water, but it didn't suddenly pour water for no reason, especially if it had been checked the night before. Stuffing boxes don't leak out of the blue, especially not bad enough to sink a boat. Then even if it had leaked, the automatic pump would have caught the problem.

I stopped moving for a second, heavy into panic, and wondered how many minutes before the stern got too heavy and pulled the rest of the *SeaBee* down. I jerked my head around and shoved my hands wildly into the water. Suddenly my fingers hit the shaft. I slid my fingers down until I felt the valves and the cool water sliding past my fingers. With my mouth near the water, I fumbled with the valves, frantic to stop the water from pushing past my fingers. Then my hands fell off and my head went down under smelly engine water, and as I jerked back and blinked water from my eyes, I stared straight into the boxed stern of the boat.

The valves were wound tight and wouldn't budge so I reached from the shaft, keeping one hand on the leak, and moved blindly in the water, thrashing in a semicircle to locate the heavy wrench I always kept nearby to tighten the stuffing box. Twice I lunged forward, missed the plywood, and fell between the ribs of the boat. I tasted diesel in my mouth and shook my head to clear the water from my eyes. I knew if I didn't find the wrench soon I would drown, but even as I had the thought, I didn't believe it was possible. So I would drown, not only in panic but also in pure ignorance, wondering what in the hell was going on.

Then my hands hit the wrench, and as awkward as I have ever handled a five-pound wrench, I did it more. I turned the valve once, missed, dropped the wrench, turned the valve again, missed again, then finally I grabbed it firmly, then *slowly* turned. *The water stopped.* I wasn't going to drown. I sat on my heels, astonished, wide-eyed, and wet faced, not saying and doing nothing. I crawled to the engine and climbed out. I was shaking, and even though the rain hit my face hard, I didn't raise a hand or turn my head. I just sat and stared at the rain and the *SeaBee* moving downwind, and the cables loose and tangled all over the deck. I didn't know how far the boat had drifted, but the dragging net had been her best anchor.

I had to get the water out of the boat, so I went down into the bilge again and crawled towards the bow. There was less water now and the plywood was easier to see. Every sound that had been drummed out of my head at the stern of the boat now was crystal clear. I found the boat battery high and dry against the side of the boat, but the automatic pump was gone. I knew where I had left it, though—aft and upright between the ribs of the boat, so even several inches of water in the bilge would float its tiny paddle and flip on the automatic switch. It took fifteen minutes of patting the water to find the water pump. I pulled it out. The wires attaching it to the battery were gone.

Finally I found them on the far side of the boat. I crawled back to the battery and rewired the pump, and immediately the pump began to pull water and discharge it through the hose and outside the boat.

I spent the rest of the evening pumping out the boat. I rewound the cables and hoisted the heavy shrimp doors, then tied them down with a rope so they wouldn't slide off the deck every time the boat rolled in the wind. The net had junked up with a ton of century-old oyster shells and smelly black mud from the dozens of dredge holes dug years ago and pocketing the bay.

It took two attempts to bring the net sack alongside the boat, but both failed to clear the deck and instead sent a torrent of black slimy mud and squashed hard heads across the deck. On the final attempt the boat lunged and a rope twisted, and block shivs in the rigging jerked the net sack to a sudden stop. Now a full net sack swung across the deck, slinging black mud and careening like a two-ton gorilla on a half-inch nylon rope. I loosened the rope from the cathead, but it was still stuck so I walked into the cabin and grabbed a butcher knife and stuck it between my teeth and started climbing the rigging. When the boat lunged in the wind, I held still and hard against the mast, with the knife tight between my teeth; then when it righted, I started climbing again.

Near the top of the rigging, I stopped altogether. For a moment I looked down at the gray churning water and heard the sound of my hair tearing the wind. My slicker whipped against the rigging, then out behind me, and where my shirt was loose the wind took that too. I was dazzled. I was tossed to the air, then plunged to the sea, and the whole time I was drunk on the idea that only one rusting mast pole separated me from it all. I would never be this free again. Only dying could do it next or do it better. Then seconds before I took the knife from my mouth and cut the rope, I laughed so hard I nearly dropped the knife.

An
Unreasonable
Woman

PART ONE

1

Dirty Secrets Revealed

I was stuck at the crossroad of Seadrift's city limits sign and looking straight into a business where I had none. Then I smiled this small and secret Mona Lisa smile and my eyes went wide, and behind me a hundred thousand dirty pipes were drilling the sky.

Red said nothing. We were at the fish house and I was telling him my dream, but he wasn't telling me his. Red was still carrying the flounder he had killed (or stole) last night. It didn't have any ice on it and looked stiff to me. At least the tail was stiff and turned straight up out of the oil bucket he had it in. Finally he turned his red head to me and said, "Dreams 'bout a chemical plant. Personally I don't mess with them. Don't dream 'bout them. Wouldn't take a fish outa their crappy water even if they gave it to me."

"Chemical plant? Nah, it was just pipes and stuff. It was just a dream anyhow."

"I worked at a plant once. Forget just what plant. Carbide, maybe."

Donna Sue made a racket behind me like she was trying to climb out the window, but it was only her boots she was taking off the desk. Red paid no mind to any of this. His face was quiet as an onion peel. He was the quietest liar I ever saw.

"That fish needs ice," Donna Sue said. She couldn't stand Red. She couldn't stand shrimpers and some she couldn't stand worse than others, so she went out the door and kicked everything she was capable of kicking.

Red looked peaceful, dead flounder at his feet. "Well, just consider yourself *reeel* lucky for never workin' there."

Donna Sue stood in the door with a shovel of ice. "She's done it already, Red," she said, and swung her whole shovel to me. "No need to tell her something she's already done. Seen it, heard it, done it . . . ain't that right?"

I had all right. It had been unintentional. A job got at Carbide, because I went with a cousin who was actually trying to get the job herself, and when they saw me, they saw a way to fill their female quota for the month. Union Carbide said, "A woman shrimper is bound to know how to work hard!" So I got a hard hat and I got an ID badge that said I was who I said I was, and every day when I came home and washed my hair, the tub water turned yellow and all of the kids ran in and took a look. That job lasted three weeks. I told the personnel at the plant that I had to quit 'cause I was going salmon fishing in Alaska and the run was fixing to happen. That was a lie. I didn't know the first thing about salmon fishing, but the gates around that plant were taking on a life of their own, so I quit and threw my hard hat in the ditch when I left.

Donna Sue shoved the ice into Red's bucket and never changed her expression from that first disgusted second she saw him walk into the fish house and proceed to tell us lies. Then Red left, straight as a poker, like nothing had ever touched him in his life. Not me and not the game wardens that were tracking him.

Donna Sue stood in the fish house door and watched Red disappear down the shell road. "Lyin' coyote! I don't know how you can sit there and listen to all that. When's he ever worked for any of those plants? And he probably stole that fish too! Or else stole the skiff to steal the fish!"

"Oh, his worst sin is he's lost," I said.

But misery didn't impress Donna Sue. She already had a world of it herself, so she sat next to the window and watched me, with her arms folded and her sea boots on the desk—white, same as mine. Four white boots on the desk like snow geese in a rice field.

I was leaning towards the bay. Actually the whole fish house was leaning towards the bay, and already a crack ran through the fish house so I could never pull boxes of shrimp out of the vault without running into that crack and throwing cold shrimp and ice halfway down my boots. My coffee cup was sitting on my legs. The coffee was cold. I had my hands around it like it was hot as hell.

I watched an egret land in the middle of the road, and without moving my chair I could see it and around it and everything else through the double wood doors that opened onto the harbor road. The fish house didn't have screens. Even after the state health department fella walked through the fish house and ticked off offenses and tapped on doors and windows and said, "Screens," and me saying, "Will do," (then, later, tacking my copy of the yellow offense sheet to the bathroom wall so I wouldn't see it) I never did screens. I liked breathing too much. Screens got in the way of breathing and a million other things I could name. With screenless windows, I could smell the sun on the docks. I could smell it when the sun went down and I could smell it when it came back up again.

I looked up from my coffee, and there on the wall were a dozen shrimp boat photographs Scotch-taped to the wall. The heat off the water had claimed half, and they listed portside like they were sinking. Me and Donna Sue had taken the pictures in the spring to sabotage whatever efforts the other fish-house owners were doing to get local boats. Getting boats (especially *working* shrimp boats and not ones where the captains were either drunk in the beer joint or asleep in their bunks, or ropes and nets were wrapped around their boats' propellers on a pretty regular basis) was a highly competitive business among fish-house owners. But being as me and Donna Sue weren't fish house *owners*, but only fish house *managers* with a missing owner that hadn't shown his face since God knows when, we weren't particular about our methods. Especially not like the other fish houses that went to tiresome places like feeding shrimpers barbecue and potato salad and red beans and beer if they weren't too Baptist that day. Me and Donna Sue weren't fixing to do none of that. We didn't want any more cooking than we were already doing at home—so it was that reason we took the pictures.

Besides, pictures didn't get destroyed and the wall wasn't a boneyard. A boat on the wall never sank in a storm. A boat on the wall never got repossessed. It never rusted or broke down, and most every shrimper in town, if he had the money to get it done, had an oil painting of his shrimp boat, high above the couch in the living room. Some even bought aerial shots taken by a helicopter, and that picture, nine times out of ten, rode on the casket with the fisherman all the way to the graveyard. Some even got buried with them. Never once did I see a wife's picture done that way.

But that was shrimpers and their boats. Every captain was God-almighty on his God-almighty shrimp boat, and today we had two God-almighty ones out. One was my brother, Sanchez (who used an alias for reasons everybody knew), and the other was Bill Bailey. Just like the song. First, Bill didn't go out, then he did and when he came back the sun was straight up. The fact that Bill hadn't come to the fish house made it pretty clear he had caught no shrimp and there was none to be had, so I wasn't even going to figure what he and Sanchez were really doing out there. Most of the other fish houses had already closed their doors. It was that kind of a shrimp season.

But sooner or later Bill would show up at the fish house, and it made no difference if he caught shrimp or didn't because shrimping filled Bill like ditch water filled a ditch. I didn't know what his excuse was neither. Bill wasn't born into shrimping. His daddy or his uncle never did it. And he didn't grow up on the coast—more like Abilene. Nope, Bill was a college-educated man, and somewhere in his lifetime he had played professional football and navigated planes over the Vietnam skies. My momma said he was the handsomest man she had ever laid eyes on, and he sure had the whitest teeth.

I saw Bill's truck and the oyster dust piled high, and when he got out and left the door open, the dust was higher than Bill's waist. Then the dust settled and I saw Bill was wearing one of those Hawaiian shirts like I've never seen nobody else do.

"Gonna run that battery down, leavin' that door open like that," I said.

"Truck's gonna give out before the battery does," he said.

Like most conversations around a fish house, ours started nowhere and meandered like a lost, starving cat. We talked about the weather and the shrimp price doing nothing and shrimp crop doing nothing, then we settled into more personal areas, like how Bill's net was working. He said it wasn't working right. Maybe he would switch nets.

"You didn't see Sanchez out there, did ya? If I thought he was stayin' out all night, I'd just lock this place up."

"Oh, Sanchez's doing what Sanchez's doing and probably not half what he'd like to do, like sticking a load of dynamite on Hynes Bay water and blowing it back into Refugio County."

Bill was in a popular area. It was about the hostility between two neighboring counties over a couple hundred acres of water, and the sometimes-fight that was drug into courtrooms, where shrimpers argued over invisible boundary lines stretching from yonder point to yonder point.

I had my own opinion and I said it. "Sanchez's wastin' his time if he just thinks it's Refugio County that hates commercial fishermen and wants them outa the bays. I imagine if this county had a choice, and didn't have to sit down at the supper table across from a shrimper at night, they'd feel the same way. Lock up every shrimp house on the bay and burn the boats."

"Ooh, are you questioning this county's loyalty to the fishermen? Fishermen aren't their favorite sons?"

"Hell! That's *exactly* what's she sayin'!" Donna Sue was watching the conversation, her boots high on the desk, and now she slung them off and looked at me. She was mad about something, but her face stayed white. It didn't get red. It always stayed white, even in the sun. Mine just got browner.

I glanced at Donna Sue, then back over to Bill. "What I *meant* to say was this county would trade off the whole fleet for just a little bitty corner of a chemical plant. Sell it all for some pipe and diesel fumes. We ain't economically viable any longer. That's all I'm sayin'!"

"*Speakin'* of which . . . " Bill started.

"Oh, shut up, Bill. I'm talkin'—"

"Oh, hold yore horses a minute. I don't want to talk about shrimpers. I want to talk about the chemical plants. Here, read it yourself. See what you think." Then Bill pulled out a folded newspaper from underneath his arm and flipped it on the desk.

"Fishermen can't read. Ain't you heard? We're stupid, besides making no money. Especially women, so take your little newspaper and hightail it."

"Now, now, now. Don't be that way. This is different. To tell you the truth, though, when I got that paper I thought I got a hold of a Houston paper. Sure didn't think it was local. Had to look twice at the front page. Go on, read it."

Generally I didn't take orders from shrimpers, but Bill had on a Hawaiian shirt that was pretty cute, so I did. I read it twice and talked to myself the whole time. On the third round I stopped in the middle and wadded the paper and pitched it against the wall.

Donna Sue gave me an irritated look she generally reserved for shrimpers. "Go get that!" she said, and it wasn't a question. It wasn't a *Would you please?* Donna Sue had been married twenty years to a shrimper, and *Would you please?* was not in her vocabulary.

I looked at the paper a minute, then got up and yanked it off the floor and spread it on the desk where Donna's boots weren't budging. She was drinking iced tea and resting the glass on her belly like pregnant women do sometimes.

I read it through again. The article was an Associated Press story that summarized a first-ever report on the federal Toxic Release Inventory, and it ranked the states on the emissions pouring from their industries.

"So what's this all about?" I said. "You're the educated one here, Bill. Why is this thing in here?"

Bill sat in the fish house window with his boots flat on the floor.

"It's part of a new federal environmental law. Industries gotta report."

"Well, I guess, but why now? I've never seen them do it before."

"Well, mainly because that Union Carbide plant in India leaked a pesticide that killed about two thousand men, women, and children overnight. Maybe more. Maybe as many as eight thousand died those first two nights. Then injured a couple hundred thousand too. Worst environmental disaster *ever*. So I guess folks in the U.S.A. got to remembering that Carbide was a U.S.A. plant, which it sure is. Carbide is as red, white, and blue as they get. Then I guess they got to figuring, well . . . maybe that could happen here. Who knows what's in those tanks out there? What's coming out of those stacks? What's in all that black smoke coming off a plant? Who knows? So Congress decided *they* needed to know. The public needed to know because we didn't need half a town dying in their sleep just because we weren't aware of something. So Congress made that TRI a part of the Superfund Act when it was reauthorized, and said industry had to report its emissions. Now it's there in print, and you finally get to know what all those chemical plants are dumping. Aren't you happy?"

I sure wasn't. Texas was in first place in most all emissions, with Louisiana breathing hard down our necks. Four times our little Calhoun County was mentioned. A piddlin' little county on the Gulf Coast that was lucky when fifteen thousand people lived and stayed overnight. The article ranked Calhoun County first nationally for toxics to the land, and said we accounted for 54 percent of the state's total of a billion pounds, and our own Alcoa was the villainous plant that landed us there.

I didn't say nothing. It was nobody's secret that Alcoa had dumped mercury in the bay so that it was in the mud and in the fish and in the crabs, but the state said mercury wasn't going nowhere, so no need for folks to get alarmed. But the article wasn't talking about what had happened in Alcoa's plant operations twenty years before. Nope. The article was talking *now. The present.* And we were ranking all over the place. Besides that first-place prize, Calhoun was third for shipping toxins out, sixth for sticking them down wells, then twenty-first for flinging them in the air. So I did the only thing you can do after winning something like that. I pretended I never saw the newspaper. It could lie down alongside the rest of the bad news that lined up so well in a dying town. Instead I listened for the sound of Sanchez's diesel engine and knew I was fast running out of reasons for being at the fish house.

Two months before the season had been different, because two months before the town was expecting The Seasons of All Seasons that would turn things all around. The shrimp season before and the season before that hadn't done it, so surely *this* was the season that would. Everybody knew about the gamble, and shrimping was a gamble, and Seadrift being the fishing town it was, it was like a whole town of gamblers with gamblers' wives' and gamblers' kids. So there were high stakes and businesses verging on bankruptcy and boats fixing to go to bankers and bankers anxious to collect, but still the shrimpers fixed their nets and hauled out boats and slapped on yet another coat of copper paint, and then they went down to Western Auto and charged towing cable and blocks and nylon rope and thimbles and chains and webbing and corks and net dip and twine and batteries—things they couldn't afford. But they were thinking high stakes. *This* will be the season they get rich.

Wrong, wrong. The brown algae (as opposed to the red algae and the green algae) moved into the bay, and eventually it came into the harbor. From the fish-house door, I watched the suffocating fish break the surface, and their silver heads were like little camera lights going off. Nothing could be done. Even scientists investigating the tides had no two ideas alike on why the algae had happened. Modern times. Lean times. Hot times. A plague on the sea.

Algae blooms weren't new to the fishermen. We'd seen them in the bays three or four times before, so I wasn't surprised when the shrimpers went to another bay, only leaving earlier and returning later.

Then the brown tide went into *that* bay, and the nets the shrimpers pulled collapsed under the weight of a billion algae blooming. Under diminishing options, shrimpers hauled their nets in and dumped them in their yards and hoped the sun and time would dry them out. Some had no time for sun and no money for another net and so resorted to more immediate methods.

Crazy Ed was one such shrimper, and he had done worse things, except this was the worst he had done with a net. He had took his algae-plagued net and tied it to the bumper of his rusting truck and hauled it down a dusty oyster road at about eighty miles an hour. What sheriff or deputy stopped him was unclear, because at that time Seadrift was in between cops, and if it had been a Seadrift cop he'd probably have been a little more understanding. So it was an out-of-town sheriff that stopped Crazy Ed for creating what he thought was a breathing hazard on a county road.

Crazy Ed came to the fish house with the sheriff and a net that smelled like a burning tire. Ed dropped the net and the sheriff at the door, then weaved his way through the maze of shrimp boxes strung out on the fish-house floor. Me and Donna Sue were dealing with a Louisiana trucker that had come to haul off every shrimp we had in the fish-house vault, and they were three-day-old shrimp and some had started to turn black and look exotic, so we were anxious to get rid of them. I ignored Crazy Ed and the sheriff for as long as I could. Ed didn't say nothing and he didn't interrupt; he just went from one white boot to the next like he was doing a dance at a honky-tonk. Then I turned and Ed grinned worse than I'd seen him do in a long time. Even worse than the time he tried to sell me the back tires off his truck because he couldn't afford gas in the truck and eat too. Only now he was grinning because he wanted to know if I could fix the net.

The sheriff stood at the door, but I didn't look there. I looked at the net and said, "Shore, I'll fix it," and acted like a shrimper dragging a thirty-two-foot net behind a truck was a perfectly natural thing to do. So I got the net. I didn't know how I was going to fix the thing without spending a fortune on new webbing, and I knew Crazy Ed didn't have the money even if I did. Maybe I could do what Ed didn't want to do and wait for the sun to do its work.

Donna Sue shook her head at me. "Why don't you burn the thing?" she said.

"Ed's already done that. Besides, it's his only net. What's he gonna use?"

Sometimes I believed nothing could save the shrimper. No decree. No government project. No ally. He was in the wrong century on the wrong path at the wrong place, and his addiction to the water was either gonna drive him crazy or kill him outright. One desperate shrimper lay facedown on the back deck of his boat in the shrimp and the muck and the hardheads and begged the dying shrimp to tell him their secret. Where they went. What they were doing. But that pile of shrimp said nothing and kept their silence to their slow gray breath.

Once or twice in my life my momma got peeved over the persistent gambling and poverty and unflagging work and asked my daddy (who had fished every day of his life except the time he was in the U.S. Navy and stationed in a lake in Idaho) when he was going to get a *real job* with a *real paycheck*. None of us knew what a real paycheck looked like, but to Momma, a real job was anything that didn't have nothing to do with the bay, because everybody knew if you wanted to make a dime on the bay you'd have to bleed *real hard*. One shrimper, who struggled every day like he was in the throes of death and lived in an ugly tan trailer with his wife and two cotton-headed boys, got his hand caught in a gear-clanging winch while he was trying to pull in a net. He had been shrimping all night for Hoppers, which is a type of shrimp that likes real bad weather or else real bad nights and seems to have a genuine vendetta against shrimpers, and on this particular night, the winch nearly tore off his thumb. To get the doors loaded and the net hauled in, the shrimper had to chew off the long white tendon his thumb was dangling from. That shrimper didn't make a dime on that trip, and that wasn't his worst trip neither. It was just a messy one.

So bad times were like the salted peanuts the shrimpers ate with their beer (good for reminding them how great it would feel when the good season returned), or else they plain forgot, same as a woman does her birth pains until the next baby begins. The motto was "Lie or just plain forget." Only I didn't forget. I had a good memory, and that was why Bill's newspaper was unnecessary. Another bullet brought home to a fishing town that just had its only son butchered and now was being told the killer most likely lived in that nice house just outside of town. Still, I wasn't saying and thinking nothing. I was on a Donna Sue tangent.

Bill wouldn't have nothing to do with that. Bill's life didn't have time for it. So he smiled and shook his fine surfer-looking head. "All I was fixing to do was get off that boat. . . . Maybe change nets. Didn't think it would help, but heck . . . isn't that what shrimpers are suppose to do? Isn't that our jobs . . . changing nets like we change our underwear? But nooo, here I go, swing by town, and then this paper. Interesting how it's showed up on your proverbial doorstep, isn't it?"

"Are you sayin' . . . it's *fate or something* that brought you and this paper down here? I could have bought that paper myself. I know how to get a paper out of the damn coin machine. I don't need a fate bearer or a proverbial nothin'."

"Oh, but would you have paid attention? Maybe the interesting part is not the newspaper at all, but *you reading it.*"

I didn't know what the heck we were discussing. Fate? In a fish house? But here we were, and since we were, I figured Bill better start putting his psychic items on a short list, and the first one wasn't the newspaper; it was Bill three months ago in a white-sheeted hospital bed in Galveston. Because the very day the doctors put a name to all of Bill's three cancers, a huge Gulf shrimp boat materialized out of thin air and parked eight inches from his sheet-covered toes. Bill said the boat hovered so close that if it had been a nurse she could have smoothed the wrinkles in his sheet.

Anyhow, I really don't recall what convinced me to call an environmental lawyer I knew only well enough to know that the fishermen owed him two hundred dollars. Maybe it was Bill. Maybe it was the dream. Who knows? I just know the whole time I was calling, I was praying the lawyer wouldn't answer, and if he did, I was praying he wouldn't ask for two hundred dollars. But the worrying was for nothing. The lawyer in his Houston office was named Blackburn, and he was *glad* to hear from me. I didn't even need to mention the paper 'cause he'd already read plenty. He knew about Calhoun County's ranking. He'd be glad to help. He had worked with shrimpers before, and what was going on down there on the Gulf Coast was a living reproach to everything every decent Texan believed in. Yes, sir, he sure would help me. It was a worthy battle. A worthy battle.

Then he said to call a meeting. "You can do that, can't you? Get one down there?"

I said, "Shore. I could manage that."

After I hung up the phone I looked at Donna Sue and said, "He said yes. Now, don't that beat all?"

"What else did he say? Did he ask for that two hundred dollars?"

"I don't think he cares. He just said, 'Call a meeting.' First thing straight outa the bag."

So we ran Bill off and finished washing and locking down the fish house, even though Sanchez hadn't come. Then I got in the van and drove to city hall. My van was an old white Sears delivery van I had bought at a sealed-bid auction, and it was the first and last time I'd ever do that. I was probably the only one that put in a bid for a thousand dollars when a hundred bucks would have bought it outright. But the van could carry a half dozen nets and five kids, so I didn't complain much.

There was no mistaking and driving past city hall. There were three flags in front that clearly marked the building as *it* and not someplace else, and there was also a huge white mast pole that was sometimes mistaken for a Christian cross by the Pentecostal crowd and had been used as such for three Easter services straight in a row.

I knew I'd be messing with women at city hall, because city hall didn't have men in the daylight hours. Not that day or any day. There were just various levels of women, and they rooted for this man and that man like they were sitting on bleachers in a baseball field and their loyalties wobbled worse than the bleachers. The men didn't need to be there anyhow. They were off on their *real* jobs: running a fish house or running illegal fish or masterminding a sometimes–auto parts place that fixed every wrecked car in the county, then resold it as new. The only thing that went on at city hall during the daylight hours was women shuffling papers. Later on and after dark, there was sometimes city council meetings where citizens got riled over the roads and the random paving that was going on.

Our current mayor, who was good-looking but who had a few women who hated him enough to kill him, was the auto parts wizard, and he came into office on the losing streak of another mayor who had been caught by the game wardens up in Hynes Bay with a boatload of illegal redfish. The former mayor's loss at the election polls didn't come from his arrest and formal charges (which really just boosted his popularity), but from his inattention to the election.

Fern Dale was the lead woman at city hall. When she wasn't working and seeing to a husband that worked part-time at Carbide and part-time on the bay, she sang in the Baptist choir and played piano and organ. Sometimes she sang solo. Fern Dale was a tall and elegant woman, and hated by half the other, shorter women in the same building, but seeing as I was nearly as tall and we both had a French grandma, and once upon a time Fern Dale had dated my sister's husband before he was converted to the Pentecostal faith, I figured we had a lot in common and it would save a lot of commotion if I went through her.

So I did, and it did just like I thought. I got the meeting date and the mayor's meeting room (and not the civic center, which was pretty dirty), and when she finished writing it in a ledger, she looked up. Her face was still as oyster stew gone cold. "Okay?" she said.

"It'll do," I said.

It wasn't a plan. It was a meeting time. Planning wasn't a sin I'd ever committed. Besides, I still had babies in the house, and they didn't like divided loyalties such as a plan would indicate, no more than they liked the furniture I piled on the staircase to keep them from climbing so they wouldn't kill themselves in a fall. But I could have saved myself the trouble, because nothing short of a fall was going to keep them from the stairs and the open roof, and my son Crockett was the worst. He rode the edge of our second-story roof and climbed at least fifty feet in the pine trees I had planted three winters ago. Crockett was four and didn't talk, and was a pilgrim in search of heights.

When I drove home and pulled the van into the middle of the yard, I saw Crockett first. In two seconds he was on top of the van, trying to see the salt grass and the sky all at the same time. I reached up and put my hand on his head, and it was like putting an iron to a dry, unwetted shirt. He ignored me and my hand and everything except the chrome antennae. The chrome excited him. He slid off the van and squatted at the front tire, and his hands moved like two wild birds tied to a string. I knew what he wanted. Crockett wanted the tire on the van. He already had two off a boat trailer, and he sent them endlessly down the dirt road.

I said, "Leave the tires alone, honey. C'mon over here." But Crockett didn't listen. Instead he climbed on the hood again and fiddled with the antennae. I got him down and took his hand and went around to the back of the house. Two of the girls were in the house and looking through the window, and we were all watching the same thing in the backyard: their daddy, Baby, walking through the trees with his pearl-handled pistol. He was under the oak trees and had stopped to look at the shrimp nets piled under a rusted tin shed. He didn't turn when I came around, but walked farther to the back and stopped at a pond half filled with water hyacinth and water moccasins.

"How many snakes did you find?" I said.

"I kilt three. Two on this side and another on the other side. I wasn't even lookin' hard."

Last winter Baby had killed thirty snakes, and now he had already that many dead. Normally he didn't like killing snakes, but the cats weren't doing their business like he thought they should, and we had, the night before, found a water moccasin under Santanna's crib. In the dark, I had thought it was a rope.

So I watched Baby while he walked to the pond, and held Crockett's hand as he fidgeted. I knew if I let his hand go, he'd walk and never stop, and then in the salt grass he would disappear and I'd have to climb the roof to track him down. I'd done it a dozen times. Never yelling, not saying, "Crockett, Crockett," but thinking *Stop, stop* and forming sign language with my hands. Still, I said, *"Look up, Crockett!"* The sandhill cranes had moved in for the evening and taken over the marsh. Their gray, dusty bodies hung in the evening sky like circus acts fixing to fall. It was not an accident that we were half a mile from the intercoastal canal and Spirit Center Bay, and that a field of salt grass and sandhill cranes came nearly to our porch. Before the babies were born, I had a design. Not a plan. A design. The design was that I could expect nobody, and nobody would come if I moved a hundred-year-old house fifty miles into the country. To get the house to the salt grass, the house was sawed in half with large chain saws (two were burned up in the process). Then it rained to beat the devil for over a month, and the house sat mired in the mud in a field a half mile from the canal. Finally the rain quit, and a Mexican man with no English and one full whiskey bottle hooked up the house and drug it the last two miles. Then the driver passed out and the house stayed where it stayed.

I didn't change anything. I kept the screen door open, and at night I laid a brick at the door to let the wind come in and the moon too—invited and warm and laying fingers of light throughout the hall.

Once during the fall after a fog had shut down the bay and the salt grass and the horizon had become a single fluid thing, a lone goose sailed into the house through the open second-story door. And that was how me and the kids and Baby came not to be strangers to the bay and salt grass, but strangers only to what lay outside and bordered our world.

2

A Shrimping Career Rehashed

I don't know why I listened and watched. He was suited and vested, his white finger crooked, and I said nothing and did nothing, and a whole wasteland of words blew over me. Then he finished, and I watched him walk back to his silver car. I was thinking it was past noon when he first came through the fish-house doors, but now I'm not so sure. He had worn a suit and his hand was white against the dark material.

He wanted to know what was going on.

With shrimpers? You want to see one of my shrimpers, I said. No, no, no, he said. Just you. Wouldn't be a real banker if I wasn't checking on what's going on down here at the bay, now, would I? So. Now. Did or did you not send out that press release? And did or did you not set up a meeting at city hall?

I said I had sent out a press release for sure. Didn't know I needed one until I found out I needed one. Newspapers want press releases. First time for everything.

So I talked, and Howdy never looked up from his shiny black shoes. I could smell new leather from where I stood. I had never talked to Howdy Doody before and would've been desperate if I had, because Howdy Doody wasn't his real name, but it was what he was called by every shrimper who ever had to get a loan from him at the bank, and worse by shrimpers who didn't. Talking to Howdy for the first time wasn't just talking to Howdy. It was talking to someone else who had more money than he did and more power than he did, and it wasn't just the bank; it was some other allegiance more powerful than *that*, and Howdy was with that allegiance even while he worked at the bank in Seadrift.

So Howdy was with somebody important and he knew it, and when he looked up from his shoes, he pranced like a preacher in a tent, who had the only exit. "So," he said. "Are you inviting me to that meeting?

You and your friends. Not thinking about making it a private little affair? Just a few select people?"

"What?" I said. "That meeting at city hall? Is that what you're down here for?"

"Just need to know, is all. On a need-to-know basis. A banker's prerogative. I just need to go back and tell a few folks that you aren't fixing to have some little vindictive meeting to roast industry alive. Not some renegade environmental group forming in our midst? Hmm?"

I laughed, or think I laughed. I felt my face stretch wide and my lips curl away from my teeth. Then I glanced over his well-padded shoulder and pretended I was counting boats or something. Something else besides getting nervous.

"So *what* am I to tell them?" he said.

"Well, tell them they're invited. Just come along. Heck, I don't care. It's just a meeting."

"Just a meeting," he said.

"Well, yeah."

"Well, good. That's good. I'll pass that on, then."

He left in his silver car, and for the next two days (there isn't nothing like a banker to put a little fire underneath you) I talked on the phone. The brownie shrimp run had almost stopped, except for the shrimpers who had taken their boats and nets and headed for the river, so nothing was going on. I didn't envy those river-bound shrimpers. River shrimping was the worst kind of shrimping, next to catching Hoppers.

I sat at the fish house and made phone calls, and while I did that Donna Sue opened the fish-house doors and made salty coffee out of Seadrift's nasty drinking water. Then we watched nothing happen. Old men that didn't fish anymore because they were either too sick or too cranky, or else their kids had sold their boats outright to keep them off the bay and from drowning, came down to the fish house and drank all our coffee. They wouldn't keep quiet even while I was on the phone, and they yelled at Donna Sue the whole time.

"Who's she talkin' to? What's she sayin'? Does Froggie know she's on that phone? You seen Froggie lately? He quit shrimpin', or what?"

I didn't say nothing, but shook my head at a particularly loud fisherman. Donna Sue yelled at him. "Can't you see she's on the phone!"

"Who's she talkin' to? Who is it?"

"It's the plants, Walt. The plants!"

"The what? The plants? *Tomato* plants?"

"No, no, no! *Carbide*, down there. You know . . . Alcoa. The *chemical* plants. Hell, Walt, you've worked there before. You oughta know what I'm talkin' about. Good Lord a'mighty!"

"Hell! *Chemical plants!* I can tell you a thing or two about them. Seen more stuff dumped . . . ooh, she's gonna get her tail in a bind. Seen it happen for a lot less than that. Better off just not askin' questions."

Walt was a semi-Yankee that retired from one of the local chemical plants on his own, but was *forced* into retirement from the bay by his grown son, and wore nothing but an old pair of coveralls with long straps and open sides, and on his feet a worn-out pair of thick rubber sandals he'd bought on a Mexico vacation years ago. Walt claimed he hadn't cooled off since he came to Texas thirty years ago.

Walt was an irritable talker and wasn't always right about things, but this time he was, 'cause while my rear end wasn't exactly in a bind the plant employee I called was furious, and his words were like razor blades coming down a cow chute. "No!" he yelled. "Call somebody else. We are not in the information business, lady. We make chemicals. We build jobs and make better lives for people in this county!"

The third chemical plant I called said they were required by law to provide information to local authorities, but not to every Tom, Dick, and Harry on the telephone. I figured local authorities might be more obliging, so I called the Calhoun County emergency coordinator in Port Lavaca, the next town over and the county seat where Sanchez, my oldest brother, had been spending so much time.

"It's lies!" the coordinator yelled. "That article's nothing but a twisted pack of lies instigated by people wanting to make something out of nothing! It's their *job* to rile up people. That's how they make their money!"

"The Toxic Release Inventory is a national report," I said. "A government report."

"Get your facts straight, lady. What do you know about it anyhow? Do you know what's on a plant's wastewater permit? Know anything *at all* about a permit? Noooh? Well, I didn't think so. I don't have time for this bunch of crap. I've got stuff to do. We do *real* work around here."

Finally I called Blackburn, the Houston lawyer, and complained about all the static I was getting, and Blackburn said he wasn't surprised.

"Just go around the sunuvubitches! Call the EPA in Dallas. Write 'em a letter and tell 'em what you want."

Donna Sue said she didn't know why I had to talk to the plants. "Just ignore the damn plants. They ignore us. Why shouldn't we do the same? Get our information someplace else." Donna Sue was in a tough spot. She didn't know which one she hated more: the chemical plants or the shrimpers. While the chemical plants were vague evils that dumped stuff she knew nothing about, the shrimpers were plain out-and-out men she knew by name.

So I sat in the office and listened to her tirade. Her once coal-black hair moved this way and that and her lips stayed grim, probably like they'd been before dawn or maybe before that. Because Donna Sue was a woman who had been in a mad-angry mood for a very long time, and save for actually killing a man somewhere, she wasn't going to be satisfied. She was bitterly disappointed, and while her rage may have started as a flicker in a dry field in Harlingen, the flames engulfed her the day she turned seven and sat in a run-down movie house with two babies and no diapers and no bottle, and a momma and a daddy long gone.

But me and Donna Sue weren't down at the fish house for our personalities. We were down there because my brother Froggie owned the fish house, but wouldn't run it because he couldn't stand messing with shrimpers. He was a shrimper himself, so he should know, and I was one when I wasn't running his fish house or fixing some shrimper's tore-up net, and Donna Sue was married to a shrimper, so while none of us liked fooling with shrimpers (being as how we knew them), my brother was the worst.

We were johnnies-come-lately to a fish-house business where women generally weren't tolerated. That wasn't to say that women didn't have their roles. They could shuffle shrimping paperwork or hustle engine parts or deckhand on the back deck of their husbands' shrimp boats the livelong day, where they were instructed to keep their mouths shut and their fingers nimble. Women were not encouraged to go on the fish-house floor, and most men wouldn't allow *their* women down at the docks, prancing around (they said) and fooling in their business. So if a woman came down to the bay at all, it was either to pick up her husband or bring down a net or a missing diesel or engine part. Some women were such wonderful gofers that their shrimper husbands bought them VHF radios for their birthdays just so the husbands could keep them informed on an hourly basis on what they might require for supper that night or what net they wanted drug out of the shed and waiting on them.

A few shrimpers, who didn't know me well enough to know better, asked Baby how come he couldn't make me stay home like I belonged. Baby's pale-water eyes stared back at them like he'd never heard the question, and he'd say nothing. It was a stupid question anyhow, 'cause everybody knew I was on the bay 'cause *my* daddy was on the bay, and my daddy was on the bay 'cause *his* daddy was on the bay, and *his* daddy was on the bay 'cause *his* daddy had pitched him over the side of a homemade fishing skiff and said, "Sink or swim. Swim or drown. Make up yore mind, boy!"

And that comes as close as anything to explaining how we all got neck deep in water and near neurotic about it. Because from the day Grandpa went over the side of a homemade fishing skiff until the day he died (or, in my interpretation, left town) he swore everything led to the water, and he wasn't talking plain water—he was talking water underneath his fishing skiff. He got up, facing it at black dawn until whenever he returned, and it was the water's heavy smell of everything it had been doing the night before that told him everything he needed to know about fishing for that day. So he didn't need to ask anybody how was fishing. He just went down to the docks and knew in a couple of seconds if he should turn around and just call it a day.

But that wasn't what Grandpa did most days. Most days he got up and ran full blind tilt to the bay. Every motion and every act was something that got him there, and if he started thinking it was something else, then he said he would put up a FOR SALE sign in the grocery store and sell the damn boat by nightfall.

But Grandpa never did, and he never owned nothing but a fishing skiff, and he didn't want a shrimp boat. "Got enough trouble with one," he said. Grandpa was one of the last commercial fishermen running the bays for big bull drum and redfish. One of the last legal ones anyhow, because Grandpa was in that era right before fishing with nets was declared illegal and the redfish became the damn sportsmen's *numero uno* game fish. Grandpa left it to his sons and his sons' sons to run the bay, with a game warden constantly on their back shoulder, watching every move they made with their boats and trucks. My daddy, who had fished since he was seven (and smoking cigarettes at the same time), finally gave up net fishing entirely because he said he got a crick in his neck from constantly looking over his shoulder. My Uncle Bud and Sanchez never quit running, and Sanchez used an alias for half his adult life.

The great-grandpa who started it all for us in Texas was a tumbleweed, and the sea was just another stopping-off place. He'd come from Arkansas and didn't particularly like the water. Didn't like the smell. Didn't like the salt sticking in his eyes. So the sea spoke to him for the first and last time and said it was all right. She didn't like him neither. He could vamoose at any time. So one day (to nobody's surprise but his wife's) he took off and disappeared, and the only thing left of that dark handsome fella is a picture on Grandpa's wall. "So *that's* him!" is what everybody says, but handsome is as handsome does, so looks aren't the thing most remembered.

Grandpa said, Weell, at least ole Mister Oklahoma (the state we figured he went to) got his family to the sand flats of Black Jack Island and didn't leave them out in the middle of nowhere to drown. Other than that mild remark, Grandpa didn't say nothing about his daddy, and nobody discussed it except when they got to quarreling over who was acting ornery enough to look like the fella on the wall. It was never figured entirely either, whether it was his rambling ways or his Indian wife with eight kids or the water telling him to get gone what really drove the daddy of us all to leave. Still, those unanswered mysteries didn't keep us kids from asking Grandpa interesting ones like What kind of Indian he was? Was it Comanche? Apache? Flesh-eating Karankawa! I was hoping flesh-eaters, but Grandpa at the same point in the questioning every time would stick his bare ugly foot in our faces and yell, "Blackfoot, you pack of heathens!"

Then he would tell us kids how he first came to Seadrift from Black Jack Island and how the price of fish had shot up to thirteen cents a pound, and how he believed he was telling us kids the gospel truth when he claimed he was stung by more stingray than anybody else in

Calhoun County. He always kept an onion poultice on the worst
wound, and sometimes he pulled off the smelly wrapping and gave us
kids the Jergens lotion, and we would rub his calf where a giant
stingray had hooked him and nearly drug him out into the wilds of
San Antonio Bay.

Grandpa was lucky. He knew his place and his time, and while it may
have been colored a bit with the skiff near-drowning and parental aban-
donment, Grandpa wasn't in Oklahoma with Mister Whatshisface,
being miserable. So Grandpa spent the rest of his considerable life
chasing big bull drum all over San Antonio and Spirit Center and
Hynes and Mission bays, and when it came time in his old age for the
sea to release him, she wouldn't let him go. She clung like a barnacle to
his chest. When he died in a rest home, where the white walls fought
with the whiter sheets and next to his bed was dried-up angel food cake,
his daughters said the only thing that had mattered to him was getting
enough wooden corks to hang a trammel net so he could go fishing. But
Grandpa was old and couldn't stand without one of his daughters
holding him upright, and he didn't know that fishing with nets was
illegal and that nobody made wooden corks anymore. So Grandpa lay
on his bed in a dream he wouldn't wake from, because the day that
schooner touched on Black Jack Island was the day a china blue wild-
ness crept in and possessed him. And Grandpa was a goner long before
his daddy was gone.

But that wasn't how it went with Daddy. There was no water talking
in Billy Bones's ear. It skipped a generation. With Daddy it was
smoking cigarettes. Before we went shrimping in the morning, all he
wanted me to do was make the coffee, and he'd bring the cigarettes. I
wrapped the mason jar we carried the coffee in with old newspaper
and Daddy wrapped the carton of cigarettes in his spare khaki pants
he always brought along for a clean change. The cigarettes were the
most important thing, though. We could skimp and get short on the
coffee, but not on the smokes. Once we traveled half the night to get
to Mesquite Bay (which was clear across the bay and almost in
another county) and Daddy forgot his cigarettes, so we turned around
towards home, using the moon to navigate with, and made it back to
Mesquite Bay just in time for the first drag at dawn.

My sole diet was coffee. Daddy never took food. Food just messed
up your focus. Fogged up your brain, and you sure didn't need to be

fogged in the head when it was already muggy enough on the bay. So it was just cigarettes and coffee: cigarettes and coffee for him, and pots and pots of coffee for me. Black or cold never bothered us, but if the coffee got too weak looking, Daddy stuck the coffee pot on the engine's exhaust pipe and left it there until the smoke from the coffee grounds boiling over drove us out of the cabin.

Having a woman on the bay was a rarity, but Daddy had his reasons. Reason one was I knew how to keep my mouth shut and I could handle the wheel of a boat in the wind and didn't cry if it felt like we were turning over. Then too, when we were letting out a net in water so black you couldn't see the net, I could anticipate orders before they were ever given. But I didn't count that as a *real* reason, because anticipating orders wasn't difficult. Most women I knew had a lifetime of anticipating orders.

Second reason, and the quality I had heaviest on my side, was I could fix a shrimp net when an experienced captain couldn't and wouldn't even if he knew how. The fishermen in town had long since given up wondering over it, and just wanted to make sure I would fix their nets or overhaul them for the winter. I became known far and wide as that woman on the salt marsh who fixed nets with nothing but the headlights from a pickup truck showing her where to cut webbing.

So I was left alone to be a fisherwoman, and by the time I was twenty-four I had my first boat, and when I was twenty-eight I had my second. That first boat was light-years behind the men's and training-pants boys', but it was mine. All mine. A boat brown as a turd and finagled from a cranky old fishermen for a bargain. I bought the boat with money I made from crabbing, and every morning the gasoline danced a jig so fierce on that flat-head engine that I'm surprised I'm living and not blown to smithereens. That first solo year as captain, my momma yelled so long and hard about me falling over and drowning and leaving her with all my kids that my daddy built rails around the whole blooming thing, except for the bow and the stern. It was a regular kindergarten boat with training wheels. Then one day the bolts fell out of the rail and the rail came off and I fell over twice and nearly drowned. I never touched crabbing again.

Still, net woman and boat captain or not, the bay and the docks were an informal Men Only club for those who were paying strict attention. But Froggie hadn't paid attention since high school, and given his inattention to detail, I was his recruit for the fish house, and probably gave my momma her happiest moment. And I wasn't just the recruit; I was the *sole* candidate. My little baby brother, John Boy, had worked at the fish house for years and was divorced and not dating and was totally disgusted over the number of hours he was having to work, so one day he threw down the ice shovel and quit.

Froggie came to the house and told Daddy. (He didn't tell me. Froggie never liked going through a woman.) He told Daddy, "She's got a job if she wants one."

Momma was there and it was her moment, and she didn't waste two seconds because she figured the fish-house job was a real step towards money and a step away from the bay. So Momma punched me several times with her hard finger, and I felt her breath hot on my face. "You better take that job. You're not makin' a piddlin' cent out there on that bay, and if you drown who's gonna take care of them babies? Me and yore daddy is too old to take care of them."

"Well, I figure their daddy can take care of them," I said.

"Oh, pooey! I'll stand on my head in the middle of the road if he does that," Momma said, and Daddy said, "Oh, Goldie. Just shut up!"

So I went to the bay and sat on the back deck of the *SeaBee*, until finally I walked over to the fish house. In the beginning I let all five kids come down and squirt water into the shrimp vat or tear down the mounds of ice in the ice vault so that it was winter somewhere in their lives. But generally I worried too much about them falling off the docks and drowning. Accidental drownings of two or more family members on the same day was a real contender for graveyard space and ranked right alongside of what seemed to waft straight from the chemical plants anchored in the wetlands.

I had my work cut out for me with the kids and the nets and the fish house, so until the shrimp boats pulled into the harbor and hauled their shrimp baskets onto the docks, I sat in the shell road outside the fish house and patched nets. The road was the only thing big enough to spread a net on, so most times I blocked the road. Old beat-up trucks loaded down with nets and overhauled engine parts would come up and shift gears, then go around my net to get down the road to their boats. (Shrimpers almost never ran over another man's net unless it was deliberate.) Sometimes instead of going around, a shrimper would drop off a wrecked net, and sometimes too a gill netter who remembered my Grandpa or knew my seventy-year-old Uncle Bud and his worse old deckhand, who were still running the bays with illegal nets and game wardens on their stern. But a net was a net and I patched a hole the same way, so half the time an illegal gill net was piled up alongside the fish-house door.

And the fishermen said the same thing every time. Whenever you got time. Whatever you wanna do. Just call the wife when yore ready and she'll come down with a checkbook. Then I'd smile and say, Shore, shore, and they'd wait a minute and say, Ain't it hot out here fer you? And I'd say, Nah, and they'd nod their heads and smile in agreement, and drive down to their boats and finally get out and haul nets, with bad backs.

Sometimes shrimpers passed me cups of coffee in the road. They especially did when they wanted nets patched in a hurry, because every shrimper knew I loved coffee and it was always a surefire way to get me to skip one net ahead of another. So by evening I often had three or four coffee cups lost in the webbing.

This particular day I wasn't working on a net. I had several piled up, but I wasn't working on them. I was surprised when Fern Dale showed up at the door, looking like a flower dropped into a rusting bucket of nails. Fern Dale stood with one hand on her dress and one hand on her throat, and she kept talking and talking until finally I asked her what she wanted. She pulled the hand off her throat and stuck it on her skirt. Now she had two hands on her skirt.

"I need you to get yore environmental meeting out of city hall. The city is trying to get a grant, and yore meeting doesn't look good. It's sending up a red flag in Washington."

I looked at her and laughed. "You want that meeting moved because it'll do *what*?"

"Send up a red flag! Really! That's what it'll do."

"Well, all right. I guess I can move it to the schoolhouse. I don't think that will hurt anything."

"No! No!" she shouted. Her voice was loud but went nowhere, and I thought maybe the fish house's tin walls just weren't used to her soft woman sound.

"I need you to take the meeting *clear* outa town! They don't want it *anywhere* near here."

There was a fleeting second where I felt I was dreaming about some-thing important, but I couldn't remember. I forgot what I said. Maybe I laughed again. I always laughed when I couldn't talk. Laughing was a language I had traded for words years ago, and so I guess Fern Dale misunderstood. She thought I said yes or she believed I thought the whole thing was funny, and really she didn't know me at all.

"All right," she said, and relief shot across her face. "You'll move this meeting out? Maybe just hold off on the whole thing for a while?"

"I don't believe so," I said.

But she was out of the fish house and not listening, and only turned to say, "You know, it ain't me wanting this. It's just folks. . . . Folks in Washington. All those red flags. You know how it is with grants. This paper and that paper, and nobody wanting any trouble. They just need a little time, is all. A little time to get things done."

What things done? Fern Dale's words didn't make any sense, so when Donna Sue came back to the fish house from hauling all her trash and mopping her floors and God knows what else at her house, I told her about the new development. She said, "Well, hell!" and launched into a tirade on city hall and Port Lavaca and half the men in her past. It was loud enough and long enough that I hardly saw Sanchez when his boat pulled into the docks. His boat was tied on the stern and he was about to throw a bowline when I walked to the door. Sanchez was bareheaded and barefooted and done up in denim everything, and when he saw me he threw a wild laugh.

"You don't have any more boats out, do you? Anyhow, I'm docking here."

I didn't answer. I just watched him from the doorway. Sanchez hadn't brought in shrimp in a week and made no pretense about it. If he caught any shrimp in his try net (and I wasn't even sure he threw over the try net), he was taking them home to his cats. He just fueled up every third day like clockwork.

"Well, Sanchez, ain't you the early bird," I said, and watched his bare feet jump from the boat to the docks a dozen times.

"Don't call me that! You want half those friggin' game wardens to hear?"

"Sanchez, I doubt there's a single soul in this county that don't know your alias, so you can dang sure bet the game wardens know it too."

"Well, no need to help them along! Hey, hand me that fuel hose, will you? Now, here. Look at this! Tell me what you think of this."

Sanchez pulled a neatly folded piece of paper out of his pocket and threw it at me. "Don't lose it! I've got the loran readings on that entire Hynes Bay area. Right there on that piece of paper. Got some clerk down at the courthouse to pull out all the old transcripts on my game-warden trial. I'm gonna check the readings with the transcript. All those idiots throwing out evidence, and I bet they didn't even read their own stuff! The morons!"

Sanchez was more legendary than most shrimpers, and while not to belittle his dozens of Vietnam medals that made him the most decorated war veteran in seven counties, Sanchez's fame was due to his being charged, ten years after the war that made him famous, with attempted murder of two Texas Parks and Wildlife game wardens. Those charges were the fallout from probably the most spontaneous act of Sanchez's life: outrunning a game warden's boat. And it cost him the equivalent of thirty thousand dollars in lawyer fees and court costs, and a more sensational trial and media circus than had ever crossed a county courthouse room.

That trial and guilty verdict warped Sanchez like rain does cheap pine. Nothing escaped the calamity. Not his health. Not his Pentecostal faith. Not his family. And certainly not Sanchez's soul. Because a truth had been violated, and the same government and institutions and beliefs and sound reasons that had sent him into a war to incinerate rice fields and jungles and blow villages into kingdom come, then land his jet like a feather on a bucking aircraft carrier, now sent him into courtrooms where judges and agencies assassinated his character.

So it was no wonder Sanchez became Sanchez and kept government moves and state moves (official, personal, and otherwise) well documented and filed in locked cases alongside a Russian assault rifle and a bayonet he kept on the floorboard of his Ford truck. Texas Parks and Wildlife was under a file penciled THE ENEMY, and the Baptist church was under GOD. Sanchez documented political corruption and obvious horsing around, and every time the government did squat and every time the government *didn't* do squat, Sanchez was prepared. He was armed. And in the chance and unhappy event that Seadrift was ever run over by government troops or corrupt game wardens from

Austin, Sanchez, with all he had stashed in his truck and locked-up toolbox, was convinced he would triumph.

It wasn't without compassion and some real understanding that I handed Sanchez his paper scribbled with navigational readings and court transcript references. He carefully folded it crosswise, then in half, then shoved it in his pocket and crammed the fuel hose into the diesel outlet fiberglassed into the deck of his boat.

"When's your trial gonna be over? I thought it *was* over," I said.

"Hey, that trial ain't *ever* gonna be over, little sister!" he said, and he looked at me briefly, then glanced back to the hose. "Stop that pump at a hundred gallons, would you? One oh oh. Would you do that for me, little sister? Oh, there isn't nothing like a little baby sister. Nothing in the world beats them! When I run for county commissioner I'm gonna put you and Donna Sue right at the top of the list on my committees. . . . Hey, now, watch that pump, dummy! A hundred! Don't want a fraction over."

Sanchez straightened up and shoved the hose straight in the air. "I win! Three days and a hundred gallons! You tell me what other shrimper can run a boat three days on a hundred gallons! You just name one!"

"There ain't been a one that's went three days in a row, so there ain't none in the running," I said.

"Well, wait till I run for commissioner. A lot of things are going to change for the fishermen. *A fish in every pot!* So tell me, what's more important, catching shrimp now or your big brother winning a campaign that busts out that yoke of pestilence we've got riding down here? Pack of morons! Probably haven't had an original thought since the day the county was invented."

"Hey, Sanchez . . . whadda you know about some economic grant going on down at city hall?"

"A lotta money circulatin' and stinkin' in politics. That's what I know. And what's this meetin' about anyhow? Why'd you do that? Who got that thing goin'?"

"You heard about *that*?"

"Hey, I wasn't born yesterday. You think I'm stupid, or what? Hell, yes, I've heard about it. Doug Lynch, who is, by the way, entrenched in that economic crowd over there, called last night and said would I please get that sister of mine outa there. Said you was heatin' things up unnecessarily."

Sanchez glared as much as he was capable, then he stepped off the boat. The harbor was like the harbor I had seen a thousand times on a thousand different mornings, except now a late-morning sun was mixed in it.

"Looky here," he said. "Surely you aren't so stupid that you expect these money mongrels to have any interests other than their own money and power. Look around you, sister! This is exactly why your big brother is running for office. Shuffle up the cards for a change. Let's see what the morons do then!"

"I don't even *know* a Doug Lynch. Who's he? And since *when* has anybody cared what a fisherman in Seadrift thought about anything? And especially a woman! Who the heck cares!"

"Are you stupid? I *told you*! Doug Lynch *is* economic development. And they don't care about *you*! What they care about is that you're messing up their little world. Some little scheme they've got hatched, and who knows what it is? It can be anything. It's no more personal than that."

"But it's just a simple meeting. Why can't *they* buzz off? Why me? Why not them?" I said.

"Because they're men, honey, and you're just a sweet, stupid little mommy. And *they're* running the show and *you're* not."

I guessed Sanchez's information was supposed to make me stop, but it didn't. It just did the reverse, and I plotted an hour more than I've ever done (which was zero), and with a little help from a three-county-wide phone book, I listed every politician I ever knew who walked, talked, and breathed in the area. Then I talked with them on the phone. Well, not actually talking with *them*, but with their secretaries, who said they would talk to them, then later the secretaries calling back and saying, Yes, Senator So-and-So will attend the community meeting. It is on his calendar. It is on his schedule. Then I sat in my chair at the fish house and couldn't think what was the second thing I needed to do.

Well, the second thing done was the very next day. The only newspaper in the county wrote an article about the chemical industry, and they quoted someone saying how harmless industry's chemicals were and how there was absolutely no health threat in the area, even though Calhoun County ranked nationally on emissions.

So industry got to do a profile on itself and nobody else was invited and nobody else commented. There was no mention made of an environmental meeting. I was beginning to believe that outside of a banker and a city secretary and an economic development man, what I was doing was no more attention-getting than a cow bellering for its calf.

3

An Outlaw and a Letter

Wally was the *numero uno* fish-house owner, the premier bandito of all banditos (the game wardens were still watching his truck), and nobody looked any further than the door Wally was coming through 'cause nobody coming *after* Wally was important. Today Wally came by himself, without none of his women (and he had *plenty*, 'cause Wally never had women-collecting problems). I didn't recognize his truck, but that wasn't unusual. Wally got into any car or truck that had keys and drove it off in a whirlwind of oyster dust and screaming tires, and the owner would eventually find it somewhere in town, abandoned like a dusty kitten.

Now Wally wanted something, and he wanted it quick. He had no time for slow women, so he motioned me with his big red hand. "Hey, hey. Who you got here? Donna Sue? Get her! Tell her I said to get in here."

"She ain't here," I said. "Went home to mop her floors or something."

Wally grabbed my arm and yanked me to the fish-house door, where he shoved his head half in and half out. He might've been hiding, but I wasn't sure. Then he turned and his face got quiet, but his eyes wouldn't stop moving. "Who you got here?" he said. "Who? Who?"

"I *told* you. I ain't got nobody, and nobody's out shrimpin'. I'm just by myself, twiddlin' my thumbs down here."

"Go look down that road and see if you see a game warden's truck comin'."

I leaned out the front door and looked down the oyster road.

"There ain't a thing movin'," I said.

"Is *zat* so? Well, looky here, if those game wardens *do* come in here—and with *my shrimp, my shrimp*—I want you to tell 'em the shrimp are forty-fifty count. None of this fifty-sixty count jazz like they're gonna tell you. Those are shrimp they took off *my* boats!

When they leave, I'll buy the shrimp back from you and give 'em back to the boats they belong to. Won't make a dime on it. Just doin' it for nothin'."

Wally stopped and looked around. He walked out the back door and onto the docks. "Where's all yore boats? Mine are still at the lane, catchin' a few shrimp. I betcha I got a lot more goin' on than you. Whatcha got goin'?"

"I ain't got a frazzlin' thing goin'," I said, and watched him move all over the fish house, starting at the office door, then going to the ice vault where I kept the shrimp boxes. "You go in there and Donna Sue's liable to cut off yore fingers. *Real* quick."

"Nah, nah," Wally said, and waved his hand at me, but he didn't open the vault. "I've got a lot better operations down where I'm at. Tell Deputy Dawg . . . hell, tell Donna Sue to tell Deputy Dawg that the next time he goes out, that I can give him a better deal. Give him a good spot right down there on the end of the docks, and ain't nobody gonna bother him. Just him and the seagulls."

"You come all the way down here just to steal one of my boats that ain't even been out? Whatsa matter? All yore boats run off or what? Gotta wrestle all your boats from your own cousin!"

"Nah . . . just cousins by marriage. What's that? And yeah, well, maybe. One or two boats left. Got another'n leavin' for the river tomorrow. Ain't gonna find nothin' there, though. Told 'em. Just wait around here a week or so. Wait and see. Why make that river bunch rich? Who's takin' care of you in the winter anyhow? Floatin' a loan and buyin' yore net? Me! That's who!"

Wally wasn't bragging; he was just telling his story. It was a story I'd heard him deliver to the fishermen a hundred times, standing in his khaki pants with his hands shoved in the pockets, messing with loose change, knocking quarters and nickels against each other, talking fishing and political strategy and who would (men) and who wouldn't (women) go to Austin to talk to the legislators about another fishing bill that would wipe out the fisheries. Then long after most of the shrimpers had already left, disgusted and angry and tired, Wally remained, oblivious to the leaving, wearing his usual impeccably ironed white shirt with the top three buttons undone and the shirt collar standing up stiff and hard against his ears, because that was the way it was done when he was young and growing up in the cool, cool fifties.

Thirty-five years later and bordering on less cool, Wally and his ironed shirt were still inseparable and it was all blamed on his momma, who for a very long, uncontested time had been Seadrift's oldest living pioneer, and easily spotted because she was the only woman in town that walked the streets wearing a long, hot black dress in broad daylight. Her husband, an injured war veteran, had died early, so when Wally and his younger brother were boys and still at home, she raised them all on ironing she took in. And the woman ironed and she ironed until she couldn't iron no more. The front porch of their ex–domino hall home looked like a bad Texas hanging, with the entire length hung in ironed pants and ironed shirts and ironed dresses, all dangling on metal clothes hangers, waiting on the owners to pick them up.

It was probably that childhood sight of women's clothes hanging off his front porch and a woman working hard as a man that traumatized and branded Wally with his knack for negating women and turning everything they said or did in reverse. So I wasn't surprised when Wally turned and did that reverse thing.

"Why don'tcha do what Howdy wants?" he said.

I looked hard at Wally and lied, lied, lied. "I ain't got *no* idea what yore talkin' about, Wally."

"Sure you do. Howdy wants you to quit messin' with those plants. Says he can get something for the fishermen if you'd just settle down and turn 'em plants loose. Heck, you do *that*, then maybe we can get the chemical plants on *our* side for a while. Help us send a few pot-shots over Parks and Wildlife's bow."

I didn't know if Wally was serious or if there was a blood vessel leaking in that head of his and the Howdy subject was just the first break in a ton of blood that was fixing to come next.

"Sounds right by me," he said. "Give 'em what they want, and maybe the fishermen can get a little bit too. It's time we get something out of Austin."

"And *a banker* is gonna do all that?" I said.

"Sure! That's what I just said! Howdy's talkin' to *big* industry. . . . And who the heck knows which ones it is. Maybe the whole mess of them! So just let 'em alone! Give 'em a little breathin' room."

"Industry is supposed to help? And maybe *not* stick another pipe in the bay and maybe *not* get another bay shut down because something *accidently, oops*—like mercury—got dumped? Who the heck needs help from them? I think they've done *plenty* already. Thank yew very much."

"Oh, you don't know nothin'! Ain'tcha ever heard of workin' underneath the table? Nothin's what it really seems."

"Maybe Howdy better quit talkin' to other men before he talks to me. I could save him a bunch of time and trouble that way."

"All righty. But I'm tellin' you, you can do a lot better for yourself if you'd just listen to a man ever' now and then. Just shut up and listen to what I'm tellin' you."

Wally shook his head, and his thin hair came unglued and the top shined, shined like one of the quarters in his pocket. Then Wally started losing interest fast, and another took its place. I could see it in his face, then coming through his eyeballs, then there it was as physical as Bill's ghost ship: the wonderment and whereabouts and conditions of shrimp boats and shrimp, captains and deckhands, fish houses and prices. Shrimping had taken over. Wally left, and the dust he left covered every mesquite tree growing in a ditch and every fence post in a fence line.

That's the last thought I gave the chemical plants. I had my meeting place. What else was there to worry over? Then I got a letter in the mail that changed everything. It was a single letter with my name on it and nothing else, like whoever had sent it had only those keys on the typewriter. I opened the letter and it said: *Ms. Wilson. Are you aware of this?*

That was it. No name. No typed nothing. The only other thing was a folded newspaper clipping, and it dropped in my lap. The clipping was a public notice on a chemical plant named Formosa Plastics. A chemical plant I'd never heard of. I read it twice and never understood a word. I figured the newspaper clipping was clearly lawyer stuff, so I picked up Froggie's phone and called our free lawyer in Houston. Mister Blackburn.

"All right," Blackburn said. "Read it again. Give me the full name of that company. What's the permit number? *All* the numbers." Then Blackburn said he'd get the full permit from Austin. They would have a file on it somewhere.

"We can ask for a public hearing on the permits," he said. "That should be a real fine start for your group. We can announce it at the meeting. You got that going, don't you? Then I guess we'll see what we'll see. If you have any trouble with reporters, just send them to me."

I got off the phone and turned the letter over and over in my hand. I put it on the desk and looked at it. The letter wasn't real like the fish house was real or the sun lying on the dock was real, so I made no mention of it to anybody. Saying nothing made no difference to Donna Sue and me anyhow. Silence was our third hand at the bay, and we could sit at the fish house for hours without a word between us. The only strong disagreement we ever had was two days after the letter, and that was over a Vietnamese shrimper who had wanted to sell his shrimp at our fish house at a time when *no* Vietnamese sold shrimp at *any* fish house in Seadrift. It was a leftover legacy from a five-year-old war between the Vietnamese and Anglo crabbers, where boats got burned and houses were torched and a crabber named Billy Joe Aplin was killed on a bluff overlooking San Antonio Bay.

So on that day, and in an argument over whether to buy shrimp from the Vietnamese shrimper, I ended up pitching the filing cabinet through the window. There was no screens on the window, so nothing stopped the cabinet's flight and the Vietnamese shrimper didn't call back. He got scared before he got a price.

The filing cabinet stayed outside, and I never got tired of looking at it when I came down to the bay to load shrimp or check on the shrimp boats and fish house. Then a week after the argument, Froggie came down to the fish house and saw the filing cabinet. "Uuuhhh," he said, and turned and went back to his truck and looked at the truck a minute, then he turned and went back to the filing cabinet. It was the first I'd seen Froggie since brownie shrimp season started, and he had cleared out then because an obnoxious shrimp buyer had showed up in an eighteen-wheeler, wanting to negotiate shrimp prices, and Froggie saw him through the window and split.

Froggie came in with the filing cabinet and sat it on the desk. "Found this outside," he said.

"Yeah, I threw it outside," I said.

"You want it outside?"

"Nah, just leave it there," I said.

So the filing cabinet was on the desk and leaning hard where it was bent, and still Froggie stayed. I figured he wanted some space, so I walked out on the docks and looked over the water and past it to the tail end of Seadrift where I had once walked in knee-high salt grass and been chased by sportsmen who saw me walking on their grass. I heard Froggie inside, fooling with the coffeepot and knocking things everywhere. Finally I went inside, and Froggie was picking up the pot and sitting it down, so I took the coffeepot out of his hand and filled it with water and stuck in some coffee grounds we kept in a rusting can. Then I turned the coffeepot on.

"Hey!" Froggie barked.

"Yeah?"

"Somebody . . . uuuhhh. Oh, shoot!" he said, and abruptly turned and left the fish house. He walked to his truck and I followed him out, not moving as fast as him. At the truck door, Froggie turned, and one boot was already in the truck and one hand was already on the wheel.

"Just watch that phone," he said. "All right? Don't want no huge telephone bill."

"Who said something?" I asked, but I said it to a truck that was already backed out and halfway to the corner. The empty shrimp baskets in the back end of his truck rolled from side to side like lopped-off heads.

I should've known the phone was gonna get me in trouble. At times like this I wished I was more orderly, or at least kept a running list of long-distance phone calls. But I wasn't and I didn't. I was more like combustion on a telephone cord. Then too, people just kept calling me on the phone. My phone. Froggie's phone. It didn't matter. That night Donna Sue called me at home on my phone.

"Turn on your TV," she said. "Channel twenty-five's got something on Formosa."

A reporter was talking about a newspaper article from a Dallas paper that named Formosa Plastics as a persistent violator of the Clean Water Act. After the reporter, the station flashed to a representative of Formosa, who said it was not true. Formosa had *unequivocally* never dumped into Cox's Creek or any creek.

Next there was an aerial shot of Lavaca Bay and, near the edge, a black, tangled structure of pipes and towers and stacks belching black smoke into a white sky—Formosa Plastics. It didn't show Cox's Creek. I wasn't sure where that was. The story was maybe five minutes, and as

I watched the screen I wondered why a Dallas paper would print something that wasn't true. Still puzzled, I called the TV reporter and said, "Is it true Formosa didn't dump anything?"

"That's what they say."

"Why did the Dallas paper print it, then? Did you check with the Dallas reporter?"

"Nope, sure didn't. Formosa said it wasn't true."

The next morning I called the Dallas paper and tracked down the reporter. "Hey, that stuff you said about Formosa Plastics being a persistent violator of the Clean Water Act. Was that true?" I said.

"Sure it was. That's why I printed it. Can't print it unless it's true," he said.

"Well, Formosa said it wasn't. Said they never dumped nothing."

"Well, now . . . is that right?" The reporter laughed and said he was sitting at his desk and looking at the documents. He had them in his hand. He would send them to me. Four administrative orders from the Environmental Protection Agency for wastewater violations.

So they can lie on TV news! And it is all right! I couldn't believe it. How could anyone know the truth? Was there a *sign*—something showing that it was a lie—or was there nothing? I couldn't remember. Did the Formosa man look ill or well when he denied it?

It was too early in the morning to leave for the fish house, so I sat in the rocking chair in a room that was part kitchen and part something else. The ceiling was high and white and shot with Sheetrock and nails. A thing started and never finished, and under it, a hundred times a week, I rocked one baby after another (Crockett until he wanted down, or Santanna until she wanted up).

Today I didn't. Santanna was messing in a low kitchen cabinet, and Crockett had two packages of weenies out of the icebox and had tore them into tiny pieces and piled them in a spot in the middle of the floor. Next he was going after the bread. I don't know what Crockett was building. He was making about as much sense as everybody else, only doctors had put a name on Crockett's condition (autism), but I didn't have none to put on mine. I just knew I had one afternoon left before the meeting at the schoolhouse, and I didn't know what after that. Maybe nothing. Maybe I would be exactly what I was under a Sheetrock ceiling.

Fear filled my head and strangled my thinking, so when I got to the bay I called Blackburn, and he said it would be all right. He had already filed with the state and requested a hearing on Formosa's permits on behalf of our group, and all he needed now was directions to the schoolhouse. He was bringing down a couple of speakers to help out.

"First meetings are always the hardest," he said. "But don't worry. You'll get through it."

Then Blackburn hung up, and I stayed holding the warm phone like it was somebody's hand and not ten minutes that had already gone. I didn't know what I was getting into, and it certainly wasn't as clearly marked as the marshes that separated the bays from the land and said this thing was the land and that other thing was the water and try not to confuse the two.

I tried to focus on the fish house, but the shrimpers had already tied their boats to the docks, then got in their trucks and stared at the windshield like walking dead. A shrimper could face poverty or misfortune, but what he wasn't willing or able to face was that minute-to-minute reality of the sun coming down on an empty deck and it barely high noon.

Sanchez came by the fish house twice and both times he brought a thermos of coffee. He twisted the thermos open as he came through the door, and poured me a cup without asking. There was no reason for his coming and going, he said. He just wanted to see two women loose as cannons. The second time Sanchez brought hamburgers he had bought on sale in Port Lavaca, and threw two on the desk and wanted to know what he needed to bring to the meeting.

"Want me to pick up some coffee? I can get you a five-pound can."

"Nope," I said. "Jus' need you to *show up*! *Comprende*? Me and Donna Sue might be the only ones there. Then how's Blackburn gonna like that? Comin' all the way down here and nobody showing. Besides, me and Donna Sue are making cakes, and there's probably gonna be more cakes than people."

Sanchez threw back his head and laughed. Then that wild length of denim he had thrown into the fish house he now flung back into his Ford truck, and he was down the road and gone and probably to a Port Lavaca courthouse he had been to twice that morning.

Me and Donna Sue stayed at the fish house until Bill Bailey came in with forty-five pounds of shrimp in an orange plastic basket. He was in early because he had to go to Houston for chemotherapy. Then if every-thing went all right and he didn't get sick from the chemo, he might just stop by Kemah or Galveston and look for his ghost shrimp boat. Bill flashed his white California teeth and said if that schoolteacher wife of his didn't get wind of it first, he might just buy that boat.

Then Donna Sue picked up her keys and purse and vamoosed, and I stayed and double-checked the shrimp tally on the books, then walked into the ice vault and double-checked the shrimp boxes there. I threw a shovel of ice on each box, shut and locked the vault door, and walked out on the docks. A gray heron, standing on one leg at the end of the pier, was startled into flight. The bird moved slowly, like a ton of baloney flung into the air, and it flew a hundred feet across the harbor, then settled on a pile of oyster shells at the water's edge. I watched the bird a minute, but the heron did a pretty good job of ignoring me.

I went home to bake a cake and haul the kids out of the scrub oak and the pond. Ramona was the oldest, twelve, and the one I counted on most, and she was out on the porch swing with Santanna, the baby. Crockett sat in the window and ran his fingers down the screen, and his eyes didn't move when I came on the porch, and his fingers didn't quit their moving.

"They were little hellions," Ramona said, and her dark, tiny face bunched behind her too-big glasses. "I couldn't make them do nothin', and you should see what Crockett did in there."

"That's what kids do," I said.

"You *always* say that," she wailed.

"That's because it's the truth. Messes are what they're in the busi-ness of."

I put Santanna on my hip while I watched Crockett through the screen. He didn't wear a shirt, and his body was as polished and smooth as a river stone. He made no sound except for the sound coming from his fingers, and his fingers were like a river diverted; a river running through him to the screen and through the lines he drew.

"Go get Crockett, Tanna. We're gonna make us a cake. Won't that be fun? Go on, go get him." I put Santanna down, and she ran to Crockett and pounded the screen with her two baby fists. *Screen ain't gonna make it*, I thought, and I went inside the house.

I started on the cake and cleaning the kitchen at the same time, and when I got the cake going, I moved from one room to the next, starting at the bottom of the house and going up. Clothes were everywhere and in various stages of damp and near-damp and sopping wet. Either the kids had been in the pond or they had dug deep enough holes under the oak trees to strike water. I washed three loads and hung them on an old trot fishing line that I used to catch catfish on the Guadalupe River, but which now was strung in the backyard between two oak trees.

I stayed busy cleaning rooms and directing kids, and tried hard not to think about the meeting. Then Ramona took the cake out of the oven and put it on the kitchen table to cool, but I told her the babies would get it there, so she moved the cake to the stove and iced it while it was still hot, and the top blistered and peeled like burned skin.

I went upstairs and found Goldie and Sarah and Santanna in front of an open door. All three girls were blond and didn't look a bit like me, and they looked up from their papers and their doll playing, and the look was so familiar I thought I had opened the door already. But I hadn't entered yet, so I stepped over their drug-out piles of paper and said, "We're fixin' to have supper, so y'all go on and clean up this mess. Go on, now."

Later as I dressed Crockett, the girls rushed in and said the chemical plants were on the TV set again. "Which one?" I said, and none of them knew, so I walked to the kitchen.

It was the same reporter on the same channel, but a different story. A local state senator was being interviewed, and he said he was not attending a local environmental meeting in Seadrift. Then an unidentified aide of Washington Congressman Laughlin said he had no plans to attend a local environmental meeting in Calhoun County. The congressman was out of the district.

I held Crockett's shirt and thought, *Now, who is having another meeting in Seadrift?* I didn't think that they were talking about me. Even when they said *Seadrift*. Even when they said *environment*. It took five solid minutes to realize that the meeting all the politicians wouldn't attend was *mine*.

4

Adversaries Approach

The best of all meetings is the one canceled. Mine wasn't, so I had no hope. I couldn't survive the talking, for silence was my religion, and I was its convert. My conversion began at the Mockingbird House, an unfinished, unpainted house with a porch that faced a single dirt road and a single mulberry tree. On one side was graveyard-lookin' trees that only a hurricane could kill, and on the other side was open fields of chest-high grass that would suddenly erupt into scrub oak and poison oak and morning glories. In this house and across the field from an old German man who constantly made my momma cry by accusing her of setting loose his old cows, me and my six brothers and sisters were born.

Before my parents lived there, the unpainted house had belonged to my widowed, short grandma, Rosebelle, who was a Christian and tithed regularly and severely all her shrimp-heading money to a Pentecostal evangelist on the radio. Before that the house had belonged to a man who sold it for the Dodge automobile Rosebelle's husband (and my other grandpa) drove to Texas in.

This is how it came to be traded our way: Grandma Rosebelle lost a son climbing into a skiff with a loaded gun. Then she lost a baby girl to a bad chest cold. Then she lost her husband, Ralf, when he was plowing a field with a mule and got hit by lightning, and the mule died and all the coins in Grandpa's pocket melted. So Grandma Rosebelle sorely hated Texas and she wanted out, out, out.

Lucky for her, my daddy obliged, and she at least moved from outside the Seadrift city limits to inside the Seadrift city limits and right into the cute little house my momma was married in. My momma had been in love with the house since it was *in town* and had *indoor* plumbing and an *indoor* toilet, and coming from nothing to nothing like she did, that cute place on the bayou looked like Scarlett O'Hara's mansion.

But Daddy swapped the house with the indoor toilet for the house without the toilet *and out in the country* (which was Daddy's criteria for cuteness), and for that my momma never forgave him. She never got her indoor toilet until years later, after a hurricane knocked down the one outside, and for years too, while we were young and driving her crazy, Momma would cross the bayou and the poison oak with all of us girls marching along behind her, toting dirty clothes a mile high, to Grandma's so she could do the wash on a real wringer washing machine in what used to be *her* house but now was Rosabelle's.

I was the fifth child and born in the middle of the shrimp and oyster season, and I never quit crying. Sometime along about the first year and well into my crying jag, my Aunt Pearlina took me to Houston to live with her and her union card–crazed husband so I wouldn't drive my mother totally crazy, and another baby sister could be born.

After my sister Janie was born and for the next three years, I quit crying and I quit talking too. In my silent world, nothing existed but the water and the marsh and someplace between the southeasterly wind as it crossed our summer porch. Then when I was five and lying alongside of my daddy's boat in the harbor, I saw the Water Lady resting. She was sitting on the shore, and her dress trailed on the edges of the mud flat and her gray hair curled around her bare feet. And when I came to her, she turned to me and her sigh was no louder than the white birds feeding on fish.

If my momma found my silence peculiar, she said nothing. She was looking for a little peace and quiet herself. So when the evening sun did its bloodletting and the shrimp boat masts showed black and high over the horizon, silence became my best game. And my refusal to talk was just the beginning. At seven I canceled the alphabet as though it never existed, at eleven I switched my handwriting, at thirteen I wasn't a team player, and by fifteen I wouldn't take group pictures or participate in class or eat anywhere near people. It was no great loss to me. My parents probably thought, *Well, at least she is in sports!* Because I threw heavy steel balls and flat wooden discuses into fierce winds and sometimes won a ribbon, but the truth be known, I was into those sports because they were solitary.

Then I spoke for the last time. In my last year in junior high, I had missed valedictorian by half a point but won salutatorian, so to accommodate the principal, I stood at long last before a crowd to speak. It was night and the lights were hot on the stage and hot on my hands, and I looked out and said blankly, "I have forgot the words," and walked off.

I didn't *willingly* talk after that. Instead I broke out windows and crawled through the glass shards to lay flat in weeds, or else prostrate on the mudflats where the salt water tugged the ends of my curly black hair. I was odd enough that my momma confided her concerns to Billy Bones in the kitchen one day (I was also a bit of a snoop). "Billy," she said, "I think somethin's the matter with that girl." But Billy Bones said nothing and smoked a cigarette. He didn't look at her. He only stared at an area somewhere between the ceiling and the wall and said, "Stupid women."

My Pentecostal upbringing fitted in nicely. I was clearly wicked and obstinate and going to hell, same as Daddy for his cigarette smoking and watching *Bonanza* and *Gunsmoke* on Sunday nights on the TV set instead of going to church. I couldn't save myself, for my tongue was tied and my handwriting locked in backwards! So I left the talking to others and contemplated my feet, and the only time I felt guilty was when I was a mother and believed I had passed on my silent gene to Crockett. I was why he was autistic.

But that wouldn't stop the meeting. I could have cut out my tongue and still I would have that cake and a lawyer to deal with. So I put the kids in the Sears van with a quilt to sit on and told Ramona to sit up front and hold the cake. Pretty pronto, Crockett went to the back of the van and pulled out all the wires of the taillight. That didn't worry me so much. What worried me was that six people would show up for the meeting and five of them would be my kids. I figured I was gonna have to tell Blackburn that I was no organizer. When I saw him, I would say, "I am no organizer, and that is the reason there are six people and two cakes in a meeting, and I am sorry you have come all the way from Houston."

I didn't believe there would be other cars. But there were, and one was Donna Sue and Deputy Dawg, and another was Blackburn. He was climbing out of his Jeep, and the first thing I saw was his black cowboy boots stepping down onto Seadrift's raw oyster road, and the second thing I saw was his everlasting confidence. That's how I knew he was Blackburn.

Then other cars showed, and I didn't know them and I didn't expect they knew me neither, so I walked past them and unlocked the school door like I was only the custodian with her mess of kids.

There were a couple of fishermen I knew, and they sat in white shirts and jeans in open trucks with rolled-down windows, and their hands moved like slow-turning leaves against the windshields. Deputy Dawg walked over to them, and the fishermen, one by one, climbed out of their trucks and settled around the fender of another truck and hitched their legs on the rusted bumper like it was the railing on somebody's shrimp boat. I knew they wouldn't come in until the last minute, and then it would be to walk single file to the back end of the room like it was only in the fringes of old buildings that they knew how to be.

Blackburn and Donna Sue followed me when I opened the door, and they turned and talked to each other with words solid as nickels on a winter floor. Apparently Blackburn was in good humor, and when he laughed Donna Sue laughed back as casual as if he was Deputy Dawg she was laughing to. I took the cake from Ramona and put it on a table in the back, where I knew the fishermen would be standing.

When I came to the front, Blackburn looked at me and said, "So. Ms. Wilson. What have we got here? And *where* are those lights?"

So this was Blackburn. He was suited in black and his jacket wasn't buttoned, but opened on a white shirt and a red tie with climbing roses. He moved like he had live fire ants on him. He wouldn't sit down and he wouldn't stand still, and finally he went with Donna Sue, looking for the lights, while I shoved open the auditorium door because it had closed again. Only Crockett stood there now and fiddled with the doorknob.

There were more cars, but the people didn't come inside; they only stood outside in bundles of quiet talk that quit when I walked past. I went looking for Blackburn, who had apparently found the lights, because every light was turned on, even the kitchen lights in a back room.

"How are we gonna handle this?" I said.

"Well, now, Ms. Wilson. How would you *like* to handle it?" he said, and he smiled, not with his mouth that was hidden behind a dark desperado mustache, but with his eyes.

"As little as possible," I said. "I've never handled a meetin'."

"Well, *that* being the case, I suggest that you introduce me first. Oh, I don't know. Say anything you want about me. A lawyer. The Houston bit. Then I'll carry it from there. I'll introduce the rest of the speakers. Later on I'll pass it back to you, and if you like, you can shut the meeting down. How does that sound?"

"Fine and dandy," I said.

"Well, fine and dandy with me too, Ms. Wilson. As for the other speakers, I suggest we work as a forum. I've taught a number of classes at Rice University, so I'm rather comfortable with that style. At the end, we—me or you, it doesn't matter—can mention that we've asked for a hearing on Formosa's permits."

Then Blackburn turned sideways, with his back to the people coming into the room, and said, "Do you know who any of these people are? Where they're from? Are some of them fishermen? It'd be *real* helpful if they were fishermen. That'd look *real* good."

"I know the fishermen, and all of them are from Seadrift. They're out there in the yard. There was supposed to be a bunch of elected officials. I *invited* them and they *said* they were comin', but some of them have canceled out on the TV. Heard it right before I came here. Might not be *any* of them showing."

"Well, that happens. We'll just have to wait and see." Then Blackburn looked at me like he was amused with the whole night. I thought he was going to laugh outright like Sanchez would have done, but he didn't. He only nodded his dark head and said, "Okay. Let's do it."

Only I didn't. I moved from some grating, hurting spot in my stomach, and it was that spot and the words coming out of my mouth that fought for my attention. I could see the fishermen in the back of the room. They had come in from the night and now they looked at me with calm disregard, as though I had momentarily separated myself from them just by being in front of the room. Just by standing there.

Three other people were up front with us. Two were activists: one from Houston who had come by himself, and another from Bay City. The activist from Houston stayed at the far end of our forum (away from Blackburn and next to me), and he had red hair. The third speaker was a doctor who said he worked occasionally on cases with Blackburn in Houston. He was an expert on environmental diseases, and talked about the controversy over the contaminant that had made Calhoun County the number one polluter in the United States.

He said he knew that Alcoa was insisting that the chemical was not dangerous and posed no health risk, and was, in fact, along with county officials, petitioning the EPA to have the chemical delisted as a contaminant and, therefore, non-reportable. "But it is a corporate half-truth," he said, "when the company says that aluminum oxide does not pose risks to the health and well-being of local residents. The *danger* is in the ability of the chemical to pick up and carry more harmful chemicals being released by the same or another area industry, and then people breathing in the stuff. And people vary enormously in their sensitivity to these chemicals. The EPA standards are based on the effect these pollutants will have on a healthy adult *male* that works and is exposed to the chemical. But what about the *children*? The *elderly*? What about *pregnant women and their fetuses*? They may be affected by a lot lesser amount."

He said it was a well-known fact that Texas, the state with the nation's worst toxic air pollution, had four highly ranked counties—Calhoun, Brazoria, Jefferson, and Harris—that lay in an arc along the Gulf of Mexico, from Port Lavaca to Port Arthur, and that region had the highest lung cancer death rates in Texas. The rates were also higher than the national average.

The meeting went from speaker to speaker as effortlessly as a wind, buffeted by nothing but its own energy, blowed down the water channel. I stood aside, not with the speakers and not with the crowd. I was in a dark corner, momentarily lit; same as a match struck on the rough side of a cheap matchbox will flare briefly, then go out.

When it was my turn to talk, I panicked and looked at Blackburn, and Blackburn never even blinked. He announced that we had formed an environmental group and as a first order of business, we had filed for a hearing on Formosa's air permits.

It was after that moment that I realized no one was going to take their hat or their purse and walk out. No one was going to stand up and shout about red flags going up in Washington. Instead they were going to sit, almost leisurely, in their hard metal chairs, as though they were sitting in the shade somewhere on a hot, windless day with nothing on their minds, but a notion to kill some time.

I forgot how it ended. I was just happy that the couple sentences I'd spoken were enough and that part of my cake was gone and all of Donna Sue's. For two seconds as I climbed into the van and went home, I felt some peace. But I should've known better.

The next morning I stood at Froggie's outside phone (the one next to the conveyor belt, and handy if you're shoving boxes of iced shrimp up a ramp and onto a truck and another buyer is on the phone offering you a quarter more a pound for your shrimp) and listened to a man holler.

He barely said who he was (Doug Lynch with Port Lavaca Economic Development) before he started. "Do you *know* what it is you're doing? Have you *any* idea, any notion of exactly what it is? And *who* is this lawyer Blackburn? *Who* is he?"

"What?" I said, and stared at a dozen names and numbers of Louisiana shrimp dealers I had scrawled in pencil on the fish-house wall.

"Are you *serious* about this hearing?"

"The one we asked for last night?" I said. "That one?"

"Oh, good Lord!" he said, and his voice quit. When he came back on the phone, his voice was quieter, like before.

"Look," he said. "It's already done. I can see that now. We just have to go from there. All right. What's your time schedule? I think I can get the permit writers from the Air Control Board, and I *certainly* can get the ones from Formosa. Then we just sit down and talk. They can explain the whole thing to you. Break it down . . . whatever. Into parts per million. Whatever. Whatever it is you want. I think I can get it together by tomorrow."

I laughed at the idea of Doug Lynch figuring all his stuff. Amazing! Between the meeting (where he wasn't) and the going to bed and having to sleep, whenever did he have time for that kind of finagling? And there I was, sleeping and thinking everything had quit at the end of the meeting, and lo and behold! Mister Economic Development was up with the night owls, thinking and plotting and scheming.

"I don't know about this idea. I'm not sure I can even get a hold of my lawyer that quick. So I'll just pass on your idea, Mister Lynch, if you don't mind."

"*Mind? Mind?* Look, Diane. Is it all right to call you Diane? Well, look, Diane, I'm just trying to save us a little time and money and nonsense, is all. A hearing is going to do nothing but put a lot of money into a lot of lawyers' pockets. *You* get nothing out of it and *Formosa* gets nothing out of it. Then too, it just gives the agencies a lot more paperwork and costs me and you, the taxpayer, a *lot* of money. So the lawyers get rich. That's it. I don't think you want that. Now, I'm *not* saying you can't bring that lawyer Blackburn. That's his name, isn't it? Well, if it makes you happy, then just bring him along. What I'm just saying is we *don't* need to get into this legal mumbo jumbo mess. I don't believe that's what either one of us are about."

I didn't get to answer the question because Doug Lynch had hung up, secure in his thinking that he was getting his sit-down meeting with me and the Air Control Board and Formosa. I was just grateful I hadn't spilled the beans on my total ignorance. I knew next to nothing, and to know *anything* I'd had to get out my newspaper clipping and unmarked envelope with my name on it and decipher its message.

The letter was still in my purse, sitting on the floor, so I went back in the office and looked at it. First one side, then the other, thinking there might be some notion, just by looking at the reverse side, what the letter writer wanted. I was scraping the barrel now. Maybe I could read the grounds out of the coffeepot.

To reverse the damage, I spent the next hour talking on the phone to the Air Control Board in Austin. It was two phone calls and four transfers: one person to another and one department to another. Then I got disconnected and had to do the call all over again. Finally I got a permit writer who said she worked on Formosa's permits, and I wrote her name and her phone number down on my newspaper clipping. Yes, she said. She knew the air permits I was talking about. Formosa Plastic. Calhoun County. She was just surprised, was all. She hadn't expected a hearing request. Nobody had.

Then she said yes, she had got a call from a Mister Lynch about my request for a meeting with the state. The staff was seeing what they could do to arrange the meeting.

"But I don't have a Mister Lynch in my group and no Mister Lynch is speaking for me. I don't know what that fella is doing. Just pay him no mind. Whatever he's sayin', just pay it no mind."

"You're *not* requesting a meeting with the state?" she said.

"Nope, but I'd sure like to see a copy of Formosa's permit."

Later I called Blackburn and he said, "Tell Lynch to go to hell! I don't even know *who* that fella is. *Who is he?* Just tell him you don't talk to *nobody* without your lawyer being present. Besides, I haven't even *read* the damn permit, let alone negotiated over it. Hell, I can barely lift the thing. It looks like a cement block they sent over here."

After Blackburn hung up, I walked to the double wood doors to see if Howdy was coming down the road. He wasn't at the meeting, so clearly he must be coming down the road. But he wasn't. It was only Baby, home from the oil derricks and the crew boats, and he was plenty mad because he had to borrow his momma's truck to get to the bay. It was a new truck his parents couldn't afford, so it was double everything he normally got when he borrowed a truck from his momma.

He said he had to get the truck back and wanted to know when I was coming home with the van. Then he got quiet and his face was caught inside the truck interior like an image reflected out of a dime store window—caught for a moment, then lost forever. I had seen it come and go like that a hundred times. Sometimes fast. Sometimes slow. All depending on the amount of time he let anybody look at his eyes.

Then Baby said something completely out of the blue. "The Baptist want money and Boy doesn't even have a headstone?"

"What? Who said that?" I said.

"Oh, that stupid preacher down there. What's his name? Asked momma when was she coming back to church, and I guess . . . oh, I don't know, put money in the collection plate. Told her it might make her *feel* better about Boy's dying. And that was the wrong thing to tell her and *that's* why she's so mad. Not about the truck so much. Just over that preacher spoutin' stuff and Boy not having a headstone."

Boy was Baby's brother and had been dead two years, and he didn't have a headstone, all right. He didn't have nothing but a paper military marker at his feet, showing he had been in the army and running trucks for the government. Boy was older than Baby by a year, and those two were the only kids their momma had, and neither one of them looked like the other except for the high forehead, which was identical and which was exactly the family resemblance that Boy blew to bits when he put the shotgun to his head. He had been dead long enough that the bow and arrows he had been an expert on (and the only thing Baby kept of his) had gathered cobwebs where Baby had stuck them high over the kitchen table. When I said something about the dust once, Baby said, "It's a relic. Bones. Let it stay up there." So it did.

In Baby's mind, it all fit. Boy's death, Crockett's autism, and the shrimping and the bays taking a nosedive all at the same time. *Everything* was a relic or bones or dead. Changed or fixing to change. "What is the same anymore?" Baby always, always said. He began saying it when he was fifteen and in his jeans and T-shirt (because that was the way he was dressed when Boy, in his white tuxedo, came by and got him), and they both crawled under a fence to chase a wild buck, while Boy's prom date sat out the night in their daddy's borrowed car. And madder than hell. Never forget that. Women were always madder than hell at Boy. Then when Baby was thirty-nine and post–Vietnam War stressed out, with three of his war buddies dead and his brother dead from his own hand, he quit saying it. He just believed it. Crawling under a barbwire fence with Crockett would change nothing.

It wasn't a coincidence that the year Boy died, Baby quit shrimping. Gave it up for good. The only time he stepped foot on a shrimp boat was when I got him to help me unload shrimp doors and nets in the middle of the spring or fall shrimp run. Otherwise coming down to the bay made Baby mad, and the truck and the headstone were just two more reasons. So Baby was impatient, and when he turned back to me he gunned the engine. He wasn't looking at me, though; he was only watching the windshield. Then Baby pulled himself in like sun to sun-stuff and went roaring off in his momma's truck.

Donna Sue had been standing at the fish-house door, watching us. She couldn't stand Baby even though he was her nephew and identical to her husband, Deputy Dawg. Those two were so similar they could have been twins, birthed twenty years apart. Then she quit looking at me and walked to the side of the fish house, where mashed crab traps and torn shrimp boxes and worn-out webbing was nearly to the top of the fish house. Donna Sue walked briskly back around to the front where our lone mulberry tree still had one end of a shrimp net tied around its base. It was a net I was in the middle of rehanging and hadn't finished. I still didn't want to finish it, even though I figured Donna Sue was thinking different. I could tell by the way she stuck her boot on the net and kicked it. So I went to the docks and leaned against a piling. The piling had three truck tires piled on it, a pre-arranged sign to shrimpers that the game wardens were at the docks.

It was some of Sanchez's doings from a season ago that wouldn't hold water now. Every game warden in the state knew that trick. I took two tires off and left the third as a bumper for shrimp boats pulling next to the docks. The harbor was full of tied boats and still as a sleeping woman's belly. There was no sound except the wind.

I stayed until Donna Sue came out to the docks, and she frowned.

"You got a customer, and he don't want shrimp."

"What's he want, then?"

"Go see for yourself."

I went through the fish house and stood at the door. I could see a car across the shell road. The sun broiled on its windshield, and there in the middle was a man, and he didn't move.

"What's he doin'?" Donna Sue said.

"I don't know. Maybe he's gettin' a gun out from under the seat."

The man stayed where he was, and I blinked like it was me out there in the sun. Then he moved, and I watched him walk across the shell road. He was carrying some papers and looked like a government something-or-other.

He came straight up to me. "Ms. Wilson?" he said. He was taller and whiter than any winter tree I'd ever seen.

"I'm Larry Peyton. The new plant manager at Formosa."

5

Of Fishermen and Politicos

It was the second week after the meeting and the second week into the fall shrimp season, and no surprise to anyone, it had disintegrated into another calamity. It was what shrimping was: a series of calamities. Then Jumpin' Junior (named for his peculiar habit of saying he was in one bay one minute, then ten minutes later showing up in another bay) hauled up in his pickup to the front door of the fish house and, with his head hanging out the window, yelled at the top of his lungs, "Why don't you gals find out what's goin' on down in that channel!"

I was sewing a net from a bent nail at the door and Donna Sue was on the back dock, and we both heard him. She came around the front with her hands on her hips and said, "Now, what in the hell do *you* want?"

"*Whadda I want? Whadda I want?* I want you gals to see what's goin' on out there in that bay! Go on, looky back there in that basket at what I got. Dead, rotten shrimp! Now, where did I get dead, rotten shrimp? Whyyy, I got 'em in the channel, is where I got 'em, and what's dead, rotten shrimp doin' out there? Tell me that, would ya!"

So I got Jumpin' Junior's dead, rotten shrimp and I stuck them in a plastic bag and labeled them with a black magic marker, and then I put them in Donna Sue's freezer. Later I would say that day was the day that something as familiar as a child's voice coming over the backseat of a car became nothing but a frozen Ziploc bag in Donna Sue's freezer.

Then on another day not much different (except that it was raining and cold), I stood on a makeshift wharf. A norther had blown in, and the rain splashed slow on the yellow pine boards. The wharf was just big enough for one shrimper to get on and off his boat in the early morning hours, so I didn't move any farther down the wharf than I had to. I certainly didn't try to go inside the cabin with the men in their wet slickers. I just turned and watched a flatbed truck haul off two dead dolphins.

The shrimpers stood on their boat, looking at me like they were deciding what they wanted told and what they thought was better left unsaid.

"How many more dead dolphins were out there?" I asked. The men said nothing. One shrimper looked down at a knotted rope like it mattered, and the rain came down off his ears and fell onto his already soaked shirt.

"This ain't no family secret here," I said, and put my boot against a rotten piling that the new boards were nailed to. It was black all the way into the water. When I looked up the shrimpers were out on the back deck and folding up the oyster sacks they had laid over the dolphins.

"Ain't it?" the skinny one said. "Who you think they're gonna blame for them being dead? First off, who's it gonna be? I told *him*"—and he jerked a thumb to the other shrimper—"we just oughta leave 'em dolphins out there to rot to pieces. Who they gonna blame but us?"

"Those dolphins didn't have bullet holes! And who catches dolphins in their nets? Nobody! Ain't a single shrimper I've ever seen. And they damn sure weren't knocked cold by a shrimp door. So nobody's thinkin' it."

"No?" he said.

"No," I said.

"Shit. Then I guess we should've got them first ones we seen last week."

The shrimpers weren't fooling. The dolphin count *had* started the week before. A newspaper account detailed the progress, saying a helicopter pilot returning from offshore spotted four dead dolphins on a single flyby. The dolphins were washed up in the shallow marshes of the bay, all male and all over three hundred pounds. Then the pilot called the Coast Guard and the Coast Guard called the game warden, and by then the pilot had counted eleven on a second check.

I didn't know how many the shrimpers found but didn't report. One gill netter left me a penciled message hammered to the fish-house door, and on the back dock a dead redfish wrapped in old newspaper. The note said, *This fish acted funny. He swum at the surface in a slow circle, and all I did was reach out and grab him. There was an alligator acting funny, but I didn't bring him.*

I took the redfish wrapped in the newspaper and froze it. Donna Sue didn't want nothing to do with the redfish because a redfish—dead, alive, or blackened in a skillet—was *big* trouble for a commercial fishing person. "You know what a game warden's gonna do if he catches us with that damn fish?"

"It's evidence," I said.

"Evidence, hell! It's illegal! They'll string us to that high line pole out there."

I wasn't worried and didn't believe Donna Sue was either. She just wouldn't admit it, and hung on to her game warden tangent like she'd hang on to an old sweater she liked. But sure enough, like an old wound that festers and heals, then festers again, the game wardens seemed to arrive overnight. I couldn't remember when I had last seen that much single-mindedness from Parks and Wildlife, and I suppose it could have been over the dolphin sightings, but the local shrimpers weren't so sure. They figured the arrival of the game wardens was to hammer another nail in their coffins, and they hung around the tailgates of their trucks and talked long and hard about it.

Sanchez figured it was him. He said if there was one thing a game warden couldn't stand worse than a commercial fisherman, it was a commercial fisherman that wouldn't stand still while they were handing out the tickets. And it didn't matter that his trial was over and done with; game wardens had mighty long memories. So I wasn't surprised when Sanchez wanted the three tires up on the piling again and he wouldn't come to the docks until way past everybody else, and I had to bring Crockett down to the bay because he was up and running the house anyhow, so it might as well be the fish-house floor he was running.

Sanchez's paranoia wasn't totally out of line. Earlier in the day four game wardens in two army-green Range Rovers stationed themselves outside the fish house under our wild mulberry tree, and there they waited out the fishermen while me and Donna Sue waited out the whole mess—game wardens and shrimpers alike. Finally the game wardens grew tired of messing with shrimpers, and they cleared out with only one handwrote ticket costing one shrimper five hundred dollars. Only Sanchez remained in the bay.

Donna Sue had been closemouthed since the game wardens left, and still silent, she swept up the dead shrimp that had fallen off the weighing bucket and ramp where shrimp are hauled from the boats. When she finished she dumped the trash shrimp outside and fed the thundering cloud of hardheads in the harbor. Then she turned on the water hose and poured bleach all over the fish-house floor. In her jeans spotted with bleach and under the raw yellow lights yawning from the fish-house rafters, Donna Sue slung water like she hardly knew what she did.

I told her to go home. I could finish up. Sanchez was tied to a piling, probably eating M&M's and drinking coffee. "He ain't sufferin' none," I said. So Donna Sue gathered her belongings; took her magazines and her half-eaten candy bar and her purse and stomped out of the fish house.

Then the fish house got quiet, and I stood and breathed in the silence. Scattered shrimp still hid in a cement wash gutter, and their bay smell and the lingering bleach smell were two things under the yellow lights of the fish-house rafters that I couldn't put my hands on. The night air did that sometimes; what seemed solid enough an hour ago—the shrimpers, the boats, diesel motors, ropes being thrown—now fled like ghosts leaving nonbelievers. I was alone with my Davy Crockett—my antelope baby. No ghost, for sure. The bayou and the high-hung nets smelt to the high heavens, and me and Crockett waited out Sanchez. Once I heard a motor and went through the fish house and looked out on the docks and down the harbor. Nothing. Ten o'clock. Eleven. I took Crockett's hand and we walked to the end of the shell road and stopped at the water's edge. The other fish houses were dark. Across the harbor, two lights hung from a two-by-four nailed to a pier. If Sanchez had seen either he would have knocked 'em both out.

Crockett was restless and grabbed my shirt to pull me down the street. He jumped on the truck-pulverized oyster shell, first one foot, then the next, then again. His hair was wet and his shirt was limp as a crumpled rose. I looked past Crockett, then beyond the docks to the boats. Above the boats mast poles and A-frames and jerked-up try nets moved slowly this way and that. Eventually it was a movement too little or not quite right that stopped me. *Then* I saw the game warden truck. It was pulled into the shadow of a closed fish house, and inside were two men, and one moved and the other did nothing.

"What is that, Crockett? Is that the game wardens? Think we oughta warn Sanchez? Should we, should we?"

I talked to Crockett, and his eyes were wide open and hot looking, but as I went to grab his hand, he was gone. He ran down the middle of the road, upright and high in the night air. Then for no reason, he stopped and his feet came together like a dance step remembered. His feet started drumming again. It wasn't a loud drum, just a low, monotonous one where the oyster dust took a beating. I grabbed his hand while he still danced and walked him off the road so the sound of our feet wouldn't carry across to the game wardens.

Crockett and I were the cavalry all war-telling is full of! Not holstered or sabered, just hoping for one VHF radio to warn Sanchez. *Beware los federales!* We went from shrimp boat to shrimp boat, tromping over winches and deck buckets and oil buckets and wet ropes and wetter nets. I rattled one cabin door after another, one lock after another. Most cabins were open, but with radios missing. Finally I found an open door and a working radio, and I shoved Crockett inside and held him tight with my knees. I reached for wires and the feel of a cold metal radio.

Twice I called Sanchez, but no answer. Then he did, and I said next to nothing. Calling was enough. Sanchez wanted to know how long it would take me to meet him. Not long, I said. You know where? he said, and I said, Shore, shore. Another secret kept from enemy game wardens. So I left the fish house lit and the Sears van in plain sight of the game wardens and walked down the road with Crockett until I found Sanchez's truck.

I was lucky I found it. Sanchez never left his truck in the same place twice and the key was always hidden. I unlocked the truck and reached inside and shoved Sanchez's bayonet underneath the seat, then picked up Crockett and set him inside. I drove the truck in first gear past the fish houses and past the game wardens. Crockett hardly budged. His tight body faced the windshield, and only two hands twisting said he was alive and with me.

We rode silently through main street, past Seadrift's city limits sign, past open fields of ranch land and rice farms, then finally across an open field and onto a dirt road that smelt of salt grass and wet cow pens. The sand was tight and puckered from rain the day before and when we drove over, little clumps of succulent plants burst like Christmas bulbs. Ahead was the intercoastal canal, and beyond that was the open bay, with its cool water and silver and black fish. When I came to the edge of the canal, I stopped the truck. The air was dead, and Crockett was quiet too. Maybe asleep. I leaned my head against the window and watched Crockett and the west end of the channel, and thought nothing at all until Sanchez's diesel motor killed the silence by degrees.

His bow came fast, high, and hard, and it rammed the canal bank, but from the stern a soft foam came like an old woman's wash water.

Sanchez walked out of the cabin in his bare feet and stood quietly near the bow. "Where's the game wardens?" he said.

"Sittin' in the dark. Waitin' on you."

I could see Sanchez's tanned face and his hair clustered soft as a woman's. His lips came away from his teeth like he was laughing at something.

"Can you keep my shrimp in my truck overnight? I can give you extra ice."

"Sure, but what's the matter with yore shrimp that you can't bring 'em in?"

"Ain't *nothin'* the matter with them. I just don't trust those friggin' game wardens. You lose thirty thousand dollars to Austin and see how much you trust them after that. I'm not giving those bastards one single excuse to screw me again!"

Sanchez turned and drug baskets of shrimp from inside the cabin. His was a common enough maneuver for a captain nervous about his shrimp. Whether his shrimp were undersized or over the pound limit, or whether the captain was just plain nervous or neurotic and imagined game wardens around every bend, a shrimper always felt better if he kept shrimp in the cabin, where a near and ready boot could dump a load in the unfortunate event that a game warden's boat surprised him on the bay. A shrimper would lose everything before he'd let a game warden confiscate his shrimp, then fine him for them, then sell the shrimp and use the money to buy *more* game wardens to chase shrimpers.

So I got out and helped Sanchez load the baskets onto the truck tailgate and sling them up next to the rear window. Sanchez filled two empty shrimp baskets with ice and I dumped them on the shrimp, then covered them with oyster sacks. After Sanchez pulled out, I watched his boat disappear down the canal. It was after midnight, but I wasn't tired. I was only stopped like a clock's second hand was stopped, and I glanced towards the truck, and Crockett's head hadn't moved either.

The next morning I caught Sanchez on his boat and told him for

that little midnight arrangement, he owed me a *big one*. I needed a
director on my environmental group, and he was my male quota. After
the conversation with Formosa's plant manager at the fish house, I had
decided the time had arrived for directors and everything legal an
environmental group needed. Right off the bat Donna Sue said she
wasn't being president, so just look elsewhere for that donkey. She did
have a daughter old enough to do something, though. With all our
connections (I had a cousin and she had a daughter and a friend), and
after a phone call to Blackburn, we made Sanchez and the daughter
directors, and the cousin and the friend became the secretary and
treasurer. So much for voting rights.

When Sanchez reached the fish house the next afternoon for our
first organizational meeting, the cousin and the daughter and the
friend had been there for over half an hour. Sanchez came in and sat
down on the edge of the desk I was sitting behind, and put a thermos
of coffee in the middle of the table and proceeded to pour me a cup
of coffee without asking. Then he looked around at the women. "Is
this the directors?" he said.

"Just you and me and Donna Sue and Sabrina. Blackburn said all we
needed was three or four. The rest here are officers."

"Nobody can sue us, can they?"

I looked up from my coffee cup and said, "Now, who in the hell
would want to sue us?"

Donna Sue's friend, who was our new secretary and a large-boned
woman with a quiet enough hairdo, sat up straight in her chair. Her
eyes got big and she said, "Nobody told me *nothing* about getting
sued."

I looked hard at Sanchez and squinted my eyes, then I looked back
at the woman. "Sanchez is just talkin' to be a talkin'. Ain't that right,
Sanchez? Nobody's got nothing to worry about. We got us a lawyer,
don't we?"

Sanchez moved off the desk and walked halfway across the room.
Then he remembered his thermos and came back. "Hey, don't take my
coffee, there. Listen, tell me what y'all decide, all right? Just give me a
call tonight and tell me what all y'all decided. I trust you ladies. I
always trust the women."

Then without a backwards glance, he went and left the door wide
open in the going. I could see the sun hammering on the street from

where I sat, then ten minutes more, I could see it again when all the other women left. We had barely made it halfway through the meeting, and half of the directors and all of the officers had taken Sanchez's direction and left. I crossed my legs and moved Froggie's old coffee cup in a slow circle. Then Donna Sue turned and all I saw was her white neck, so I listened to her white neck like it was her mouth that was talking. She said, "Well, why don't we just put out an open invitation in the newspaper? Just invite everybody in!"

Donna Sue was looking through the door at a man standing in the middle of the fish house. It was the county commissioner, another elected official that didn't make my meeting. He didn't move out of his spot in the fish house. It was like he was superglued. Then after he still said nothing and didn't move any closer, just giving Donna Sue a sideways glance now and then, Donna Sue frowned and said she was leaving. Then she went into the ice vault and slammed the door.

"Looks like y'all gonna need a traffic cop down here just to let the traffic past," the commissioner said. He looked around the fish house, then at me, and for a second we were face-to-face. There was something about the lines around his mouth and I thought he might be fixing to smile, but he didn't.

"What can I do for you, Mister Hahn?"

"Well, nothing really. I've just been meaning to come down here, is all. Tell you why I didn't make that meeting of yours. It went all right, didn't it?"

"Sure, Mister Hahn. It went just fine."

"I figured it would. That's what I was thinking." He stared at the floor awhile, then he looked up and his words seemed to hit out of nowhere.

"You know I went to Taiwan, don'tcha?"

I said I sure didn't. So he proceeded to tell me how he and a few of county's best had went to Taiwan on a business deal, intending to get a little offer of a few million dollars for a chemical expansion and instead got billions. Billions. Myyy, but wasn't that chairman a wonderful man. Even sent him a birthday cake down to the office without nobody having to say so. Just up and sent the cake.

"Who's this Chairman fella? I've never heard of him."

"*The Chairman!* You've never heard of Formosa's Chairman? Whyyy, he's one of the richest—eleventh, I believe—richest men in

the world! Comes from Taiwan. Great humanitarian. Great. Just
great. Builds hospitals, chemical plants. Into all kinds of stuff. Real
name isn't the Chairman, though. That's just what they call him 'cause
. . . I guess he's such a great fella and rich and all."

The commissioner was talking pretty fast, obviously thinking my
question was a plenty good avenue to say what he really came for, so
I got the spill on Wang Yung-Ching—*the Chairman, the owner,
builder, man extraordinaire.* In a world where large, faceless multinational corporations were the norm, Formosa was one of the biggest
family-owned dynasties around. Probably in the world! And it was his
family that owned the Formosa chemical plant that my environmental
group was requesting a hearing on.

The commissioner stopped talking and looked at me, like if I
wanted to jump in and say something, then I could, but I didn't, so he
blurted out, "You know why he left Taiwan and came all this way
down here to Texas, don'tcha?"

"Are you talkin' about the Chairman *and* Formosa? Why Formosa
has all those permits out there?"

"That's it! That's it!" the commissioner said, and his face got red like
a woman had slapped him good. Then that same hand that had got
the commissioner was now up to my face, and I saw either I ducked
or I got slapped, so I backed up.

"Look, all we went to Taiwan for was a little county business. A
little something extra going on at that tiny plant of his down here. But
what we *got* . . . what he *offered was three billion dollars! Three billion!*
We nearly fell out of our chairs. He offered us more than the whole
county's worth! *And he did it because he hates communists.*"

"Three billion dollars' worth because the Chairman hates communists? I didn't know there were communists in Taiwan," I said.

"Whyyy, shore there is. Wang just figured, why not get out of
Taiwan altogether? Come to the United States. He got his start in the
first place from us. Got a little economic starter loan after we—well,
it wasn't we, not me and you, it was U.S. *bombers* flying during World
War II that blew his rice mill to kingdom come that did it. So after
that blowing-up deal he got his half-million-dollar loan, and here we
sit in Calhoun County, three billions dollars richer."

The commissioner stepped closer and said he had to get real personal with me. Formosa only had one window of opportunity. Things

had to be put into motion fast. The Chairman had asked them—well, them that went—to *personally* see to a few things. See if those state and federal agencies couldn't speed up the permitting. "'Cause, you know," he said, "you gotta go when the train leaves the station, or else you get left behind."

"So where did y'all go to do all this asking?" I said.

"Oh, Austin. Dallas ... that's where the EPA's regional office is, you know. Dallas. We were *quite* a little delegation. Told those agency heads, 'We may be little, but we've come a *long* way, and you can't just go around holding up economic development like this. Let's put a little *grease* on this thing!' 'Cause it's not like we're getting this three-billion-dollar offer for nothing! We have to give a little too. That's what the Chairman said. A few incentives on our part. Besides, Formosa could just as easy take this deal to Louisiana. We don't have it sewn up entirely, and I don't think Louisiana would kick him out either. Probably offer him a better deal, is all. So you see what I mean? What I'm talking about. It doesn't hurt to have a little friendly persuasion coming down the tube on our part. Make things friendly. What does it hurt?"

Donna Sue opened the ice vault and came out with a bottle of bleach and poured it on the fish-house floor. I watched the bleach trail get closer and closer to the commissioner's shoes, until finally he said, "Well, I won't pester you no more." His breath came slow—not easy, but slow like it was borrowed air to begin with and it didn't know the way out. Then he turned and went through the fish house in a cautious way, as though he thought at any moment Donna Sue might hit him with the water hose she was washing everything down with. But Donna Sue payed him no mind and looked content over the fact that a man interrupted was a man stopped. Then, as I watched from the door, the commissioner got in his official county car with the words COUNTY COMMISSIONER stenciled in black so nobody in the county would ever be confused over whose car it was, and the smell of bleach came over my shoulder like near-rain right before it hits.

6

Knocked Clean out of the Ring

It went this way: I had left the fish house at noon and a fog still covered the town and the roads and all of the bay. I was driving Froggie's ton-and-a-half diesel truck that he kept at the fish house so he could unload his shrimp without actually coming into the fish house and talking with us women. (Froggie shrimped in the middle of Lavaca Bay, on top of Alcoa's mercury-contaminated mess, and trucking his shrimp instead of hauling them by boat saved him a couple hours.)

I was depositing the fish-house money at the bank and had just unzipped the cotton money bag that carried cash from shrimp peddlers and checks from Louisiana shrimp buyers and half a dozen IOUs when Howdy showed up. He grabbed my elbow and pulled me aside and said he'd heard so much about what I was fixing to do that he just had to hear it for himself. Besides, he was getting concerned about my lawyer. Who was paying that fella anyhow? What kind of deal did I have going on?

I said it wasn't no deal. Just a free lawyer. Howdy looked at me and laughed and said he never heard of a free lawyer. Who ever heard of that?

"He's pro bono. That means he's a free lawyer. Doing it for nothing."

"Oh," Howdy said. "Nobody does anything for nothing. You just have to look harder for the reason, is all. See what agenda they've got. Who knows if it's the same one you've got. Then there's this other deal. You're local and he's not. What's that do? Messes everything up, 'cause you dredge up a lawyer, *then* the other side's got to dredge up a lawyer. Maybe two or three of them. Don't you think it's just better if the *local* folks sit down and put their heads together? It hasn't gone so far that we can't do that, has it?"

"We're asking for a hearin' on Formosa. If that means we've gone too far, then I guess we've gone too far."

"But nothing that can't be reversed? You're not so *wacko–wacko* you wouldn't listen to a little reason if it was offered to you? Not if we offered you your *own* little community group? You know, something industry could be involved in too, so it wouldn't be so one-sided . . . but it'd be yours. There's a few folks in industry and some outside of it that would go along with that idea. You can be the chairperson or whatever. . . . As long as the *whole* group was involved in the decision-making process. And it would go without saying that things would be kept confidential. There would *need* to be an assurance of that. Maybe sign something or other 'cause we *certainly* don't need to be airing our dirty laundry, now, do we? You do that, then I don't see why there couldn't be some sort of financial arrangement made. A salary of sorts. You could have a whole different crowd of folks tippin' their hat to you every morning, saying, 'Good day, Missus Wilson. And how are you doin', Missus Wilson?' You could have people *respecting* you."

His head hung in front of me like a mirror over a dashboard. Neither one of us blinked—not him, not me. And if the sun rose in the morning or was pinned to an afternoon sky, it mattered not a bit 'cause we were just folks talking and lying at high noon in a bank. Then Howdy leaned forward and touched my hand. "If you scratch our back, then we'll scratch yours. Give 'em their permits. Nobody gets hurt. Nobody. And you can make a little money too. I bet that bank account of yours could use a little cash flow, now, couldn't it?"

I stood with my hands on my hips and laughed, and the money bag almost fell. Then I laughed a second time. I was at the door. Then there was the bank sidewalk and the street, and I'd have seen clear to the bay if I had left already.

Later at the fish house, I ruminated like a cow over the whole sad affair. I figured nobody was tellin' me to "Quit, quit, for God's sakes!" except half the county. The other half was making a point of not talking to me. And I hadn't heard from Blackburn. I didn't know where that free lawyer was. So I sat at the fish house and told Donna Sue she could deliver the money bag from there on out. I wasn't going down to the bank again. I didn't tell her about Howdy; instead I said I didn't like dealing with money. Then to get her really off the subject, I told her there was a full moon out so maybe some of the shrimp that had been hiding out in the upper bays and bayous might move out. Maybe Deputy Dawg could find them.

The next day was Saturday. Once upon a time in my life, Saturdays were quiet Sundays done inside out—but all that was gone. I certainly remembered this Saturday and what it brought. She was an old woman with a black scarf, and she came into the fish house at midday. She moved like Grandpa, except Grandpa was dead and this old woman was only dying, she said. She came in and stayed and stayed, and her hands were folded on a round, hard knot that she said was cancer. She was ripe as a melon, she said. Then she took a piece of paper out of her purse and handed it to me. It was the same kind of public notice that had came in my letter, except this old woman was no letter bringing it.

There was nothing cryptic or mysterious about it. It was a public notice on Union Carbide, another chemical plant in our county. It was the plant closest to Seadrift and the one I had worked in for three weeks. She had cut it out of the newspaper, she said, and she sat in my office chair and hardly moved, and when she did, she moved both her knees at the same time, like a bolt was through them at the joint. She lived next to Carbide until her bad health drove both her and her husband off. Her husband had been a cotton farmer long before Carbide came along, and the farm had been in their family for years. Now every time her husband planted cotton, it wanted to ramble clear to Mexico. No cotton. Just a pile of rambling vines. She could probably plant the thing like a wisteria vine and let it clamber all over the front porch if she had a mind to.

"Ain't you the gal takin' care of this kinda stuff? That gal that was in the paper?"

"Yes, ma'am. I sure am," I said.

She wanted to know what Carbide was askin' for. She could tell it was something, but she didn't know what. I didn't need to talk. I just kept quiet, nodding my head ever' now and then as she talked about farming and roads taken over by a chemical plant and the smells and the fires at night and something she called Stinky Ditch.

"Why do you think this notice was in the back end of the paper, honey? Were they tryin' to hide it? You think they were thinking nobody would look there?"

I had learned a thing or two in two months, so I said, No, ma'am. Formosa's permits were back there too. Companies are required by law to put a public notice in the paper if the company wants to build or expand and it's gonna put out emissions. Lets the public know, and you can fight it if you want. Well, try to fight anyhow. I'd see what I could do. Get a hold of the permit. Talk to our lawyer.

When the old woman left the fish house her fingers were pinched around her belly like it was a rag doll she carried under her skirt instead of a cancer that had come through her window one night and laid a nest in her belly. I stayed long after she left, wondering about the new road I was on and just where the experts were to warn me in plenty of time. Saying to me, "Do this thing, then this thing, then this." I hadn't seen the experts, but they were bound to be somewhere.

Otherwise nothing changed. The shrimp boats still went out on moon time, caught nothing, then came back and tied ropes to their boats. Me and Donna Sue watched from the fish-house door and stayed until we saw their trucks leave, then we turned and went inside.

I was impatient for things to happen. So I got on the phone and called the county newspaper reporter. She was new in town, a Quaker woman from Kansas who sometimes wore a hat, and she wanted to know if I had a press release.

I don't need one, I said. I just want to talk a minute. Then I told her that our environmental group was fixing to have another meeting down at city hall. It was a spur-of-the-moment meeting that even I didn't know about until I said it, and Donna Sue sure didn't know nothing, so she shoved both her fists on her hips and looked at me real hard.

The reporter said, "Oh, the new environmental group. I've heard you were being handled. I've been told I shouldn't worry myself about you."

"Who said that?" I said.

"Oh," she laughed, and her voice was like fine china coming over the wire. "Let's just say I heard it through the grapevine."

"Well, I have about half a dozen men *tryin'* to handle me. Maybe that's what the grapevine's sayin'. Somebody *tryin'* . . . but nobody's doin' it just yet."

"Well, that isn't what I've heard," said the reporter, and her voice wouldn't let go of the laugh she probably started when she first heard she was coming to Texas.

When I got off the phone, Donna Sue was still standing with her hands clinched on her hips. "Now, *what* city hall are we talkin' about here?"

"The same city hall we was run out of the first time," I said.

• • •

So I arranged another meeting, and the town got rained on for about a week. Then the fog set in on a hundred different shrimp boats that were all in some form of disrepair, some rotting, some sinking, some generations old, some in the middle of a resell (shrimpers traded boats and skiffs and engines the way other men traded horses or trucks or tractors or dogs). The weather was saying something, and I should have listened. But no, my intuition was flat on its ass from inattention, and I went about my business like I knew exactly what I was doing.

The documents from the Dallas reporter arrived in the mail and I took them to the fish house and spread them out on the desk. Stuck on top was a note from the reporter saying the newspaper had compiled its list of the most persistent Clean Water Act violators based on information from the EPA files in Dallas. The reporter listed an EPA telephone number, so I called and got informed on the EPA's definition of a persistent Clean Water Act violator.

The man on the phone said the EPA didn't issue an administrative order unless there were serious violations, and companies were allowed to dump a certain amount of chemicals and metals through their outfall. It was allowable and on their permit. Everything from sewage to arsenic to benzene to oil to vinyl chloride. Some cities even had forty outfalls . . . like Houston, for instance. Then some companies just had a few, and some had a lot more than a few. It was in their permit application how many outfalls were allowed and how many pounds of a particular chemical was allowed.

"It's pretty much self-policing," he said. "You know, companies monitor their own wastewater and report violations."

"Self-policing? How can y'all trust a company to police themselves? I don't see a driver policing himself out there on that highway. Fishermen down here don't get to police themselves."

"Do you realize the kind of money it would take from our budget to put inspectors down there in those facilities? Checking on a regular basis? We are backlogged and scrimping for money as it is, and doing real well, I might say, if we can get an inspector into those companies once a year. We're pretty confident self-reporting works. But talk to your congressman next time you see him. That's where *our* budget comes from. Congress."

I didn't argue. I was in foreign territory and I just had a native tell me I was supposed to trust them and drink the water. Later I made copies of the EPA documents at city hall for the meeting, and paid twenty cents a page (which I thought was highway robbery), and pulled the money out of my salary at the fish house. Until then I hadn't figured expenses or the phone into the picture. I figured the phone would be dealt with when Froggie got the bill and blew his stack.

I didn't go down to city hall until the day of the meeting. I didn't want to run the risk of bumping into a city secretary. Then too, we were busy enough waiting on our few boats and the truck coming for what little shrimp we had, and putting up signs all over Seadrift and in the fish houses and even past the city-limit signs at Wally's fish house near the intercoastal canal. We didn't post signs in Port Lavaca, after a couple of store managers looked at our handwritten signs and shook their heads. They said no and gave no reason.

On the evening of the meeting I left the two babies with the older girls, all standing on the porch, and their thin dark shapes looked even thinner in the shade of the porch. Crockett howled when I left and ran down the road after me, so I stopped the van and took Crockett by the hand and led him back to his sisters on the porch.

I didn't bake a cake for this meeting.

Some weary wind was blowing across Seadrift, coming from the bay and going through main street and leaving whip marks in the parking lot where nobody was. I got out of the van and took my white copies and went inside. The room I had rented was the entertainment side, and it hadn't seen entertainment in a long while. The floor was dirty and smelled of pencil shavings and small, unwashed boys. I hunted for a broom, then turned on three lights, then swept the floor. I pulled metal chairs folded against a wall into three rows and pointed their gray backs to the ceiling. Finally I drug a school desk out from a wall and put my papers on it.

Ten minutes more, Donna Sue showed up with her daughter: our two directors. Later still, a half-dozen people arrived. One was the secretary in our group, and the others I didn't know. They all sat in thin-shouldered silence and kept their thoughts to themselves. Sanchez never came, so I made coffee in an old shiny percolator I found in the closet, and sat it on the floor. I waited until a quarter after seven, then I got up and stood in front of the scarred school desk.

What happened next was not fear exactly. It was more like a dozen black cats had crossed my path and I was going to have to forgive myself for *ever* thinking I had seen trouble before. Clearly I hadn't. A dozen people arrived. They were dressed nice, but with the slightly rumpled appearance (it wasn't in their clothes; it was in their faces!) of tourists from a dull packaged deal, who had unexpectedly careened into an interesting crowd of lowbrow natives. And myyy, weren't things looking up.

The *arrived* people moved together and talked together in a shuffling mixture of laughter and fine clothes, and when they turned, the fluorescent light from the ceiling laid varnish thin as nail polish on their arms and faces. They glittered like gold underwater.

I reacted like a knee pounded with a mallet, but they crossed their arms and legs and made sitting noises with the metal chairs, almost as unconcerned as babies throwing forks at a picnic. One woman wore round white earrings the size of half dollars. I had never saw earrings that big. I was amazed at the confidence of such earring wearing, and it neatly matched the shotgun effect the *arrived* crowd was having on the meeting.

I stayed where I was, but my concentration was rattled and any introduction I had planned was gone. So I leaned over the desk and tapped the EPA papers beneath me and said, "I got a little piece of information that might interest y'all."

One of the men smiled, then two women on either side of him turned to him and smiled, then *all* of them turned back to me so it was three who watched and two who smiled, and one who was fixing to say something real important.

"Oh," he said, "and *what* little piece of information might that be? Is it to explain why you are trying to turn Formosa into polluters? What is your agenda there, may I ask?"

He was dark-haired and I was so struck by his slick-headed hairdo that I forgot what he said, so I said, "What? What?"

"I thought an environmental group *helped* a community. I didn't know its purpose was to tear down everything the community leaders were trying to build up. You know, Formosa's window of opportunity is *limited*! You're messing the whole thing up by what you're doing right here this very minute!"

I saw it was planned. One cloud moving north, then another

straight behind him. The thundercloud behind him said, "Are we supposed to sit here and believe everything you say? How do we *know* it's true? Maybe you're making this up."

"I don't even like chemistry, so how can I make it up? Where am I gonna get information like that?"

"Maybe you got it from Louisiana. They want this plant worse than we do, so maybe you're working for them. Why else would somebody come out of the blue like you are and knock down everything we've done for over a year?"

I said, "I've got information right here. Formosa was fined sixty-five thousand dollars two years ago, and another twenty-five thousand dollars this year for wastewater violations. And that was in Texas. Not Louisiana."

"That's the *old* plant! What Formosa's building now is technology based. It's state-of-the-art, for Christ's sake! Things aren't done the way they used to be. Ask the mayor there; he's got a construction contract with Formosa to work over there, unless you shoot the whole deal down. He should know. You can't do things the way you did them ten years ago. Besides, the environmental agencies won't let you. The EPA's got people watchin' every little thing you do. . . . Saying 'No, no, no' all *over* the place."

"EPA told me they didn't have enough inspectors for what you're talking about. None of those agencies do, probably. . . . So that's all I'm talking about here. Just watchin' things, is all. Being a watchdog."

"You're *shutting it down*, is what you're doin', and that's *all* your doing. It hasn't got a thing to do with the environment. You're a shrimper and antiprogress. Wanting to stop everything that doesn't have to do with fishing. Why, your outboard motors put more oil out there into the bay then all those industries do. It's a fact! Look it up!"

"What about all the cancer and illness we've got around here?" I said. "What's causing the learning problems we've got with our children? Don't you care to know what's causing it?"

A woman in the front row leaned her head to one side, and her two penciled eyes stuck in her pale face like moons in a sad land, and she didn't even wait to draw a breath before she stood up. "You know," she said, "I'm involved with the school system, and I've never read a report that suggests industry's pollution causes mental retardation. I've never seen anything of the kind. And while I can understand your concern, there is a lot more evidence supporting defective genes. Especially in rural areas. Intermarrying between cousins, that type of thing. That's really the more scientific approach, if you're actually looking for causes and not just wanting to blame someone."

The woman watched me steadily and didn't change her expression. "Sometimes we have to look for the enemy in our own mirror, and I can understand your reluctance to look there. I had a husband that worked for twenty years at one of the local plants, and just as he was planning on retiring, he got sick and died of cancer. Now, I could blame the company, say they killed him. But I think, *No*. No. He smoked cigarettes. He didn't eat right. So you see, I could blame the company, but I don't. I look closer. Do you think for a minute I could sit here and support Formosa, or any other industry for that matter, if I thought that it was the company that killed my husband?"

Then the woman quit, and before I had time to move my face from her face, she turned and smiled sadly at the rest of the group, and it was like the sky opened its mouth and swallowed them whole.

Now the second man (the thundercloud with no women) got up again and he spread his arms wide and said, "*This* is exactly what we've been trying to tell you. You're making a mistake. Somebody's leading you down the wrong path. I don't know, maybe it's you. Maybe it's just simply you. But it's *wrong*. And it's no way to conduct any kind of scientific inquiry. You don't even follow rules of protocol, for Christ's sake! You're running on pure emotion, and you *can't be emotional about a scientific inquiry! You just can't do it!*"

I felt like I was sitting in a big, bright wind where I couldn't retreat. The man was nearly screaming, and tore from his place. "You cannot do this! How on earth do you expect to convey any type of sane meeting with this type of emotional hysteria?"

The women around him shuffled and rearranged their skirts, and the perfect line of their legs was like chalk marks on a chalkboard. I was observing myself now, comparing myself; I was outside looking in, and I wished I had better clothes. If I had better shoes I would stroll across to the man who flung his arms to the dirty ceiling and I would stand in openmouthed amazement at his rage. Maybe I would laugh.

Instead I stood behind a child's desk and put my fist flat on the stack of paper. "Look, Mister," I said, "I don't know *who* you are, but I don't think there's nothing wrong in us loving the things we love. If

I put a little life and blood and bones in the things we love and call it home and you want to call it emotional . . . well, get on callin' it that, then. I ain't saying I'm sorry, because I feel for that bay out there. And I dang sure want to make sure somebody don't kill it no more times than it's already been killed."

"Kill it? Kill it? That bay isn't killed! If that bay's killed, then I'm a Nazi submarine captain. . . . And I'm a harbor captain for the navigation district, so I know these things. I run ships up and down through that ship channel all the time! I see your shrimpers out there all the time. I know about shrimpers! I know they're having hard times. That's why I'm so confused. Why would a shrimper wreck confidence in a company this county—and in our hard times too—is tryin' to do business with? What you're doin' is killing the gravy horse! This county's got unemployment up around fifteen percent! Are you prepared to feed those people this winter when they still don't have jobs? What about all of those snowbirds out of Kansas and Missouri, wanting to come down here for the winter and spend a little money? Do you know we're *already* getting calls from them about the pollution down here? I tell them, 'What pollution? It's all in the head of one woman down here. That's who's doing all the trashing. It's *certainly* not us! We're working our tails off to make this county attractive, and a crazy woman out there is blasting it to smithereens!'"

I looked at the captain and saw no sea there. No water showed in his eyes or how he moved his smile. I smelled no salt water. I saw only a man who strolled the lengths of metal decks in canvas shoes and white pants and white shirt, and what sun he knew lay in a triangle at his throat.

I didn't know where I retreated in that room, but wherever I went, the man pursued and the group followed. A man. I wasn't surprised. It was *always* a man. Then I retreated once more and I was a hundred yards away, then more yards, then more until finally I wasn't there at all. I didn't know where I was. I was farther away than I had ever been, and where I waited there was no fear.

Fearing nothing (and in my bad-looking shoes), I walked to the captain with the women who watched me calmly and turned their heads like white birds on the salt flats, and I folded my arms and leaned into his face. "Buzz off! Mister Captain or whatever you are. Just buzz off!"

That ended the niceties and all polite talk. I told the mayor of Port Lavaca to shut up, and to a snippy woman with a question for the newspaper, I said to look up her own damn answer. I wasn't taking anymore. I had my fill. Evidently (and new to me) I had a line that they couldn't cross. So while the entertainment side of city hall hadn't produced an orderly meeting that the sea captain wanted or even an informative meeting that I did, at least I found my quaking hidey-hole and ripped myself out whole. I hardly knew myself.

7

Negotiating with the Enemy

It was the second time the Houston activist called, and I couldn't remember nothing about him except his red hair. The first time he called, me and Donna Sue were loading boxes of iced shrimp onto the ramp of an eighteen-wheeler truck headed for Louisiana. The truck driver was inside the office, tallying up what all he owed us and what all he was fixing to cut us, because he didn't know if he liked our shrimp today and he didn't know if he liked our fish house neither. He yelled out the window that there was a call, and I yelled back that whoever it was to just call back. That was the first time.

The second time was hours later, and I was sitting with my boots in the window.

"It's Rick Abraham," he said, and I said nothing. And he said, "You remember me. I was down at that meeting y'all had."

Oh. *That meeting.* I narrowed my eyes and said, "That second one? Are you talkin' about that one?"

"I'm talking about that first one, I think."

"Oh. All right," I said. "Because if it was that *second* one, I was fixin' to say—"

"No, no. That first one. I was the environmentalist from Houston. We've got an environmental group in Houston. A statewide deal. We've got maybe twenty-five organizations such as yourself. You know, grassroots groups that are affiliated with us. I thought I'd call and see how things are goin'. Maybe see if you can get a couple of folks together for a little meeting. I could come down and we could go over some strategies."

"Well, we got us a lawyer," I said.

"Yeah, I know. Jim Blackburn. But a lawyer isn't an activist. Jim and I are two different birds. Lawyers talk one talk, and activists talk another. I'm not sayin you're not going to be needin' a lawyer down the road somewhere. I'm just sayin' there's a lot more things that can be done before you need a lawyer."

Then Rick wanted to know if there were any other state or national environmental groups in my area.

"Nope," I said. "Might be something down in Corpus Christi, with all the birds and everything. Maybe the Audubon Society. But that's a lifetime away from us. Eighty miles or so."

"That's what I thought. Something national like the Audubon. There aren't any groups like Texans United? Concerned about local grassroots issues? Greenpeace isn't down there?"

"Nope, and what's this *grassroots* thing?"

"It's local groups like yourself. You know, grass *roots*. Up from the ground. Local people. Just ordinary people like yourself. Politicians and agencies tend to be a little more sympathetic to an environmental issue if they think the concern comes from the local folks and not some big national organization out of Washington. It's votes and political turf and all that. So how about it, then? Get a few folks and give me a call."

I didn't remember what all I said. I always had a difficult time saying no to a friendly voice, but I also wasn't sure of what I'd complicate. How did an outside lawyer and an outside environmental group fit together? Was there some rule that I didn't know about, and if I messed it up I'd be making a couple more men mad as hell? Still, I wrote down his phone number and told him I would talk to a few folks.

I didn't do none of that. I was actually trying my best to forget Rick and Blackburn and meetings *entirely*. That last meeting at city hall had tuckered me a bit. I sat in the fish-house office with my boots on the desk, and Donna Sue sat on the blue shrimp box reading an advertisement about renting condos in Colorado. She had a pencil and was figuring on a piece of paper how much it was going to take to get her out of Seadrift and into Colorado. The wind had shut down, and through the edges of the cold open window, I could see the *SeaBee* hardly moving.

Then Blackburn called. "How are you ladies for a ride?"

"A ride? To where?" I said.

"Houston. Formosa wants to talk."

"Talk about what?"

"Well, hell. Those *permits*, of course! Where's your mind, Wilson? I think one of your local senators told Formosa to talk to us and see if we couldn't resolve some of our difficulties. I don't know—maybe it was Formosa's corporate New Jersey office talking. Who knows what it was? But whoever it was, it's going down at one of the biggest law firms in Houston. A lot bigger than mine. You think y'all can drive up to my office and then we can go over there together? Think you can manage that? Doesn't one of you drive in traffic yet?"

"I've never driven in any place that had a lot of overhead hanging lights. Not any freeways neither."

"Well, get Donna Sue, then, and get on up here. We've got a lot to talk about."

Donna Sue and I had to do some figuring. Who was gonna run the fish house while we were both gone? The only hands we ever had were a couple of boys, and they were gone because shrimping was so slow. I called the house and found Baby was not going to the Gulf with any supplies to any oil rigs that he knew of, and he was available if Donna Sue wasn't going to be there to bug him.

No, I said. Donna Sue wasn't gonna be there. So I hired him on the spot.

In the meantime, Formosa was sending out press releases to everywhere and everyone, or at least talking to senators in the know and our own state Senator Armbrister was interviewed on TV and said any delay in construction of the new Formosa project would be disastrous to the area's economy, and that he had requested that Formosa meet with the environmental group fighting their permit.

The next day I was running Baby through the ropes on the fish house, and Donna Sue had left in disgust at Baby being present, and Sanchez was coming through the door with his thermos of coffee. He had seen the story on the TV and wanted to know when we were going to the meeting. He thought he ought to be there. He was a director and, besides, he wanted to see Blackburn about a little legal problem. He would drive me and Donna Sue to Houston.

The next day Sanchez arrived, driving his diesel car that he had bought to save money when diesel was cheaper than gasoline. I sat in the front seat, blinking back early sunlight, while Sanchez drove about a hundred miles an hour and broke every speed limit on the highway. He had propped up a copy of *Time* magazine on the steering wheel and was reading and driving at the same time. I felt alarm creeping up my spine as I watched his hands and his copy of *Time* dance together on the steering wheel.

Two hours later, Sanchez caught the tail end of Houston and drove straight for the middle. The traffic didn't even faze him. He just kept moving and yelling, "Move over, moron!" then occasionally turning and gesturing at some car he saw, dipping his head and grinning and frowning alternately. I kept one hand tight in my lap and the other hand hard against the window, and I didn't look to see whether Sanchez's grin had stopped or if it had just stretched into another grin. At last Sanchez stopped and pulled onto a quiet narrow street with Blackburn's building the tallest around. It wasn't tallest by much, and I was real surprised there was a quiet *anything* in Houston, least of all Blackburn's office.

We went up to the fourth floor in an elevator that began in a wide oasis-like room and finished in a rat's maze. Then we walked straight into a lady Buddha sitting at a computer screen. "Well, how are y'all?" she said, and her face was smooth as the wide, wide sky.

"Oh, fine, fine, fine. Fine as a fiddle," said Sanchez. "Where's Blackburn? Where's he at?"

"Oh, Mister Blackburn's around here somewhere," she said, and with that Houston air-conditioning and her wind-clinking voice taking her somewhere down the hall, she reappeared with Blackburn. "Whyyy, here he is," she said.

Sure enough, it was. For two seconds I was caught in a confusion of black eyes and white face and white shirt and black hair that came walking down the white hall of his office. Inside his open jacket was a red tie with blue and green fish. "Well, now," he said, and smiled with his eyes like he'd done before, and his mouth didn't even need to move at all.

Then we went down to his private office for a minute, then we came out and down the elevator, then all of us climbed into his green-and-tan Jeep covered in bumper stickers of ANN RICHARDS FOR GOVERNOR and Galveston Bay for saving. Then we barreled off for something a little farther on downtown.

It took twenty minutes to get there, and it was a place in Houston where the sun didn't want to shine and only the Jeep (where Blackburn parked it across the street) was in any kind of light. The sidewalks looked permanently cold, permanently old, and they led us to a gray slate building that opened into vaulted ceilings made of brass and tinted glass. The carpet was blood red. A row of elevators was laid into a wall of black marble, and we took one and went up to the sixth floor.

Blackburn got out first and turned to us with his finger to his lips. "Don't say anything in here," he said. "There are spies around. Ssshh."

"Well, I can if I want to," Donna Sue said, and she looked at me, and we both laughed, and Blackburn turned again and said, "Ssshh!"

We walked to a pair of double swinging glass doors, and inside was a man in a dark suit, standing with a cigar. He came to us, saying, "Well, good! This is real good!" and he took the cigar out of his mouth and rubbed his nose with the same hand, and the cigar's tip was bright with a red light like a red eye. He pulled us down some quiet hall and into a large room with a long dark table, and against one wall were black-and-steel carts covered in white linen cloth and carrying brass urns reflecting dull light like moonlight off a truck fender.

I never once thought to ask Blackburn on what solid ground or under what sun we were operating. Never once did I think to discuss in the Jeep coming over, or any elevator we went through, what, if any, were the words we were going to live by in that room. I tried hard to think, but my head hadn't arrived. It was still leaning against a fish-house door and looking out over the bay. I sat down in a heavy chair at the dark table and reached over to the brass pot to see if it was hot and if there was coffee in it. Blackburn didn't sit. He dropped his briefcase on a padded chair and stood with one hand on his black hip and one cowboy boot caught in the chair's mahogany rung. He was watching the door and everybody who came in.

Donna Sue didn't move. She sat in her chair with her purse in her lap and both hands on her purse, and she barely breathed.

I poured coffee in a cup and tried to hold as many sentences in my head as I could, but they quarreled like cats strung on a clothesline. Then I lost the whole quarreling mess when ten men in dark suits and each holding papers and briefcases filed into the room. Two I had seen before: one at the fish house and another from a dozen TV interviews.

The plant manager looked at me briefly. He acted like he wanted to sit down but thought different, so he came over and talked polite talk, brief talk, then turned and went back to his chair. An Asian man followed behind him, and he smiled and his whole head was in the smiling as he bent and took one of my big hands in his two small hands, and he said, Miss Welson, Miss Welson, Miss Welson.

Formosa sat on their side of the table and we sat on our side, and a man in the middle with hair bright as a bonfire got up and said who he was and what law firm he represented and which way was to the coffee and which way was to the restrooms and whoever needed parking vouchers to be sure and clear it at the front desk before they left. Then he turned to the plant manager and waved a white hand as though he were waving to two attendants in the parking lot. Mister Peyton, he said, was going to take it over from there.

The plant manager stood up. First, he wanted to make it clear that Formosa's environmental commitment was equally as important as their economic commitment. Then he leaned forward with a dead serious look and said, "However, having said that, I must make *absolutely* clear that our communication problem must be resolved *today*."

I squirmed in my chair and looked at Blackburn, and he had taken a pen and a lavender pad out of his briefcase and written down *today* and underlined it.

The plant manager said the plant was about three months behind on its target date to begin construction. "Now," he said, and looked across the table at us, "this is *not* due to Missus Wilson's group request for a public hearing. That is not the reason. We have had a few small problems. A few. But we are confident that any agreement that comes out of this meeting today will set a precedent, because, predominately, these issues end up in a court battle with everyone slugging it out."

Then it was our turn to talk, and Blackburn leaned over the table with his eyes not smiling and the pen's edge hard and lavender on his paper. He said his clients wanted to discuss emission sources and toxic pollutants in the ambient air. Then we could go into the plant processes more. Discuss the units. We'd begin with that, for starters, then we'd see.

The plant manager stood motionless for a moment, then he nodded his head and his eyes moved to one corner of his brain. He turned to the men at the table. "I believe we can provide that. Right?"

He said basically what had been touted as the largest single investment in Texas's history, and the largest in the nation in over a decade, was a new plastics factory, with seven linked plants, which would make it one of the largest producers of polyvinyl chloride in the world. By their own estimate, the plant would cost more than 1.5 billion dollars to build, would employ as many as four thousand workers during construction, and would add twelve hundred permanent jobs to Calhoun County's economy.

Blackburn leaned forward at that point and said, "Mister Peyton, no disrespect intended, but we can read that in any month-old newspaper. This is not the Chamber of Commerce you are talking to here. If you don't mind getting to the gist of things."

Mister Peyton said, "Rest assured, Mister Blackburn, with *all* these plans we are touting, there goes a corporate philosophy that seeks *constant* improvement, and this includes environmental excellence. We stand behind this philosophy one hundred percent. As for the seven air permits that Ms. Wilson's group has requested a hearing on, Formosa will be using the best available control technology. The technology will limit Formosa's releases to ten percent of that allowed by the Environmental Protection Agency."

I leaned hard on the table and said, "So how much are y'all talking about? A couple hundred pounds? A couple *million*?"

The plant manager looked at me. "Well, it's a *bit* more complicated than that, Ms. Wilson. But I can guarantee you, the EPA and the Air Control Board are not wimps. They are tough in dealing with industries, but they can be easy to work with if you do what they want. We are going to be watched every minute of the day. It's not like we function on our own timeline. It's the agencies' timeline, and we are going to be watched like hawks!"

"But exactly *how many pounds or tons* are y'all talkin' about? You never said that yet."

"Ms. Wilson, we do not take this as a lark. We *will* have plant personnel to inspect every flange and pump seal and valve packing and threaded seal monthly, to make sure small leaks do not go undetected. We are leaving nothing to chance here. We might have made a few mistakes in the past, but believe me, the Chairman intends for his Point Comfort plant to be the jewel on the Texas Gulf Coast. We are very proud of what it will be."

He stood quiet for a moment, fully flushed and breathing hard. Both of his hands lay on either side of a stack of papers that were now spread so that one or two touched his hand. He looked like he might read something from one of the papers, but he didn't. He jerked his head up like one of us had made a noise and that noise was his job to stop.

I blinked and looked at Blackburn, and he leaned on his elbows and wrote on his pad. I didn't know if he listened or not, or even if what the plant manager had said was genuine or if it was a lie. Was I standing in the middle and they were to the right or left of me? Or was I to the left or right of them and *they* were in the middle? I didn't know if it was possible to be as ignorant as I was. I figured I was setting records somewhere.

Finally I leaned over the table and said in a voice I didn't recognize, "Have y'all got any environmental problems? I was wondering if you could tell me that?"

The plant manager's eyes said, *What? What?* Then he turned and looked to nobody in particular, then turned back to me and said, "Why, sure. Lemme think. I don't *believe* we've really had any problems. Not any that I can think of. We had a little pop valve release last week. . . . You know, kinda like a garden hose springing a little leak."

He looked over to one of the men sitting next to him. "Wasn't that when it was? Last week? Yeah. That was it. But that's about it. I don't believe that release was enough to be reportable. We've got to turn in all of these releases to the agencies, and some are reportable and some aren't."

"Nothing else? No bigger releases or spills or dumping or anything like that?" I was remembering the EPA documents sitting at the fish house, but I didn't know enough about chemicals and permit limits to not sound more stupid than I felt, so I said nothing else.

"Nooo. I don't think so. You know, maybe a long time ago. But that was before my time. During start-ups and after turnarounds, when you have to take a few units down and fix them, well, then we may have had a little problem. But on a regular day-to-day basis? Nooo. It's really pretty quiet out there."

So we all invented stories. At least I invented one about what was going on and what was being said and if it was the truth at all or just more things we didn't know about and didn't even know how to ask about. Blackburn got me in a corner of the conference room and said, "How are we *really* to know? We just have to trust that they are telling the truth. Besides, it's the first time." The first time? I didn't know if he meant the first time for him or the first time for me.

Blackburn asked more questions about toxic pollutants, and the plant manager was now allowing (seeing as how the worst was over) other men around the table to stand up and talk, and the one speaking next was a baby-skinned newcomer looking as young as my oldest girl. He said the permit allowed thousands of tons of nitrous oxide, and many hundreds of tons of volatile organic compounds and benzene, and so many tons of sulfur dioxide and particulates. Much of this I knew nothing about until months later. Nitrous oxide is the chief ingredient of smog. Sulfur dioxide, the principal pollutant in acid rain. Benzene is linked to leukemia. Volatile organic compounds to brain cancer. So it went on and on, a litany of chemicals I knew nothing about. Chloroethane. Chloroform. Ethylene dichloride. Vinyl chloride. Chlorine. I couldn't believe the amount of chemicals allowed to be released on permits. And Formosa hadn't given the numbers to me; only to Blackburn had they finally dished them out.

Then Blackburn said, "Isn't that nitrous oxide level way high? Four-and-a-half million pounds? That would put the ozone levels in the area near the EPA attainment level, and could possibly limit other future industrial expansion."

I was thinking, *And everything else too!* The chemical names whirled like sun motes through a broken window shade. Still, crazy or not, we negotiated monitoring on this chemical and on that particulate, and where in the Sam Hill was the Air Control Board on all this! Then Formosa's executives leaped from their chairs and left us, saying they'd give us a chance to talk. Talk all you want. Take your time. But *sometime*, today. We want to wrap this thing up today.

Blackburn turned in his chair with his pen in his hand and his lavender pad on the table. "Okay. What else beside the monitoring for chemicals do y'all want?" he said.

Sanchez had said nothing the entire time. For the first time in his life, he was not talking or commanding or laughing, but only sitting and drinking coffee. I looked at him, and he just shrugged his shoulders.

Donna Sue said, "I don't suppose we could ask for an outboard motor?" and Blackburn laughed and said no, no.

I said, "How about we do a health study in the community?"

"Where? In the county?"

"No no. In Point Comfort. Right next to Formosa. How about that?"

"Well," Blackburn said, "Let me see what I can do."

Blackburn took his pad and left, and we stayed where a ton and a half of God-colored light did our breathing for us. I waited with my hands on the table and thought, *Yes, I have done this before. The waiting is nothing new here.* Donna Sue's hard white fingers were wrapped around the handle of her purse, and she wouldn't look up. She breathed hard, down-frowning on her rough hands.

Then Blackburn came back and said, "Well, they agreed to most of it. But the health study is a no go. They said it's a can of worms."

"Well, I *like* that one. How come we can't have that one?"

"Well, Wilson, they just said emphatically no to that one. Like I said, they consider that one a can of worms. Opens up all kinds of stuff for them."

"Can of worms in what sense?" I said.

"In the sense that it's a can of worms, Wilson."

"Well, I don't know if I want to accept that or not."

"Well, hell," said Blackburn, "I guess I gotta work for my money. Lemme just see what I can do here. This is what lawyers are good for, Wilson. Figuring out something in between. A little compromise here. You think you can compromise a little here, Wilson?"

"I like the health study, Blackburn!" I said.

"Well, I *know* you like the health study, but Formosa *doesn't. Comprende?* So let's just figure out something we all can live with. How about liver screening? What about that?"

"What about it?" I said.

"Well, Formosa's a polyvinyl chloride plant. I'm sure they've had releases of vinyl chloride sometime in their life, and vinyl chloride can cause liver cancer. A whole lot of other bad stuff too, but the liver cancer is a real zinger. Also, it's one of the few chemicals you can link directly to a disease. Like benzene to leukemia. So how about it? It's not a full-blown health study, but at least it's a step in the right direction. You know, Wilson, sometimes you've got to take little steps before you take those huge ones you're so concerned about."

"Well, Formosa wants things done *today*. Not tomorrow. *Today.* And everybody in this county and half the state seems to be helping them to get it done today, but when I ask for something for the people or for the bay, all I get told is I need to take real bitty little steps."

"Oh, Wilson!"

"Oh, Blackburn!"

So he took his pad back to Formosa, and we sat in the heavy air again. I didn't even remember Donna Sue sitting there until she whirled to me and said, "I don't see why we have to give them anything!"

8

The Press Arrives to
Liars and Fools

The rest of that week I nursed some kind of unbridled anger. The meeting and consequent agreement with Formosa wasn't all of it, but it was close. The newspaper was the other part. The only newspaper in the county had written an article about the whole affair. First, it congratulated us somewhere in small print, then in huge headlines it took it all back, saying: GROUP BACKS DOWN FROM FORMOSA.

I sat at the fish house with my hands on my head. *Backing down? Scared?* That had nothing to do with it. We were stupid, but we damn sure weren't scared. And why didn't people make up their minds? First, they blasted us because we didn't negotiate, then they blasted us because we did. I was thinking of all the dozens of coin-operated newspaper machines in town and how I'd like to take every one and haul them to the bay and dump them.

Then Blackburn called and laughed. "Wilson, you're gonna learn the ropes sooner or later, and you're gonna find out that newspapers aren't always your buddies. How do you think they make their money anyhow? They just don't get it donated to them for being civically minded. No, Wilson. It's *advertisements*! Paid for by industry and by companies—businesses. You ever heard of that? But let me see what I can do. All right? That paper is totally out of line, so I'll call Formosa and see if I can't make things clearer to them."

When Blackburn hung up, Donna Sue said, "I suspected this all along."

"Suspected what?" I said, but she didn't answer. Instead Donna Sue got in her car and went home, where she went to the bathroom because she wouldn't go to the one at the fish house. Then Donna Sue returned. Then she went home again for the night. Then for two days she stayed in the I Have Been Ambushed mode, until it was Saturday and then she didn't come at all.

I brought Crockett and Santanna to the fish house with me and left the vault door open for them to play in, and bought them a new package of crayons and stuck it and a coloring book on the desk. The babies went back and forth from the ice mound to the colors, sometimes moving out to the open door to watch me while I patched a net in the street.

At midday a man from Formosa showed up with a copy of the agreement we had signed in Houston, agreeing to drop our hearing request. He needed a signature for a final legal paper. Crockett gravely held a hose and watched the water pour into a cement gutter until the man's black shoes moved into his path, and then Crockett, silent still, directed the water hose over the man's shoes. The man jumped, kicked one foot, then the other, and held the papers high in the air like he thought Crockett might water him and the whole thing down.

"Oh, he don't mean nothing by it," I said. "You just got your shoes where he was watering, is all. Isn't that right, Crockett?" But Crockett didn't say nothing, and he held the water hose where the shoes had been and watched the water move across the fish-house floor to the bay.

I had been in the net, so I pulled myself out of the webbing long enough to glance through the agreement and sign it, then I sat back down on the net and I wouldn't even look up when the man drove off. Signing my name made about as much sense as it did a week ago, and in the end I felt just as disturbed. Donna Sue and I weren't that far apart in our thinking.

Finally I got up from the net and went to the harbor. At least *that* was the same. The water hadn't changed. But the docks had. They were stumbling, they were begging *please, please let us fall in the water.* And one of these days the docks were going to fall, and when they did they would take the whole blooming fish house along with them. But for now the docks just leaned and flirted with the idea that one black night a few nails would fail and the water would crack open its dark mouth and swallow everything whole.

I stayed at the fish house until I finished the net, then I left it in a corner outside so that if the shrimper it belonged to came by and saw it (which ever' shrimper did—driving slow and checking out every net on the premises), then he could take it. I left a note, hammered on the back fish-house door, for Sanchez. Then I took the two babies and drove home and never got farther than the porch swing. I was sitting with one baby on my lap and another baby climbing the chain the swing was dangling from when Donna Sue drove in the yard. She sat in her car and honked the horn. I watched her for a minute, then I walked out to the car and leaned against the window. Three of the kids followed, and Crockett squatted at the front tire and tried to shove a tiny metal car underneath.

"How come you don't answer your phone?" she said.

"It's been disconnected or broke. . . . Don't know which. Only working phone is the fish-house phone."

"Well, get it fixed, 'cause I don't want to have to drive all the way out here anymore just to deliver you a message. Some reporter's been driving me crazy with phone calls. It's one of those Houston ones. I think that's what he said. I wrote it down somewhere. Wants to talk to you on Monday. Said you was *the lone opposition* out there."

Then she switched the car key and looked out the window to make sure I took Crockett's car out from under her tire, and said she was leaving. She just came to deliver the message anyhow, and she wasn't fixing to sit around all day so forty of my cats could climb in her window. She'd see me on Monday.

Sunday I didn't go to the fish house, but stayed home with the kids. I figured they'd patter their hands in applause when I walked past, but they didn't. They howled and yelled and ran into the oak canopies and buried themselves in hand-dug sand holes, and all day long I saw floor tracks pale as animals' paw prints. Then that night I walked out on the cooling porch in an old loose dress I used for a nightgown, and I saw two deer crossing the yard. One deer stayed and lifted its head briefly in a yard it seemed to have forgotten. Before I could call the kids, it left.

Monday morning it rained, and I sat down at the fish-house office and wondered if a reporter would make it through all that rain. I had sat in boats through plenty rainstorms, and I always felt the same way; unremarkable and invisible and not a curtain moving in my house. Some things just never change. Donna Sue came in, and her white skin was twice as light in the rainstorm than I ever remembered it in the sun. "Why don't you call him or do somethin'?" she said.

"I'm thinkin'," I said.

"Yore thinkin'?"

"I sure am," I said.

"Well, then, all right. All right."

"All right," I said. "There you go."

Then I took my hands from my eyes and saw the reporter had come. And he had. He had come through all that rain and all that Houston traffic and drove a hundred and fifty miles in a rented car and a rumpled suit, and said he had already been to Formosa.

Now he sat in a broken-down chair that Donna Sue had confiscated from the fish-house closet to sit all the company we had been having lately. He was a big man in a half-dried suit, and I could imagine him, scrunched over and intense in his small rented car, driving in the rain. He had a notepad on his knees and a foot of papers at his feet, and he scribbled something on the pad, then he looked up.

"You know I've been investigating Formosa. That's what I've come to talk to you about."

"Didn't know it, " I said. "I don't believe there is anybody that really knows one thing about that company. . . . Except that it's pure as the driven snow."

"Oh, it's a whole lot dirtier than that. What stirred my interest in the first place is that our state is *paying* an outlaw polluter—you knew that one, didn't you?—*hundreds* of millions of dollars to build a plant in your little county. It's one of those perverse ironies that once these same giant corporations clamored for the privilege of building a plant in Texas, and now we've gotta pay them."

"We're paying them? Now, how did that happen?"

"Well, first, the Chairman invites a small delegation from Calhoun County to his far-flung empire in Taiwan, and they presume it is to foster goodwill. Maybe they're even thinking they can persuade the good Chairman to fund a ten-million-dollar expansion of the existing Formosa plant in Point Comfort. But lo and behold! The Chairman offers *two billion dollars' worth*! A virtual Disney World of chemicals! I imagine that little delegation believed they had succeeded beyond their wildest dreams."

"Yeah, I've already heard about that. But where's this paying part? I didn't hear that one."

"Well, it goes this way. Now that the Chairman has dangled the carrot, you know, the two-billion-dollar chemical plant . . . then he produces the whip. He wants tax breaks. He wants speedy processing of the environmental permits. He wants visas for his Taiwanese engineers. Without such assistance, he says, he will have no other choice but to build his multibillion-dollar plant somewhere else—like Louisiana, for instance."

"Oh yeah, Chamber of Commerce thinks I'm a spy for them. Then the county commissioner has to have a talk. Everybody's spouting economic development and windows of opportunity! They're preaching it pretty hard."

"Oh yes," he said, "Economic development will heal us from our miseries. Economic development will put people to work and diversify the economy. It will probably even balance the budget. And you're right too. I'm surprised the preachers haven't invoked economic development in their sermons. But, Lordy! Unemployment fifteen percent! In spite of the fact that y'all already have four or five major chemical companies? Now, does that make sense that another chemical plant is supposed to turn things around? Am I missing something here? But, good Lord! *Two billion dollars' worth!* Well, well, that should make it a horse of a different color. Don't you think? Isn't that what they're saying? But then too, two billion dollars is much too much for a little county delegation to handle. Forget them! Now we gotta get the Texas Department of Commerce involved; move in and start calling the shots. Call it another home run for Texas. And you can bet with that much money and fifteen hundred promised jobs, every politician in the state wants to rush in to bask in the glory. A Taiwanese multinational is bringing plastics and a gob of money to Texas! They're probably cheering themselves in the back boardrooms. Even our governor wants to hog the spotlight with Senator Gramm. And they all say the same thing: All Texas has to do is a little deep digging into the public pockets that's been so empty for years from oil-field recession and real estate busts."

"So all this cheerleading, and how many million dollars' worth did we throw out?"

"Two hundred fifty million! The state of Texas is giving Formosa around two hundred fifty million in tax breaks and incentives! Think long and hard on that one. They gave ten million dollars to work on your navigation harbor and the ship channel. Broaden and widen just so Formosa can get their many, many big ships in and out . . . and by the way, isn't that the same ship channel where all Alcoa's mercury lays?

That's interesting as heck. What happens when a dredging operation starts chewing on that methyl mercury on the mud bottom? I can't even begin to guess. Then there's all those school taxes. . . . A hundred million dollars being promised from your little school district . . ."

"*Our school district?* That one my brother Froggie is sitting on? How can they do that when they've already told a couple schools they might be shut down because of funds? The newspapers said they were going to eliminate seventeen teachers, for God's sake!"

"Sorry, I didn't come with the answers. Those are some of the same questions I'm asking myself. You'd think a state department or agency supposedly working on behalf of the people of Texas would bother with questions like that. But apparently not."

The reporter looked at me for a minute and his eyes were bright. "Does any of this surprise you? The incentives offered? Any of it?"

I said I was surprised that nobody had mentioned a price tag in all the meetings I had been to, and apparently, as much as I'd thought I'd been a player, all I had been was a spectator, and there were a lot more reasons than communists that were driving the Chairman. Donna Sue was shuffling at the door, moving one boot, then the other, like she was fixing to do something with either or both of them. "I should've known it was another lie," she said. "Sounded like it the minute I heard it."

"Oh, wait, wait," the reporter said, and he smiled so quick and shoved himself so near the edge of his chair that two black bony knees stared me straight in the face.

"You heard he hated communists? Well, I was told that Wang started in the rice fields in Taiwan, then World War II came along and along with World War II came the B-29 bombers that destroyed his fields. So to compensate for that, the U.S. government made him a little postwar loan of three-quarters of a million dollars, and it was that postwar development grant that changed the course of his career from rice to plastics, because when he left the rice fields and went the direction of plastics, he never looked back. Some engineers that worked with him said Wang was so ignorant in the beginning that he didn't even know what the *P* in PVC stood for. Heck, I think he's still proud of that fact. Tells it himself when he talks to corporations."

"So he's repaying our American generosity with a big fat chemical plant in our backyard?"

"That's what he says the deal is. He'll tell you himself if he's with
his interpreter. You know he doesn't speak English? Well, at least he
says he can't, and I don't think he even finished school. Doesn't seem
to have hurt him, though. A self-made man at seventy-three, worth
over six billion dollars, and a company budget that amounts to several
percentage points of Taiwan's gross national product. And he's got a
better workout regime than a lotta men half my age, and I'm not that
old. Gets up at four in the morning! Push-ups! Laps in the swimming
pool! He's like one of those old robber barons I read about in
American History 101. The long-gone kind. The Carnegies and the
Rockefellers. I checked Wang's horoscope out too. Hey, I checked
everything out! He was born the year of the dragon. Probably thinks
he's a descendant of the Chinese emperors who believed *they* were
descendants of the real dragons. Why else call himself the Chairman?
In my book that corners the market on egomania."

"Yeah, but what's so special about the year of the dragon? I thought
dragons were something mean. Big teeth!"

"That, my friend, is the difference between the Western and
Chinese mind. To the Chinese, the dragon is *all* male and it spreads
good fortune. Imagine that's why the emperors made them a royal
sign. It sure might explain Wang's tendency for acquiring wives. He's
got three, you know. But that dragon thing doesn't explain it all. He's
got this curious work/body ethics. Some kinda toughness. I read
something about it in one of his business speeches he gave. Wang
talked about his earlier rice mill and a neighboring Japanese man who
had a lot of advantages Wang didn't have. The Japanese man would
close his mill at six and go home and rest in a warm bath, and Wang
would work until ten thirty or later, then take a cold shower out in the
open weather. Winter or summer didn't matter. Wang claimed he
earned three pennies more a day, and that was about the equivalent of
selling three bags of rice. So Wang outdid his Japanese neighbor even
though the neighbor had a lot better conditions."

Then the reporter stopped and he leaned his big face towards me.
There was no wrinkle added or subtracted to the scrubbed arrangement of his high forehead. It was buffed and clean as a dog's bowl.

"Everything in his apartment in New Jersey is supposidly *plastic*.
Plastic window frames. *Plastic* dishes. Some engineer told me that the

shark fin in his soup is plastic. . . . You think the man's got the beginnings of a plastic fetish? Or does he just like *cheap*? Someone who knows him pretty well told me his wives have to throw away his old clothes to make him buy new ones, and his idea of entertainment is drinking five beers a night in his New Jersey high-rise."

The reporter hadn't finished, but I couldn't think where else he could go. Donna Sue looked like she was deciding: inside or out. Quit or not. Then she apparently decided, because she came in and gathered her magazine and her half-filled tea jar and a sweater she didn't wear and left. The rain had stopped and yellow light came up the crack in the cement floor and moved to where the reporter's hand rummaged through a stack of papers. He sorted through two piles, then restacked them into a single one. Then he yanked his hand out of the yellow light and sat up.

"Look, everybody knows Wall Street's mantra of 'Greed is good,' and I know we've got this idea that development, even at great costs, is fine and dandy, but *not* questioning why a man's been barred from doing business in his *own* country is beyond me. If you ask me, *that's* the real zinger."

"Wang was *barred* from Taiwan? His own country?"

"Well, let's just say he originally wanted to build the ten-billion-dollar chemical plant in Taiwan, but a thousand angry farmers climbed down his throat and pitched rocks at him. They were fed up with all the pollution from his eight other plants. Even Taiwan's Council for Economic Planning and Development—which isn't known for stuff like this—came out and accused Wang of serious pollution problems. I guess that showdown with the farmers made Wang pretty hoppin' mad. Mad enough that he hauled his investments off to the good ole U.S. of A."

"Has Wang got plants besides the ones he's got here? Besides that one next to Lavaca Bay?"

"Oh, Wang's got chemical plants everywhere. In Delaware a judge got so furious at the constant problems with his vinyl chloride plant there that he sent an order to have twenty-seven permits jerked and the facility shut down. Then Formosa wouldn't open the plant gate, so apparently the state had to fly a *helicopter* over the plant and *drop* the order in."

"The same company we're letting in down here? That's the one? Somebody that won't take orders from a federal judge?"

"That's exactly who y'all are letting in down here. But Formosa's side of it was, Oh, well, the Delaware problem was something they inherited along with the property title when they purchased the plant. So it's my guess they'll say the same about why their Baton Rouge plant in Louisiana has groundwater so contaminated that if somebody wanted to drink the water they'd have to dilute one glass of it with a quarter of a million gallons of clean water. The ethylene dichloride level—another one of their hallmark chemicals besides vinyl chloride—in that groundwater is thousands and thousands of times the federal drinking-water standard. And EDC will melt a hard hat. A Louisiana official told me he just hoped when they built the plant in Texas, they dismantled the one in Louisiana."

The full meaning of the meeting in Houston was starting to hit me, and I wished I had never heard of Formosa. Every word coming out of the reporter's mouth damned this county farther and farther down a dirt road that was going nowhere. Calhoun County was destined to be a carbon copy of the abuse the Chairman had done elsewhere. If it wasn't already!

According to the reporter, it was. The old vinyl chloride plant on Lavaca Bay had had releases everywhere. Land, air, and water—you name it. The Air Control Board had given them orders for air violations for every year the plant had been in operation since 1983. The releases of vinyl chloride (and that chemical did nothing but rot out a worker's liver, or make his wife spontaneously abort her babies quicker than you could sing Dixie) were too numerous to count. He'd read files reporting a green, bubbly liquid floating from the plant down Cox's Creek, then out underneath Highway 35. Files that talk about chromium and vinyl chloride and ethylene dichloride being discharged into the creek behind the plant. He guessed it eventually ended up in Matagorda Bay. Eight million pounds of seafood and a hundred twenty million dollars' worth of recreational fishing put at risk. A whole fishing community. No wonder the fisheries are in a crisis.

When he stopped talking, he shook his head and said, "It looks like I ran off your friend there. Didn't mean to come down here and depress y'all."

I couldn't think of a word to explain Donna Sue's leaving, so I stood up and messed with a cold cup of coffee. After he put his papers down on the floor, the reporter looked at me. "Oh, don't take it too personal.

Nobody else checked up on him either. The secretary of state told me—he admitted it, actually—that not *one* public or private official, or even one journalist, for that matter, questioned whether it was in the best interest of the state to bring down a polluter. But at least he was honest! The Department of Commerce pleaded ignorant as a goat. They said they weren't the regulatory agency for the environment. It's not *their* job! So the deal comes down to this: Our great state of Texas handed an outlaw polluter over two hundred fifty million dollars in incentives just to come here. That was one hundred twenty thousand dollars for *every* job Formosa promised to bring in. We pay it. And that money is going to a polluter that would have come here anyway, because it isn't the incentives or the tax packages that draw these companies. What draws them is our cheap oil and our plentiful land and our fresh water and the bays to dump their waste and carry their plastic products hither and yon. They probably had a psychological profile on you people done—probably on file somewhere—saying nobody would oppose them. Little rural community. Fishermen. Not much education."

So the reporter left, and I thought it was later than it was, but it was only two hours gone. Somewhere in my head was the agreement I'd signed, and outside of it were the sounds of shrimp boats moving into the harbor and bumping into wharfs and pilings, and ropes being slung from hand to pole. I didn't look at that signed page in my head or write another word on it or scribble a sign or say out loud "When did the sun go down on us and I didn't see it?" I merely watched slow, tired captains wander into the fish house, not bothering to check the scales or watch me count shrimp. They shoved their yellow tickets in their pockets and walked out into the night.

Donna Sue returned disgusted and showed it by slamming ice into shrimp boxes and glaring at the shrimpers like she wanted to check their pockets for IDs to see if they were from Houston.

"It ain't their fault," I said, "We just went into that meeting knowing nothing. It might be small-town thinking and living. Maybe breathing. Maybe it's in the air."

"Then what's Blackburn's excuse? How come *he* didn't know about Formosa? Wasn't he smart enough? Wasn't he big-town thinking enough for you? He should've known Formosa was lying in their teeth just so they could get us out of their way and on with what it was they were gettin' on with before we came along. He should've known! I didn't know. You didn't know. But what was Blackburn's excuse?"

"Blackburn said it was the first time. Maybe he ain't used to liars neither." I stopped sweeping shrimp off the fish-house floor and leaned hard on the broom and looked down at what was so alive that morning but was so dead and tangled now.

"Besides," I said, "He's doin' it for free. You or me give him a dime yet? I guess we just gotta do more than depend on one man in Houston with a lawyer shingle. Gotta get us a filing cabinet and file stuff. Get us a camera and take pictures. Do our own checking. We can't depend on Blackburn for everything."

Donna Sue stood quiet for maybe five minutes, then she said real low and real slow, "You've got waaay too much trust in Blackburn. He ain't *nothin'* but another man. How do we know he ain't just playin' us both for fools? He's a lawyer, ain't he? *A man and a lawyer!* That's two strikes already."

She stayed at the fish house for a while and finally simmered down. If there had been an edge to her before, it was gone now. Finally she grabbed her car keys and walked out to her car parked underneath my net-hanging tree, and stood there under the brittle branches.

"You want me to wait aroun' awhile?" she said. "Don't need nobody blowing you away down here."

No, I said. The only one who might murder me was the truck driver tomorrow, if the shrimp numbers didn't tally. So I turned and didn't watch her go. I was tired, suddenly wishing I was gone and already pulled into a yard with lights in the house. Instead I leaned the broom against the whitewashed walls (Donna Sue's idea to keep back the night) and walked into the fish house and sat down.

9

Texas Water Commission Files

I stood under the front porch awning of an environmental enforcement building that gave no shade, and I took my time about going in. Blackburn had said if I wanted information I should try Corpus, so I was trying Corpus. It was my first encounter with the Texas Water Commission. I figured the officials would see I was incompetent and send me straight out the door. But they didn't. The two inspectors (not officials, like I thought) just looked at me, their eyes round and deadpan and serious as doornails. They were holding files like busy was something they did all day, and one of them was handsome in a blond kind of way, and the other one was handsome in a dark kind of way. I looked at one, then the other, then asked them both if they had any files on Union Carbide or Formosa. Either one, I said. It don't matter.

The inspectors passed some kind of eye signal just by the way their eyes widened and narrowed, then they turned to me. The blond one said, "Where's that Carbide plant located? We know where the Formosa one is. Is it the Texas City Union Carbide plant you want or the Seadrift plant?"

"Seadrift," I said.

"Oh," they both said. Then the dark-haired one said, "Are you the lady that's asking for a hearing on Formosa?"

"Yeah, or I *was* anyhow." I could feel the sun burning on the back of my neck. I thought I had closed the office door, but I hadn't. I was practically in the street under the sun. The inspectors were fiercely neat in their permanent-press shirts, and they hardly caused a wrinkle when they slowly turned to each other and passed the eye signals again.

"It's a complicated story," I said, in a rush to explain. "We *were* doing the hearin', but now . . . well, we've just got some kinda liver screening going on. Some monitoring. Stuff like that. I'm still involved. . . . I think."

They both gave a soft *ohhh*, then asked which files I wanted first: the Carbide files or the Formosa ones. I said, "Oh, give me the Carbide ones," so the blond inspector took me to a room where I could view the files, and the other went looking for the files on Formosa. Five minutes later he came back with an armload of folders. The blond inspector stood at the door and watched. Then they both left.

I was halfway through Carbide's files when the blond inspector came back in. "Are you finding everything all right?" he said. I looked up and said "Sure. I appreciate it. I really do."

Still, he didn't leave, only stood at the window and watched. Then he came up to me and leaned close and said, "I got something you ought to see. Maybe you should come with me a minute."

Only a woman standing stark naked with just her hands to cover herself was more nervous than me, but the man knew exactly where to go and what file to pull. He said, "Try to do something with this if you can. We've tried sending it up further in enforcement to the state or the EPA. . . . But it just gets caught in a bottleneck somewhere. I don't wanna guess what's the deal there. So see what you can do. It can't hurt."

"What is it?" I said.

The man opened the file and put his finger on the first paper. "Here. See that chemical? Normally the smallest amounts of these chemicals that would ordinarily merit a response are in the range of one-hundredth or one-tenth parts per million. These samples here show concentrations that are hundreds and thousands of times higher. We are talking vinyl chloride and ethylene dichloride. Chloroform. Nasty chemicals. All of them. There's at least thirteen of the fourteen priority pollutants here that the federal government regulates. . . . And that ain't good. The government regulates them for plenty good reasons. So any way you look at it, it's a heck of a lot of contamination in the groundwater at Formosa's plant in Point Comfort. At this point we don't know whether these contaminates are seeping into the drinking-water wells or not. There's no survey out there to tell us. So we don't know. We just don't know."

He said that during an inspection several years before, the EPA had caught Formosa with real high levels of contaminants in their storm-water basin down at their wastewater unit—into the thousands of parts per million of ethylene dichloride. A couple hundred parts per million of vinyl chloride. It was the real ugly stuff and not pretty consequences. EDC could damage the liver and kidneys and other organs. It could cause internal hemorrhaging and blood clots. It could also explode. Vinyl chloride was worse. It caused liver and stomach cancer. Brain cancer. Spontaneous abortions. Increased rates of birth defects.

The EPA had told Formosa to clean up its act and get the stuff out of there. The EPA inspector suspected that there might also be groundwater contamination caused by the leakage and said so in his inspection report, but nobody knew for sure because nobody investigated.

"Sooo, what did Formosa do?" the inspector said. "Well, they *dutifully* put down sixteen monitoring wells, supposedly to detect if there was a breach from the storm-water basin to the groundwater. You know, to actually check for groundwater contamination. So here we come, the state, doing our inspection a few years later. We go out there and check, and there are the monitoring wells, all right. All sixteen, except either the wells were knocked down or they were covered up. Looked like somebody had backed over them a couple of times with a backhoe. One or two of them I don't even know how Formosa got a sample out of them. But they were clean as a whistle on contaminants. No chemical showed up except in three wells, and Formosa's tests showed these were only real low concentrations. This goes on for about a year until one day we find this well that Formosa never told us about. The well had never been mentioned or drawn on a diagram or been a part of any of the data we had requested. So we asked Formosa, 'Hey, what's the deal here?' and one of the supervisors finally admitted that the well was drawing groundwater out from underneath the contaminated site. So we proceeded to do our *own* sampling and took it back to our lab in Corpus and had it tested. And this here, you see? This is what we found."

He put his finger on the test results and tapped it a couple times. "I was thinking to myself, *Is this possible fraud and misrepresentation on the part of Formosa?* Heck, I don't even want to think about it. You go figure it."

I was starting to feel the nubby hot wool of something being jerked over my head again, and it said loud and crystal clear, "This is about the eighth time you've been had, you stupid idiot!"

I stayed in that Texas Water Commission office, with its white walls and white floors and papers everywhere pegged with colored tacks on cork bulletin boards, for nearly a full day. Long enough to get files on Carbide and Formosa, and long enough for the inspector to copy me the entire file on the contaminated well. When he handed it to me, he said he just did the grunt work. He found the stuff. That was the level he was on. He guessed it was that *other* level, and he tossed his blond head to the ceiling, that seemed to just want to lose stuff.

I started rereading the file just to make sure I had what I thought I had. The inspector had given me internal memorandums for every visit they had made to the wells at Formosa and what their conclusions had been. I couldn't believe I had information a lot more important people than me needed and, apparently, didn't have. And why they didn't, I had no idea, but I was sure going to remedy that little problem. So the next morning I took the papers straight to the fish house and got on the phone and didn't do a lick of work first. I didn't even check the ice vault to see how many shrimp boxes were there. For all I knew, somebody could have come and ripped us off of everything.

I called the county judge and the secretary answered, and got my name and proceeded to tell me the judge wasn't there. *Maybe he is and maybe he isn't,* I was thinking. The judge didn't call that day or the next, so I called again, and the secretary hesitated a second like she was trying to decide whether she wanted to be irritated by my second call or pretend she was confused and had never heard of me. So she did a little of both, going first one way, then another.

Finally I hung up the phone and told Donna Sue I was going to the judge's office to deliver the file personally. Donna Sue barely looked up from her magazine and said something like "Oh, hell." So I went to Port Lavaca and to the brick fortress they called the county courthouse. I went up a flight of stairs and walked straight into the judge's office. Nobody was there, but the door was wide open, so I went in and left a copy on the judge's desk. Before I got back to the fish house, the judge called.

He was cool and formal like he was sipping iced tea, with his best suit on, out under a magnolia bush. He said he was just returning my call, and what was it I needed?

I said, "Did you see those papers on Formosa I left for you?"

Yes, yes, he said, but he had called Formosa and they had assured him it was nothing but some small readings from an old abandoned pipe they had left in the ground. Apparently the monitoring well was close enough to the pipe to pick up the readings. There was nothing to be concerned about.

"Besides," the judge said, "those were little bitty numbers. That's part per billion, part per million stuff."

"That ethylene dichloride concentration is about seventy thousand times the federal drinking-water standard," I said. "I don't think that's so small. You think that groundwater might be on a level with some folks' water wells out there? How do you know those wells are not contaminated?"

"How do I know, young lady? Because Formosa *satisfied* me with their answer, *that's* how come I know. I trust Formosa. Do you realize all what Formosa is doing for this county? What it *can* do? Have you any idea how many *jobs* they'll provide just at that new plant alone? You've just got no idea, no idea of how big a strain this county is under. . . . Why, the mental cases alone is staggering. These are people who have literally gone *crazy* worrying over a job. That factor, alone— just reducing mental cases—is enough to justify Formosa in my books, and it makes me a very ready and willing listener."

"Are you sayin' folks are gonna go nuts if we don't get Formosa down here?"

"That's what . . . well, in a roundabout way."

"What about askin' questions? Will askin' questions drive them nuts too?"

"I believe that's all I need to add to this conversation, young lady. I can spot a smart mouth when I hear one."

I started to say I was forty years old and probably older than he was, so I wasn't a young lady, but the judge hung up and I sat in the fish house with a dead phone. Donna Sue stood in the fish-house door in her white boots and bleach-stained jeans.

"Hell," she said, "it ain't gonna get any worse. Call the rest of them. Call the whole damn bunch."

So I called the county commissioners and listened when the phone went dead or else the commissioners went stone deaf themselves. They wouldn't say nothing, so I had to do all the talking and pretty fast too, so they'd stay on the line and not run out the door and across the grass to get into their cars.

Eventually I made a call to one of our elected state representatives, and he was cold, cold, cold. He didn't like me in particular, and he didn't like commercial fishermen *at all*. The fishermen had embarrassed him at a function once and he had never got over it. He just listened, said a brittle "thank you" like ice breaking up, and hung up.

I called Blackburn, and he said, "Well, we can always ask for an environmental impact statement. That might be something that can slow this Formosa thing down a little bit until we get better answers on what's going on out there. Formosa's got federal projects involved in this expansion, and when you've got that you've got a federal law saying an environmental impact statement is required. So Formosa wants to dredge that ship channel. That's Corps of Engineers. Then there's probably some water-pipeline deal going on. That's Bureau of Reclamation. I think we can figure out a law or two to do battle on."

"So we can ask for an environmental impact statement? Just like that?" I said.

"We can try. Nothing out there saying we can't try. It's just getting anywhere with it that's the problem. Getting it into the right courts and before the right judges. In the meantime, just keep pushing that information that you've got there in your hands. Go call Rick Abraham. Give him something to do."

Blackburn hung up, and I sat at the window of the fish house. Outside the window and beyond the shell road were mudflats and a tiny bayou with sun and birds and tall grass. If I had time I could sit and contemplate the silence, like old times. But I didn't have time. And I was riled about tracking Rick down.

I called Houston, and the Texans United volunteer on the phone said Rick wasn't in Houston, he was in *Austin*. Or fixing to be in Austin. A few environmental groups, plus a political party or two, were taking the temperature of the environmental movement in Texas. Willie Nelson might show up, so it might end up in a party.

Donna Sue said she wasn't going for sure. And *who* said Willie was gonna be there? She didn't believe that. Besides, her car wasn't running right, and Deputy Dawg was suddenly getting stubborn about totally unrelated things.

"Such as?" I said.

"Such as me frying a whole damn chicken before he goes out shrimping at three in the morning, is what. You ever cut and fried—

double the egg and double the batter—chicken at three in the morning? Then I do that, and he wants biscuits next. Then I ain't gonna to tell you what he wants next. I'm still trying to clear my mind on that. It's all tied to this Formosa thing. He wants me out. He just ain't sayin' it. He says other things instead."

So I asked Baby to drive me to the Trailway bus station that was forty miles away in Victoria, and he said, "How come you don't get your buddy Donna Sue to do it?"

I shrugged my shoulders and didn't say nothing about Deputy Dawg, because I didn't want that blood-and-personality connection to harden some notion already starting in Baby. "She can't always do it," I said.

"You always do it, so why can't she? What makes her so special?"

"I *need* you to take me! There ain't any other way I'm getting to Austin except on that bus, and it's either you takin' me to the bus station or me drivin' all the way to Austin in the van, and I don't believe that van will make it."

Baby's smell was hard as the walls in the house, and around his shirt collar and his hair was a scent of the sea, and against his wrist was a layer as thick as my hand. I looked at him and my hand went out to his hard hand, and at length I touched his shirt. He stepped back.

"I'm gonna do it, Baby. I *am*."

"Yeah, I know. You'll do it no matter what I tell you. No matter what *I say*."

Baby took me, but he didn't talk the whole hour it took to get there. Finally I opened the door and got out at the bus station, and Baby shifted gears and never looked back.

I sat on the bus, dirty and tired, and my teeth tasted like I had eaten the vinyl seat I sat on. I watched the space at my feet until the bus started, then I leaned back onto my couch and watched bits of Texas drag by the window. Cars and trees and dried winter fields came, then changed into old towns and old buildings and older signs. Sometimes a man or a child looked up, startled at a bus rider looking out and staring back. Old dried Texas stayed in my window the whole ride. The sun slanted in my window, and I went to sleep sitting up in the thin dust of winter.

When the bus reached Austin, I walked outside the covered entrance and into the street and looked for the big pearl-colored dome of the capitol. That was all I knew of Austin. The capitol. I had been there once with the fishermen when they were fighting yet another fishing bill.

I walked down the street; first one way, then another. The wind yanked at my jean legs, and picked up bits of litter and dirt and flung them far into the air. Then a dusty Austin city bus came and jerked open its door, and I got in. I got off three blocks from what I figured I was looking for. It wasn't the capitol, but it was bound to be close. So I walked several blocks. There was the open door, and above it on a long white banner stenciled in green letters were the words TEXAS: WHERE ARE WE GOING?

Inside the entrance hall had the air of a flea market, with dozens of tables filled and overflowing with papers and articles and hand-printed pamphlets. There were posters taped to every wall and leaning against every table. The posters decried toxic landfills and plastic baby toys and medical wastes and shipment of wastes and agency foot-dragging and seal deaths in the Arctic Ocean and dolphin deaths in the Gulf. One poster lambasted a toxic landfill outside Houston, and another had graphic drawings of a site in Dallas contaminated with lead that was filling black babies' bodies. Another poster was a black-and-white drawing of a Vietnam vet holding a baby, and both of them were drenched in orange rain. T-shirts filled a long table and were tacked to the wall behind. Slogans stamped in blue and green dyes shouted: EXXON SPILLS, CARBIDE KILLS. SAVE OUR CHILDREN. MOTHERS AGAINST PESTICIDES. PROTECT OUR AIR.

Two old women with white cotton bags and GRAY POWER stamped on shirts covering their ample breasts milled around a table. They picked up this book, then another, then looked at something else. A boy with a ponytail and a bag over his shoulder picked at pamphlets crammed on a small card table. FOR SALE BY AUTHOR. MUST SEE TO APPRECIATE. GAIA APPRECIATES YOUR HELP.

They were shopping. Hunting down hope. Wal-Mart couldn't have done it better or had wider aisles. Pick what you want. Children's cancer statistics. Emission controls. Self-help on organizing. Self-help on grant writing. Secret plots and sweetheart deals of government and state agencies. Green scorecards rating legislators and Common Cause rating legislation. Vietnam vets were against Agent Orange, and housewives were against the nonlabeling of canned goods.

But the real deal was inside, behind closed doors. The evangelizing. I saw it pretty plain, so that's where I went looking for Rick. I went in and sat near the back. I didn't see Rick anywhere, and thought about getting up and looking for him. I watched speakers come and go. They walked to the podium, laid down their notes, then either talked off the tops of their heads or straight from the notes for twenty minutes. I sat in my gray metal chair and twice I tried to move, but twice I didn't. Six speakers came and went, then another came to talk. The speaker was thin and in a coat too big, and he carried his notes to the podium and read them all. His voice was a slow, tired wind on its way to Waco or Laredo, so I finally got up and went back into the hall. There I saw Rick standing and talking with two women. When he saw me he said, "Hey! Look who's here. I was just thinking about you."

PART TWO

10

Dirty Facts Revealed

The first bad thing about working with two men is that they're two men. The next-worse thing is that their war playing was liable to be different as heck from mine, and it was. Rick believed in hand-to-hand combat and gouging the opponents' eyes out, and Blackburn believed in guerrilla warfare.

"Light one fire and if that doesn't work, then light another one. Keep your number of options going. Surprise the bastards behind a tree. That'll keep the enemy off balance."

Blackburn was in his office. He leaned back into his latest theory and yanked his eyes to see if the thought he was thinking in that leather office chair was going anywhere.

"Oh, hell, where are they now?" he said, looking down the hall for one of his legal aides, and turned back around. "Look, Wilson, all I'm saying is we don't *always* have to have a frontal attack. And *if* there is a need for a full-frontal hand-to-hand thing, then *please, for me*, get Mister Rick out there in front. He's in Houston. He's got distance. He can afford to lead the front attack for criminal charges on Formosa, if that's what he thinks you ought to be doing. Let him have some worries about assassins at the door for a while."

Blackburn stopped talking and smiled like he found something vastly amusing about me and my plans and the white boots that I wore and the bay that lay at my very doorstep. He tipped his chair back and leisurely peeled a pink wrapper from a hard candy and shoved it in his mouth. His black boots were on the desk, and in the space above his shoes, a redfish tie hung loose around his neck.

"I worry about you, Wilson. How many people do you have anyhow? Ones you can count on? You? Donna Sue? Who else? That brother of yours?"

"I *had* twenty signed-up members, but I lost a couple the other day.

A woman wrote and said her husband told her to get out. It was getting too hot."

"I rest my case. I'm not so sure asking for criminal prosecution as the first dogie out of the chute is the way to go. I know Rick wants you to do it and wants you to get a petition going down there, but that's a real heavy accusation there. . . . Claiming Formosa has criminal intent on their releases, then forcing—oh, excuse me, *petitioning*—the state to enforce. Lordy, Wilson. And I don't care what that reporter claimed or what those documents showed. . . . You live down there and you're pretty much on your own. Rick isn't the one going after names where the enemy lives. It's different for him. But you *could* get those fishermen off their rears. *That's* the ones you really need to get help from. If these agencies look at anything, it's those fishermen's names. And start thinking about that environmental impact statement. Think more on that one and less on the criminal prosecution. An EIS might not be winnable, but it sure as hell is doable."

I started to defend Rick and say I didn't think Rick minded bullets so much. The problem was I was just one of a hundred projects Rick already had going on. But I didn't say it and I didn't tell Blackburn that I couldn't call Rick anyhow. My phoning days at the fish house were numbered. I'd have better luck talking through a tin can from here on out.

The phone business had started mild enough. Me and Donna Sue had gone after parts to fix the conveyor belt, and I had been waiting in the truck for I don't know how long. Froggie walked up to the window without warning. "When are you payin' that bill?" he said.

"What bill?" I said.

"Ohhh, you know what bill. All those calls. When are you doin' it?"

"Hmm . . . how 'bout . . . next week? How 'bout then?"

"Next week, then. You'll get me three fifty?"

"Oh, that's what it was? Sure. I'll get you three fifty."

Then Froggie walked down the sidewalk and started across the street when I yelled, "It was three fifty? Three fifty even?"

"Three fifty!" he yelled. "Next week!"

I didn't like dealing with money. But there I was, in the middle of the road and acting like I was fixing to go someplace, only I didn't have the money. My purse didn't have the money and my next-week salary wasn't enough and I was sure Howdy Doody would tell me my bank account was busted. So any calls to Rick in Houston were out of the question, and telling Blackburn I needed three hundred dollars by next week was about ten words too many. I would have sooner cut out my tongue.

But too damn bad for me. I still needed the money, so I went down to the canal where I had hauled Sanchez's shrimp more times than I could count, and pulled into Wally's little ponderosa.

Wally's place was a fishing mess made up of opened oyster heaps and sand dunes and old tin buildings doing nothing and holding nothing, and one lone abandoned railroad car that was drug out there for God knows what reason except maybe to house the illegal Mexicans that constantly walked the Gulf beaches, looking for decking jobs.

Across from Wally's and sharing the same canal and the same road was a sportsmen's camp with a dozen travel trailers that went nowhere, and sometimes they were vacant and sometimes they weren't. Next to the trailers and out front on prime water property were three beach houses, plus one lone store/bait stand that had the only gasoline pump around. A white bait flag was almost always out. We got bait. We don't got bait. It was better than a neon light.

There was a simmering war going on. The sportsmen in the one camp hated the commercial fishermen in the other and, most spectacularly, they hated Wally. Most shrimpers felt confused and angry about the declared war, but Wally didn't care. He flaunted his fish house and his illegal gill nets as exuberantly as a big momma with her big ugly baby. Wally was *proud* to be a fin fisherman (and sometimes outlaw), and wasn't *nobody* running him off the bays. Commercial fishermen were on the water and making a hard living long before the "damnsportsmen" came along to spoil it. So even as hard and troubling as the times were, Wally wasn't defeated. Not when he had a Louisiana shrimp buyer and an eighteen-wheeler truck backed up and loading his shrimp, and stashed in the back end of the fish house and in an old rusted refrigerator truck, the illegal redfish his daddy-in-law (my seventy-year-old uncle) had brought in the night before.

Anybody with any real understanding of war-telling knew it was late for the fishermen, but there was no pitiful hand-wringing on Wally's part. Nope. Wally just grieved inward, and the internal hemorrhaging colored his skin as deep red as the illegal fish he hid in the refrigerator truck.

But I didn't go into fishing calamaties with Wally. I needed his help on organizing the fishermen to fight Formosa, so I went that direction. "Oh, nah, nah, nah," he said, and brushed my words off like he was swatting flies.

He didn't sit still at his desk, but reached over and spilled a rusty can filled with nickels and quarters and frayed dollar bills. He grabbed a couple of quarters and said, "Get me a Coke over there, would ya? Here, get yourself one too." And he tossed me some change.

I went and got Wally a Coke and sat down on his desk. "I mean it, Wally. I want you to help me on this Formosa thing."

"*Everbody* wants my help. I can't even go into town without some-body needin' me for somethin'."

"Yep. You're the man, all right."

"Nah, nah . . . I know where you're going with that, and I ain't goin' there. I ain't got time in the day, girl. I'm a busy man. Got waaaay too many irons in the fire, and none of them makes money unless I keep the pot stirrin'. And shrimpin' don't look good at all."

"Maybe if you help me with Formosa, we could have a chance of things getting better on the bay. Ever wonder why the seasons are the way they are? No cycle to it anymore. All those dolphins dying. Then all those pelicans they found dead out there on that island."

"Nobody pays attention to that stuff! Besides, whadda they say? Cold weather! Dolphins freezin' to death. Now, how much sense is that? It's *money* that gets listened to, girl! Just like Howdy said down there at the bank. Give 'em their permits. Maybe those plants will help for a change. Somebody sure needs to 'cause it ain't gonna be the shrimpers helping themselves. They're too busy just trying to stay alive in the hours they got left. Jus' ask me—I know all this stuff! I've had a life brimming over with fightin', and I'm tired of it. Tired, girl. Real tired."

Light spilled from his picture window and filled every crack in the wall, but still Wally wasn't finished. "C'mere, girl," he said, and he waved me out of his office with his red face and his red hand leading. I suspected it wasn't just Coke Wally had been drinking, and when he took out a whiskey bottle, I knew it for sure. He uncorked the bottle like I wasn't standing there and waved it around.

Wally was a private drinker (which everybody in town knew). The whiskey's original use—to keep him warm on the cold winter nights he sat in his skiff, waiting out the redfish and the big bull drum and maybe even a game warden's boat prowling the bays—was forgotten, and Wally's skiff and nets had been outlawed by Texas Parks and Wildlife regulators, and what nets that weren't confiscated now rotted in the sun like everything else. But still Wally's bottle remained as young as the day it was born, and it was only Wally, worn out and tired.

At the moment, Wally wasn't worn down. Wally was excited about the illegal redfish hidden in the cold, dark interior of the abandoned refrigerator truck.

"Whadda you think of that?" he said. "My old daddy-in-law catchin' that mess of fish!"

"Looks like a pile, all right," I said.

"Well, I think *so*! But try to tell that sportsmen crowd over there that there's plenty of redfish in the bays and just see what they say. 'Not there! Not there!' That's what they say. My hind foot! They're everywhere and eatin' every shrimp in the bay. It's just 'cause those stupid sportsmen can't *catch* 'em is what the big deal is. So we're not suppose to catch 'em either!"

Wally's eyes bulged in his round face and his eyes said the same thing as his mouth. I didn't want to get into that long-gone redfish fight. I had others lined up and waiting, but Wally wanted to die a little that day and remember when Seadrift sat stunned and the grief she felt was not only for outlawed nets and skiffs but for young boys and daddies and grandfathers arrested and rotting in jail for still being fishermen. And outside the courthouse? Fishermen's wives and daughters walked the grounds and didn't even know where to park their trucks.

So Wally was remembering and uncorking his bottle, and I was shoving a petition in his hands.

"Here, sign this," I said.

"Oh, heck, what have you got now? What is this?"

"It's a criminal petition on Formosa. We're trying to get the state to file criminal charges on them. Make 'em do somethin'."

"Well, heck, get 'em to do sumpin', then. . . . But gettin' the state to do *anything* when you don't have money to get it done is a lot bigger job than you think. Jus' ask me. . . . Oh, heck! Maybe you do know. Maybe I ain't tellin' you a single frazzlin' thing."

Wally flattened the paper against my back and signed the petition with a flourish. "I don't know *nothin'* about nothin' anymore. A woman might can do somethin' where a man can't anymore. They might listen to a woman. . . . 'Cause those legislators *shore* don't listen to me in Austin anymore. You can tell they don't want to hear it. They're tired of my face or somethin'. I don't know what it is."

"They gave me and Donna Sue the same kinda look. . . . Only difference was a senator on the Natural Resource Committee told us we might get a vote or two if we slept with some senators there. At least you didn't get that one."

"Nope," Wally said. "Never said that one to me."

"Well, see how lucky you was!"

"Oh, pooey. What else you need, or was that it?"

"Well, I need some money. Froggie's fixin' to shut off my phone if I don't pay him some money."

I watched Wally fumble with his pockets, trying to figure which pocket his money was in. Then he yanked out a fat green roll and pulled off two hundred-dollar bills. "Is this gonna do?"

I took one bill and shoved the other back to him. "One's enough, Wally. I'll get some of the other fish houses to help."

If I'd known then that Wally's place was the last fish house on Easy Street, I'd have took both of Wally's hundred-dollar bills just like he offered. That was the last bit of money I got without bleeding for it. The next fish house I asked, the owner looked at me and said nothing. Then he stared off to the side of my head until he finally said, thoroughly tired, "Well, hell, how much did Wally put in?"

"Wally gave me a hundred."

The fish-house manager gave me another bad look, then another long sigh, then he slowly drug out his long black book of blank checks. I left soon as I got the check and before the owner turned sullen and started bleeding all over his desk. Back at our fish house, I called Haynie's fish house across the harbor. Haynie, I sorta knew. Haynie had went to school with my brother, Froggie, and rode around in a truck with Froggie and had a joint fish account at the bank with Froggie and privately owned the only boat launch in town plus his own fish house. The boat launch was where all the Vietnamese crabbers and most all the sportsmen who drifted into town launched their boats, and anytime anybody put a skiff in the water, Haynie got two dollars.

Haynie said hell would freeze over before he gave me any money, and I was the most ignorant sonuvabitch in town. And don't *never* call him again. Then he hung up.

Donna Sue was real patient explaining Haynie. "His wife works at one of those plants. Maybe Carbide or British Petroleum. She's somebody's executive secretary."

My life was getting to be a succession of cut-downs and blown-to-hell looks, and I was turning cement in my resolve never to ask for money again. "I think I can get seventy dollars from my fish-house check," I said.

"Baby's gonna kill you, he finds out you're using that money," Donna Sue said.

"Froggie's gonna kill me faster if I don't. I ain't askin' another fish house. Not another one."

I stayed on that roost for a while and said I wasn't coming off no matter what. I didn't want none of their damn fish-house money. So Donna Sue came and Donna Sue went, and where she went she didn't say. When she came back she thumped a hundred-dollar bill down on the desk.

"Now. Don't that make three hundred? And don't ask where it come from, because it ain't from me and that's all you need to know. I know some fishermen too, you know. Froggie can just swallow that other fifty. It ain't gonna kill him."

So I picked myself up and slammed myself right back where I started before I had the money problems. I hardly contained myself two whole minutes before I called Blackburn in Houston.

"So what's this environmental impact thing that we want?" I said. "What's it do?"

"It's a federal law," he said. "One of those innumerable environmental laws we've got around out there, but a fat lot it does us. It's *enforcing* laws and making judges and agencies pay attention to them that's the bummer. But this one, in a nutshell, says the public has a right to know about projects that might impact them. It's preventive. Precautionary. So if Formosa has any federal projects associated with its expansion and that project has the potential to impact the health and well-being of the citizens and the environment . . . well, *by law* they're required to do a study on the impacts."

"So Formosa does a study. So what?"

"Well, for starters, Wilson, it isn't an everyday kind of study. It lets the public in. You—the public—get to speak your mind. Then too, it requires EPA and National Marine Fisheries and the U.S. Fish and Wildlife and the Bureau of Reclamation involvement, when a company like Formosa would just rather do their *own* little report without any interference at all. Just get their construction contracts in order and get the hell on building and up and running. That's their idea of a perfect world. So if you're wondering will Formosa be pissed off about the whole thing, well, hell, yes! They aren't going to volunteer for it! But then, they aren't really gonna be worried neither, because we don't have a snowball's chance in hell of getting it. And Formosa knows it."

"I thought you said it was federal law," I said.

"It is. Legally. *Politically*, it's something else. It's kinda twisted. It's the law, but it isn't. You get my drift? It just depends on what side of the fence you're standing on, and I dare say you and I are on the *wrong* side. People like you are always gonna be on the wrong side, and I just *choose* to. And whether or not that makes me stupid, I don't know. But if stupid's the case, then I guess I went to college to get that stupid."

"Donna Sue doesn't figure you're stupid. She just figures you're corrupt. She saves the stupid for me and her."

"Well, be sure to give Donna Sue my congratulations on that *wrong* but astute judgment. Tell her she should be happy to know that I'm as stupid as y'all are."

But Donna Sue wasn't happy about anything except me causing more problems, and every call I made on Froggie's phone seemed to raise her spirits that much more. I'd never seen such a twice-removed troublemaker in my life. Then, continuing her pattern, three days later and two weeks after my visit to the Water Commission down in Corpus Christi, Donna Sue brought a newspaper from her second run of the morning into town. She laid the newspaper on top of my coffee cup. "What's this, you figure?"

"Don't know. Says it's something to do with a reinvestment zone in Point Comfort . . . whatever that is."

"Don't you think you need to be there?" she said.

"Now, why don't you go tell Baby that? Pick up that phone and say you think Diane's gotta run to another meeting."

"Baby should've picked himself a different woman. It's his own fault for gettin' the wrong damn kind of woman."

That's a fact and a lot of people knew it, but Momma said it different when I went to pick up the babies. She was in the kitchen, and Daddy sat in his chair at the kitchen table and did absolutely nothing except smoke a cigarette and drink his coffee.

"You don't deserve somebody like Baby," she said, and she wasn't even going to talk about Formosa. She refused to discuss that subject, saying her eye was hurting and the arguing was gonna cause her head to explode.

So I drove home to Baby, and he was still mad about the bus trip to Austin, so I got the two babies dressed, and fed supper to the girls, then I left to go to the meeting in Point Comfort, and Baby never raised his head. He was watching *Killer Snakes* on TV.

The ride to Point Comfort wasn't complicated. It was exciting if you were a kid and liked bridges. I looked out the window and pointed out the old pilings of the first bridge to the babies. With all that water surrounding the town, you'd have thought Point Comfort was a fishing town, but it wasn't. It was a company town with a capital *C*, and the only dock worth noting was an industrial one, and it ranked fourth behind the Houston Ship Channel, which ranked first.

Point Comfort was born out of the barn-red side of an Alcoa bauxite refinery, and in the fifties it gained cityhood and proceeded to lay down two roads: one coming in and one going out. The town had two companies besides Alcoa: Formosa on the north end of town, then another out on the mudflats where the company's name was still printed on the side: BEAN. Now the tide lived there, and Bean was gone.

Although Point Comfort was a company town and part of the triad in our three-town county, the majority of the plant workers came from outside the county, and on any given morning a long line of headlights could be seen on the highway, coming from Victoria County and beyond. (Even Union Carbide's birthday billboard outside Seadrift's city limits read THANK YOU VICTORIA! It said nothing to the town or county where the plant had spilled its chemicals for fifty years.) But that was the way it was in a county where it was either heavy-duty industry or unemployment. Apparently the meeting I was heading for was a variation on that tunnel thinking.

A woman older than me and smaller than me met me at the city hall door. She had yellow hair cut at some earlier time, and now it was growing out in certain spots and in certain spots it wasn't. She took both my brown hands and looked me square in the eye.

"You've got no idea how much I appreciate this," she said. "I need *all* the help I can get here." Her eyes said she was serious, all right, and she refused to smile and she refused to budge from the door.

"Do you know how much I've had to go a-beggin' to them? *Them! Them* who've come to *our* town. How many times I've said to Formosa, 'Just please, please, please think about it. Just please give us a little helpin' hand here.' But no! Nothing is what I get!"

"What are you sayin'? Formosa—"

"Yes! That's what I'm sayin'. They're right across the railroad track! Breathing fumes down on us! And now they want to build this billion-something-dollar plant to add to that *other* one they've got. You'd think Formosa would figure they owed *us* something for all that commotion. But no! I went to them and said, 'Look, the city's got this little problem right now. Alcoa wants to quit providing drinking water the way they always did before.' And who knows why . . . maybe the liability. Maybe they're worrying about the bays polluted with mercury. *I* don't know. I just know our water source is drying up and we've got to get another one, and *nobody* wants to help."

She stopped long enough to fling her hand into the night air. "Just look there! See what we put up with."

I couldn't think what to say. But she didn't care. I took both babies by the hands and went inside to a near-empty room. Crockett dropped my hand and sat on the floor and fiddled with a metal ring on the metal chair, and was faster alone than I was. I stepped over him and sat in the next chair and pulled out some Crayolas and paper from my purse and gave them to Santanna. Then I handed Crockett a small metal car, and he turned it over and spun the tires.

A ceilingful of long fluorescent lights (some working and some dead and mildewed) turned the room into bright afternoon. Dogs would have run howling from such a light, but it didn't seem to drive anybody away. The light just pulled them in from the night outside. A man and his wife walked in, then two more men, then four more. One woman turned and looked at me, then glanced down to Crockett on the floor. A man pulled a metal folding table from off the wall, slammed it flat on the floor, then drug it to the front of the room. A woman went to help and the man shooed her away with an upraised hand.

Santanna cried about something. It was still not too late to leave. The feeling of leaving was more profound than rain, so I leaned over Santanna and whispered into her hair, "Hush, hush. We will go home soon."

Then Formosa arrived in the doorway. Not rushing, not moving; just being in a doorway while everybody else was sitting. They were two men, tall and without coats, and seemed to be watching the room. Then the plant manager said something to the other and moved, but whatever he said confounded the other, because he stood at the door and shook. Even from where I sat, I could see him shake. He was the man Formosa had sent to the fish house and the man whose shoes Crockett had watered down with the hose.

When he saw me, he lifted one hand and started towards me, but the plant manager stood again and frowned hard and called from his chair. "Fred," he said. "Fred." They sat three seats from me and the plant manager said nothing, but Fred leaned over two empty chairs and Santanna's head and said low and fast, "All of those wells . . . "

"What?" I said.

"*That* information on the wells. The ones you gave the judge, we . . . "

The plant manager shoved Fred's shoulder, then turned and stared straight ahead. Fred was docile for two seconds, then he hissed across the empty chairs, "We *didn't know* that report was out there. *I didn't!*"

There was no pretense now. Fred was skipping any part that said him and me were regular folks on a quiet evening. Nope. Fred was jumping straight into mayhem, and his whispers were louder than the mayor's mayoral talking as she started the meeting.

"Where did you find those documents? Austin? I can't find them anywhere!" Fred was leaning on his arm at some angle he couldn't possibly lean, and deep breathing in a way he couldn't possibly breathe. Water or not, Fred was drowning in his own white shirt.

The plant manager turned around in his chair and grabbed Fred's shoulder. "Fred! Fred!" he said. Then he jumped up and took Fred's arm and drug him past the row of chairs and out towards the back.

I was beginning to see I had an influence after all, and if not from what I did, then at least from what I *said*. It certainly made people go in different ways than what they planned. The meeting, however, was going right along without me, and this meeting was over money. Formosa was asking for the thing it didn't have yet: a two-hundred-fifty-acre tract of land within the city limits of Point Comfort designated a reinvestment zone. It was the first step in a series that would qualify Formosa for a tax abatement from the city of Point Comfort. So its mayor had been up and down twice, and a councilperson once, and now it was Formosa's turn to talk.

The talking was Fred's job, and he said the request boiled down to a couple of points. First, Formosa needed a reinvestment zone declared on a couple of hundred acres between Formosa's gas plant and State Highway 35. Second, Formosa needed to construct a tank farm. The talk lasted about twenty minutes and didn't mention chemicals.

A man who had watched Fred deliver his speech turned in his chair. "We hear what all Formosa *wants*, but what kinda chemicals are y'all talkin' about out on that tank farm?"

Fred stood. A queer look formed around his eyes. "We'll have *all types*. They're permitted, though. Allowable limits permitted by the state."

The man faced Fred now. "I just wanna know what kind of chemicals y'all are gonna have. What are they?"

"Well, all right. Most are basically harmless. The state defines them as nonhazardous. Take ethylene, for instance. You can put green unripe bananas from your home into a paper sack and let them ripen, and right there you have created ethylene. Right in that paper sack."

"Ethylene's one of the chemicals, then?"

"Why, yes. We need ethylene. Ethylene's a basic building block for chemicals."

That appeared to be the full disclosure of the tank farm. Not much questioning was happening, with the city council sitting behind their vanilla-colored foldout table, so I turned slowly and looked at Fred. "Aren't y'all a vinyl chloride plant? And isn't ethylene dichloride, or EDC, your primary product? So won't that be stored out there in the tank farm too?"

Fred acted like a gate had swung open onto some field he wasn't sure he ought to be tromping on, so he *uhmm*ed and swung around and looked down at the plant manager, who was thumping a hard finger into an open manual in his lap. The manager lifted the book and handed it to Fred. "Here it is very clear, Fred. Right here," he said.

Fred read from the manual about ethylene dichloride, calling it 1,2 dichloroethane instead, and saying it was an intermediate product in vinyl chloride production and used as a solvent and an antiknock agent in leaded gas, and if the chemical was released it was quickly destroyed by sunlight, and did that answer the question?

If I hadn't known different, I would have believed him. Fred looked sincere, so Formosa, with its dirty, gritty flares and its big smelly tanks and its half a zillion pipes, seemed like it was producing nothing but rotten bananas. I was surprised Fred didn't declare they were building a nature trail through the whole benign mess and planting native plants like lantana around the tanks.

So I reluctantly spoke again. "I think what this man really wants to know, Fred, is what are the health effects of those chemicals out there. . . . And those besides ethylene. He probably wants to know if it's gonna affect his kids if they get exposed to it out there on the playground. And what does happen if his kids breathe it?"

Fred stood with the manual over his arm, and his eyes looked like they had gone from daylight to dusk in a matter of seconds. "I wasn't *finished*!" Fred said.

People moved in their chairs and rearranged their feet, and the man who had spoken first and still watched Fred turned to me and said, "Go ahead, Mrs. Wilson. Formosa's had their turn. It's your turn now."

"Formosa's got a lot of things that you folks have a right to know about. For instance, what's gonna be the health effects of these chemicals—and *all* the chemicals, not just the ones they wanna talk about—on your children, since this plant is gonna be practically in the schoolyard. I don't believe they're playing fair. Formosa wants reinvestment zones and tax abatements and don't seem willing to tell you the whole truth. I wouldn't give them *anything* until I got the whole truth out of them."

The plant manager jumped to his feet. "We *have had* a *half dozen* meetings with these people! I'll have you to know, *Missus Wilson*, we have explained and reexplained time and time again this expansion in *significant* detail! In minute detail! There is not one thing we have kept from them!"

"Then how come these people don't seem to know the chemicals y'all are going to be storing? Or their health effects? How come they don't know that EDC, what you call 1,2 dichloroethane, can melt a worker's hard hat and it's cancer causing and damages the kidneys and the liver? That it can cause internal hemorrhaging and blood clots. And if it explodes—which it can pretty well do because it's real flammable—

then it can create poisonous gases like hydrogen chloride and phosgene. Kinda like what wiped out thousands of people in Bhopal, India, in a single day a few years back. *Did you bother to tell them that?*"

"I *believe*, Missus Wilson, that we don't need *you* telling us what we should and should not do. We have done just fine with this community."

A woman got up from her chair and said, "I thinks she's right. How do we know how much you're *really* not sayin'? I didn't know all that about that chemical she was talking about. Whoever heard that? And we're expected to give everything! Tax relief. Buiding in our community, next to our schools. Well, whadda y'all giving?"

"We have *told* you the truth! I can't believe you would ever think something like that. We are *investing* in this community! Formosa is spending a *fortune....*"

The mayor, who had been standing quiet, now seemed to look down a straight line of unbroken light. She said in her tightest mayoral voice, "Weeehll . . . maybe Formosa's spending a fortune, but it sure isn't on this community. I'd just like to *see* the money y'all spent here. And now y'all want more out of us! Well, what about this community? We've got our kids' futures to worry about. How's this town going to survive with all this construction going on around us? We need *all kinds* of services. . . . It's not just the water treatment plant. Now, apparently we don't even know what we'll be breathin' when we wake up in the morning. As elected mayor of this town, I need to say, we need to think on this. This town isn't ready to deliver a decision on the reinvestment zone. Not tonight anyhow. So if there is a motion raised to table this item, then I'd like to adjourn. Do I hear a motion on that?"

A man raised his hand and said he was making a motion to table the request. Then the plant manager again jumped to his feet and yelled at the mayor, "I protest this motion! This is a *simple* request that has been blown *totally*—"

"Your protest is denied, Mister Peyton. We will take it up at another time. This meeting is adjourned."

Fred never called to me as I left the room. He only looked like he had watched the fluorescent tubing in the ceiling lights for too long. So I left. The two babies and I went into the night. I turned once before I climbed into the van, and the good people of Point Comfort were still at it, busy as all get-out figuring how long they were going to keep Formosa waiting.

11

A Dream Is a Dream Come True

This sheet-wadded dream had a long silver tanker in a bayou clearing, and that barrel of steel was as fat a figure on that desolate bayou as any I had ever seen. So the first thought stinging my sleeping head was if a skiff could muck up a bayou, what would an eighteen-wheeler do? Baby said nothing to my dream, like it was going to cost him the sun or something to haul a word to me. But dreaming, while no account in Baby's book, meant plenty to me.

I wasn't actually waiting on the tanker, 'cause the first thing that happened after my Point Comfort meeting was the dolphins. Again. Only this time a game warden and not a helicopter pilot sighted the dead dolphins. The game warden had circled an entire bay with an airboat in the dark, then upped the number of dead dolphins found in a month to twenty-one. Next he alerted the only group that held a federal permit to handle live and dead marine mammals stranded on Texas's shores—the Mammal Stranding Network in Galveston—and by Sunday morning they *all* arrived. Stranding Network volunteers. Hordes of media from across the state. Texas Parks and Wildlife biologists and game wardens. Hoist trucks and flatbeds. Coastguardsmen and university researchers. It was an intense three-day effort to find the answer to the question they all wanted to know: Why did the dolphins die?

On the west end of Matagorda Bay, Coast Guard volunteers worked from a borrowed johnboat and ran as far as possible into the shallow bay, then waded ashore to rope a dolphin, then towed the carcass to a makeshift boat ramp. On the north side Parks and Wildlife biologists loaded their boat with four dolphins at a time, then made a run to the intercoastal waterway. The dolphins had been dead for a while, and on a scale of one to five, with one being a live dolphin, they were all fours. Most were large adults, with only a few weighing less than three hundred pounds.

For three days helicopters from Houston-based television networks crisscrossed the bay in search of footage and interviews. Carloads of tourists and locals stopped continuously by the bay and walked out into the water and stared at nothing. Then they shook their heads at the sorry business and got back in their cars and drove off. One researcher ventured to guess that the entire population of dolphins could have been wiped out.

Using a hoist truck and a flatbed, it took almost a day to deliver the dolphins to Galveston Island. There they were weighed and tags checked and measurements taken before they were carried on stretchers to a necropsy table. There a series of four samples were taken from each animal's liver, kidney, muscle, blubber, bone, and heart. Stomachs were removed whole and sent to a national fisheries service in Florida. The heads were frozen for future study.

The researchers said they had no idea. They couldn't say what killed the dolphins, but they had found a whole fish in the forward stomach compartment of a dolphin, so they knew the dolphins didn't starve to death. But it worried them that the dolphins were found dead on the shorelines of the local bays instead of the barrier island beaches, where dolphin carcasses were usually found. Tests could take months and the exact cause of death might never be known. That was unfortunate, because the bottlenose dolphins could be a biological indicator of the health of the Gulf of Mexico. After all, the dolphins are on top of the food chain. "They're eating what we're eating," a biologist remarked.

I was getting a death count from another bay. Red brought me a red-fish for the third straight day, and when he handed it to me, wrapped in newspaper, he said he had just slowed down the skiff and scooped it outa the water. So I stuck the illegal fish under the van seat and took it to Donna Sue's freezer, like I had done everything else. Donna Sue wasn't in a pleasant mood and said if it was Red's fish I was bringing in, she wasn't freezing the damn thing. There were three already in the freezer, and there was bound to be a con in it somewhere.

I figured Donna Sue was either tired of oystering or she was tired of Deputy Dawg. It was a common enough condition when married folks worked the same boat day in and day out, and Donna Sue and Deputy Dawg had been oystering on their boat as a two-man opera-tion for over a month. I ignored Donna Sue's complaints and gave her the fish, and she stuck it the freezer underneath a dozen packages of frozen deer meat. She wasn't taking any chances, she said. Game wardens had more rights than drug agents. They didn't need a warrant for anything. Carried a gun everywhere they went. Once a game warden came straight into her house and went through her clothes basket, slinging clothes everywhere, looking for a turkey he heard Deputy Dawg shot out of season. Never found it, though, 'cause it was under the bed, and wasn't that too damn bad for them.

I didn't blame Donna Sue for getting cranky. I was getting tired myself. All that frozen evidence we were hauling back and forth from the fish house to the freezer. I had called three different state biologists on the coast and they all had said, "Hang on to it for a little bit. Freeze it if you can."

"That's what I've been doing. I thought y'all wanted something fresh to test."

"Well, hang on to it for a bit. We'll give you a call."

A gill netter I knew only because of the ice he bought in the early morning hours brought in an oyster sack of dead fish and sat it upright on the fish-house floor. He was a young fisherman with a wife and three kids and a broken-down truck, and three years before had been arrested for the very same thing he was doing now. I could bet there was fifty redfish out in his truck in another sack, and when he got home he'd dump them all in the kitchen sink and fillet and sell them to anybody who'd meet him out in a pasture somewhere. That or deliver the fillets to their front doors. Only thing he'd worry about was burying the highly recognizable fish skins deep enough so the neighborhood cats didn't drag them out on the main street.

So I took the gill netter's fish and wrapped them all separate, then took the sack to Donna Sue. She started to say something, then stopped and just shook her head. She shoved the entire load as far down in the freezer as she could get it.

Since Donna Sue had left the fish house to go oystering with Deputy Dawg, I took turns bringing the babies to the fish house. Sometimes it was Santanna and sometimes it was Crockett, then sometimes it was both. As the oyster boats started to pile into the harbor, I'd fix the babies a wide, high pen made of oyster sacks, and threaten to skin them alive if they climbed out. The oyster men would get off their boats and ramble in and lean over the sacks and mess the babies' hair and feed them their leftover bean burritos or baloney sandwiches.

Sometimes a captain and his crew would take the babies to the cabin of their boat and let them turn the wheel or mess with the radio or some shackle or a small piece of chain.

Days I waited with the babies, Seadrift was like a little island smelling hard of the only thing she had to offer: oysters. Then other days I swore gun smoke was what I smelled, and I became so convinced of it that I told Donna Sue we needed to hire someone to stand guard outside the city limits sign so when the gun toters or the bad dream really came, we'd know it in a minute.

I was at the fish house when a certain rotten dream walked into my life. I had finished with the oyster boats and was cleaning up, dragging oyster sacks around and wooden pallets in and out the fish-house door, when a famous barn burner showed up. Allie was famous for other things, but mainly he was famous for barn burnings. At the moment he was cursing under his breath with his matches safely tucked away. SUMABETCHES, SUMABETCHES, SUMABETCHES. A wild arm flew one way and another got thrown in the air, then yanked back and stuck in a dirty shirt that was a good six inches longer on one side than the other. On the short side I saw his red hand trying to get out as fast as he put it in.

I figured a fire was going on somewhere. But I didn't know for sure so, curious, I walked to the open door and looked out. There was no truck anywhere, and only one fish house across the harbor with a lone light wired to its tin roof was still open. Allie brushed past me and ran down the road with both arms flying. He leaned into the road, and shell dust mingled with his feet and up his legs and finally it settled in a quarreling cloud in his hair. At the end of the harbor road, Allie changed directions. He cut into a ditch, tramped knee-deep in saltgrass, then veered onto a foot path on the edge of the marsh. I could see Allie disconnected from the trail, stark as a white rag thrown down a well.

I followed, half curious, half thinking the thing that had set him off might make sense to me. Still, I was surprised when it did. There next to the bayou was my dream: the tanker truck with its long barrel of steel attached to its cab like the shiny black back of a cockroach to its head.

Allie never stopped moving; he just added the sound you make when you run into a truck. He barreled straight into the door of the truck, pounding his fists and yelling SUMABETCHESSUMABETCHES to the high heavens. The driver's-side door opened and a man leaned out and hollered at Allie to get the hell away or he'd knock the gotdang tar out of him.

I was getting dizzy from it all. Allie was pounding and cursing, and the driver was waving his hand, going Hey, hey, hey, and I didn't do nothing but get dizzy. Then the driver saw me and his mouth opened a little, then jerked at the corners like a rubber band snapped. He yanked himself back in the truck, then leaned out the window and yelled, "Lady, yew better get that nut outa the way or I'm running this truck cleeer over him!"

Now, how could a truck that big get in a bayou that small? I had an image of a three-hundred-pound woman climbing into a pimento jar. Then the truck rumbled to a start and the man slammed a gear, threw the truck in reverse, then rear-ended the sand bluff. Inside the man swore, but never looked up. Then he jerked more gears, gunned the motor to a high whine, and the truck made a wild leap in the dark. It was all slow motion, a dream of a dream and not nearly as real as the hard sand I stood on. I had forgotten Allie. It seemed hours since he had ran flailing against the truck door. But all Allie had done was start on something else. In a great bearlike lunge, Allie had thrown himself so far onto the hood that for a few seconds he was a crazy hood ornament gyrating in the wind.

The driver yelled, and Allie's body only rolled from side to side and made little hollow sounds like *pong-pong-pong-pong*. I ran to the truck and grabbed Allie's feet, and his feet were worse than grabbing fence posts, so I yanked on his shirt and the buttons gave way. Then the truck lunged and Allie went with it, his arms splayed out like chickens loosed from a chicken coop. I pulled on Allie's one arm (a pale, sad arm as thin as the skinny moon above us) and held tight.

The truck moved up the edge of a low bluff without its headlights on, but the sheen of its stainless steel tank was bright as the moon. Then it hit the paved road, and the headlights came on. I watched from the bayou's edge, knowing the roads and the route the trucker would probably take. So I grabbed Allie's hand and jerked him down the path, yelling C'mon, c'mon, c'mon, and Allie ran in the salt grass and he ran in the water and he threw water like it was seeds he was sowing in the night. I tromped in the water after him. He was soaking

wet and the water shone on his head and on his bare shoulder. Finally
I left him trembling and silent in the salt grass and ran to the road and
the van sitting at the side of the fish house. Allie had stumbled up the
edge of the path, and I took his cold hands and pulled him along and
shoved him in the van.

Allie had quit most everything he had been doing before, and now
it was just his head that rolled and muttered about the sumabetch that
I was. I imagined his mouth would get tired of all that cussing, but it
didn't seem to work that way with Allie. It was just me that was tired,
and I hadn't done near what Allie had. So I started the van and shifted
gears and slung the van in a backwards arc faster than I had ever done.
Then I hit the road. Allie leaned over, and his wet hair hit me on the
shoulder.

I was speeding through main street. Half a dozen empty storefronts
with sagging porches and interrupted cement sidewalks slid past me.
The street was empty. No brake lights. No lights boiling off a stainless steel tanker. The van's lights picked out bits of Seadrift; a bare lot
needing mowing, a house with a missing porch. Another empty oyster
road. *Then red brake lights.* I shoved on the gas pedal and felt in the
seat for paper, for my purse, for anything I could write something
down on. Numbers off the side of the truck. A license plate number.
What was the color of the truck? What was it? Oh, yeah, yeah, red
and white. That was easy to remember. I scooted my foot on the floorboard, but found nothing. Maybe I could scratch the numbers on the
dashboard with my fingers.

I looked at Allie as a streetlight came hard across his face and
filled it like a hole. It was the first time I'd seen Allie's face immobile. It was just me going faster and faster. I could see the truck and
its row of bottom lights strung like Christmas lights. I didn't know
how far ahead the truck was, but it was just a matter of time before
I caught it. So what was I going to do with it? Was I going to stop
it? Was I going to run the van into the side truck fender like I'd seen
on a TV show? Could I make a citizen's arrest? Was that *only* in the
movies too? I figured when I got level with the truck, *something*
would come to me, clear as a bell. Like God talking in a tent and
giving directions.

The road's final turn and where a truck could lose itself wasn't far
off, so I increased the speed, but instead of going faster, the van shook

violently. I held the steering wheel tight with both hands like it was a mean hog I was pinning down. Maybe I should have stopped and called it quits right then. Enough was enough. Who was I in a race against anyhow? Who appointed me, besides some old dream spinner? That's what I wanted to know.

Finally a tire exploded, and I slammed on the brakes with both feet, and me and Allie did a little whirly-whirl on the black-paved highway. I shut my eyes, hoping for a quick death and hoping my head wouldn't go through the windshield with me feeling every glass sliver. But it was just that silent black circling thing taking its own sweet time to get around one full circle before it started on another. At the end of the second cycle, it quit. Everything quit; not even the motor made a sound. I looked over at Allie, and he was staring at nothing in particular.

"Well, Allie, how'd you like bein' nearly keeled? Did that feel all right?"

12

Losses, Gains, and Petitions

I was at the fish house with the phone hard against my ear. Outside the occasional truck came up and down the shell road. It was cold and the cold came from a white sky, ran through the front doors, then out the back. I was wearing a yellow slicker and expecting rain anytime.

I was talking with Blackburn. His voice was switched off so hard I couldn't recognize it. Maybe my working with Rick (even when it had been Blackburn who suggested it) had done it. What's the matter? I said, and he said nothing was the matter. What made me think something was the matter? He was having an off day. Then Blackburn asked how my criminal prosecution petition on Formosa was doing.

"Well, it's damn hard! We've got plenty of evidence. . . . Least *we* think it's evidence. Records that say Formosa doesn't seem willing to prevent spills, or else they don't report them like they're supposed to. One inspection report told where Formosa built an earthen dam to store some acid spill, then when the Water Commission came along, Formosa broke a hole and let it all go. And you think the state fines Formosa for something like that? Heck, no! The files are full of stuff like that, and that's not even mentioning the files those inspectors down in Corpus gave me. Where's the enforcement on *that* one?"

"Wilson! Try a little honey for a change. Sometimes you can catch a fly better with honey than you can wielding a ten-ton sledgehammer. Stick a petition for an environmental impact statement out there! That one isn't near as intimidating for people to sign, nor for the state to get involved in. Who have you got to sign that criminal petition anyhow? Anybody?"

"Plain ole fishermen. Had to talk their legs off to do it, though. But what else you gonna expect when Formosa's already got millions plunked down for construction out there? They've given out forty-five contracts, and God knows how many went to the local politicians. Mayor in Port Lavaca's got one. Justice of the peace's got one. That woman mayor in Point Comfort won't talk to me anymore. Remember her? She loved me for a while. Now she works for an ex-mayor who's got a contract. And remember that little reinvestment zone problem Formosa had a month ago? The deal the city council in Point Comfort turned down? Well, forget it. The Chairman himself flew down from New Jersey after that city hall fiasco and gave a big shindig at the Formosa guesthouse, and before you know it he's telling that Point Comfort mayor he's gonna just buy her that little wastewater treatment system she wanted so bad. Yeah, the Chairman just walked up to the mayor with that interpreter in tow and tells her he's gonna build it. 'Cause wasn't that what she wanted—a million-gallon-a-day treatment facility? He's gonna donate the whole shebang to the city—the water plant and the land underneath—right after the construction on the Formosa expansion is complete. So Point Comfort turns over the rein-vestment zone deal and Formosa gets what it wanted. Next, I guess, it's the abatement on taxes. Another giveaway thing."

I knew something had been off with the mayor. A mayor just isn't fine as peach wine at one meeting and wanting your input and wanting your support, then a month later meeting you at the door and telling you to mind your own business and stay out of Point Comfort. But remembering that blistering hot conversation with the mayor was nothing compared to what Sanchez brought. It started with my second directors' meeting and Sanchez bursting through the doors with his face looking fit to explode.

"Look at all you women just sitting and waiting for the boom to fall! Well, they've sued us, ladies! They've sued us!"

"Who's sued us?" I said.

"Are you *stupid*! Formosa! Formosa!" Sanchez threw down a news-paper and nodded his head vigorously towards it. "Go ahead. Read it. Just don't take too long, is all. You wait and you're gonna be writing your *own* epitaph."

I looked at the paper but didn't read it. "Formosa's not gonna sue us. They're just talkin'. Whadda you think we got a lawyer for? Formosa just wants to shut us up."

Donna Sue didn't need any convincing of Formosa's intent and said if that was the way it was gonna be with Formosa, then she didn't want her daughter being a director. Her daughter didn't have much, but whatever it was, Formosa wasn't gonna have the satisfaction of getting it. She told her daughter, "You go, but I ain't leavin'. Nobody's running me off. I ain't got nothing Formosa wants. An old rotten boat? See if I give a hoot. Tell them to come on and get it."

Sanchez stayed at the fish house until the old dead afternoon fled, and all the directors and officers with it. Then he went too, but before he went he drank all my coffee and laughed when he quit. Donna Sue sat in a corner with a rain jacket that covered up everything but her white face, and said nothing.

I was beginning to discover the difference between women and other women, and it wasn't measured by filling in their weights or their shoe sizes on a piece of paper or knowing what color of house they were washing their dirty dishes in. A woman's difference was measured by whether she listened to herself at all.

So I got Donna Sue, and here was the plan: The agenda was the water. I couldn't see the map much, but I sure could read a wastewater permit. A thirty-inch steel pipeline (stamped FORMOSA in grass-green paint) shoved into one of our sleepy bay bottoms with three foot of mud on top, and who knows how many thousand cubic yards of bay mud and shell reefs dredged just so Formosa could dump millions of gallons of wastewater into a watery cradle meant for shrimp and fish and crabs.

Formosa's wastewater permit and pipeline was standing and smoking a cigar around the corner, but what already had a foot in the door was a ten-million-dollar grant from the state of Texas. That grant had been drug first through the corridors of the Department of Commerce, then through the Calhoun County Navigation District, just so the Lavaca Bay Ship Channel could be dredged to forty feet and in the process become part of the grand package that lured Formosa to Texas in the first place.

Blackburn was amazed at my political naïveté. "No wonder they're threatening to sue! I'm surprised they haven't hired hit men in masks!" he hollered over the phone. "They've got water permits and dredging permits and pipeline permits all in one big, ugly balancing act, and we're out there throwing hardballs at them. Criminal prosecution! Environmental impact statements! How do you think that makes their contractors feel? Warm and fuzzy about the project? Of *course* Formosa's gonna threaten to sue. Every minute we delay their project costs them thousands of dollars!"

But we weren't all of Formosa's problem; part of its balancing act was failing from its own gravity. Too many balls in the air, maybe, or a slew of scientists investigating the dolphin deaths. Or just the sudden spotlight on an otherwise dark corner of an otherwise done deal: the complicated, sorry mercury mess (fixing to be a Superfund site) that was Lavaca Bay, and working on getting worse with Formosa's dredging project.

Some of it had to do with overcaffeinated economic planners thinking Lavaca Bay's Ship Channel could run second behind the Houston Ship Channel, and when the Houston channel was shut down because of a barge accident or because the channel had ignited, then the Lavaca Bay Ship Channel could be the port of choice. To the economic thinkers it was a mere fly in the ointment that part of the dredged twenty-five miles that was gonna create this harbor dynamo was an area that the Department of Health had closed to the taking of fish and crabs because of Alcoa's mercury contamination. Flounder still had levels of mercury five times what the health department wanted, and one health department official even warned that a single fish taken from that area and eaten by a pregnant woman could possibly damage her unborn child.

But not enough to get folks riled over. People were working on the mercury problem in Lavaca Bay! Local county officials and Alcoa (who was responsible for the mercury problem in the first place) were fighting tooth and nail to oppose the EPA's listing of Lavaca Bay as a Superfund site. That should help the publicity problem. And as for that minor worry of contaminated mercury sediment being spread by the dredging for Formosa and prosperity, the mud dredged from that particular Superfund area would be stored in containment ponds the Navigation District had leased from Alcoa. In other words, the navigation district would be paying Alcoa to store contaminated bay spoil that Alcoa had contaminated in the first place.

A problem arose. What was to be done about the Wisconsin and Kansas snowbirds when they rolled into the county in their mammoth RVs in the dead of winter and viewed EPA officials in moon suits, taking samples from the bay? That question was a Chamber of Commerce question, and they decided they weren't lying down for any of that bad press about Superfunds and ranking high in national reports. So the captain of the harbor and twice-elected president of Port Lavaca's Chamber of Commerce, Larry Robinson, put his finely chiseled head together with Formosa's, and they launched the Formosa, Chamber of Commerce, and Agriculture Environmental group. That effort spun a series of pro-industry letters to the newspaper, and Captain Larry wrote the first and he wasn't no dandelion tiptoeing around the issues.

If Alcoa was so toxic, he wrote, then how come there were so many birds nesting around the plant, and abundant fish in the waters adjacent to the plant? And dolphins? "Dolphins don't swim in polluted water!" he wrote. If Alcoa was the most toxic plant in the United States, then he was a Nazi U-boat commander! "Let's get serious! Can anyone seriously believe that?"

The county officials saw the pollution-airing problem as serious (millions at stake and money to lose) and knew instinctively which side was buttered and which side wasn't—and it *most certainly wasn't* the fishing industry, which had once been first in the county's pioneering days and now was a casualty and a possible scapegoat. The county judge (a lawyer on a political sabbatical) said that most likely it wasn't pollution that caused the fishing calamity. It was overfishing. Without a trace of irony to stop his train of thought, he continued that it was written on the walls that the county couldn't rely on the fishing industry as they did in the past and would have to look at other sources for survival. People were going around like the sky was falling. It was all gloomy and there was no chance of hope, but with the coming of Formosa, everything had changed. The psyche of the people just changed. They all became positive. The county had something to believe in.

I spent a lot of time keeping track of political talk like that. Who said what and who did what. Every day I went to Pic-Pac grocery store and fed thirty-five cents into a coin-operated newsstand for the local paper, went back to the fish house, and cut it up with an old pair of scissors. I had a file that filled up one corner of the fish house. Sometimes Sanchez came to the fish house and forgot he'd quit as director, and forgot he was running for county commissioner in an election fast approaching, and forgot the only time he had been to his boat in a week was to pump the water out. One day I cornered him, and it took the whole afternoon and I didn't convince him.

"Don't you know where you go, so go half . . . hell, Sanchez, *all of the directors*! What am I suppose to do with no directors? No officers!"

"Hey, honey. This is money. If it wasn't, then it'd be different."

So Sanchez left, and the only thing that had changed between the time he was a shrimper and the time he became a political candidate was that now when he came to the fish house he parked his truck in front and not hidden halfway across the harbor or down the road. I knew what Sanchez was thinking. He was running for *county commissioner*. What did he have to be afraid of anymore? His streak of bad luck had come to a merciful end.

I had ran out of answers on what to do with my missing directors and officers. Maybe I wasn't even legal anymore, and if Formosa found out I would be hung out to dry. So I called Blackburn, and before I told him my troubles, he told me his. He said he had spent the whole day talking one pair of clients into *fighting* a chemical company on the Houston Ship Channel, then another pair of clients into *settling* with a chemical company. Both his clients, he said, were wobbling like newborn colts on their first legs. But even with that complaint, Blackburn was in a wry, comical mood and found my tale of missing members and Formosa's lawsuit vastly amusing.

"Wilson, don't you have any women down there with *nothing*? If you don't have anything, then you're not scared of losing it. It's simple arithmetic."

"Well, *then*, they got husbands. There's *that* problem."

"Well, get *divorced* women! And you know how to get people, don't you? How Cesar Chávez did it. He went *person to person*! Just person to person. You got to be a little willing to be a people person, Wilson."

I was in deep trouble. All I really wanted to do was pull up to a table with just one person sitting at it. Me. Me and maybe the water and the sun, and the sun not stretched like a trotline across a river, but like a current that ran how the water ran, and it was only the sun with yellow eyes that looked down on us. I didn't want no more company and no more talking.

I didn't tell Blackburn that. He was already sounding squirrelly every time I mentioned my dreams, so I told him instead that the only divorced woman I knew was somebody brought to my house by a cousin. Not ever wanting to risk familiarity, I think of them as Woman Number One and Woman Number Two. They had been at the house and I had been working for a while on getting them to leave. Plotting,

plotting, plotting. I sat way back in the rocking chair until the six bars in the rocker hit my back and I nearly had the women gone.

Woman Number Two was a slow blonde with sleepy green eyes, like she'd just woke and couldn't wait to go back to bed. She I knew least of all, and they were nearly gone until I said something about a dream that was driving me crazy.

Woman Number Two said, "Dream? Dream?" like it was a song, and the tilt of her eyes was pronounced and her smile turned whitely upwards.

"Oh, that," I said, like lightning had struck my eyeball. "It is a dream. Over and over. Again and again. Maybe not the same house . . . but *a house*. Unpainted. Weathered. Old and solid. And the furniture! The furniture and the jewelry and the gleaming wooden boxes and the treasures and the beveled glass bouncing and reflecting off one thing after another! And I walk through it all. One room after another. Balconies and French doors. One leading to the other. I never grow tired of seeing it and wondering over it, and outside I know the water and sand comes clear to the porch."

Then there in the middle of leaving (and in the middle of the French doors) the blonde woman said, "It is yourself. The house is yourself, and you are valuable."

That was all she said. At the French doors with the two of them in the middle of good-bye. I didn't have a thought, but my body reacted like I was a funeral pyre burning like hell.

The sleepy-eyed one said, "We women have to stick together. We're valuable too. You know that, don't you?"

"Oh, I'm just a little chunk of gold sitting out here," I said, and laughed.

Her name was Kathy, and she was different from me. She was from Nebraska, but more Southern acting than I ever was. She was a natural. She said when she was a girl the summers would go on forever and the nights rolled even longer. Longer still in cars. "I dated at fourteen," she said. "Once I dated three men in the same day. Not *boys*. *Men*." Then she looked at me slowly and smiled. "There were a lot of open windows."

Then one day she packed her dresses and her jeans and her high heels and her nylon hose and a yellow autograph dog with GUESS WHO? penciled on the ear, and she left Nebraska through the last open window. Her mother found her diary later and ripped the dirty pages out. "My mother was probably expecting more," she said. Then she headed for Texas. Headed for the beaches. Put her face in the direction of whatever wind was blowing, and licked the salt off her skin when she got here. "It was just like having an afternoon margarita," she said.

After Kathy left my house, one night went, then two nights, then on the third night my life changed forever. I dreamed of a long-dead Pentecostal preacher I had loved better than Jesus and who cried when he read Psalms, which he quoted from memory with his finger stuck in the Bible in the right place. All my young religious life, Brother Bob had been in Seadrift, and he often went down to the beer joint and talked to the fishermen sitting at the tables with their dark bottles of beer and with the doors wide open to the shell road, and the fishermen would nod their heads when Brother Bob talked about Jesus.

So I said to him, I thought you were dead. And Brother Bob smiled and shook his head no, and we walked into a forest and I dreamed around us was a mess of tall trees, but inside the clearing with me and Brother Bob was a tall old building that men were working on. And at the top of the spiraling house was the *face of God* in glass. Brother Bob looked at me and he leaned down and whispered: *"Just be careful around the edges."*

Well, if my battle with Formosa was the face of God, then I wasn't being careful! But I was a woman that was returning by degrees. I didn't know how long I had been gone or *how* I knew I had returned, but plates and missing crockery in a house I once owned now sat at the place where I ate, and what rags I used to wipe my mouth smelled of old, familiar things.

So one raw, cold winter evening I took the face of God further. I called another environmental meeting (with no directors and no officers, only Donna Sue and the divorced Kathy), and instead of Sanchez, I got Formosa with their stash of video cameras and tape recorders and a stenographer carrying her machine in a black leather tote case. The men set up their equipment in the back of the room behind all the folding chairs, and the video man leaned back and looked at the ceiling and said, "This light isn't helping." The stenographer came to the front row and unfolded her machine into a miniature desk.

There is sometimes a silence that comes from noise you don't recognize, and it carries no weight and it has no name. So this new unnamed noise arrived: Jack Wu. Jack was a wasp of a man: much smaller than me, much much smaller than my wrist. I don't know, he might have been cat-boned from birth.

"*Excuse me,*" he said. "*Excuse* me. We would like you to know that we are taping your words. *All* that you say. Every word you say, we will tape. And if there are lies . . . we will tape those lies. That is all. That is what we have to say to you."

Three trucks pulled up outside the civic center, and seven men got out and milled around the door. They were oystermen, and I saw them through the glass doors in their oyster clothes, hunkered down against the cold with lit cigarettes and struck matches and nothing in their posture saying they were doing anything more than waiting for a smoke to finish. Finally they filed into the room and sat together, and I picked up a petition I brought with me and took it to them and showed them where to sign their names. They looked tired—as though the wind and the cold had blown out the light in their eyes, and when they signed their names it was slower than a schoolboy would sign his name. When they finished, they picked at their sore hands, torn from throwing oysters and handling heavy dredges all day.

I walked back to the front of the room and I glanced over at Formosa's crew. The woman with the black typing machine had her hair done in a French twist, and she watched me closer than a lover. She mouthed the words as I said them and typed fast on her black machine.

I said our environmental group was officially asking for an environmental impact statement on the Formosa expansion, and we were putting out a petition to collect signatures to send to state and federal environmental agencies and our elected officials. An environmental impact statement was federal law. We weren't asking for nothing more than the law required, and we believed that the two-billion-dollar chemical plant expansion, with its half-dozen federal projects, had the potential to create impacts none of us could foresee.

Captain Larry Robinson sat with the Formosa crowd. He lifted his head and he looked at the faces around him. He stopped when he saw the fishermen. "You know, I've always been the first to defend you shrimpers. Look at *all* the restrictions on y'all. I say to myself, Now who's initiating all these laws? Who? Who? Why, we know the answer to that one. It's the environmentalists! That's who! And who do you shrimpers have in the enemy camp . . . huh? Why, it's one of your own smack-dab in their camp! So if any more restrictions come down on y'all's heads, just give Miz Wilson the credit there. . . . 'Cause it's her swelling those enemy ranks. So maybe what we ought to do here is see about getting an impact study done on her. Maybe that's what we ought to do."

Jack Wu stood up next, and his voice was thin and reedy and came from four rows back. "Formosa has already submitted an independently prepared environmental document to the EPA. It was filed last April. Another impact statement like you have suggested will only be a tiresome repetition of our original document and could delay this project fourteen months to two years. Is that what you want? More delays? A study costing millions more?"

I shook my head. "There's a big difference between what y'all filed in April and what an environmental impact study with EPA oversight would do. What kind of public comment was involved in your study in April? None, I bet. So who knows what was in it or where you got your information!"

"We do not tell lies, Missus Wilson! It is all science! Facts! We get our facts correct. It is not like you tell everywhere. 'PVC is harmful! PVC is harmful!' We can tell you that PVC is, in fact, *harmless!* It has the same consistency as sugar. Look! We have a little bottle here. Smell it! Pass it around! Smell it! Do you smell an odor? No! It has no odor! It is harmless! So why do we need to be burdened with another long study? It is silly. A waste of time. At this very minute we build a very fine administration building. We have made many landscaping plans that will only beautify the area. Much money has already been spent. We have planted many, many trees! How can this be called damage?"

I could see we weren't going to agree on anything. We might as well have been from separate planets, with each defending a cause the other knew no words for and wouldn't have appreciated even if we had. I supposed it was why wars were declared.

13

Money, Money, Money

He was a mad old man who said he had been so tore up when he went to Austin recently that he couldn't even sit up straight in his supper chair at night. He had to hold on to the edges just to keep from falling over. The old man called me twice on the telephone, saying first that Chocolate Bayou that was right at his very doorstep was polluted to the high heavens and he had aerial shots to prove it. From the air, he said, it looked like a great arm had come down and tore through there.

On his last call the old man suddenly quit, and it wasn't until a week later that Wally told me the old man had died with a heart attack. Dropped dead with the receiver warm in his hand.

"Guess you keeled him just talkin' to him," Wally said. He was sitting at the fish house, his round face flushed from neck to hairline, and I was sitting up to my cold, blue mouth in a yellow slicker. Wally's shirtsleeves were rolled up and three buttons were undone on his shirt, and he looked like a hot potato fixing to explode in my broken-down chair. Wally scooted his chair until our knees nearly met.

"Forget that," he said. "I want you to put down what you want from Carbide. You *want* something, don'tcha? Want a permit or somethin'? Like Formosa? Get a piece of paper! Write down whatcha want!"

"Why?"

"Why? 'Cause I'm a man, and men like talkin' to other men and they don't like talkin' to women. Why you think it's *me* all the time doin' the talkin' in Austin and not you women? They need a man. . . . Somebody that knows the business and can talk the talk about money without cavin' in until you need to cave in!"

"Who you been talkin' to, Wally?"

Wally's hands fiddled with a jelly jar wrapped in silver tape. It was Donna Sue's tea jar and it still had tea in it.

"Ain't talkin' to a frazzlin' soul! Okay, okay, two. But they came to me first! Hired me! I didn't go to nobody. Don't need to. These companies ain't stupid. They know who to talk to. So hey, I think one of them chemical companies wants to hire me; maybe another does too! Maybe I can negotiate with every one of them you're messin' with. What does it hurt? But don't go tellin' nobody, all right? Don't tell Donna Sue. It's just me and your little secret."

Donna Sue said she saw it coming. She just wondered what took Wally so long to take Formosa's money. But if Wally ever came through those fish-house doors again, she was going to take an ice shovel and kill him and bury him somewhere in the vault under ice.

"Whadda you think he's been hired as Formosa's consultant for anyhow?" she said. "How many fishermen he can get off your side and on Formosa's? How much he can shut you up? I ain't worried none, though. Wally can't survive this. I know him, and he ain't gonna be able to live with himself. You just watch. It's gonna eat him alive."

Sanchez thought Wally's new job was funny as heck and said he knew there was a reason he had come seven miles out of his way to the fish house. Just so he could tell me a fisherman bought out was nothing new. "There's lots worse things than *that!*" he said, and he leaned back his head and laughed, and the sound went straight up and threw spiders out of their holes with the racket.

Donna Sue stood in the door and glanced sideways at Sanchez, then back at me. She tightened her eyes till mine hurt. "Wally's gonna ruin you with the fishermen," she said. "You can bet that's why Formosa's hired him. Cut off your contacts and make 'em theirs. So you better get what links you can and quick! Else . . . wham! Shot in the foot by ole Wally bird."

"Hey, now, just you wait on your big brother," Sanchez said. "When I win that election next week, I'm going to get *all* of those stinkin' cahoots by the nose ring and haul them around so we can smell something different for a while. That's half the problem down there. Smelling the same ole stinking thing day in and day out."

"Sanchez, waitin' on a politician for something is waitin' on *nothin'!*"

"I am *not* one of those idiot politicians! It's gonna be different!"

Sanchez's anger rose and fell like an elevator. He was amused. "Hey, go after those rich sportsmen down in Port O'Connor. Wally isn't in that circle, and if they know that Wally is working *against* you, then that might be the incentive for those dumb rich bastards to work for *you*! They think they're working against some gill netter, and they'll launch a fleet of lobbyists right at your doorstep. . . . Just don't act like a stupid woman and confuse them with more facts than you need to. And for God's sake, don't tell them you build shrimp nets!"

So I became the infiltrator of the rich white sportsmen in Port O'Connor, and I had Sanchez to thank for it. His Mad Hatter insistence became an intolerable rub. I waited half a day to get rid of Sanchez, then another two days just so I didn't look like I was taking orders from a man walking fast to completely mad. Then I called the only contact I had in Port O'Connor: a tall, skinny part-time shrimper named Benny that I once patched nets for. When Benny wasn't shrimping for himself, Benny ran plumbing in rich folks' houses, but his big bucks came from taking rich sportsmen from Houston and San Antonio fishing and charging them a hundred dollars a head.

For Benny that was a lot of money. Then if he got three of them on the boat at the same time, that was three hundred dollars! And when was the last time a bay shrimper like himself made three hundred dollars clear in single day? He sure couldn't remember it. It was more like three hundred dollars worth of *expenses* he remembered.

"Besides," he said, "those rich sunuvubitches just *love* to pay big bucks. If they don't, then they think you aren't any good. So I just oblige them."

When I handed the petitions to Benny, he looked them over a couple of minutes. Then he looked up and said he didn't think the sportsmen he knew would run with the criminal petition, but they might on the environmental impact one. "They might support you there," he said.

"These fellas are real funny about stuff like this. Half of them are lawyers, and the rest have businesses of their own, so they might end up empathizing with Formosa on the criminal one."

"Don't those fellas fish down here?" I said.

"Sure, they fish, but they also come out the front door of a million-dollar condo in the morning. They aren't your *regular* sports fishermen. Not pole-and-bait folks. And I ain't real sure how much I need to tell them about you. Who you are and what you do for a living might be a pretty big wall for them to get over."

"Just because I'm a shrimper?"

"Sure, that . . . but also because you've got that cousin Wally that's the biggest outlaw they've ever heard of. Then your Uncle Bud, who's a bigger outlaw than Wally. *Then* they get word your brother went to court in Refugio for trying to run down game wardens with his shrimp boat! Wow. Much as I sympathize, Diane, they hear attempted capital murder and, bingo, the lights go off in their little noggins. These are conservative people, Diane. And they don't like commercial fisher people."

Benny looked at my half-open mouth and my eyes starting to squint, and he rushed headlong into his next words. "Hey, now! Don't you worry none. Sometimes after I take the fellas out, they invite me and the wife over and we drink wine out on their front deck. Watch the boats go up and down the canal. I'll bring it up next time. See what they say."

For a week I sat at the fish house in total disgust and drank black coffee that wasn't even hot. I had quit counting who was on whose side and how many it made for me and how many it made for them. But I figured if Formosa was going to get any more dogs, then they were going to have to get a kennel to handle all of them. I was losing hope about anything happening in Port O'Connor and felt my comfort zone eroding like the Guadalupe River at flood stage.

Maybe I just needed to handle the petitions I had. Focus on that. So while the oystermen stood outside the office door in their boots and told me how much fuel they had took on and how many sacks of oysters they had brought in, Donna Sue and I stuffed petitions into envelopes and wrote every congressman and legislator we knew. In hindsight, there were only two mistakes. One, our petition-stuffing jump-started the opposition's letter-writing campaign, and two, every politician in the state avoided my call or else had secretaries say they had never seen the petitions.

Then one cold morning Donna Sue drove down to the bay and she didn't get out of her car. She sat and watched me from the window. "When's the last time you heard from Benny about those petitions?"

"I ain't heard from that fella," I said.

"Well, you have now," she said. "He called and wants you to come and get 'em. Said he's finished."

Two days later Donna Sue and I rode to Port O'Connor. Donna Sue wasn't in her best mood and she didn't care if I knew it. "So now we're talking to the folks that probably gave the damn game wardens the money and the ammunition to run Sanchez down. I don't care if they run Wally down fifty times a day, but I don't like thinking it was Sanchez."

She was referring to commercial fishermen's long-running gripe over the coveted position rich, influential sportsmen played on the Texas Parks and Wildlife Commission, and their programs like Operation Game Thief and the Redfish "Sting" Operation that jailed ten local Seadrift fishermen. Commercial fishermen often felt the rope hand that hung them belonged to a sportsman.

I looked over at Donna Sue and didn't say nothing. It was a sad day, all right, when I had to romance the people who were partly responsible for the half-dozen tragedies in Seadrift. But now wasn't the time to go looking over old graves. Instead I thought of every place I could leave a petition and wondered if the Baptist church would take one and whether they would act like the Pentecostal preacher if they did. The Pentecostal preacher had took a look at the petitions in my hand and, without extending his own, said he'd have to ask Jesus first. And I said, "Well, tell him not to take too long," and I laughed. And the preacher, who was standing at a gas pump filling up his Toyota truck, looked me squarely in the eyes and said, "Honey, we're all on Jesus's time."

It was the second day of a norther and it wasn't raining and it wasn't overcast, but gale force winds were out. Even in Sanchez's heavy old truck, I could feel the wind shove and squirm and run up and down the frame like a crazed squirrel looking for a hole. A rust hole is what it found, and it burrowed up and into the cab. The old worn rubber from the floorboard lifted twice. Up and down and up and down. Even the outside mirror twirled so fast I had to stick a wad of paper behind it.

Port O'Connor is a quiet town in the winter—worse than Seadrift. If Seadrift lost half its residents in the winter like Port O'Connor lost its tourists, Seadrift would fold up and die from grief. When Port O'Connor did lose them, it just breathed a sigh of profound relief. Coming into town, we were the only truck on the road, and I didn't see nothing moving and I didn't expect to see nothing moving.

Benny had said to meet him on the docks of one of his sportfishing clients. The client was a corporate lawyer out of Dallas who had a thirty-eight-foot sportsman rig that he didn't know beans how to run.

That was one of the reasons he hired Benny. The others were to guide the lawyer to the hidey-hole of the golden redfish, and do maintenance on the boat. I turned off the main road and drove the three blocks to the intercoastal canal. The route was easy to spot. People around the water always gave dead giveaways to what was actually only a block off and didn't need no announcement at all. It was like someone hollering, "Water is just around the corner!" and the water was already lapping at your feet. A smorgasbord of nautical castoffs— old rotting boats and abandoned boats and half-finished boats and anchors and ropes and buoys of all kinds—cluttered every yard and lot. The sea stuff perched on every lot corner and was strung from pillar to post to lamppost to porch, and on every square inch of a beach owner's property.

The last block from the intercoastal, the cutesy items stopped. Now million-dollar condos and tennis courts and cemented entryways and private boathouses with matching docks boarded up for the winter lay full out in the sun and weather. There were at least fifty flags with different nautical messages on every one, and a dozen top-heavy palm trees eerily waving their fingers. It was the only part of town that was landscaped.

Here was where buying and selling was done by the square foot, and grown men threw hissy fits over property inches lost to currents or boat wakes. Every condo and oil franchise lining the intercoastal had a huge sign promising dire consequences for any fast-moving vessel. It was zero wake tolerance!

The intercoastal canal, with its old, oily eroding banks, was a moneymaker for everything from the plastics and nylon manufacturing industries, hidden behind the trees on the Guadalupe River, to the oil and gas franchises, with their minidocks and chain-link fences and towed-in-and-tied-up three-tiered mechanical rigs. Here also were hundreds of millions of dollars in real estate (condos with their matching boathouses, where owners could yank out five-hundred-thousand-dollar boats after an evening's ride) and a dozen dank and dirty Gulf shrimp rigs tied to a shrimp house going broke.

And congesting and churning down the brown intercoastal water: the barges. Sometimes the barge traffic was worse than downtown Houston at morning rush hour, with only the carrying load different: watery routes bound for the chemical plants downriver, carrying gases and lethal fluids that could kill every shrimp embryo within a ten-mile radius. The barges made little noise—slipping and sliding and moving water from hull to bank to hull again. And they carried their cargo as effortlessly and unconcerned as a mother carried her baby on a Saturday afternoon.

Donna Sue and I didn't talk. We just watched what slid past our window. A half-dozen flags flew wild in the wind. In the last big hurricane, twenty-five years before, the town had been 90 percent destroyed. Now there was no fear. If a storm came to these homeowners, somebody was gonna get sued.

It was somewhere among that stretch of houses we were supposed to meet Benny with his oil rag. Donna Sue rolled down her window and made me stop at a house where the garage was bigger than her house in Seadrift. She started to say something, but stopped when Benny came up to the window in his baseball cap, and smiled and stuck his hand through the small opening where the window was down. He looked at Donna Sue looking over his shoulder, so he turned and looked at the house, too. "*Ain't* she something, though? Dang it!"

Benny laughed and looked over at me. He said, "Those fellas are gonna sign off on your impact petition, Diane. But that other one . . . they ain't gonna get anywhere near that one. Ain't Formosa suing you over that one?"

"Oh, Formosa's just trying to scare me. It ain't nothing."

"Well, you're only gonna get help on the impact petition. Hell, Diane, I believe these fellas probably want this bay as clean as the rest of us. They're just real careful what they choose to take on as an issue. But I can tell you what a couple of them told me, if you won't get mad over it."

Donna Sue wasn't looking at the house or its curved cement driveway any longer, but straight at Benny, and she wasn't smiling. "Go ahead. It ain't gonna bother her. She's heard a lot worse, so just say what you gotta say."

"Well, a couple of them said they'd heard you had connections with the net fishermen around here. Said if you wanted to work with them you was gonna have to disassociate yourself from the commercial fishing folks. If you could do that, then I think they'd turn the milk wagon loose."

"What's the milk wagon?" I said.

"The money! The dough-re-mi."

"I grew up with those folks you're talkin' about, Benny. Some of them are my kinfolks."

"Well, I believe that's their point, Diane."

"I could sell the *SeaBee*. You figure they want that too?"

"Oh, it's just the gill netters they're after right now. That's the connection they want severed. I don't think they're after the shrimpers just yet."

"Well, they don't want much, do they?"

"Diane, this is *real big* money we're talking about. They've got the means to help—and you and me may not agree with how they want to do it—but it's dang big money! *Way* big."

Benny stopped and shook his head. Then he handed me the petition with eight names on it, and they all had Houston addresses except one that said San Antonio. I thanked him, shoved the petition in the seat, then drove back to the fish house. I didn't go into the office. Instead I walked out on the docks and looked over the reefs and the mudflats. The fish house was facing the sun, so the air was hot and heavy. I breathed hard. Then I told Donna Sue to call Blackburn and hand me the phone through the window. I was talking outside so I could breathe right.

The minute Blackburn came on the line, I blurted out, "You ever get donations from big sportsmen?"

"If we're *lucky* we'll get a donation from them. I'd be happy as a clam if we did."

"Well, you get one, you just better tear it up. I won't take it! I better never see any of their money or any of their checks neither."

"Wilson," Blackburn said, "you're getting mighty particular over something we really can't afford to get particular on. You know *some* of these lines you've got drawn, you might have to cross one of these days."

"The fishermen ain't one that I cross. I turn on the fishermen, then I might as well turn on myself."

"Wilson," Blackburn said, "I *admire* your willingness to stick to your roots. But you gotta know your loyalties to the fishermen can be dangerous. Those are dangerous friends to have in the environmental fight. Newspapers would love to hear stories like that."

After Blackburn hung up and the oyster boats started dribbling in, I got twisted inside. I hadn't expected one cause to splinter another, and somehow I knew I would steal the boat and cut the line on anything that drove me there.

• • •

Next to Formosa, my piddlin' petitions looked like squashed bugs. Formosa was in full swing and said they expected four thousand construction workers on the site in a year's time. It was the culmination of a lot of hard work by many people, and the beginning of many years of opportunity in Calhoun County. Then the county judge said he was ecstatic about the project, and even though it would put a strain on the area schools and roads and jailhouses, he didn't have any doubt the county couldn't handle it. "We welcome this type of problem. Lordy, we look forward to it."

Still, while some businesses had been touched by industrial growth spawned by Formosa, the Chamber of Commerce worried about the ones that hadn't. Even though hotels and motels were filled to 90 percent capacity and restaurants were doing incredible business (filled for both dinner and supper) and the grocery stores were doing great, and the service stations and the convenience stores were doing just terrific, little was being done to prepare for the wave of four thousand temporary construction workers fixing to descend on the county that coming summer.

There seemed to be a fundamental problem. Builders were leery about building homes and apartments on speculation, and money lenders were nervous about financing them. The fear, said the economic consultants hired to do some speculating on the problem, was the result of the question over whether Formosa would receive environmental permits for the expansion and whether they were going to have to do a complete environmental impact statement.

Suddenly, eight months into a campaign, I was media material. The *Victoria Advocate*, a local newspaper with readership in the tens of thousands, called and wanted to know my frank impressions, now that I had stymied Formosa's progress. Before the business editor began the interview he said, "Now, I want to warn you. This is going to be negative." Sure enough, the first headline read FORMOSA CRITICS SHORT ON SUPPORT IN COUNTY, and the second headline read EFFORTS OF INDUSTRY SUPPORTED IN CALHOUN. Then the articles proceeded to justify the headlines, and all I did was watch with stony bewilderment. Donna Sue came down to the fish house and said, "When was the last time you heard from a politician about the petitions we mailed out?" And I said, "I ain't heard from a one. I guess death has sealed their mouths shut."

"Congressman Laughlin ain't got his shut. He's givin' a talk at the café, and everybody's welcome. Come and meet your congressman. It said so right there on the café sign."

To be fair, Laughlin wasn't the first congressman I hadn't heard from; he was just the closest. I had made one fledgling attempt at contacting a politician in person (the man had black-and-white framed pictures of Martin Luther King and Bobby Kennedy on his office wall, so I figured he was safe), and after I talked with him for about ten minutes on the county's environmental problems, then asked him to take a stand on the environment, he told me I was known as a maverick and a nut and he wasn't about to commit political suicide.

So I was fed up with politicians and didn't even pause when I called the Washington congressman's office in Victoria. I told the secretary, "I just want you to know that I have repeatedly tried to get a hold of Mister Laughlin about the situation down here, and he just doesn't seem to want to talk. So we're finished talkin'. You know that little cake-and-coffee thing he's doin' in Seadrift this evening? Well, we're gonna picket it! You tell Mister Laughlin, and I'll tell the press."

Then I hung up and asked Donna Sue to go to town and pick up some poster board and Magic Markers. We were doing a demonstration. I said, "Who do you think would picket with us?"

She had her keys in her hand, and not an expression crossed her face. "Me. That's one. Get your kids . . . that'll be a crew."

After Donna Sue left, I walked out on the docks and looked down the harbor. Across the docks, two men squatted around an old diesel engine on a broke-down oyster boat. Red was one. I guess fishing had finally starved him out. I walked around the harbor, then up the plank to their boat. Red watched me while I explained what I wanted them to do, and neither man looked amazed, but squatted with hard, greasy hands across their knees. "I guess it'll be all right," Red said, and raised a wrench when I left.

Donna Sue was waiting at the door when I got back. She had thrown the poster board on the floor. "That D.A. fella called," she said.

"What D.A. fella?"

"The *D.A.*! District attorney! I don't know. He talked like you knew him. Said he wanted to talk about what you were fixin' on doing. He wants you to call him."

"Well, it's too late. What we got to say will be said on the picket line."

Next Howdy called and said, "What kinda fool thing are you doing now?"

And I said, "Every fool thing I can think of that I ain't thought of before."

Howdy said, "Let's talk about this tomorrow."

And I said, "What I got to say I'll say from a picket line today."

"You know you're not just picketing *any* politician on a campaign trail. You are picketing key people in the Democratic party here in Calhoun County. A congressman, a district attorney, a county judge. I myself am running for that county judge seat."

"Howdy, I'm gonna hang up."

"All right. How many folks do you figure you're going to have out there, if you don't mind saying so?"

"Oh, I got a dozen at least, Howdy."

Donna Sue snorted. She was sitting on the fish-house floor with a Magic Marker in her hand, and she looked up long enough to laugh. "That's what I like about you," she said. "Your daring-do."

Two hours later, there we were: two dirty oystermen, two women, and three kids I had brought from the house. Then four men came through the fish-house doors. Howdy got straight to the point. "What do you want?" And he eyed the two fishermen hauling signs to the van. "What's it gonna take to settle our little difference here?"

The congressman was the bigger politician, but Howdy was the one who knew me more, so somewhere on the ride over to the fish house, they must have decided Howdy would do most of the talking. Halfway through the talking they switched strategies, and the congressman stepped in front of Howdy and started talking himself.

"Look, Miz Wilson. Let's talk frank. What is it you want me to do?" Then he turned to Howdy and said, "Stay outa this, Howard. I believe I can handle it."

So I hurled myself into a face so white it was like holes cut from a sheet where his eyes should have been. I took him step-by-step through months of information and piles of petitions and levels of contamination. When I finished, he said, "So? What is it you want me to do?"

"Do? What I want you to *do* is write a letter to the EPA asking for an environmental impact study on Formosa's expansion. That's what all those petitions I sent you were about."

"*Just* a letter."

"Sure, it's something. . . ."

"Yeah, yeah, I know. All right. Look. Howard, write down 'Requesting study from the EPA.' The one in Dallas? That one or the one in Washington?"

"No, just Dallas is all right," I said.

Two days later I found out I had had two days of low romancing and nothing else. Because not only did the congressman *not* write a letter to the EPA, but he made a statement to the press saying an environmental impact study on Formosa was needless and would only damage the economy on the mid–Gulf Coast.

Well, the congressman wasn't my first political sweetheart, but he sure was gonna be my last. I went to the fish house and rummaged around in my spiral notebook until I found my page with politicians' phone numbers and addresses, and I tore it out. I told myself, "Now, how many times does it take for you to be in a stinking hellhole before you recognize the stink?"

I didn't have a healthy attitude about the election. Howdy was running for county judge just like he said he was, and the D.A. was running for D.A., and Sanchez was running for county commissioner. I was tempted to go into the curtained voting booth and deface the table. I saw Howdy once before the election, and he winked and said, "Don't forget. Just give me enough slack to get out of Dodge City."

If I had lied to save his skin, the results would have been the same. Howdy won and the D.A. won. Sanchez, the only one I voted for, lost. I waited a week to hear from Sanchez. He didn't drive down to the fish house, and he didn't go to his boat. Once I looked out the fish-house window and saw his truck, but before I got to the door, he was gone.

Maybe the fact that he didn't stop caused me to wait another week, just like it was another afternoon. So I was busy with the oyster business rising and falling and tired men arguing on the docks about whose boat had pulled in first when Froggie came into the fish house. He said, "Sanchez's boat is up for sale."

Momma had the cleanest knife. When I pulled into the driveway to get the kids, she met me at the door and pointed a shaking finger at me. "If you don't stop that stuff you're doin', you're gonna make your brother lose his job. Just see if you don't."

I walked inside, and Daddy was sitting at the supper table with his knees crossed and smoking a cigarette. Momma was still behind me and shaking her finger. "Billy, tell her. Tell her she better quit."

Daddy didn't look at neither of us; he just gazed through the haze of the cigarette smoke at a brass barometer nailed to the wall. "Oh, shut up, Goldie," he said.

If I live thirty more years, I still won't know how the blow came. Was it one word or a string of words, or was it me finally turning to Daddy and saying, "Who's Sanchez workin' for that he's gonna lose his job?"

Momma answered for all of us. "Formosa! Formosa! He's got a good job now, and you just better leave him alone. Tell her, Billy. Tell her."

I was told, all right. And when I got quiet and stopped breathing long enough to hear it, what I was told was that a woman can pass up ribbons and beads, but she better never pass up her home-sewn dress. Because if she did, she was gonna pay dearly for it. If she did, then everyone was gonna desert her, and who's gonna care? Hell would freeze over first. A woman could just sit there, alone, by herself, until Judgment Day.

14

The Informant

Donna Sue and I said nothing about Sanchez leaving. Even the times we saw his truck drive past the fish house to his boat in the evening after he got off work from Formosa, then go past again without stopping, we said nothing. I didn't know why Sanchez stayed away. I had already forgiven him. As for Donna Sue, Sanchez was the only man she had ever given an ounce of forgiveness. We were catlike in the way we skirted around talk of Sanchez.

Baby said it was my fault Sanchez wouldn't come around. If I didn't demand some gotawful high levels of everybody, then people wouldn't stay off. Where on earth did I get those harebrained ideas anyhow? Baby watched me from a distance, like distance was all we had between us anymore. Nothing was of his making anymore, he said. The bay wasn't. Shrimping wasn't. I sure wasn't.

I could have told him that even if I went home and stayed home and did nothing for five years, it might still be the same. It might be worse.

Baby thought different. When things changed, they always went bad. Same as when Boy died and all the markers shifted. Or else got stole. So Baby went underground for cover, and his brother's dying was the glue that sealed him in.

"Don't you know there's a limit to what demons do?" I said. "Ain't everything a death sentence."

"What," he said, "you readin' a highfalutin book now? You doin' that now?"

Baby said I quit trying to please him. But that wasn't it. It was more that I wasn't doing a good job of it, and it was getting painfully obvious. Because Baby didn't like me reading books or talking to Blackburn. He didn't like lawyers. Lawyers had screwed around with his brother, screwed around with the fishermen. He didn't like men in suits. Or women in suits. Or people with high degrees. He thought places like Houston should be burned to the ground. Austin was worse. Austin was where the game wardens were. That town should be scattered to the wind.

"Game wardens didn't have nothing to do with Boy killing himself," I said.

"Well, they held the gun while he pulled the trigger."

I was amazed. Two birds could leave a branch at the same time and one could remember leaving, and the other would drift forever in his ghost tree fashioned from wisps of thin air and bits of nothing. It didn't even matter that the original branch was dead and gone.

Two days later an oyster buyer drove into town. He sat on a blue plastic shrimp box while all around him tired and weary women dropped like flies. Then he drank a whole bottle of spiced rum, climbed into his white Lincoln Town Car with the gold leaf trim, and wheeled the hell out of town. Two more days and the oyster price dropped through the floor. Most of the oystermen stayed in, disgusted, with their boats tied to the pilings.

I walked across the harbor and sat on their back decks and tried to talk about the pollution from the plants and how the fishermen oughta get involved.

Their argument was, How was gettin' riled gonna help? Wasn't nothing gonna stop things the way they were goin'. Only thing it was gonna do was scare folks into believin' there was something the matter with those bays out there. And then there go the markets. Shot straight to hell in a breadbasket.

Talk like that ran hard down some dirt road in me, and sometimes I believed them. Sometimes I didn't. Now I didn't, so I got up and walked back to the fish house. The day wasn't fit for nothing but cleaning, so I opened the vault and all the doors in the fish house and put sticks in the window to keep them open and let in the salt air. I was scrubbing the fish-house floor with a hard broom when the phone rang, and I turned my back to it and let it keep on ringing. Finally I went and yanked it up. "Whadda you want?"

A voice said, "I'll tell you a few things, Missus Wilson. But I won't say it over the phone."

"Who is this?" I said.

"Let's just call me Douglas," he said.

"You're sayin' that like it's not your real name."

"I won't say anything over the phone, Missus Wilson. I thought I made that clear. I'll talk, but not here. Someplace else."

"How about at least tellin' me what this is all about?"

"Oh, I think you already know that."

"Ohhh. So it's Formosa."

"I will *not* talk over the phone, Missus Wilson, but I will say that you are correct there. You are correct."

"So you live around here? You work over there?"

"That's a few of the things we can discuss when we meet. Don't bring anybody else, though. I won't talk to anybody else. This first time, I want just *you*."

I was wondering if I was talking to a man with a waiting gun, and wondering how close I had to get before I actually knew. But what counted most with the man on the phone was if I was going to meet him and where it would be. "Do you know Victoria?" he said. Little red flags shot up in my head. How about a dark country road? How about a vacant house with handy telephone wire to wrap around your throat? Then the man hung up with no more answers than a sermon. I thought, *This is no call from a man. This is a call from a shadow, and I don't know whether I trust him or not.*

So I called Blackburn, and he said not to meet with the man.

"How am I ever gonna get any information if I don't meet with the people who call?"

"Hell, Wilson! At least make the meetings a little more visible. Not so cloak-and-dagger. You know there's a vast difference between a lunatic and a real worker. You might try figurin' which one they are before you dive in headfirst."

Blackburn sounded irritated about the whole thing, but finally he said, Well, oh hell, he knew a private investigator he used sometimes, and he'd give him a call.

"Only *don't move* until the investigator calls you. Stay put for a minute, if you can. Try not to do anything, if that is at all possible. You think that's at all possible?"

So yes, I was listening, but no, I couldn't wait. It was late in the oyster season and late in my life, and besides, I didn't know what Blackburn was fixing to do. Then too, the man on the phone wasn't waiting either. He called me again using the code name Douglas. It is our private code, he said, and he didn't laugh once. He wanted to make sure I was coming to the meeting. There were no changes of plans? Nobody else coming?

I said I wasn't backing out if that's what he meant, then we changed the first meeting place and arranged a second, then we changed the time. Later in the day, he said. He had some things to do first. Dig a hole. Buy a gun. A million details to take care of.

The man was getting crystal clear in my head and I hadn't even met him yet. A little alarm was going off in my head every two seconds, hollering, *Wait! Wait!*

The next phone call threw the same leery feeling over me, until he said who he was. It was the private eye and his main office was in Houston, but he had an associate based in Victoria, so anywhere my informant (code name Douglas) wanted to meet, our mutual friend could case out first. Before the meeting.

I gave the detective the details of the meeting and the time and the place, and he told me where to meet his associate. In the parking lot at Wal-Mart.

"Wal-Mart is good for a lot of reasons," he said. "A lotta commotion going on and nobody paying attention to anything but their own shopping cart. You two can discuss what you need to right there."

I was not spying. I didn't know what it was, but after I met the private eye in the Wal-Mart parking lot and got in his black Ford truck and he showed me the miniature tape recorder and how it worked and how it slipped into his pocket so little and black, I figured it was pretty dang close. It was kissin' cousins to spying.

The private eye (he liked being called a PI) said his name was Mike, and with his red hair and his black leather bomber jacket, he was about as obvious as a Christmas tree in June. I would have turned and looked and said, "He sure looks like a private detective I saw on TV just last week." (If Donna Sue had saw him she would have asked him, first off, if he had a girlfriend, then second, if his truck was paid for.) Mike the PI was full of instructions. First, we had to locate our man, then he would follow a few minutes later. He'd sit nearby, but far enough away that he could observe the whole thing. I was to put the tape recorder in my purse. Then put the purse on the table. This was important, he said. The recorder picked up voices better the closer it was to us. Then I was to remember the tape ran only *forty-five* minutes on one side, and when it was close to ending, the tape recorder would start beeping. I was to leave *before* that happened.

"You don't want the recorder beeping there on the table, do you?" he said. "That might cause a few problems. So get up and excuse yourself. Say you're going to the bathroom. Say anything. Just get up and leave. All righty?"

After the spying lessons, I got out of his truck and back into my van, then both of us drove to a coffee shop where Douglas wanted to meet. I didn't know the place, but Mike did. He had driven past it a couple of times.

I went in and did as near-blind an entrance as I had ever done. It took everything I had to stop and not walk clear across the room and out the other side. Then I saw Douglas sitting in a dark hole at a corner table, with his tiny legs crossed and his hands lying quiet as two old cats. A manila envelope was flat on the table.

I walked over. "Douglas?" Well, he was Douglas, all right, and that was about the easiest thing I got out of him. He was a man who had a hundred Phillips-head screws holding him down. Nothing dangled, nothing flapped. His hair was neatly combed and his hands barely cleared his shirt cuffs. He wore a coat over his shirt, and neither one was wrinkled. Douglas didn't look like the wrinkling kind. I felt like a flaming gypsy next to him, and I put my purse on the table and smoothed my hair.

Douglas watched me sit down, then he looked at my purse briefly, then he looked at me briefly, then he looked away. His face said he was a man full of secrets and he was tired of keeping track of them all, but his mouth didn't say nothing. He just tapped the envelope on the table. "This is some of it," he said. "I can't let you keep it, but you can look at it."

Then he leaned towards me and said in a real tidy way, "It's not me. It's other people involved. Some are real sick. Some are dead. One we'll speak about isn't working for Formosa any longer. They fired him when his liver-enzymes tests came back running around four hundred when it's suppose to be around thirty." He looked at me and said, "You know anything about vinyl chloride? What it does to a person?"

"I don't know a whole lot."

"About the only thing you'll find a company admitting to is

angiosarcoma. Cancer of the liver. That other stuff a worker complains about? Forget it. If it doesn't cause cancer right off the bat and bad enough for them to see—bad enough, a worker's sick in the hospital and dying from it—then they think the worker's just complaining. Trying to get outa work. Look at the fella I was telling you about. He was fixing to be promoted to foreman, and they told him all he had to do was get a physical first. Then his liver tests come back, and out the gate he went. He was a good welder too. Cutting into lines all the time. They said the enzyme count was high because he was a druggie. A pothead. How'd he do his job so well before, then? He did fine for them when he was cutting into lines and getting drenched with vinyl chloride or EDC. When he complained about being dizzy or not being able to breathe, they just give him cough syrup. I suppose they keep it in gallon jugs just for that purpose."

Douglas said he worked in the vinyl chloride monitor control room in the old part of the Formosa plant. He had no idea what they were gonna do with the new part. Maybe try to destroy the whole place. The drinking water. The air. A lot of people over there were scared. Thought the place was like a napalm bomb fixing to go off. The last time he was in the control room, twenty-six automatic shutdowns were bypassed. He quit counting how many instruments weren't working. Maybe twelve or thirteen.

Douglas hardly moved in his chair. He was a careful man, given only to small movements and showing what he needed to show. Everything else was battened down like a ship in a bad sea. When he drank his decaffeinated coffee, he barely glanced at my purse.

I was in a fit of paranoia and wondered if I looked more suspect taking notes or if I didn't, so, undecided, I yanked paper out of my purse. I held the paper up and asked him if it was all right to take notes. Mentally I calculated how many minutes I had before the recorder started beeping.

Douglas stopped talking and laid his hand flat on the envelope. "Well, since I'm not letting you keep any of the papers, how else are you going to remember everything? It's not like you got a tape recorder. Right?"

Right, right, I said, then out of the corner of my eye I watched it all unravel. Two tables over, Mike had suddenly decided he wasn't just watching anymore. Mike was getting up and moving to our table. I looked at him, bewildered, but he kept coming. I wondered just how long before we were both thrown out.

Mike stood at the table and said, "I'm an associate of Diane's. You mind?" Then he sat down before he got an answer. I said nothing, and to give Douglas credit, he said nothing. He only gave Mike the same look he had took to giving my purse. Then Douglas pulled out his papers. They were internal memos of every kind. Accident reports. Employees documenting low oxygen levels from equipment failure. Leaks falsified. Notes from a plant audit listed four pages of problems. Employees exposed to vinyl chloride not monitored, workers exposed to vinyl chloride not being notified, vessels with holes venting gases, inspections needed for cracks in vessels, pump valves not working, exposed wires plantwide.

I picked up each document and read it, then handed it to Mike. It was a lot of words. I debated whether I needed to take detailed notes or hope I'd see the documents again. My focus on the documents was being blurred by the tape recorder winding its way to a screeching halt in my purse. I didn't know what Douglas's threshold for bizarre behavior was, but I figured me and my PI were close to bottoming out. Midway through the documents and a second cup of coffee, Mike kicked me hard under the table. "Don't this coffee sure run through a person!" he said.

I stared back. "Oh, oh, oh," I said, and got up and grabbed my purse, and Mike turned to Douglas and smiled a big, loose grin. "*Women*," he said. "Women and their dang purses." Then they both turned and watched me leave.

Eventually I told Douglas about the recorder, but he had known all along. "That was one huge purse," he said. I met him four times, and it never was in the same place twice. Once he visited the fish house and showed me where a bullet had been fired through the back window of his car. "It wasn't for me," he said. "That bullet was for my wife, for causing production to stop." He said his wife worked in the incinerator area in the old side of the plant. In the old part where corrosion was its middle name. He never mentioned her name.

The old part of Formosa always seemed to have relentless problems: incinerators failing, equipment bypasses, pipes and valves and flanges corroded by acids. Toxic waste gases were vented to the atmosphere on a regular basis. To anyone who had bothered to read the history documenting the problems in the Air Control Board's annual investigative report filed in a regional office in Corpus Christi, those things weren't surprising. "But who does that?" Douglas said. "What citizen goes to that length? Or what politician?"

Douglas said one report said the waste gas incinerators at Formosa had not only been overloaded, but were beset with severe corrosion and faulty construction and design. The corrosion was caused because the hydrochloric acid in the waste gases destroyed the waste gas blowers and whatever was left. In 1985 the incinerators had failed so consistently and released such huge amounts—sixty-four bypassed releases—of vinyl chloride that the state forced Formosa to install a third waste gas incinerator so that at least one waste gas incinerator was up and running at all times and a backup waste gas incinerator was available.

"Heck," Douglas said, "before the ink on that agreed judgment was dry, the plant had a major power failure, triggering an emergency shutdown of the plant, and seventy-four tons of vinyl chloride monomoner went into the atmosphere. That's *a hundred and forty-eight thousand pounds of vinyl chloride in one day!* Now, remember, this vinyl chloride isn't baby powder. It's explosive and one of the worst cancer-causing chemicals in the world. It's so hazardous the government says you're in violation if a single pound is released. But here seventy-four tons of vinyl chloride were released within one mile of an elementary school right across the road from Point Comfort. And if that wasn't enough, Formosa, in the same breath they were polluting with, asked the state to permit a tenth reactor while the ninth was violating production permits. You tell me the state is getting it? You exceed permits and you're rewarded with more?"

Douglas said he didn't wonder that every man, woman, and child didn't wake up in Point Comfort and touch their own hand and wonder if they might be dead already. Or how much longer. It was the end for him, but it hadn't happened fast enough and he was glad, glad, glad he had spilled his guts and documents to me. He didn't care if they were company documents.

On our last meeting together, Douglas gave me the name of a worker. "Let him call you when he's ready. He'll call. He's not going anywhere."

"How do you know that?" I said.

"Because he's sick. Who's gonna hire a sick worker? Where's he gonna go?"

• • •

Overnight I became a conduit for workers. The calls came from every direction and from every plant in the county. A few workers came by the fish house, carrying a photograph of a chemical spill or a rusted pipe buried deep in the ground; another horror tale of another chemical. Cyanide. Arsenic. Acrylonitrile. Benzene. One day after a few subtle, hush-hush telephone calls, a large, rotund superintendent from Union Carbide brought a map to the fish house and laid it across my desk. That's where the contamination of the county's source of drinking water occurred, he said. That's where they leaked benzene: right under the noses of the Guadalupe–Blanco River Authority. The superintendent's grandson was mentally retarded, and he could no longer live with himself.

Most workers just wanted to pass on information. They didn't trust the company to fix it, and didn't trust OSHA (the Occupational Safety and Health Administration) to protect them. Every worker that walked in the fish-house door snorted when I mentioned OSHA. They believed any information a worker delivered to that agency would eventually wind its way back to the company, and then the worker would be fired. "Hell, woman! There's no job protection there!" they said.

Most workers said they got job security by taking matters into their own hands, and complaining to OSHA or the company certainly wasn't high on the list. Some workers kept a "black book" where they documented releases and injuries, then hid it in a safety-deposit box. Then when push came to shove, they'd see who could push hardest.

What about agency inspections? Don't that uncover some stuff? I said. Another laugh. First off, they said, when a company was *finally* inspected by an agency after either a complaint or for a yearly inspection, it was common practice for the environmental or safety agency to give the company two weeks' notice or more. Often a state politician would give the company a little friendly call warning them to look out. By then problems could be tidied up. Records materialized. Spills cleaned. Workers vanished. One worker said Formosa bused workers into another section of the plant when a scheduled inspection from OSHA arrived. Workers were discouraged from talking to OSHA inspectors.

So I called the OSHA office in Corpus Christi and filed the incidents that the workers wouldn't. Most incidents were unsafe working conditions created by rotten vinyl chloride monomer (VCM) or EDC lines that should have been shut down and pipes replaced or work permits okayed over the telephone, instead of the safety personnel coming to the plant to check it out. Then there were complaints that serious leaks were stopped by makeshift methods like wire and duct tape, and in the process often soaked the workers with VCM because the vessels were still in service. Most important, workers were often just not qualified to do the work.

OSHA reviewed my letters, rewrote the complaint, then sent a copy to Formosa with the cautionary words: WE HAVE NOT DETERMINED WHETHER THE HAZARDS, AS ALLEGED, EXIST AT YOUR WORKPLACE; AND WE DO NOT INTEND TO CONDUCT AN INVESTIGATION AT THIS TIME. So Formosa answered the complaint—word for word from the plant's standard operation procedures—and sent it back to OSHA. Case closed.

One OSHA inspector admitted the problem, saying worker injury was one of the great "unders" of American health care. It was under-recognized, underreported, undercompensated, understudied, and underprevented. A hundred thousand workers died a year, and another hundred thousand were hurt. Occupational disease was clearly one of the most significant causes of premature death in the country, although it was not recognized as such. More workers died from illnesses they got at work than in car accidents.

And the reason it wasn't recognized, he guessed, was that the diseases the workers came down with had such a long latency period, and mimicked other illnesses, that often workers didn't realize that they had first contracted the disease from their own workplace. Compounding the issue was the financial starvation of the enforcement branches that should have stopped some of the practices from continuing.

At some point in my phone calls to OSHA and my griping that inspections at the plant weren't included along with the form letters sent to Formosa, I realized I knew nothing about workers and their rights. I knew about as much as that time I left Seadrift's city limits for the first time, and there hugging the bayou and lighting up our lives was Union Carbide, with fifty acres of blinding lightbulbs heating up the cold night sky. I decided I needed to talk to the union. *Any* union. I didn't know *who* they were or *what* they were, but I figured unions had to be political. So I picked the most political spot in Texas: Austin. And Austin couldn't help its political saturation. It just flowed from the capitol steps and spilled in the streets like Kool-Aid seeking its lowest level. And when Austin was in the middle of a legislative session, it was doubly political, so me and Donna Sue picked a legislation-filled day and drove around the capitol six or seven times looking for parking. Finally we abandoned Donna Sue's car and started walking.

Three blocks from the capitol and six blocks from the car, we found the union in a spread of magnificent oak trees. In a huge white banner across the full side of a building were the letters: AFL-CIO/LULAC.

Later on and far beyond the outskirts of Austin, Donna Sue said, "Just how many union fellas did you find in there?"

"I think you got to approach the union just right. You don't just walk up to any ole union man. Who knows what they think?"

Well, I could have waited forever to get understanding. After all, fishermen didn't unionize. In fact, they'd sooner go down the hell tube than get together and agree on something. Still, I began to get a glimmer of workers' lives, and especially after I got the call from the sick worker that Douglas had told me to wait for. The sick man said I was gonna have to come to see him instead of the other way around. It was getting worse and worse for him to go anywhere. He wanted to know if I needed any directions getting there, and I said no. I had been to Point Comfort before.

So that was one reason I found his house so easy. The other reason was he lived right across the street from Formosa. Chairman Wang, visiting, probably could have seen us from his office window. There was a fairly new truck sitting in a tiny driveway, and I went around it to get to the door. The worker's gray, calm face stopped me. He leaned out and said, "Do you see my truck out there? It's for sale. You don't need a truck, do you?"

No, I said. I didn't believe so. Then I came in and sat down in a small chair in a small house with wall-to-wall Christmas lights. I looked around, and he watched as I looked. "That's my wife's doin's," he said. "She'd never take 'em down if I left it up to her."

I nodded my head and watched the lights smear like colored water on the ceiling. "Once," I said, "when it was Christmastime and I first got my driver's license, I drove around a big town for the first time and I ran every traffic light, thinking it was Christmas lights."

"I can appreciate that," he said. "I come from a small town too. A traffic light wasn't in my vocabulary neither." Now, he said, sometimes he thought it all was just a bad dream. That somehow he would wake up and it would be nothing but bad dream. Be back in his own bed in a small town.

"Now, I ain't nothing but sick all the time. I'm almost finished. I know it. I can't perform my craft anymore. I can't weld. I can't hold my arm up to burn a rod anymore. I have to use my other arm to hold it. My shoulders, my forearms, here. My knees. Everything. I got pains where pains ain't been invented yet."

He said he had worked at Formosa for seven or eight years, and all the workers ever thought about was the future of that plant. They knew it was getting worse every day, and that was what worried him. They had two fellas that got hepatitis while working out there. Formosa blamed it on family history and needles and stuff.

"Heck," he said. "I knew those fellas. I knew they didn't use needles. But that's what the Chairman would say. That's what the safety man over there would say. And you are fighting a losing battle trying to blame it on Formosa. Everything is negligence on the part of the hands.

"Sometimes I got called out two or three times in the middle of the night, and the safety man, he wouldn't come out in the middle of the night. He would every once in a while, but most of the time he would just okay your permit over the phone to go do this hot work. Not even knowing if the line had been purged. If it was ready for you.

"I would work thirty hours without a break. Go home. Rest a little bit. Go back out and do it again. And the whole time you are doing it, you are opening up reboilers. Exchangers. And they are never purged. As soon as you break a seal and pull it apart, you throw up. There were lots of times I would go home and wake up in the middle of the night and just throw up. Run chills. And just be sick. All the time from what I did that night.

"One leak we had out there was this vessel. I couldn't believe it. They called me out. It was the middle of the night. I couldn't believe it. I just live across the street, so I got all the calls out. I am making eighty, ninety, a hundred hours a week. Year after year. So when I go in, I seen all the lights were flashing. I seen this cloud going north. That vessel had a real nice rust hole. Well, not rust. It was eat out from the chemical. But they didn't want to shut it down. And all I had was a slicker and a face shield to go get into that. I didn't have any kind of face mask, you know, any kind of breathing or fresh air or anything. I got soaked in it. It was EDC.

"What I did was I got . . . I had to break into the shop that night because I didn't even have a way to get into the shop. I went in and got a whole bunch of hose clamps. I put them together to go around this big vessel. It was, heck, ten, twelve, feet in diameter just across it. By myself, now. I had to start here and get this clamp all the way around. Put some tape in there. Tighten it up. And that's the way we sealed that leak.

"Another time we run a four-inch PVC line from the plant all the way out to the wastewater through this field. And this was in the middle of winter. You know what plastic pipe does when it freezes and stuff? We run that line, and a day later that PVC line was all over the place. I guess it got to moving around and pulled apart at the joints. We glued them together in different places. The pipe shattered. It was out in the middle of a dark field. And everything they were pumping into wastewater was just going into the ground. We knew that was a joke when we were putting it there. Plastic pipe."

He took his time talking like there was nothing left for him but a cold, clear morning and he had somebody's gray mare to ride him through it, if he wanted. He sat on the couch, his hands perfectly still over his belly, and two pink-and-white pompom pillows tucked behind his back. Ever' now and then he reached and pulled out a pillow and patted the yarn balls back in place, then tucked it back.

He said he didn't know what he wanted. Maybe make it so every man that worked in a chemical plant was told the truth and tested on a regular basis in the proper way. Maybe make it so a man didn't have to die just to go to work. He said it was probably too late for him. He thought it was. His wife couldn't bear to look at him. She couldn't sleep without tranquilizers. Gave up her sewing. Baking. He pulled the pillow out again, looked at it, then left it in his lap. "This little thing here was the last thing she messed with. Said she wouldn't touch another one. Ain't no use, so what for? About the only thing left is those Christmas lights there."

I never saw him again. He was in the hospital for the last three months of his life, unable to speak and eventually getting so he couldn't even nod his head. His wife went to the hospital every day, and they would write on a pad. The bad dream never quit for him; he never woke up from nothing. Then, at forty-two, he died and left behind a wife, a truck, and a houseful of Christmas lights across the street from Formosa. The company said his cancer was from nitrates. "Nitrates!" his wife said. "They asked me how much barbecue he ate."

15

Battle Lines Are Drawn

I was on the dark end of the roof where it was quiet, and there was nothing in the field. The helicopter was gone. Baby had given me the night watch and said, Watch that sky. Don't do nothing but watch that sky. Anything comes, just pull the trigger. Then Baby was gone to the Gulf and the only thing left was the shotgun in the closet, so I waited inside until the helicopter sound, *whom-whom-whom*, came over again at eleven, then I loaded the shotgun carefully and climbed on the roof and waited. It was cold as I waited on the roof and waited for the night to throw something back at me. A truck I never saw (but heard) came on a nearby road, so I pulled back the trigger. I wondered why men in a fit of wrong wished me harm. That notion I colored so raw in my head that even when the truck left and didn't return, I couldn't uncock the trigger. I waited instead. One more. One more. When it never came I climbed down from the roof and laid the cocked gun beside me on the bed, because truth be known, as trigger-happy as I was on the roof, I was an amateur with guns. The next morning, I fired the shotgun out the window and woke up all the kids for school.

By noon I was on regular time, sitting on the fish-house steps and mending a net for a shrimper while Crockett and Santanna played at my feet. Crockett had a screwdriver and was wrecking an adding machine, and Santanna had my old netting scissors and was making baby attempts at cutting webbing. When Blackburn called, I drug the telephone cord twenty feet out of the office and sat on the cord while I talked with him. I told him about the helicopter, and he wondered why I didn't bring the kids up to Wimberly and stay in his camp house. I said hiding wasn't going to help.

Then Blackburn said sometimes media attention offered more protection then a gun, so maybe it was time for a little guerrilla action on our part. He'd even call Rick himself and bring him in on it, if Donna Sue and I would drive to Houston for the meeting.

The next morning Donna Sue and I hauled two blue shrimp boxes of files out of the trunk of her car and into Blackburn's office. Who knows which of us in that office was the most aggressive and wanted more to come out of that meeting: Blackburn with his AA meetings and search for a higher power over an earlier alcohol problem (maybe something too that could whack a hundred-man lawyer firm he couldn't abide), or Rick, who had done civil rights in the bad old days and now was doing Texas's bad old days with its man-made chemical hellholes lining the Houston Ship Channel, and nothing for himself except staying single and chewing his nails until they bled. Or my agenda, which was simple: I hated the sight of chemical plants on the water and fought their plastic-and-steel birth.

We wrote five letters. Two went to the Air Control Board, asking them to revoke Formosa's air permits because Formosa had misrepresented to us in negotiations the true extent of the emissions from their expansion. Then we requested a public hearing on Formosa's marine terminal. The last three letters were intent-to-sue letters and sent to Formosa and the EPA and the Bureau of Land Management for violation of federal environmental laws and allowing Formosa to continue construction without an environmental impact study.

So the coffee got drank and a jarful of candy got ate and refilled, and Blackburn and Rick never had a better time together; they were near and almost buddies. Almost friends. After we set a date for the public meeting in Point Comfort announcing our efforts, Rick left and Donna Sue and I drug the shrimp crates into Blackburn's office. Blackburn sat at his computer screen, his fish tie loosened and his coat gone, and he ad-libbed his way through three intent-to-sue letters. Donna Sue and I (barefoot and sitting on his office floor) fielded documents as Blackburn yelled questions. Where is a description of that permit? What's the name of those units going up? Where's that EPA document on their federal water violations? Where's that press statement from the EPA? Get me that administrator's address!

Then Blackburn yelled, "Hey, Wilson, how close is that chemical plant gonna be to Lavaca Bay?" and I said, "It's gonna be pretty dang close," and Blackburn laughed and typed *pretty dang close* into his intent-to-sue letter. Blackburn was happy and said a dozen times to us, "Y'all like this? Does this make y'all happy?" Then he looked at us barefoot on his office floor, and acted like pleasing us was the only test he had to pass in a town where winning was the only deal left.

I had three weeks to plan the meeting in Point Comfort, and Rick called and warned me not to cut it short. "These things need at least a month of preparation. You do less and you'll end up looking like an amateur. So none of this rambling on stuff like you got till Christmas to get it done."

Rick was long gone past thinking my shoot-from-the-hip style was working, so he gave me his new grassroots activist speech. You need a plan! he said, and showed me how it was done. He wrote a long list of tasks on a yellow legal pad, and I nodded my head yes, yes (and took no notes), and when I finally believed he had quit wondering if I was listening, I quit listening. Then I just smiled and looked at a spot in the middle of his forehead and went and done it my way.

I believed in *not* so much organizing. There were other worlds out there, and sometimes those worlds had winds same as ours, and when they got bored or disappointed with our reality they stood at our plain pine doors and knocked. It was to this other world that Blackburn gave my name, and it knocked when I was standing at the kitchen sink in my faded jeans.

It was *48 Hours*, and the producer wanted to do a piece for Earth Day. He asked me questions for an hour, then declared himself about 90 percent sold on the story. By the way, he said, do you have any big action coming up? Now, not on *our* behalf, but something you might already have in mind? Why, shore, I said, and he said, Perfect! He was 100 percent sure.

Sometimes there are things that the mind refuses, same as the stomach refuses, and until the moment they arrived in two vans, and panic clambered through my body worse than two babies running through the hall, I never believed *48 Hours* would arrive. I should have; everybody else did. All four mayors in all four towns. Formosa executives. Chamber of Commerce. Economic Development. The county's chemical plants. Reporters. Especially reporters. Houston sent a helicopter and a television crew, and *China Times* sent a reporter from New York City (he flew to Houston and rented a car), and they all showed up on the front porch at the same time. They were friendly, handsome men in coats with pockets bulging with rolls of film and spiral notebooks, and dragging wires everywhere. The children bolted like a cloud of chickens, except for Crockett, who grabbed every flashing light and every boxed anything, and when the Chinese reporter squatted down and held the video camera so Crockett could see the lights, Crockett's fingers ran tenderly over the lens.

For three days the reporters crammed wires up my shirt and around my collar and followed me everywhere with huge silver photo moons taller than my head. I couldn't go into a bedroom to dress a squirming baby without the cameramen following. "This is realism," one reporter said. "The viewers *love* it!"

Then they drove all over the county in a van marked 48 HOURS, and chemical plants seemed to stop running. The discharges stopped flowing and the incinerators quit flaring. It was as though the chemical industry had declared a holiday. The Point Comfort mayor was furious, and in her TV interview (wearing a brand-new pale yellow pantsuit, with her blond hair stiff and lips bloodred) she said so. "It's horrible! This quiet little town!"

The chamber's president mused and fumed in his chamber role. Formosa's violations should be discussed behind closed doors and not in front of the entire countryside! He feared the publicity would damage the county's seafood industry, and hadn't the poor shrimpers had enough grief? Then Wally and a Formosa representative met my two brothers (and thereby antagonized Baby in the process, because he was *the husband* and not invited) and warned them to quieten their sister down, or the fishing community was going to know *who* was responsible for dead seafood markets. My brothers did nothing. They would have been exceptional brothers, if they had.

Then it all converged: Stars lined up with planets and moons got in the middle, and *48 Hours* filmed it all. It had all the ingredients of a huge success for a film crew: There was action, there were fights (live action!), and there were government and agency people galore (standing slightly off center and trying not to draw attention or get asked questions).

Then there was Formosa—trying hard to make up its corporate mind. First they were not sending nobody to *that* hoedown! Then they were because *somebody* had to represent the company, and Lord knows it wasn't going to be that outsider group putting on the show! So paranoia won the day, and Formosa and her corporate sponsors and supporters showed up in droves. Employees. Politicians. Business leaders. Chamber of Commerce. Economic Development. Navigation district. They brought handwritten signs and poster boards and congregated in the middle like Formosa's pep squad. Formosa's executives, in shiny black suits, sat in the row behind the Chamber of Commerce like hunched-over, primed quarterbacks in a high school gym.

Three hundred people crowded the city hall in Point Comfort. Some stood in the back and around the sides and a few stood outside, but close enough to the door to hear. Reporters were everywhere. They pulled up in vans and drug out their cameras and wires that snaked across the lawn and down the aisles. A helicopter circled the plant, and one reporter climbed Formosa's chain-link fence near a roadside park.

Division ruled the day. The mayor forgot she wasn't leading the meeting and kept interrupting. What were Blackburn and Rick Abraham doing there? They didn't live here. They were instigators of trouble. Finally I got tired of the mayor and walked to the microphone and said I was kicking the mayor out of the room if she didn't shut up and let the speakers talk.

Blackburn spoke first about the work our environmental group had accomplished on Formosa's permits, and that didn't go well because nobody in the audience wanted to hear what the other side had done. Suddenly a big baby-faced man, sitting behind the Chamber row and obviously in Formosa's row, lumbered up and identified himself as Joe Wyatt, a former congressman who was working for Formosa. He questioned Blackburn on what our group really had contributed to the permits.

"Now, Mister Blackburn, that isn't how I see it. The Air Control Board would have requested the same changes as you all did, so that issue is moot. Then as far as the liver screening we agreed upon, Formosa planned on doing it anyhow. So that is a moot issue too."

That produced a heated exchange between the two, and Blackburn shoved his hands on his hips and walked farther into the audience and said the Air Control Board was one of the worst state agencies he had ever seen in his life and the state Air Control Board was totally unsympathetic to the public. Someone in the audience said that Mister Blackburn didn't need to tell that to Mister Wyatt, since Mister Wyatt's wife, Mary Ann, was a member of the Air Control Board. Mister Wyatt knew all about the Air Control Board.

Rick came next and read a list of state and federal enforcement actions against Formosa, then another list of violations that had never been enforced. Rick said Texas was being ruined by industry, and someone in the audience wanted to know what was the basis of his statement, and someone else wanted to know why we were meddling in something that was none of our business. State and federal agencies took care of environmental problems. We should just let them do their business and mind our own.

That business about agencies taking care of problems hit home, so while it wasn't my turn to talk, I went to the microphone anyway and said that groundwater contamination reports had been given to me by state inspectors because the agencies were reluctant to pursue enforcement against companies. I had even been given contamination data the EPA didn't have and apparently didn't want. Just how was that possible in a world where agencies took care of environmental problems?

All sorts of accusations got sent back and forth, and when they didn't come fast enough, Joe Wyatt in the back row passed notes to the chamber president in the front, and the chamber president hopped up and asked Joe's questions. Why did Calhoun County Resource Watch have so few county members? Where was their support?

I said perhaps if Formosa quit videotaping every meeting I had and quit hiring half the politicians in the state as contractors, then maybe the county folks wouldn't be so scared to be members. Then I told Joe Wyatt to ask his own questions and quit passing them to the Chamber row.

Like all battles, there were fights inside and out, and the outside one was worst, so the police were called. I was worn out from the arguing. Blackburn looked over at me and shrugged his shoulders, so I went to the microphone and said the meeting was over. We'd done as much damage as we could in a three-hour stretch. Then the reporters and camera crew did a few final interviews in different corners of the room with the local citizens and with Formosa's representatives, and finally they walked outside and into the yard and filmed their commentaries against a backdrop of incinerators and cooling towers. Later the film crew gave me their cards and said to let them know how things developed. Then they drove off.

• • •

Blackburn and I were the last to leave. We stood in a newly mown yard with a couple of trees, and Formosa a street away—as visible at night as it was in the day, only louder and brighter, and a thousand lightbulbs burning along with everything else in the night air. Blackburn was as frisky as I'd ever seen him. He said nights like this made him feel good about being a lawyer again. He loved the politics of South Texas and fighting the good fight. Fighting the odds. Not scratching the surface of the law like it was chicken scratch and he was just one of a dozen chickens.

After he left I drove over the bridge and went home. It was after midnight, the kids were asleep, and nothing moved, so I walked barefoot out onto the porch and sat on the swing and stared into the yard. Then for the same reason I sat on the porch and did nothing, I did nothing when the phone rang. It rang three times before I opened the screen door and walked into the kitchen and picked it up.

"Miz Wilson?"

"That's me. What can I do for you?"

"Miz Wilson, they're burying drums at Formosa. I know it's late, but I thought you might want to know. I talked with one of the bulldozer operators a little while ago, and he told me the blade of his bulldozer hit one of the drums and some of it splashed and burned him pretty bad. When he went and told his supervisor about getting burned, the man just said *that* was a good way to lose a job. The bulldozer operator didn't say no more. He just came to me."

"You think the worker would talk to me? Would you give me his name?"

"No, ma'am. I can't do that. But I think if you go over there and look, you're gonna find out the information is true."

It was a long time before the man quit talking and hung up. I could imagine him sitting in a dark room in one of those big sweaty armchairs.

The next day I went to the fish house, and Donna Sue was in an uproar over the night before. She blamed Wally 'cause none of the shrimpers showed up, and I told her shrimpers not showing up was nothing new. They didn't need nobody for that type of disinterest. A dead dog in the road would have got that one going. Anyhow, that meeting was over. What I wanted now was a camera or a video camera. Either one, I didn't care. I needed to get pictures of bulldozers working on Formosa's property.

Donna Sue said, "Get Sam Clegg's plane. He's got one and a pilot too. I think that secretary of his is a pilot."

I hesitated for a second because I didn't believe I'd make it past the secretary to get to Sam. Wasted thinking. The secretary put me straight through to Sam, and Sam laughed and said his secretary *was indeed* a pilot and he already knew about the bulldozers. One of the operators had called him. Sam said he was sending his pilot up that night to fly over Formosa with an infrared camera.

That took care of some of the problem, but I figured names and phone numbers of bulldozer operators would be important, so I called Wally and said I needed a favor. A little bit of information. I'd owe him *big time*. Wally wanted to know what I needed the information for. What was I up to? Pure as the driven snow, I said, and besides, no tellin' what kind of information he could get out of me later on. Then I went over to the *SeaBee* and waited like all the old men who didn't fish anymore did: sitting high and dry on old boats with dirty rags nailed across their cabin doors to keep out the fog.

Only no fog came, just Wally, and he was an hour late. He was in a peach-colored car this time and it looked brand-new. He got out of his car and walked to the *SeaBee* with papers in his hand. He stopped on the back deck of the boat, still wearing the same woman-ironed shirt and the same pants, and looked exactly like he'd just walked out of his own fish-house office and not some air-conditioned office of a chemical plant a dozen miles away.

"You have any trouble getting that list?" I said, and Wally said, "Naw. It was slick as a whistle." Then Wally stayed awhile and we talked about nothing except what all the oystermen weren't doing and weren't catching in their dredges. He didn't mention the meeting, and I didn't mention the papers. I didn't want Wally thinking I had more than a passing fancy for the list of contractors. Anything more would have sent him figuring and I didn't want but one of us weaving a scarf out of that piece of paper.

When he left I called the only independent bulldozer company listed on the paper. I told the secretary I had a small company and needed to hire a bulldozer somewhere down the line, and how many operators did they have anyway? The secretary said they had three operators, but they were already tied up at Formosa. Sometimes they hired another independent out of Bay City, which they had for the

Formosa work they were doing now, but he was off for a day. Call him. Maybe he could give me an idea of the rates and how long a job took.

I called the man to make sure he was home, then I went home and fixed an early supper for the kids and got them bathed. I told Baby I was meeting a worker. Baby was watching TV, and above his head the whirling Sears fan displaced hot air with more hot air, and under the supper table Crockett spun a tiny alternator fan over and over and watched nothing at all.

I made Bay City in two hours. It was dark when I knocked on the door. A woman who answered looked hard at my face. She stood with one hand on the door and the other on her hip, and when I asked for her husband, the woman said he was just sitting down for supper. She stared while I stood silent, then finally she stepped back and opened the door. As I walked through the open door a chair scraped hard against a wooden floor and a man came out.

The operator was a man who never drank and never gambled, 'cause how else would he have acquired a house like he had unless he never touched his vices, only looking like he might had if he hadn't known that the minute he did, he would backslide into the mud he came from. He wasn't glad to see me. He knew my type—we were kin that way. He was just sitting down to supper, he said. I was keeping him from it. What did I want? He didn't smile, and a deep weariness was staked around his mouth.

I didn't say I was a shrimper or an activist. I figured either one of those words would have slammed the door on me. So I said, "You're a bulldozer operator working at Formosa?"

"I work at Formosa sometimes. What of it?"

"You been working out there the last couple of nights?"

"Yeah, that's right," he said and moved to the door and looked outside to see what I had brought along with me. Then he walked back in and turned around slow to me. "Whadda you want to know all this for? Who are you workin' for?"

Working for nobody, I said. I was a fisherman from Seadrift. I'd been fighting some of Formosa's permits. "We had a meeting a couple nights ago. Down in Point Comfort. You hear about it?"

The man's face got quiet and his mouth worked like he was still chewing supper, only he wasn't sitting at the supper table. He leaned towards me and put up a hard finger.

"Look, lady! I'm not doin' anything out there. Okay? I'm not doin' one damn thing! I don't know where you got . . . " Then he stopped abruptly and threw his hands into the air.

"I ain't sayin' nothin'! I don't have to talk to you. Just go on. Get on out of here!"

"Look," I said. "I got a call, and let's just say I know there's a few bulldozers out there burying something. Okay? I just want to know what it is. I'm not out to cause you any problems. I just need somebody to talk to me."

"Talk? Talk? Lady, I *can't* talk. Somebody like me with my piddlin' little operation starts to talk, and that's it! I'm blackballed. Quick! I'd never get work again. Might as well put a FOR SALE sign up in the front yard."

He turned, and the imprint of a hard hat worn all day showed against the back of his head. I stumbled behind him, not going fast, just not retreating. In the background were supper sounds. A woman's voice. A dish. A child talking.

"Listen, I know you got kids. I can hear them in there. Don't tell me you don't care about them. Maybe it wasn't you that called, but one of y'all sure did, and one operator got exposed to some kind of chemical, and if that operator got exposed, then don't you think it's possible you got exposed too? Are you riskin' getting sick later on just because some company doesn't want to deal with their wastes right?"

He whirled around and shoved both hands on his hips. "Look, lady. I *wasn't* burying drums or whatever it is you think I was doin'! I was just cleanin' out the . . . okay, okay. Maybe I was out there. I ain't sayin' I wasn't, 'cause I've already told you I was. I'm just saying *I don't know what it was or if it was legal.* Maybe it was. Maybe it wasn't. Who's keeping a rule book out there, anyway? The foreman just tells you to do something, and if you want to keep your job you do it. Okay? No questions asked. And you talk about my kids? Well, it's all for my kids! That's all it's for. I grew up with nothin', so anything past that is great! It's for my kids I want something different."

He stopped talking, but his lips moved like he was wanting to say more. Somewhere in the room a clock struck eight times, and the man dropped his hands and the palms looked hard as supper plates against his worn jeans. Then he spoke slow and the words moved out of his face as irreparable as water moved from the dam where it was blocked.

He said, "I know what you're thinkin'. *But I ain't a polluter!* I care as much as the next fella about what's goin' on down there. I grew up down there. Don't live there anymore, but that's where I started. Even had an ole uncle that was a shrimper—doesn't everybody got one? Been dead a long time, though. Drowned way back when I was a kid."

The man stood near his brand-new shiny walls, and high above him on the wall a fake ivy poked from the plaster head of a golden baby angel. He seemed out of place; a cutout picture from the Monkey Ward catalog pasted into an issue of *Southern Living*. I didn't like seeing his face that clear, so I glanced down at my feet.

"I ain't gonna stand here and say I didn't think what was goin' on was a little strange. Two or three in the morning and moving and shovin' stuff around? First, they said, 'Clean out this ditch and go haul it there in another hole.' Then in that hole . . . and I'm tellin' you the *truth*. I nearly lost my dozer a couple of times. I don't know what all was in there. It was kinda a reddish liquid. It wasn't drums, though. I wasn't the one doin' that one. The only reason I heard we were out there was because of some kind of EPA inspection or something. We was to work every night until we got the job done. Didn't know what the EPA inspection was about and I didn't ask. Had a question or two about why they wanted that dump area raised about four foot, but I shore didn't ask it."

I stayed nearly an hour and waited on him to get a piece of paper, then he sat down and drew out the perimeters of the plant with the highway and the creek that ran behind and out into the bay. He marked an × on the map where he had dumped what he had cleaned from the ditches and outfalls the last three nights. When he finished, he shoved the paper across the supper table to me. His plate was untouched and cold. "Is that gonna do?" he said.

"I believe it will. We've got somebody else trying to get pictures from a plane, but anytime you got someone who can give you information firsthand, it's always better."

The man never said for me not to give his name and I never said I wouldn't, but as I stood by the van and looked into his face, I tried to say I wouldn't. That night, almost as much as I wanted information and bulldozers to stop, I wanted not to give his name.

16

Union Carbide Blows;
the Fed Arrives

Union Carbide blew up, and the only mistake was I told Baby my dream.

He said, "How'd you know it was Carbide? One plant exploding is just like another one exploding."

"Well, it was Union Carbide, all right, because right above the explosion and the fire, in big black letters, were the words UNION CARBIDE. It was night. Carbide is fixing to explode!"

He said, "Well, don't tell nobody, or they're damn sure gonna think you done it somehow."

Then in early March and two weeks before oyster season ended, I woke up after midnight and went to the window, and there Union Carbide filled the night and shook the house. There were three explosions. Three fires. It was my dream, except the black words UNION CARBIDE weren't there. I wondered if I wasn't dreaming a second time but I wasn't. It was the real thing. The paper said Carbide was lucky it only had a skeleton crew that late at night, and only thirty-two were injured and one man dead. One man. The rest were lucky. So, so lucky. Carbide had been named the safest plant in Texas by the Texas Chemical Council a few scant months before, and it was even on a plaque on the wall that blew through a cylinder. Three workers on the edge of the blast climbed Carbide's eight-foot chain-link fence and ran all the way to Seadrift.

Nobody knew what all was burning that night, but shrapnel as big as vehicles was hurled across the road and into the surrounding countryside. An ethereal chemical substance no one knew the name for bathed the night. Later a Houston paper said it was only by chance the whole countryside didn't go, because a hundred and fifty feet from the blast (and already taking a hit) was an ethylene oxide tank storing the equivalent of fifty-eight tons of TNT.

The fishermen threw their arms in the air and shook their heads and walked to their boats. Who knows about these things? Who can tell? It was a good thing they had their boats. It was a good thing they could steer their boats away from the town and the land and the chemical plants and head for open water—but still, if a deckhand walked bird-light and unannounced into the cabin, the startled shrimper shouted, "Stand back! Stand back!"

Who was he kidding? The water wasn't a safe hidey-hole anymore. Accidents, sickness. Then more dolphins washed up dead on the shores. Nobody knew what it meant and if anyone ventured a guess, then somebody else came along to cancel it. The fishermen were bewildered. They knew dolphins only as boat junkies, following along beside the boats and eating whatever the nets stirred up. The fishermen could recognize the ones that trailed their boats through the landlocks and followed them into the bays by the cuts and scrapes and scratches on the trailing edge of their dorsal fins. They were moments of light, flashing in the water like coming and going butcher knives pitched in an underwater honky-tonk fight.

And they died like flies. Some blamed deadly pesticides and speculated that the spring's heavy rains and flooding had washed pesticides and other contaminants into the bay. Some went even further and nailed the pesticide Aldicarb, but other biologists and scientists came out and said that finding was misinterpreted. Perhaps polychlorinated biphenols were affecting the dolphins. The levels detected in the dolphin tissues ranged from a low of 4,000 parts per million to a high of 150,000 parts per million. The significance was unclear, however.

Then two biologists came to Seadrift to test the channel where Jumpin' Junior's dead shrimp were found. The men came in a truck hauling a skiff and trailer, and they launched their boat in the middle of a squall. Due to the severity of the weather, the biologists only tested three sites, and all for arsenic (the biologists said, "That's the chemical that was found in the dolphin tissues.") Later the state sent the report back, and arsenic levels were exceeded in two of the three sites, but their finding: overfishing.

A simple case of victim fingered as perpetrator. Only fishermen weren't making any money and were on nobody's calling list, so nobody cared what they were called. *Bay rapers* was just another name on a long list next to *outlaw*. So name-called and unaffected, the oyster boats left for ports like Galveston or Freeport or Louisiana. The captains took on two hundred gallons of fuel, flipped boat lines, and headed for the open seas. Going all the way, they said. Might get there by midday of the next day or morning of the next. Another few boats changed rigs and started shrimping for the most dismal and dark of all shrimp: Hoppers. Black seas and rough nights, and you were lucky when you brought in two hundred pounds of stinking shrimp. Mostly you brought in a worn-out body jittering from too much boiled coffee, and a torn, smelly net wadded up on the back deck.

Hoppering required nothing on my part at the fish house. I either found a shrimp basket with an oyster sack thrown over it and sitting at the back door of the fish house, or a shrimper had broke into the fish house and left the shrimp on the scales. Either way it took one shrimping crate and two shovels of ice to take care of it, so I had a lot of free time on my hands. I brought the babies down to the fish house and let them have the run of it. When I wasn't on the phone and trying to get somewhere with EPA investigators, I was keeping an eye on the babies' heads.

Finally an EPA investigator called and said they were sending down two agents and they just wanted to know where to meet. So on a day it rained, two women in business suits met me at the café outside of town. We talked at a table, and the women agents payed no mind to the congestion in the café and calmly drank their Dr Peppers. I gave them the pictures Sam's pilot took, and pointed out the trucks and the bulldozers and the special fender that the operator out of Bay City had on his bulldozer. Then I gave them a copy of the map and showed them where my contact had drawn an ×.

The women were unemotional and detached. They said they were the first string. They just took information. Checked out the area. The primary investigator would come later, "sometime later. We'll let you know."

A few days later, a woman from the state attorney general's office called and said she wanted to help. Did I know the Water Commission was going to levy a huge penalty against Formosa? The biggest the commission had ever filed against a company in Texas. Over two hundred forty thousand dollars for wastewater violations.

"Unfortunately," the woman said, "the commission is also allowing the violations to continue. Business is business, you know. You might want to show up for the commission hearing."

The woman was right as rain. The penalty made headlines in the newspapers, and a local politician I had informed months before about the contamination and who had curtly dismissed me was fuming. He wanted to know why the state had failed to notify him! Personally! He didn't appreciate hearing through the paper. Didn't they know he was the legislator who had introduced the bill that required local officials to be informed first of contamination in their county? And that reporting never happened! Notification did not occur! He had other issues too. Did the Water Commission know if Formosa's contamination had entered the local drinking water? Did they believe it had?

A Water Commission spokesperson said although organic compounds found were suspected to cause cancer, the contaminated water was fifteen feet below the ground and not at a level most wells were dug, so the water was safe. However, they hadn't actually surveyed the area to see if there were wells.

I called Rick about the enforcement hearing, and he said I should consider presenting my criminal petitions to Chairman Bucko. Without opposition such as the petitions would show, the Water Commission would most likely let Formosa off the hook. Two hundred forty thousand dollars in penalties is nothing to these companies, Rick said. One of their smallest units in Point Comfort probably made four or five times that amount every day.

So I threw caution to the wind and got up at six one morning, and with my pile of petitions drove the van three hours to Austin. It was uneventful driving down. The van didn't blow a motor, and I didn't get lost, and I found the Stephen F. Austin building easy enough. The room was huge, with tall windows curtained in heavy purple velvet, and onstage heavy purple curtains stood ready for somebody. Texas flags were draped in every corner, then pasted on anything that stood upright or had a flat surface was the big round symbol of the Water Commission.

After the room filled, Chairman Bucko came to the microphone. He was a charismatic speaker with an actor's dark good looks, and he fairly danced across the stage. He said due to the length of the meeting, the general rules were not going to be followed and no oral comment from the audience would be allowed on Formosa's hearing. Just put it in writing, he said.

Rick sat beside me and jabbed me hard in the ribs. "*That's* for us," he said. "The chairman saw us and doesn't want us to talk!"

Then from that nest of sticks, a whole pile of contradictions and ironies rose like flames in a barn fire: The commission decided that even though Formosa's fine warranted something in the seven-figure bracket, they would calculate it thirty times lower, and although Formosa continued to violate their wastewater permit on a daily basis into a body of water they had already degraded, the state would allow the wastewater permit and violations to continue.

It wasn't the Water Commission's fault, Chairman Bucko said. The blame lay squarely with the federal agencies who prevented the Water Commission from dealing appropriately with the environmental issues at Formosa. Maybe now the agencies would back off on their demand for a comprehensive EIS and let the state regulatory process work.

A lawyer representing Formosa got up and said that until Formosa received their new wastewater permit, their problems could not be corrected and Formosa was far from being the worst chemical company on the Gulf Coast. I waited until the end of Formosa's speech and stood with the petitions to my chest and asked to speak. The chairman looked at me with surprise, annoyance flip-flopping on his face. Then he dismissed me with a glance and began to talk on another subject. I interrupted him and said I had driven three hours to get to Austin to say something before the commission, and I wanted permission to say it.

The chairman leaned into the microphone and said, "Sit down, young lady. This is my hearing. I'll say who'll speak and who won't."

I said I wasn't gonna sit down. I had come a long ways, and I was gonna deliver the thousand signatures I had collected on a petition. "That's what I came for, and that is what I'm gonna do."

The chairman got agitated and hunched over the microphone and said in a harsh voice that if I didn't sit down he was calling the capitol police.

I said, "I don't care, Mister Chairman. I'm not leaving until I finish."

So Bucko was upset, and I knew what riled him. The commission was going to take heat for being so light on Formosa, and I wouldn't shut up in his commission meeting. What else riled him, I don't know. Maybe Rick standing up and saying loud enough for anyone to hear that the commission could try to shut us out, but they couldn't shut us up. Bucko called it a publicity stunt and stormed off the stage and out of his own meeting to call the capitol police, while the other commissioners sat around a table, looking confused.

An impromptu press conference was created outside from the fallout, and Rick told the press that the Water Commission was playing footsie with industry, and Bucko, caught midstream by a reporter in his search for campus cops, retorted that if any party was guilty of practicing politics, then it was that environmental group doing their little publicity stunt to raise money to pay their own salaries.

In the middle of the press conference, Blackburn waltzed through on some unofficial business (he never said what) and found himself in the middle of Act Two of something Chairman Bucko was calling environmental street theater. Then the press scrambled and left just like they had arrived, and I turned around and Rick was gone too. Blackburn drug me into a capitol coffee shop to discuss my role in Bucko's wrath.

"So our little Miss Margie's come to Austin, has she? And she doesn't appreciate the commission's tact in dealing with the public. Wait till we get our hearing at the Air Control Board. Oh, the wonders and the marvels you will see then." Blackburn laughed and placed his briefcase on a chair between us.

I said I didn't think it was a bit funny that the commission acted like the public was interfering in their business. *Their business!*

"Which you were, Wilson. These agencies are in the business of permitting. The sooner you learn that, the better. Who do you think beats the drum for cleaner air or cleaner water anyhow? It sure isn't agencies. It's not the Texas Chemical Council. Any time the public— we the people—work to get the Clean Water Act or the Clean Air Act a little tougher, industry is out there griping their heads off. Saying, 'They're gonna bankrupt us! We've gotta run off to Mexico where things aren't so tough!' Oh, it just breaks my heart, those poor, poor babies. Then you and I get trampled to death when they run to the bank."

Blackburn smiled (probably thinking how Bucko was still riled and roaming the halls) and said before he left Austin, he'd go talk to Bucko and see what he could find out. Bucko wasn't so bad. He was a terrific fishing buddy. Then Blackburn got up and went to the cashier and said he wanted to pay for both coffees. He turned to me and smiled broadly and told the cashier, "This is the cheapest thing I've ever done for her."

The next week I restricted myself to old nets I'd never finished. I stretched worn-out, wire-showing cable between two oak trees in the front yard, and as the babies ran underneath a hundred times, I rehung nets for the next shrimping season. Blackburn called off and on about the hearing we were requesting and about no news on the lawsuit front. He left messages with Donna Sue, and she drove down in her car and delivered them in her flat, dry voice.

The house phone got disconnected and Baby said he was glad, glad. First good thing he had seen in he didn't know when. Still, he stopped asking when I was gonna quit. He stopped everything except walking through the trees with Crockett, and once he came to me and said he saw an owl and it flew down to him. Was that supposed to be Boy? I said, and Baby said he had no damn idea. It was just an owl.

I stayed in the hot sun and stabbed the net with my needle of twine, and thought it was a good thing it wasn't night. In that mucky darkness, I talked to myself worse than Crockett moved his whirling hands. Blackburn said I was in a funk because I was stuck down there in that little backwater place called Seadrift. No need to be down and out in Seadrift, he said. There was plenty going on. I told him there was a million miles of difference between a fisherman at the front door of Formosa and a lawyer in an ivory tower in Houston. And it wasn't just that, I said. That woman part drove us another million miles apart.

Ohhh, that woman part was Blackburn's favorite, and being a man, he could say that. *Yes, yes!* He'd read books on ecofeminism! Might have even taught it in his Rice University classes, except the mere mention of the word sent his male students howling. He had to call it by another word. *Ecofeminism* was too spooky for Texas men. So Blackburn lectured on life cycles instead of goddesses, and environmental ethics instead of spirituality, but his tone was still as feverish as a preacher with a message scribbled in his pocket.

Blackburn was tired of what the law profession demanded of him and the moral canyons he had to walk every day of his life. He was sick of dominance and aggression and inflated egos, and sometimes he saw in the male flesh he was born to a semblance of the thing that was killing the earth. It was in company executives' faces when they talked of progress and economics and risk assessments, and in agency hearing transcripts that measured a bay's worth in carrying loads and parts per million of allowable wastes.

The only flaw in his ecofeminism argument was his own testosterone-riddled body. A Houston Astrodome wrestler lived in him. Blackburn was Blackburn's own worst enemy, and I just hoped he never saw the flaw when he was fighting for me. I had no time for it. I wanted his aggression to be full-blown.

Besides, Blackburn didn't know a woman's flip side—that curious blend of savagery and pity, of yearning and hatred. So what if a woman screamed to the high heavens when a washing machine broke or a tea jar got spilled or a baby got born? It was only her way of saying, to those who were sensitive to that kind of listening, that it was her one kingdom left and what else was there?

But Blackburn didn't see that side. So that was why he didn't get too concerned like Baby did when I had two secret meetings with men I didn't know at all. My first meeting was at Whataburger in broad daylight with an EPA criminal investigator, and I couldn't have got more people looking than if the man across from me had hired them. He was a big man wearing boots with shooting stars, and was about the fartherest thing I could imagine from a federal anything. He said he was once a Houston cop, but I didn't see that one either. He might have been a sheriff out of Laredo. Or maybe a snake handler in El Paso.

He took up the whole table with his notes and his coffee, and I was trying hard not to spill my own coffee over the whole thing. I was nervous as heck. We were the only table drinking coffee while everybody else had Cokes and Dr Peppers and Whataburgers and french fries. When he finally got his notepad and his coffee situated, he looked at me real serious. He said, "Now, I need to tell you right off that you can get into a lot of trouble lying to a federal investigator. It's just like lying to the FBI. I'm not saying you are; I'm just warning you."

"Sure," I said. "Consider me warned." But lies weren't what I was worried about. I was nervous about giving up the names of workers. I didn't like saying them even if I had a whole notebookful with my coffee sitting on top. I could tell the EPA investigator thought names were gonna be the dessert on the table, though. Facts, facts, facts, and none of this other bullshit. This is serious stuff, girl. Serious. And if you don't think it's serious, then just see where it lands you first time you tell me a bullshit lie. Then he stuck a tape recorder on the table.

"Now, I got a problem right here," I said, and pointed at the recorder.

"What's that, darlin'?"

"How do I know you're not gonna take everything I say and hand it over to Formosa's lawyers? Call it disclosure or something."

"Well, call the gotdam attorney general's office, then! Get that federal one! Call him!"

"Well, who is he? Maybe that one's crooked too."

The big man leaned across the table and put his hand on his coffee to hold it still. "Lissen, darlin', we're deputized U.S. marshals. We work with the United States federal office and chase environmental criminals, for Chrissakes! I'm not just a sack of small potatoes they send down here. I could arrest someone if I wanted to."

But I was a wary woman and had come full circle from trusting everything and everyone to trusting nobody and nothing. I had wrestled the long arm of politics on a hundred different tables, and maybe now on this Whataburger table with this federal marshal.

The federal investigator was just as concerned with my qualifications. Why were the workers talking to me anyhow? That's kinda strange. Workers talking to the troublemaker. He looked at me and laughed, and his big white cowboy shirt with the pearl buttons hardly moved. He had a mile-deep chest, and I just heard the rumble.

"Now, why would they do that? I'd think it'd be like putting a gun to their head."

I told him there were a couple of truths I could count on. First, that I was gonna be contacted after a worker got hurt and generally not before. Second, I was the least of three evils, and the first of those three evils were the company and OSHA. OSHA might be out there to protect them, but they sure weren't trusted.

"Now, the company I can understand," the inspector said. "A company is notorious for having profit foremost in their minds. They don't get paid for being nice to their workers. It might make things smoother, but it's not a money-breaking deal. But that OSHA one is interesting. That's their job."

I said most workers didn't know their rights. Wouldn't know them if they walked up and bit them. One worker called and said he worked a ten-hour shift and fell off a scaffolding that wasn't tied down, and the company said they were firing him because he was drunk. That worker didn't know what to do. What were his rights? Go tell the company they're not fair? Write a complaint to OSHA?

The inspector said his investigation didn't cover worker safety. What he was looking for were criminal acts that involved hazardous waste and dumpings and wastewater. The Clean Water Act. Resource Conservation and Recovery Act. That type of thing, he said. And even calling it criminal was pretty tough because the investigators had to prove intent. Show that there was a *knowing* intent by the company to commit an illegal dumping.

"You do that, then you've got a ball game. Any knowing violation of the Clean Water Act—where some person knowingly introduces a pollutant to the water—could get them jail time up to three years. Then a pretty hefty penalty too. Five thousand to fifty thousand dollars a day for some of the offenses. But you've got to *prove* intent."

"What about an action that's got the potential to create an environmental release? Workers talk a lot about the quality of the construction going on out there. Say it's moving too fast, and four hundred contractors working right on top of each other at any given time. Too many short cuts. Everything rush, rush, rush. Welds aren't X-rayed on tanks and pipes, so who knows if they're any good or not? Training for a worker is nonexistent. That's a joke. And who knows who is being hired? They just want workers. Anybody! Don't need to be qualified, and if one worker doesn't do what they want done as fast as they want it done, then there's three hundred other men standing at the gate, waiting in line."

The man shook his head and wrote nothing down. I guessed construction wasn't his jurisdiction either. "There's always talk like that around a construction site. Especially one this big."

"Are you saying it's just talk?" I said.

The man laughed. "Oh, no, no, no. You're not gonna get me to say that. I just *do* my job. I can't do OSHA's job. . . . Which it sounds like it is. I can't do anything about quality of construction problems. Maybe there's some agency out there that keeps track of it. Sets up some sorts of standards. I don't know. Maybe you've just got to *trust* that they're gonna do the right thing and not blow up the plant. Do their own quality control. Something like that. That might be where you need unions. They could influence the quality of construction out there. But then that's not my job and I ain't advocating unions."

We stayed at Whataburger until the dinner crowd left and I gave him every contact and map and photograph I had. Then the investigator turned off his tape recorder and stuck it on top of his notepad. He'd stay in touch, but he couldn't give me the details of any interview he'd do. That would violate confidentiality, and besides, if I was too involved in his investigation it would only complicate the case. "We don't need any legal mumbo jumbo going on, now do we, darlin'?" he said.

I didn't stay around to watch him leave. I had better things to do: a fish house waiting, and some union representatives had called and wanted to talk. I got to the fish house as an eighteen-wheeler backed up to our long metal conveyor ramp outside the fish house. The shrimp boxes were shotgun scattered from the vault where Donna Sue had kicked them to the door where the ramp sat. Ice was everywhere and the smell of Gulf shrimp was strong.

We were almost finished—with four shrimp boxes left on the fish-house floor—when the union men walked in the door. They were wearing Arrow shirts crisp enough to eat, and as we slung the last 120-pound boxes on the ramp, all four men rushed up. "Honey, honey, honey!" they said. "Let us give you a hand there!" And I said, "You fellas just stand back there. We can handle this."

The men laughed and smiled wide, clean smiles, smoked Winston cigarettes, and shot the bull ever' which way while Donna Sue and I finished loading the truck. Donna Sue shoved me on the shoulder. "Go take care of your union fellas. I'll handle the truck driver."

I went in the office and the four men followed me. In the office we fought about the chair: me trying to give it to one of them and all of them trying to give it to me. It was a courtly war that people in the South loved to fight, and no better way to tell a Yankee was in your midst than their lack of enthusiasm in the war. Finally to shut them up, I sat down in the chair.

The men sat on overturned shrimp boxes like it was a front porch and they didn't mind the mosquitoes or mind the dust; they were just sitting to be sitting.

"Y'all sure look like plain ole down-home boys," I said.

They grinned and nodded their heads—yhah, yhah, yhah—and slung that Texas charm like it was gravy in a skillet. No, ma'am, they didn't disagree at all. Down-home boys was just about what they were. "You know where San Angelo is, don'tcha, honey?" the oldest man said. Little ole hick town outside of San Angelo? That was where he was born. Another was raised in Channelview and worked at that Phillips 66 plant in Pasadena when it blew up.

The oldest man was Gary Weatherby, and he was the Oil, Chemical, and Atomic Workers's International representative. He said while they were all just country boys, the worst hick in the bunch was from a place out of state, in Ohio, called Round Top, known only for the smallest nuclear reactor in the entire countryside. Other than that reactor, Round Top wasn't nothing but coal miners and black lung and black lung and coal miners—as side-by-side as two people holding hands and kissing.

The men were from the Oil, Chemical, and Atomic Workers's International union chapter in Texas City, a place of wall-to-wall chemical and oil refinery sites and put on the map by the same explosion that blasted five hundred folks off it in the late forties. There was nothing the union men hadn't heard and seen. Knew every same ole sad story up and down the Gulf Coast, and what else could you expect from an industry-dominated Right to Work state like Texas? The Texas legislature had at one time offered an amendment on the house floor to not only abolish unions and confiscate their property and send their families to concentration camps, but also put members up before a wall to be shot.

Sonny, the secretary of the union, said, "I can give you our toll-free number down at the union hall, and those Formosa workers can call me day or night and I can tell them right over the phone, 'You're screwed!' It's that simple."

He said there was no job protection in a nonunion job, but a worker didn't see it that way when he was being hired. He thought he'd work forever. Last forever. Stay healthy. Stay strong. Nothing was gonna happen to him, so why should he pay dues for nothing? And even if something happened and he got injured, the worker thought he could depend on workers' compensation or the company to take care of him.

Sonny looked at me, his dark eyes like pencil points, and said, "You know what workers' compensation is, don't you? It's insurance where a worker supposedly gets paid for his injuries in exchange for not suing the company. Well, in Texas, workers' comp has become a money-making machine, and there isn't another line of insurance that has a better rate of return."

But he wasn't at the fish house to tell me that a union would right every wrong. Nope. That depended on the workers. The members. A union was only as good as its members. "You know what they say," Sonny said. "The amount of oppression is about in direct proportion to what you will put up with. In other words, to be a doormat, you gotta lay down first."

"Believe me," he said, "we've got our own problems. If we didn't, then the unions in this country wouldn't be losing members and on the downswing trying to come up."

Here I thought was a strange kind of hope. Questions to ask every worker I came across. Why all the needless pain? The needless dying? There was an escape and it was sitting on two shrimp boxes in a hot fish house. Men working together.

Sonny said it was up to the workers wherever they were: on the bay in their fishing boats or halfway up a reactor in a chemical plant. They could do something or they didn't have to. He said he could talk to them on the phone, cite OSHA regulations out the wazoo, or he could go through the maze of workers' comp laws with them. But really, nobody was gonna save the worker but himself. Then the union could really do something in this country.

An hour had passed and whiffs of hard smoke hung like curtains from the ceiling. Then the union men rumbled alive, gathered their long legs and their cowboy boots. They hugged me several times, then hunted down Donna Sue in the cold interior of the ice vault and hugged her.

Donna Sue was red and blushing to her dark hair roots. She looked rumpled and young as she stood in the fish-house door and waved, yelling, "y'all take care of yourselves driving back." Donna Sue and I stood alone in the fish-house doorway. No reason for us being there; every reason gone when the shrimp left and the union men drove off. So I went home and faced trouble for being gone all day. It wasn't big trouble, nothing that would break bones. Only the windows were broke where Baby had smashed them and cut his hand, then smeared the phone with blood. Baby said nothing when I came home, and he wouldn't eat supper. Finally I walked out into the dark to the oak trees to find him and said, "It was only the union I was talking to."

Baby said it was the union that made prices so high. What else but them? Strike for higher and higher wages, and what are you gonna get but people like him having to pay for it all? Then when they weren't striking, they were off taking coffee breaks. Everybody knew that. He said nobody knew how to work. He'd like to see one of those union fellas work a day like a fisherman did on a boat. It would kill them dead.

I said, "You've never even been around a union. You don't know what they do," and Baby said, "I got ears, don't I? I can hear, can't I?"

That night, I slept with both babies. One baby for each arm. I lay and stared at the ceiling with the old chipped paint until it was nearly daybreak.

17

We Strike at the Heart of Formosa

He was a night man from Louisiana sent in to do a job all else had failed. He sat with his hands together, the fingers crossed and locked. He said he was gonna get serious. What was it gonna take for me to drop my opposition to the marine terminal permit?

I said, "Frankly, Mister Andre, negotiating isn't worth it, 'cause y'all ain't honest. About the only starting place in our negotiations is when y'all agree to do an environmental impact statement."

We sat at a table in a café, and his face was hard and never once looked right with his tailored business suit. "Look," he said, and spread his big white fingers out in front of me. "This cumulative-effect *environmental impact* thing is blown way out of proportion. All these projects! That Matagorda Bay dredging issue doesn't have a thing to do with us! That project has been completely removed. Besides, it's a different ball game now. We're being watched with a microscope. And the problems we've had before, you can rest assured we'll be aware of next time."

"Yeah, like y'all constructing without an impact study. Violating the law right there."

"The EPA has warned us that we are proceeding at risk if we construct without the permits. So that's what we are doing. It is no guarantee we will get the permits."

"And who said that . . . y'all proceeding at risk? The EPA administrator in Dallas? Senator Gramm's former campaign manager? The same Senator Gramm getting all the glory for bringing Formosa to Texas in the first place? Isn't that a bit too cozy?"

"Miss Wilson. Let me *assure* you that the EPA has questioned us at length. Why, tomorrow we're having to host over a half-dozen state and federal agencies. . . . "

"Tomorrow? Really? Where at?"

"At the new administration building . . . why?"

"How about I just sit in on the meeting?"

"Now, *why* do you want to do that?"

"Just curious. I'd like to see what the agencies' concerns are."

"All right, but how about you having some thoughts on forfeiting the marine terminal permit? See what you think might convince you or your group or your lawyer."

"Oh, I didn't come here to negotiate on that one."

At that instant, the conspiratorial rapport that existed between us was gone and we sat at a table with his untouched coffee cup and mine drained and finished and cold, cold, cold. I saw his teeth briefly. They came and they went.

I went to his meeting anyhow, and wore a black dress and black high-heel shoes with leather straps, and half the men in the room came to my shoulders and the rest of them hit me about eye level. There were fifteen men at a long shiny table, and half worked for Formosa and the rest came from Fish and Wildlife, National Marine Fisheries, Texas Parks and Wildlife, and the Texas Water Commission. The agency men sat in jeans and coats and took notes, and throughout the meeting they turned to each other, serious and astonished, as if they were saying, "Now, did you hear *that one*? Be sure to put *that* down."

The Fish and Wildlife man never smiled and his questions weren't friendly. What were the cumulative impacts of the extraction of freshwater from Lake Texana, plus the Formosa discharge, plus the deepening of the ship channel, plus the Colorado River diversion on the salinity of Matagorda Bay?

The Fish and Wildlife man wanted to know about the contaminants already present in the bay. What of the mercury? Sampling indicated that the mercury was moving up in the food chain in seabirds. What would be the impact of Formosa's discharge if the ethylene dichloride and copper present there collided with the mercury from the Superfund? Did the combined effect of the several chemicals cause a rise in toxicity to the marine life? And what of the aromatic hydrocarbons and the PAHs and the PCBs? Those contaminants were already in the fish in the bay. What kind of chemical cocktail would Formosa's discharge be creating?

The National Marine guy raised questions about the potential loss of wetlands, and what alternatives were there to the discharge of toxins into the bay. It was certainly one of the questions an environmental impact statement could address—alternatives for potential problems.

Joe Wyatt looked up from his note-taking and glared at the men. He said most of the questions regarding Formosa's discharge and possible spills were only "What ifs" that couldn't be definitively answered, and the questions were asked in such a way that any answer could be followed with ten more questions. An environmental impact study would do no good because Fish and Wildlife would not accept one that didn't provide the answers they wanted. It was self-defeating. A waste of time and money.

It was a stalemate, not an indictment of the expansion, but a joy for me. I had forgotten what it was like to sit among friends, to have your complaints and concerns voiced. Then two federal men (one from Corpus and another from Galveston) got me in a corner and handed me a study they had mentioned: the effect of copper on mercury in a marine environment. Then they gave me their cards and said they wanted to slip me some inside information. The EPA was fixing to announce an eight-million-dollar penalty against Formosa for hazardous waste violations. It looked like all my rabble-rousing had done some good.

I didn't betray a sound leaving that administration building, already built on a project not yet permitted. Flower beds were dug at the entrance, and workers in hard hats and jeans drug plats and plats of begonias and periwinkles out of the back end of a truck. I went home to the cement of the fish house and a dry, dry bay. Two days later a Houston reporter called, and again I heard my insider tip: the EPA was handing Formosa the largest penalty they had ever dealt a company in their five-state region. An 8.3-million-dollar penalty for hazardous waste violations.

If there was fallout from Formosa's fine, I didn't see it. The construction didn't stop. The injuries still happened. It was the same ole, same ole stuff. But Blackburn knew more of the players, and he said it was a time when rotten fruit fell hard from the tree. It was our time to strike.

"Think guerrilla, Wilson. We're little, so we've got to make little work for us. While Formosa and those agencies are lumbering around in red tape and politics and taking ten years to do something, we can zip around like those Africanized killer bees y'all got down there."

So we announced our lawsuit against the EPA and Formosa, and for two whole days Blackburn and Rick got along all right. Rick and I were listed as plaintiffs on the suit, and Blackburn was the pro bono lawyer working for nothing. Blackburn was beaming. He had swapped his spiritual ecofeminist mantle for killer lawyer instincts. "I just *love* it!" he said, and he couldn't wait to get to Calhoun County and kick some butt.

Two days later we wrote a press release and had our press conference in Point Comfort. Blackburn and Rick drove down in separate cars, and at nearly high noon in the heat and with the high white fog coming off Formosa's cooling towers, we flashed and glared. Our teeth were like razors.

But the night before, Joe Wyatt did his work. Joe told the newspaper that he didn't think there were ten people in the county that Diane Wilson represented, and he had no idea what we were going to say. Now he stood with two men in black suits, silent and hot. It was hard to tell who they hated most.

Four television crews arrived and bounded out of vans and cars. They milled around, pulling wires and hauling cameras, and followed us wherever we went. Into the city hall auditorium. Out into the yard. One reporter wanted a shot of me next to the water. "You're the shrimper lady, aren't you? Where's your boat? Can we get a shot of that?" Another television crew drove me to Formosa's fence line and had me stand in the ditch. "Don't smile," the cameraman said. "Frown like you mean it."

For Blackburn the press conference was just another round of Rice students he was lecturing or a courtroom he was commandeering. He was in his element and lounged in front, while Rick crammed notes in his hard metal chair and I sat with legs shaking. Blackburn went first and passed out the letters he had written to Formosa and the EPA warning of our intent to sue in sixty days.

Blackburn said he had never seen such a mess as Formosa. Their environmental compliance was in such disarray that only by stopping construction could Formosa correct the current problems and come into compliance. He announced that Calhoun County Resource Watch and Texans United intended to file suit under the Clean Water Act, the Endangered Species Act, and the National Environmental Policy Act if the corrective actions were not taken. Not only had wetlands been disturbed, but the whooping cranes and the piping plovers and the brown pelicans, plus five varieties of endangered sea turtles, could be threatened by the Formosa project. We were seeking to have all construction permits revoked and Formosa's construction shut down until Formosa agreed to do an environmental impact statement and the study was completed.

A number of people wandered in, and someone in the audience yelled about job losses over a few frazzling turtles, and Rick got up and said if there was any blame for job losses, the blame should be placed on the politicians and promoters who weren't honest about the problems associated with the company. The man who stood next was Formosa's cat-boned Taiwanese executive, and his voice sounded like rain on fish-house tin. "It is so unfortunate the plaintiffs are continuing to mislead the public with these unfounded charges. Our opponents have portrayed our company as less than concerned about the environment. Nothing can be further from the truth. Our present construction is in compliance with applicable environmental regulations, and we do not anticipate any halting of construction."

I walked to the microphone. "One of our biggest concerns is that all of the hundreds of millions of dollars that you have already spent constructing will prejudice the EPA's final decision on the permit. How is it fair to this community or this county if the EPA gives more weight to the fact that your whole expansion is already built and the workers hired?"

The Taiwanese man leaned forward and shrilled, "We are building *at risk!* It is our fortune we gamble with. The EPA can declare it null and void tomorrow."

The room had now acquired an entire Formosa workforce, and they were on the point of rising and walking out of the room. Most were the same type of men who had talked to me in their homes or sent me documents or called late at night about a release at the plant. They stood with hard eyes and arms folded, and they didn't care what I saw in their faces.

After the press conference was over I slipped into the bathroom and ran cold water over my face and talked a long and hard line to myself: *Don't you cry. Don't you cry. Nobody never said this was gonna be easy.* When I came out Blackburn was talking with Joe Wyatt and a reporter at the same time; Joe and Blackburn were animated and tossing their arms, and the reporter was hanging onto his microphone. Rick fumed in a corner and was getting redder by the minute. No one looked as I walked past and went outside to watch the high white smoke from a cooling tower drift in the wind.

That night I told myself I had hurled iron-old traditions as thick as my wrist long enough; I was going shrimping. Donna Sue could run the fish house by herself for a while. There weren't a lot of days left in the season, and Baby said, "Why are you concerned now?" I didn't explain. Didn't say no, no; instead I went to the porch and the babies piled on the swing, and fiddled with my hair.

I took two days off from the fish house and worked dragging one net off the *SeaBee* and hauling another on; then I switched try nets and did half a dozen other things to get the *SeaBee* ready for shrimping. That night I pulled the *SeaBee* over to the fish house and fueled and took on ice. At four the next morning a line of squalls out of the Gulf hit, and I sat in the kitchen with a cup of coffee and a filled thermos. I watched the rain through the window and listened to the wind howl around a corner. Thirty minutes later a shrimper called and said, "Diane, your boat is sinkin'. I'd get down here if I was you."

I hung up the phone and ran around the house, looking for a rain slicker and a water pump. Only now the pump was rusted and sat in a wet, sandy corner of the barn, half covered in a net.

I ran back into the house and slammed the screen door, and there standing on the kitchen table was Crockett, trying to reach the ceiling fan with a broom. I grabbed Crockett off the table and yelled upstairs to Baby that I was taking Crockett to the bay and the *SeaBee* was sinking.

It was near dawn and the sky looked like it had been rubbed with a wet fist. The van windows fogged up, so I rolled them down and Crockett clambered over me with bare, hard feet and stuck his head out the window. When I got to the docks, I could see the *SeaBee*'s stern level with the water. Nearby a truck was parked with a door flung open. A man was hunched over the engine, and when I got out of the van, he stood up and yelled something, then bent over the engine again. When I got on the boat, he stood up and we both went down below in the engine room.

"Girl, don't you have an automatic pump?" he said, "I looked all over and didn't see one. I tightened up your stuffing box there . . . that thing was loose as a goose. I come down a little while ago to check on my boat and I seen yours there. Guess it was that stuffing box. That and the rain and no automatic pump."

I said, I got an automatic pump. And that stuffing box wasn't leakin' last night when I repacked it. He said, Well, girl, you better get it looked at. Gonna find yourself sunk out there one of these days.

The shrimper stayed while I poked my hand at the bilge water, hunting for the water pump I knew I had. I found it eventually, lying on its side between two scuffords in the hull. I never found the wires connecting it to the battery. Now there was too much water in the boat—even for a working automatic pump—so I took Crockett and we drove all over a wet town, looking for a bigger pump. I talked to every shrimper who thought he might have one out in his barn or in the garage or maybe in the back end of his truck. Finally I talked a county worker into letting me borrow one from the county barn, and I spent my first shrimping morning pumping out the *SeaBee*.

18

Beauty Queens, Banquets, and Spies

She was a former beauty queen wanting cigarettes, and she stood on the back deck of the *SeaBee*, nervous as heck. Twice she threw her black head over her shoulder and asked, "Do you think anybody can see me?"

I said, No, no. Nobody cares you're out here. At least the shrimpers don't.

"The Chamber's gonna *kill* me. I know they are. . . . But I don't care. I *don't!* I'm sick of seeing them turn a blind eye to Formosa. Just bring in the jobs! Bring in the business! *Good God!* Give me a break! Give me a cigarette too. You got a cigarette?" She laughed again and the sun laid a heavy hand on her hair.

I told her it took guts for what she was doing. A lot of people walked on the other side of the street when they see me coming. One woman closed the doors to her café.

"Oh, I'm braver than *that*. I can speak my mind to our chamber president, Larry Robinson, anyhow. I told him the other night when this whole thing came up about giving a banquet for the Chairman to offset that fine they got from the EPA. . . . I said, 'What for? They deserved it, for Chrissakes!' Then on top of that, I hear Wang's bringing down a dozen Taiwanese reporters to see this little jewel of a plant he's got down here. What a laugh! What a big joke!"

"You ever think about taking that notion of giving Larry a piece of your mind a little further?"

"Oh, nooo," she said. "You're not getting me for that. I'm just delivering a little information. . . . Besides, somebody needs to spoil Larry's Chamber party."

She stayed for another twenty minutes, giving out the same warm energy I was sure she poured out everywhere. So she left unrecruited, and I walked to the fish house and called Blackburn about the Chairman's party and said I was going to do a counterdemonstration outside the banquet hall. Somebody needed to get information to those Taiwanese reporters so they didn't just get Formosa's side.

Blackburn wasn't happy. "Wilson, haven't I done enough? Isn't a lawsuit plenty? Why all this extra *extra*?"

"This isn't about you, Blackburn! This is about this county celebrating a polluter! Making like he's some kind of a movie star. And bringing all that press from Taiwan—what's that about? Maybe he's trying to build another chemical plant over there again."

"Well, I can see you're not going to listen to me. But I guess you'll call your lawyer when you're ready to get out of jail, won't you? You figure your ole lawyer can be handy then?"

"Maybe so. Maybe I'll call Rick too."

"Oh, hell, get him, then. It is about time Rick did something besides complain about lawyers who wanna be activists. Isn't that what he says?"

"Rick thinks you're doing a good job on the lawsuit."

"Oh, sure."

It took a whole afternoon to reach Rick. When I told him about the Taiwanese reporters and the celebration party in Port Lavaca, Rick said he'd had an interesting morning too. It wasn't just reporters the Chairman was bringing to Texas. About thirty or more Taiwanese officials were coming too.

"It seems Wang is trying to win home support for a seven-billion-dollar chemical complex in Taiwan. That last one he wanted to build got a lot of local farmers mad as hornets, and they put a quietus on it. Now I guess the Chairman thinks the situation's changed. A Taiwanese I talked to this morning said that the project Wang wants to build would increase Taiwan's chemical production over one hundred thirty percent. And that on an island that's already overwhelmed! Maybe he thinks he can convince the villagers and the government by showing them how wonderful his Texas plant is."

Rick said he couldn't help me with the demonstration for the Chamber party, but if I came to Houston he could at least help me get information to the Taiwanese officials flying in from Taiwan by way of Hawaii. We could also talk to a man who headed up a Taiwanese association for expatriates in the States.

So I did something I never did before. I drove in Houston traffic and rode the freeways begot by Houston. This begotten freeway ran past chemical plants and oil refineries and tanks and towers and pipes, and all plunked down on the Houston Ship Channel. But it didn't stop there. The tanks and chemical units and pipes in turn spilled out and gave birth to liquids and weird chemicals that filled the barges along the Houston Ship Channel and the stainless steel tanks of eighteen-wheelers that ran up and down the freeway. I rode the concrete ramps and the ten-lane roads, jam-packed between trucks loaded with ammonia and ethylene oxide and hydrogen sulfide and phosgene and nitrogen peroxide. The fumes rose off those tankers and drifted through my window and they stayed on my cheekbones like they owned 'em.

I found Rick and we drove six exits in the opposite direction to the office of a man named J. S. Chien. He had his own engineering company where he said he did well enough, but his real work was fighting for his countrymen in Taiwan.

"Isn't that right?" he said, and looked at me. "You don't forget your fisherfolks because you come to Houston or because you go to Washington. It is the same with me. And even though I will probably never be allowed to return to Taiwan—as a former dissident, the government will never allow me a visa—still, it does not make me any less Taiwanese." He shrugged his shoulders, and his wide mouth came together in a soft knot. "Ah, well . . . I can fight from Houston. Mister Rick fights from Houston. So I can fight from Houston."

Chien was part of a larger group of native Taiwanese who were fighting in exile for the environment of their homeland, and Formosa Plastic and Wang Yung-Ching were a part of that fight because of their enormous pollution over there.

"Constantly building! Wang buys land and builds another plant, then another. Always another. He lives in luxury in New Jersey, far from polluted Taiwan. So what does he care that the new plant he wishes to build could send hundreds of tons of toxins into the air and water every year? So very dangerous. A few years back an engineer struck a match for a cigarette, and vapor that had seeped up into the air from the contaminated groundwater exploded. Eighty-five percent of the engineer's skin was burnt off."

That incident was not uncommon. There were no groundwater pollution laws in Taiwan to protect the people. There was nothing to protect the water. Oil sludge content in Houchin groundwater was six thousand times the American standard!

"Can you see why we are so concerned? Taiwan has *enough*! *Enough production and enough pollution!*"

"But I thought the villagers fought Wang off!"

"They did!" he said. "The Ilan residents protested, and even the county commissioners denounced it. Wang just threatened to take his business to China, and the Taiwan government panicked and promised to find somewhere else for Wang."

Chien seemed apologetic and waved his hand towards the window. "The Chairman is part of your world now. In your Texas streets. That is too bad."

I felt unsophisticated, naïve. I didn't know enough of Houston to get onto its Gulf Freeway, but Rick was all business. He sat with a notebook on his knees and a nail-bitten hand on top, and he thumped his fingers impatiently. "So how many officials can we expect on this trip, Mister Chien?"

"Thirty-two, perhaps. That is unless they lose someone on the trip." Chien laughed and his mouth went smooth as a woman's. "Wang Yung-Ching has spies, but we have ours too."

"Because of your spies, you knew they were coming?" I asked.

"It is also how we know the itinerary. From Hawaii to Los Angeles. Then to Houston for one night. Then bused to Point Comfort. We have just now found out—through you—about the party being prepared. That part we did not know. Oh, it has been very sly. No one knew nothing. Even one of the Buddhist officials invited was taken to a temple before the trip and made to swear not to divulge one detail. Our spies tell us many things."

I was a Siamese twin to Chien's childlike delight of his spies. So I smiled at his smiles and laughed with his laughs.

Rick wanted details. Who was Chien's contact? When was he calling? What airport was the plane arriving at? Which hotel would the men be staying at? Then Rick turned to me and said, "How much material have you got with you? Any news clippings?"

"Our little lawsuit," I said.

"All right. We'll make copies at the office. Then we'll just wait 'em out. What time do you expect them, Mister Chien?"

Chien looked up from his chair. "Very late. By the time they land at the international airport and get their luggage and go downtown, it will at least be two A.M."

I called Baby and told him I was meeting a busload of Asian men at two in the morning at a hotel in Houston, and he said I needed to be given the Mother of the Year award, and he wouldn't be staying up and waiting, and if there was a door that could be locked, he would find it. So I wasn't just meeting men in hotels; I was making a marriage as stiff as a fence post.

Rick and I spent ten more hours together, and the high point was a restaurant in Houston where redfish, imported from God knows where, was on the menu. I was amazed how bones of a fish could end up in a dimly lit restaurant in Houston. One day it was Seadrift's fish bones and future, and the next day it was fishpond product, with me sitting on a red vinyl seat beside it.

After midnight we drove down a damp Houston street to the hotel. Nothing moved except eight skateboarders who came out of nowhere and skated down the middle of the street. We had a half hour to spare, so we got a corner of the lobby and went through our documents about a hundred times until we stacked them in a single pile in front of us and waited. Our plan was simple enough. Hand out the documents. We weren't going to protest or hold signs or block the way into the hotel. It was probably the most passive thing Rick had ever organized.

So when the bus arrived, we got up and went through the hotel's double glass doors and stood at the bus door. The bus door opened and two Taiwanese men got off, then looked at us standing not fifteen feet away and immediately got back on the bus. Then they shut the door, and everybody on the bus peered out the window as we looked back and waved our papers a couple of times.

After fifteen minutes of us standing there and them sitting and watching, the door cracked again and one man squeezed through and ran to the lobby. Then several more did the same thing. None took our papers. They looked at the documents we waved like it was fire from hell. Finally, in a rush of limbs and bags and averted eyes, the whole bus emptied, and it wasn't until Chien arrived with another Taiwanese man that we managed to talk with anyone at all.

"Formosa's spies are taking notes," Chien explained. "Whoever talks will have his name written down. We must wait until they go upstairs to their rooms. Then they will talk."

So we waited thirty minutes more. Then Chien and Rick and I sneaked from bedroom to bedroom and sat on hard beds and hard chairs, and in between we handed out our documents. In the early morning hotel hours we pressed our heads together and talked Taiwanese politics and clandestine meetings and the Chairman's coming and goings. It seemed dreamlike; somewhere between the yesterday of five kids and the now of the night hour. The first and second worlds had blurred so that I couldn't find the horizon dividing them.

Our talk was not so dreamy. One man sat in his shirtsleeves and his black wrinkled pants and said if there was a war they were fighting in Taiwan, then Wang Yung-Ching was the General Patton in it. This frugal Patton would sit in his company conference room with his frugal dollar-and-a-half lunch box and summon his executives and get from them what was Wang's goal in the first place: to know every detail of every operation, just as a general in a war would want to know every pothole and every blown bridge on his road to victory.

"It is no coincidence that the doctors at the Chang Gung hospital in Taiwan label the mysterious high incidence of stomach problems among Wang's top executives as the Formosa Plastic Syndrome. And as for his own children? The Chairman won't send them to American schools. He says they are not disciplined enough. No! Only English schools that are run like the military! The American schools are just more of that moral decadence he worries so much about. The minute you relax your grip or your hardworking habits—there it goes! The advancement stops! The profit stops! You are left behind!"

The man seemed tired and his shoulders slumped under his wrinkled shirt. He briefly touched the papers we had spread on the bed, and shook his head. Wang had met with five Kuomintang legislators in his home in New Jersey not long ago. He told them there were still many land plots that could be developed into petrochemical plants in Taiwan.

"The man never stops!" he said. "How many more plants can he build to choke our poor polluted island? It is so predictable. Your officials should have asked *our* opinion of Wang Yung-Ching first. Perhaps then it wouldn't have turned out the same for you and me."

He said the sixth naptha cracker plant that Wang wanted to build in Taiwan needed as much water per day as a city of a million and a half people. And water was already a serious problem in Taiwan. Then as the groundwater was depleted, the ground sank. In some places in West and South Taiwan, the ground had sunk so much that the whole first floors of buildings had sunk into the ground and the second floor was now the first.

Then as the rivers' levels grew less, the concentration of the pollution in the water increased, and when the first rains of the wet, stormy season came, all the heavy metals, such as mercury and arsenic and copper and lead, that had sunk to the bottom of the near-empty rivers during calm dry seasons were suddenly stirred up. People wondered why all the fish died after the first rains, but it wasn't really all that strange.

The man stopped talking and looked quietly at me. "There is only miles that separate us. You and I are much alike. We both fight for our homeland. Even when Wang Yung-Ching pays for my plane fare and pays for my lunch—even a visit to Disney World—still, I will fight. He has much money, but he cannot buy my heart. I know he cannot buy your heart either. So you see, we will win."

19

Raining on the Chairman's Parade

If I'd learned one thing, it was to keep the people who despised even the shadow you make on the sidewalk guessing. The next thing I learned was not to leave anything until mañana, because mañana was way too late. Donna Sue told Wally (the same man she said she'd see burning in hell before she'd talk to him again) that we were fixing to picket the Chairman. Then, Wally being the paid informant he was, I got only a half-day head start on a demonstration permit where I should have had a week.

I went to the Port Lavaca city manager first, and his face was white and cold, and his eyes were flounder eyes looking up from the mud of Lavaca Bay. He wasn't much help, and kept his words clipped and blunt and said things like, "I've got no earthly idea," or "You better check with someone else." When I asked him, "Well, who, then?" he said, "I've got no earthly idea."

I was barely out of the city manager's office before Donna Sue tracked me down and told me that thing about Wally knowing. And I said, "Well, then Formosa makes three."

So I had to move *faster* than a city manager and *faster* than Wally, and nothing moved faster than Wally. He had filed more twelfth-hour injunctions against Texas Parks and Wildlife's fishing regulations than any fisherman alive. And my permit wasn't even a piece of paper yet.

Hours later and after leaving a city lawyer's office with two pearly eyed looks on two lawyers' faces, I still had no paper. Only a vague "Okay, but you better keep your people behind the parking lot and not stepping on the path around the lighthouse, because if you do that, then you're gonna be obstructing the right-of-way of visitors who have come to see the lighthouse and *then* you could be arrested."

Wally had already arrived at the fish house. He didn't even let me get out of the van. He came across the road and slammed his fist on the hood. "You *can't* do this!" he yelled. "This is . . . *crazy!* Who do you think you are? *Protesting!*"

"Why, how do you think this country got anywhere? Because we said 'Pretty please'? *Heck, no!* This country's got a whole history of disobedience, and I'm about as American as your apple pie."

Wally shoved his face close to the window, and I could see where his neck was sweating and his scalp pink and wet from yelling at me. "Do you *know* how stupid you will look! A demonstration! Where? Are you gonna do it hangin' off all the cars that are gonna be comin' in? 'Cause *that's* what's gonna happen. Lots of cars! Lots! People *want* the Chairman. They *like* him over here!"

Then Wally threw his arms over his head. "All right! You've done it! You've left me no recourse. It ain't my fault no more. Don't blame me if the fishermen come down on you." He whirled in his smartly ironed khaki pants and stormed across the road and drove out of town.

I don't know what Wally did next after he drove out of town. Whatever it was, I was busy enough making phone calls and trying to find demonstrators. In between the planning, I drove to my momma's and picked up the babies and never asked her to be a protester. I knew better.

I stopped at the Western Auto to buy poster board and Magic Markers, and I put one kid on my hip and grabbed another by the hand when I went inside. To cut expenses, the owner had shut off the air-conditioning. Now the doors were wide open and the owner sat in a chair with the back leaned against a wall and the front legs up. His hair was nearly as black as mine, except it was straight and lay flat like it was painted on.

"What kinda flowers you want?" he said.

"Flowers for what?" I said.

"For that funeral yore fixin' to have," he said.

"Oh, folks have got high hopes," I said, and walked around to a wall of dusty bins with dustier merchandise. I picked out a couple of markers and a box of Crayolas for the kids and all the poster board he had.

Back at the fish house I turned the coffeepot on and turned five or six shrimp boxes upside down in the doorway to keep the babies in. Donna Sue went back and forth from her house to the fish house, once bringing a sack of mayonnaise sandwiches, and another time a jar of iced tea. Then she'd climb over the boxes (still in her rubber boots, even though she'd been home a dozen times) and drag out a wet rag and wipe down the kids. After about the fifth time of doing that, she turned and looked at me. "How many people you got?"

"Four or five. Then we got the kids. With everybody, I guess we got a dozen. Depends, though, on how cranky the babies get and how many of them might need naps."

"Get that Chamber woman. Wasn't she interested? Didn't she come over here and tell you the whole mess anyhow?"

"Larry Robinson keeps tellin' her trash. Says there's gonna be trouble. And if she wanted to come so bad, he would just get her a ticket for the inside shindig."

I didn't really care. Ten or one was the same difference to me. I'd do my demonstration no matter what, because I was staying on a path that was the purest and clearest road I'd ever seen.

Five hours before the demonstration, Wally proved someone can die without being a corpse. He flung himself into the fish house, and when he couldn't get through the door because of the piled-high shrimp boxes, he leaned over and waved a paper at me.

"Now! Do everything you want to do! Go ahead . . . but *it ain't gonna be our fault what happens!* This paper takes care of everything!"

I glanced up from the phone. "What is it?"

"It's a *disclaimer*! Formosa told their workers in *writing* not to lay one little finger on your crazy head. So you just go on ahead and let the chips fall where they may. *Legally* see whose fault it is."

"Wally . . ."

"Don't matter, don't matter," he said, and held the paper tight in his hand and high above his head. If I had touched a match to the paper, Wally would have went up in smoke. Then he flung himself out of the fish house and shouted something in the street when he left.

An hour later I found out what Wally hollered. It was retribution. Something out of a dark corner of Revelations. Then Doug Lynch called and said there was nothing dark about it at all. It was just a corner of the parking lot. They had already marked off an area for my demonstrators with yellow cop tape, and it was right next to the banquet hall where everything would be going on. I couldn't get any closer.

I said, "I thought the lawyers told me not to get on the parking lot over by y'all."

"Oh, you know lawyers. Everthing's gotta be just so-so with them.

This is *us*, Diane. We're clearing a little spot, and you can do all your protesting to your heart's content."

I didn't buy none of it. Leopards didn't change spots overnight, and neither did Doug Lynch. I just didn't have no place to go with my suspicions except head-on. I figured I'd find his marked-off area soon enough.

Then two hours before we left for Port Lavaca with ten demonstrators to my name, Joe Wyatt called and said the Chairman wanted to talk to me.

I said, "The *Chairman*?"

Joe said, "Yes! Yes! The Chairman!"

I said, "Why do I want to talk to the Chairman when I'm fixin' to demonstrate the fella?"

Joe said. "Don't you understand? The Chairman just doesn't talk to *anybody*! And he wants to talk to *you*!"

"I don't know about all this. I'll get back to you."

So I called Blackburn and told him I didn't want to meet with the Chairman. "All the talkin's been done," I said.

Blackburn said, "Listen, Wilson, you wanna know how to negotiate? You talk! You talk! You open your little mouth and you talk to the other fella. Besides, if you don't, then the Chairman's just going to tell the press you were unreasonable. You wouldn't talk to him."

"He just wants to stop me from demonstratin'!" I said. "Wally and Joe's been all over the county, talking with the fish houses and tellin' them I'm shutting down the bays. How do you like that? Those plants can damn well pollute, but *I'm* the one shutting down the bays just because I say something about the pollution! That's a kill-the-messenger thing if I ever saw one."

"Why, sure, Wilson. What do you expect? For them to welcome you in so you can shut down their private little projects? Hell, no. They're gonna fight you!"

After I finished with Blackburn, I looked over at Donna Sue and said, "Well, I guess we'll see the dang Chairman."

So me and Donna Sue drove over in silence, and it was hot, and when we went over the causeway the heat rode on the wind and got caught in our hair and blew our hair as wild as we felt. I didn't put my hand up to stop it. I was way past caring what I looked like, and figured if the Chairman could give his own executives stomachaches then I wasn't dressing up for mine.

When we got to Formosa's guesthouse, we got even quieter. We sat in the van in a cement parking lot and looked at the blocklike two-story building. I wasn't sure about the building. It was the most uninteresting and hot-looking block of cinder that I had ever seen. Joe had given me directions, but there was nothing on the building that said it was a guesthouse. Every window was covered with a hospital-white venetian blind. They could be killing cats behind those windows, for all I knew.

Then I figured lots of windows meant lots of rooms, so we walked down the sidewalk and past some burnt and whacked-at legustrum hedges that ran along the side. We went up the three cement steps to a heavy white door and went inside. It was air-conditioned, and could have been the hall of any hospital needing repainting. No pictures. No knickknacks. No furniture. Just cold, sterile air.

We stayed a minute, huddled in indecision, not knowing if we hadn't walked into the back door of somebody's business, when a Taiwanese man came around a corner with an armload of papers. He jumped when he saw us. He was in a suit without the coat and looked like that was the closest he ever got to undressed. Then something flashed across his face and he smiled and bowed and gestured with arms loaded down with papers.

"Come," he said. "Come. Come." Then he led us down the hall to a door and he opened it with one hand, still smiling, still dipping his head. "Yes, yes," he said. "It is all right. Come in. Come in." When we walked in, the man shut the door and left.

So with three hours left to an afternoon, we sat in a room that was nearly as impressive as any twenty-five-dollar hotel room I had ever seen. But instead of a bed and mattress, we had three couches. The couches filled up one whole white-looking wall. Couch after couch after couch, and every couch was different. The only thing they had in common was that they were all the same color. Same as the walls. Same as two plastic knickknacks on the wall with fake green fern sticking out. It made me dizzy, so I sat down near the only other piece of furniture in the room: a hard blue Formica dinner table. I decided we were either in a storage room or we were fixing to be served dinner. To make sure I didn't have to eat, I scooted back my chair and waited.

Donna Sue fumed in silence. She crossed everything she could cross, then uncrossed them.

When I thought we had waited long enough, a side door opened and a fiftyish woman walked in. She had smooth black hair pulled back in a hard bun, and she wore a dark blue silk dress. She smiled and nodded her shiny black head a couple of times and asked if we wanted tea. I said yes, and Donna Sue looked up, said no, then looked off again.

The woman's face was absolutely calm and absolutely beautiful, and even when Donna Sue said no the woman acted like she said yes. Then she left, and when she came back she brought three glasses of iced tea and a sullen teenage girl.

They both sat at the table and the older woman said nothing and held her two white hands in her lap, and the young girl looked over now and then and acted like she'd like to put arsenic in my tea glass if I'd let her. We were probably the four quietest women ever stuck together in a room.

The Chairman arrived like any old king who wouldn't smile and everyone died until he did. He was dressed in hard gray from the top of his iron-colored hair all the way down to his iron shoes. And he wasn't happy, or else his steely gray insides had declared our whole meeting silly. Even when he looked at his wife he still didn't smile.

Then Jack Wu entered, as shiny as a clear channel on an old black-and-white TV set. He was the interpreter and explained in a cold and prissy voice that the Chairman spoke very little English. "A few words. Words like *welcome* and *no problem*. Things like that. The Chairman's rise from poverty to riches has required a concentration that does not leave much time for book learning. I'm sure you understand."

When Jack turned and said something to the Chairman, the Chairman nodded his coiffed sphinx head. I could see there wasn't gonna be no digging in that face. I'd find concrete easier. So I sat in my chair, not knowing which man I was supposed to talk to, and looked half at Jack and half at the Chairman. Jack said the Chairman wanted to know what I wanted. What did *I* want? And I had thirty minutes to tell it. How high did they want me to go? How many moons did I have to climb?

I looked at the Chairman and sighed. I wasn't mad or aggravated. I was just worn out with the question. How do you explain a bay and the pain and dying of a town? How to talk of fisherman? Or Formosa's own workers? What words make invisible worlds seen and not sound like pure nonsense and thrown out faster than bad milk thrown from a baby's bottle?

The words came hard and fought and bled red on the floor. The storage room became a birthing room. I was glad there wasn't a mirror reflecting faces. But I knew what Donna Sue would say. Pained or not, she'd say the same thing she said when Deputy Dawg went on trial in a small dark courtroom of a justice of the peace's office and Deputy Dawg insisted on telling his story. She said, "Just let him do it. He's gotta do it. Ain't nothin' else to be done." I forgot what all happened in that JP's office, but I know he lost his shrimp and net and gained a five-hundred-dollar fine.

In my two hours of talking, I didn't know what all I lost, but I sure knew I gained nothing. I knew that look on Jack Wu's face. It was a polite Oriental expression saying, *Hurry up and shut up.* I didn't know what the Chairman thought 'cause he never looked at me. Was it a deliberate snub or just common Asian courtesy? Maybe he was disciplined enough that he could sleep with his eyes wide open, and the whole point of the meeting was to make me late for a demonstration.

The ice in the tea glass was gone, and Donna Sue wasn't even pretending she wasn't aggravated anymore. I wasn't surprised when she whirled her legs out of their locked position, slammed them hard on the floor, then looked at her watch. Then she punched me hard on the arm.

"I know, I know," I said, and put my hand in the air. Suddenly Jack perked up and his eyes got blacker than before and he leaned and said something to the Chairman, and the Chairman leaned and said something back. Then Jack, rod straight in his hard aluminum chair, said the Chairman wanted to invite me to see his chemical plants in Delaware and Louisiana. Perhaps Taiwan. Maybe then I could see how well the Chairman handled his operations.

"There is such a lack of communications in the Texas plant," he said. "All the Chairman wants to do is fix the problem and have all of these sad, sad environmental issues go away. There is nothing the Chairman would like better. So if you can be patient, you will see how Formosa's other facilities are run. Then you might change your mind? You might be willing to go to Delaware and to other places? The Chairman is a *very* gracious host."

I looked at the Chairman, but that wasn't what his face said. His face said I was a woman in a cotton dress, standing at a door, and the door would open if I wanted it to. I didn't need to break the door down. The door was gonna open, and I wasn't the first one he had let in neither. No. The Chairman had already let in forty-eight county citizens for an eight-day tour of Taiwan. Judges and mayors and school board members and businessmen and newspaper editors and navigation-district representatives and county commissioners. Wives and friends. An information-gathering tour, paid for by Formosa, where the most deserving came home carrying Wang Yung-Ching's mementos from Taiwan. Rolex watches and fine china.

I looked carefully at Jack, then at the Chairman, who for the first time was openly watching me with dark, hooded eyes. I said nothing for a minute, then as clear as I could, I said, "I can't accept the offer. I have more than I can bear to see right here in Texas."

I don't remember what else was said. We shook hands with everybody. The Chairman's handshake was surprisingly tiny, small as his beautiful wife's. We kept moving until we were out in the parking lot.

The time we had lost suddenly became clear. The sun was lower and Formosa's plant shift had ended and another was beginning, so when we went over the causeway, hundreds of workers were with us. We drove past the lighthouse and the city swimming pool and stopped at the Bauer Community Center. Our area was roped off just like Doug Lynch said it would be, only across from it and four times what we had was another roped-off area.

"*That* don't look good," Donna Sue said. She slid out of the van with me and came to where I started making protest signs on the hood.

She pointed at a carload of men leaving and the back window full of construction hard hats. "Did you see that?" she said.

"Sure I saw that. They want to tear our heads off and stuff 'em in their hats."

"You figure they're coming back?"

"Figure they will. And probably got a lot more where they're coming from."

I was right. By the time I finished printing six or seven signs, a large white storage van pulled into the parking lot across from us and unfolded one side into an instant concession stand with upright racks and rows and rows of potato chips and candy bars and salted nuts.

Five or six little black levers ran along the edge and made a Coke bar to pour Cokes and Dr Peppers and Pepsis to whoever wanted them. A huge blue sign with white letters was on the van's other side and it read: THANK YOU, CHAIRMAN WANG AND FORMOSA PLASTICS FOR THE JOB OPPORTUNITIES!! I was dumbstruck, so I stood with my black marker and my protest signs and didn't move one inch towards our roped-off area.

Then the side parking lot got a lot busier and started filling up with dozens and dozens of trucks. Men got out in hard hats and dirty jeans and coveralls, and their shirtsleeves were rolled up and their boots were hard looking and big as mountains. They moved slow, heads bent and shoulders rounded, and looked like they might've been remembering where they put that last beer or where that last gun was fired. Suddenly, as though some agreed-upon magic number of tired workers had been reached, they moved in a fluid motion to the roped-off area across from us.

Donna Sue said, "I'm gonna call the cops. I know somebody—and he better come." She threw my documents and the protest signs out of the van and drove off. I stayed a second, but finally ran out of things to do that could keep me out of our roped-off area, so I picked up the documents and shoved more signs underneath my arm, and as casually as I could, I walked to our area. Just my walk seemed to make the men mad. Some of them yelled and walked to the rope line and shoved on it.

I stopped and looked at them. All right. So that was how it was. This was where they wanted to take it. There were thirty or forty feet of pavement between us, and the only thing in the middle was a man in a business suit with a video camera, and it was pointed directly at me.

I don't know who Donna Sue hoped to save with her county constable, but in ten minutes' time, he was the second man in the middle. Then I quit counting. Three police cars showed up with lights flashing, then more cars, and none were people I knew. The policemen strolled up like they knew me; men in dark uniforms sayin', "Everything all right, miss? No trouble yet?"

I wasn't looking for nobody to save me from the workers! Somehow it had gotten twisted and the War with the Chairman had switched to the War with the Workers. I stood watching the night get closer and the bay get darker as more and more cars piled into the parking lot, and every time I tried to concentrate on the protest, a vast irony overwhelmed me: elected officials in fine suits and women in satin gowns getting out of expensive cars in a parking lot where all around were the working-class poor with dirty hands, protecting the guests from me. On their way to the banquet hall, invited couples sometimes stopped—a woman long enough to touch her hair or a man the hood of his car (once and briefly, like a man touches a woman's neck). Then both of them would walk fast past the ropes, eyes averted, and through the double glass doors of the Bauer Community Center.

When I looked at the workers gesturing and shouting at me, I thought, *Did you see that couple?* But I figured they didn't. Why else were they on the opposite side of a rope if it wasn't because they didn't understand or couldn't see what marched between us?

Later my troops arrived. Kathy showed up in her old pale Oldsmobile with a kid in every window. Some were hers and some were mine, and counting them and the couple of senior citizens and tired fishermen, we had twelve demonstrators. I figured there were three hundred construction workers on the other side. I stood at the edge of the rope with my documents and my babies and tried to pass out information to anybody who would stop. None would, and after a while nobody would even walk close to our roped-off area. Donna Sue was our road warrior–sage, and she punched me on the arm and pointed with her finger. "Don'tcha see? They're goin' through that side door there."

They were, all right. People were pulling up in their cars to a far parking lot, getting out, and walking as fast as their fine suits or their floor-length gowns would allow. A few cars didn't even stop, but drove up to the side entrance, dropped off a woman or two, then sped off.

That side-door entrance was just another thing I hadn't planned on, and the demonstration was now about the biggest unplanned thing I had ever done. It was only the sheer audacity of this protest that rattled anybody at all. That and the fear I might do something *worse*. I could see their fear clear as rainwater on glass. "Lord! She'll do anything! Anything!" That was how I realized the power of action. Didn't matter what kind. Planned, unplanned, misbegotten, undone. Action could make you believe. Actions could make heroes of us all just by saying "It is so." No wonder the Bible was filled with such terrible actions.

So I forgot who I was and stood in a parking lot and watched a thing unfold. Behind the glass doors of the community center, a mariachi band strolled between the guests. Dark Spanish women, with pretty skirts furled and their hands held high, advanced with erotic intensity, and men sang and strummed guitars hanging from wide red bands around their necks. Sometimes a door would open and a lost chord from a Spanish song would trail out like smoke escaping from a fire.

Then Senator Armbrister walked out to our roped area and he was smiling, and he came up to Donna Sue and me and said, "How's my girls?"

He put an arm on both our shoulders and didn't look rushed and didn't look fake, but stood, leisurely and effortlessly. A handsome man and a popular senator. I liked him too. I knew what side he was on, but I didn't hold it against him. I knew him back when he was just a young cop from Victoria and he brought down his pretty wife and family to the dirty old fish house so he could talk to the fishermen about why he was running for representative, the first statewide office he won. Tonight he was Formosa's Master of Ceremonies, and in front of five hundred strong he would introduce the Chairman and say, "Here is the man that is saving this tri-county area!"

The senator blew us some kisses and smiled a couple of times (and probably meant it too), then he quit and walked past the ropes and never turned again.

All I wanted was the day to finish what it was doing and for the night to get black. It was then that my ex–beauty queen showed up. She slid under the ropes and stood beside me. She had stayed undecided and afraid at home. Should she come? Should she stay? Then Larry called and told her, "Go see your little protester friends if you want to! They aren't *nothing* compared to Formosa's side. There are enough workers paid overtime for what we wanted. So go on! We've pulled their little claws, and they can't even meow now."

So she came, and I think I smiled. I might have said a word or two. I had Crockett by one hand and a handful of documents in the other, and almost casual, almost asleep, I turned my back on the workers and looked past the lighthouse and past the swimming pool and watched muddy Lavaca Bay do absolutely nothing. Then I turned back and saw the causeway and saw what must be the Chairman. Seven black limousines (three preceding and three following, and one odd limousine in the middle) had their headlights on and little flags on their hoods, and they came at a measured pace straight over the causeway, not moving fast and not moving slow, just moving at a middle speed only a president or a foreign king would. And just slow enough for people to notice.

The cars moved together across the causeway, down the highway, and into the community center parking lot. Then two things happened: Six cars split off from the procession, and the Chairman's limousine moved to the covered side entrance of the building. Fifty or sixty Taiwanese men in dark suits ran to the car and surrounded it, chanting, "Formosa, Formosa, Formosa." There they remained, chanting and bowing, even while the car stopped. I forgot how long I stood watching that scene. It was long after the Chairman got out of his limousine and went inside and the construction workers climbed into their trucks in their heavy boots and left. The concession van packed up its peanuts and Coke and drove off. The mariachi band disappeared from behind the glass doors, and Kathy took a disgusted Donna Sue home. I was left with the babies and my girls and the ropes. The older girls sat barefooted on the cement parking lot, their shoes long gone, and they quietly complained.

What subtle plotting and politics were going on inside that building? I didn't know and I didn't care. I was washed out and done in. I pulled the babies and the girls to the van and was getting inside when a bevy of eager boy reporters, just like Clark Kent's redheaded sidekick, rushed to the van door.

They were the reporters from Taiwan and wanted to know why I had refused the Chairman's gracious offer. Wang had briefed them on our conversation earlier, and the reporters were puzzled. Why did I refuse? Wasn't I seeking answers to my questions? Did I simply want to fight and that was all?

It was dark, and I looked at the young confusion at my window and felt suddenly very tired. No, I said. It is not that. I am a mother and a shrimper. I don't have *time* to fight. It is the bay I care about. The bay and the water and fishermen's lives. Workers in the plant too.

"You're a momma," they said. "A momma. And a shrimper."

Sure, I said. And that wasn't all. There were a lot of violations that Formosa had committed. They had just received one of the highest penalties the EPA had ever given. Almost nine million dollars.

No, no, no, they said. The Chairman had said he had taken care of the EPA. They were not to worry. No problem.

I shook my head, sad that the boy reporters were so mistaken. I passed out my documents and left the parking lot.

Later I found out *I* was the one that didn't understand. I was the one that couldn't see the light. Donna Sue read it first. Then she said, "Yez, sirree. Pretty damn stupid."

"Just read it," I said.

So she read the paper and twisted her mouth so hard I couldn't recognize it. The Chairman had taken care of the EPA. No problem. No problem. The nearly nine-million-dollar penalty had been slashed in half, and Formosa said they neither admitted nor denied the charges in the EPA order. In fact, they welcomed the settlement.

20

A Hydrochloric Cloud;
a Worker Talks

Doomsday don't always stay doomsday. And sometimes it gets reported by the press. For a few days after the four million dollars were whacked from Formosa's penalty by the EPA, it was. A reporter from Houston wanted to know what I thought about Formosa giving campaign funds to U.S. Senator Gramm, the man who appointed his former campaign advisor to the head of the EPA Region 6, and who was now the final authority on Formosa's penalty and all their permits.

I replied that Phil Gramm had been real helpful to Formosa and he'd been real helpful to the EPA administrator and the administrator had been real helpful to Formosa, but none of them had been helpful to us. Then a San Antonio editorial writer said it "appeared" that the Gramm contribution was an attempt to purchase political influence, and he hoped that EPA Administrator Layton did what was right for Texas. There was no good reason for the EPA to reduce Formosa's fine.

Gramm's press secretary said he wasn't familiar with the Formosa-connected campaign contributions, and if anyone thought that Senator Gramm would interfere in a decision of that sort, then they were either deluded or smoking them funny cigarettes.

This went on for a while: bare-boned politics careening through the county. I got a dozen calls from Washington reporters thrilled to death with all the zany politics in Texas. Why, it was *crazy!* Those political footprints were clear enough that a blind man could follow them. They just wished they were down there in the middle of it.

I was used to the cash flow business. It was old hat now. Some had money and some didn't. The rich got richer, and the poor went downhill. I believed it was even in the Bible somewhere, and more than likely some part of a Pentecostal Sunday sermon I heard. How else can you console people except make it biblical, make it inevitable? I was tired of it being local newspaper headlines, though. I was tired of Formosa's smiley executive faces on the front page of the local newspaper, handing out typewriters to the libraries and T-shirts to the kiddies and money to the police department to buy cars and money to the county and city EMS to buy defibrillators. They sponsored health fairs and Fish-o-rees and Boy Scout can recycling. They fixed the roof on the local Port Lavaca theater to provide "spiritual happiness to the people," and gave banquets to groups like Ducks Unlimited to save the waterfowl. They approved an eighteen-hole golf course to wind through a housing development, and in a partnership with an energy corporation and Formosa subsidiary, they created fifteen acres of marsh habitat for the world's only breeding population of wild whooping cranes.

Then, as an unprecedented door prize at a Sunday-night supper, Wang announced he would donate five hundred thousand dollars each to the Memorial Medical Center in Port Lavaca and the Edna Independent School District, and would endow a one-million-dollar trust fund to aid religious programs in Calhoun, Jackson, and Victoria counties.

Formosa was everywhere and into everything, so the question became if my house was empty and the lights infrequent and remote, was it because I was a heretic in the religon of Formosa and the rest of the county was on Formosa's milk wagon, going to a plastic gotdam heaven?

One hot, muggy night I dreamed. A kamikaze pilot with a leather flight hat around his head and goggles around his flashing eyes dropped something terrible from the skies. Then the terrible thing became something else—a fog that covered and scorched the ground. I awoke from my dream and told myself I would take it to Kathy. Let her diagnose it, from her Oldsmobile car, like some doctor of dreams. But I didn't have time, because that night a worker called and wouldn't give his name. His name didn't matter, he said. He wanted to let me know that something bad was going on at Formosa. It might be hydrochloric acid. He was in the cloud at the plant and his throat was burning. He didn't know for sure what it was, but the plant had disappeared in it.

So I made two calls. I called the twenty-four-hour EPA hotline and the state hotlines and I told them if they hadn't heard about a Formosa release yet, they were hearin' it now and they might oughta check on it.

As acid clouds go, this one had sprouted suddenly from rusting bolts and a block valve in the vinyl chloride monomer unit in the old portion of Formosa. Like a seed flowering in a rush, it tumbled gate and sod in its unbridled hurry to show itself: 10,370 pounds of a gaseous hydrochloric flower.

The flower pulsed and advanced, pulsed and advanced—a chemical equivalent of the real thing. Cattle bawled and ran wild in the fields. A field man at Formosa's tank farm saw the cloud and got in his truck and drove to the leak. There he parked and watched from inside the cab. Finally he got out and started hooking up nitrogen and water hoses to spray at the erupting pump, but that wouldn't work because the amount of hydrochloric acid gas pouring out was too great. So the worker put on a breathing air pack and tried to close a block valve to isolate the leak. Nearby a worker delivering sample bottles to the incinerator area came out of the control room and saw the cloud. He ran towards the cloud, and when the fog lifted for a brief second, he saw the worker trying to the close a valve. He ran to the the nitrogen hose and tried to blow the vapors away while the first worker stayed on the valve.

Then another worker stumbled upon the two and became concerned over their safety. He tried several times to pull back the worker trying to shut off the valve. "Don't do it!" he said. "Wait until we can get full enclosure suits to protect ourselves. Let that pressure come down on that vessel!"

A passing police car noticed the cloud and stopped long enough to announce the release over the police scanner. Then the county judge, standing in his pajamas in his home in nearby Port Lavaca, looked out the bay window overlooking Lavaca Bay and saw the cloud. A short time later he heard the alert over the police radio. He said later that he attempted to get more information on the release, but he could never get enough to determine whether an evacuation was necessary or not.

A seven-mile section of highway running past the plant was closed down, and seven miles from the scene a man sat in an air-conditioned car, waiting. His eyes smarted and his throat hurt. He saw a security man sitting in a truck off the side of the road, and he pulled up to him and asked him if he knew what was being released. Should he just stay there in his car and wait, or would it be better if he just turned around and went back?

The security man looked at him and said, "Man, I ain't got no idea."

A half mile downwind from the plant, a woman received a call from her daughter saying she had seen a dark cloud coming from Formosa and was calling to warn them. She had no idea what it was, but they better get out quick.

The husband grabbed a video recorder and went outside in the dark yard and filmed the cloud moving across their ranch. Normally thousands of bright lights coming from Formosa were clearly visible from their home, but tonight there were no lights. They had disappeared, and only a whitish cloud remained. As the man recorded the huge fog rolling into his yard, his throat and mouth began to burn and he raised his shirt and held it against his mouth. Slowly the lens on the recorder clouded and the man used his shirt to wipe the lens. Then the plume enveloped him.

Nearly an hour after the release, the Calhoun County Emergency Management Coordinator left a message on Formosa's neighbors' answering machine. They should evacuate immediately.

Later a volunteer fireman sent to the scene from Port Lavaca called his wife and said, "Honey, what's HCL?"

The next day in Point Comfort, the incident came home to roost. Formosa issued a statement saying that the plant had a release of hydrochloric acid that reacted with the high humidity in the air to form a cloud that the wind carried north and away from the nearby community. The gas dissipated by late evening.

The company said 727 gallons of HCL acid were released when bolts let go on a plug valve, but at no time was Formosa unaware of the release, and residents in the path of the release were phoned by the Formosa Plastics Security Department within five minutes of the release.

Within the dugout of the plant, it was another story. Boys, boys, boys! Don'tcha know this kind of thing just won't fly? Where's your heads, boys? First, we've got to upgrade all those block valves and all those bolts. Then we've got to have full enclosure suits in the VCM room, and if we *don't* have 'em, well, fellas, we've gotta *get 'em*! Plus we've got to get safety out here to train you boys on how to use the things.

Second, we need more air packs in the control room. And for God's sake, don'tcha think we need a control-room breathing air system that's functional? What's the matter with a little function? Tell me that!

Now, the third thing we need is to let security hear the emergency alarm system! How is security gonna know to take incoming calls from the mayor and the EPA if they don't even know there's an emergency? You don't want 'em knowing it just 'cause they happened to look out the window and seen the damn thing comin', do you?

A couple of personal items, here, fellas: We don't want the lab personnel driving their vehicles to the gate when they're evacuating the plant, and we sure don't need unauthorized people driving vehicles around the vapor-release area. That's all, and let's don't do this again, okay?

That did seem to be all of it. A few days after the incident county and city officials met with Formosa, and the mayor issued a statement saying they had received a positive response from the plant manager and now everybody just had to wait and see how it worked out. It wasn't going to do any good to call names and point fingers, because nothing would be accomplished that way. After all, the citizens had to work with Formosa. They were their closest neighbors.

The agencies were not so cheery-eyed. An EPA spokesman said they were concerned that the incident was not reported to them until twenty hours after it happened. Regulations requiring industries to report their leaks immediately was interpreted by some courts to mean within one hour and *not* twenty hours.

Two weeks later the state Air Control Board wrote a letter to the company, saying an investigation conducted after the HCL release confirmed a nuisance condition had existed and that Formosa should call the office to arrange a mutually agreeable date and time for a formal enforcement conference. A full five months later Formosa was fined twenty thousand dollars—a fraction of the money that a single unit at Formosa made in a single day.

Nothing came of an "unofficial" report from the sales representative of the valve-manufacturing company, who said he warned Formosa that the valve wouldn't work. The sales representative had been concerned enough over the valve malfunctioning that he had called a local citizen and the citizen called me, and I called the EPA investigator, and the EPA investigator said he'd look into it, but it really wasn't his jurisdiction.

So it was obscure information I was trafficking in. I took notes and kept files and talked to anybody who would talk to me. I even followed one phone call to a man's house in a high, dry field of corn, and he showed me the window where aliens were taping his brain waves. I was worse than a pack rat dealing in tinfoil, and figured soon I'd be stacking newspapers in the hall and marking my path with coffee stains.

I had two shrimp boxes completely full of Formosa's violations and inspection reports and obscure reports filed by even more obscure companies. Subcontractors of subcontractors sent by the EPA to do on-site inspection. The reports were meant for burial. Formosa claimed they'd never heard of them. Never saw the inspectors. Never saw the file. Sometimes one paragraph from the report was enough— but there were hundreds. Chromate water discharged to surface waters. Release of untreated process water containing high concentrations of ethylene dichloride, vinyl chloride, and other chlorinated organic compounds to Cox's Creek. One report noted a green, bubbly material flowing off Formosa's site under Highway 35.

The reports didn't make headlines in a paper. They were only notes in a dead file in Austin or buried on some microfilm in a vault in Dallas. I argued once with the plant manager, saying there wasn't a fair thing about it. A man could make the arrest column in the local newspaper any day of the week for running his truck with expired license plates or no insurance, but let a chemical company, half a mile wide and with a thousand unknown chemicals zipping through their pipes, release eighty tons of a baby-aborting chemical into his neighbor's backyard, and it would be lucky if it made a note in a report. The plant manager sounded startled over the phone. "Good God!" he said. "Of course we *can't* put that type of information in the paper. Do you want old Mister Weaver across the street to have a heart attack?"

With all my blue shrimp boxes, I figured myself a walking encyclopedia on Formosa. I knew more about Formosa than Formosa knew about themselves, and was beginning to think it was no wonder that Fred Olneck or Joe Wyatt or Wally called with no other purpose than to pry information out of my shrimp files. I was better than a private eye, and they didn't even have to pay for it.

Some information I didn't mind telling Formosa. Old press releases. Proposed dam projects and their second stages. Even a chemical release I didn't mind divulging if Formosa already knew but just couldn't settle on how big it was. Was it an insignificant release or not? Was it a pinhole or big as your fist? Formosa was just doing a little troubleshooting, was all. They were thinking: Should they report a release as a half pound when they knew I had talked to the worker and knew it was a couple of hundred pounds? How much trouble was out there?

In late August, when all the flowers were wilting on the bougainvillea bush and the peaches lay rotten underfoot, I learned the rock-bottom of a worker's despair. This time it was a supervisor. He needed to talk. He had talked with everyone there was to talk with, and I was the only one left. Him and his gun would show up at the fish house if I waited around long enough for him to get there.

So I waited until dark, and when he pulled his truck along the side of the fish house and came through the back door, I could see his hands shaking. He was dark-haired and young; a long-legged man with a button-down shirt. His name was Dale and he was head of Formosa's security. Before that he had had a stint as a cop and a little plant work. He had lived in Point Comfort for a while, but after the hydrochloric release, both he and his dog got sick and they had moved.

He started out in safety at Formosa and said he was given no safety training. He was told he didn't need it. He was at the plant during a shutdown when a huge leak of Freon in the refrigeration unit across from VCM was sent into the atmosphere. The man in safety who tried to shut it down had his hands freeze to the valve.

That first winter he had seen blue barrels from the VCM unit being hauled in a truck and dumped into the creek behind the plant. "It was either excess or contaminated vinyl chloride from that area," he said, "but they told me it wouldn't hurt nothing. They didn't like dumping in the ditches because the Water Commission tested the ditches."

Then Dale stopped and leaned his head on the fish-house wall like he was fashioning some phrase in his head to make me believe his story more. I *knew* exactly what he was doing. I had done it myself when I talked to reporters about horrendous incidents and had to watch the disbelief growing, minute by minute, on their faces.

Dale's hand trembled on his knee, and he picked it up and laughed. "I'm shaking. I can feel it clear inside my head." Then he started talking. He had been in Regulatory Affairs for a while, and knew Fred and the new plant manager that had been hired after Formosa had started having problems again. The two previous plant managers had been given different positions. Heck, he thought Larry Peyton was the third plant manager. But still, the problems continued, so those two, Larry and Fred, started going into the plant and taking pictures. They thought maybe there was some kind of obstacle in the regular channel of communication, and their intent with the pictures was to go around the block and take it directly to the Chairman's daughter, Susan Wang. But then somebody put *them* off-limits from the plant.

But his job was security, and that was his real concern. He had noticed for a while that a huge profit had been going to a security company that Formosa had contracted. Triple D Security.

He said, "Normally a contract will go to the lowest bidders, but this company had one of the highest bids, and still Formosa gave them the contract."

Then too, the security company hadn't had a competitive bid in a long time, and by all appearances it looked like they got whatever they asked for. He said he thought it was part of his job to notice things like that. So he did some figuring on his own.

"What it boiled down to was, by eliminating Triple D Security, Formosa could not only save nearly a hundred thousand dollars a year, but the employees would receive full benefits and this would attract better-qualified personnel and cut down on turnover. Coemployment litigation would probably cease. *That* was what I thought."

He sent his report and recommendations on the security contract to the corporate headquarters in New Jersey. Two weeks later a personal and confidential memorandum from New Jersey arrived, acknowledging that one of the main problems with the high cost of security in Texas was that one local company had had the contract for a very long time. The memo said it turned out that the local security firm, Triple D, was in fact one of the very high bids, and there had been no competitive bidding for a while. The memo agreed with everything he had found. However, the memo said, it turned out that the security company was owned or managed by Ken Armbrister, at the time the Texas state representative for the area, and because of the sensitivity of dropping the contract with him, Susan Wang, the Chairman's daughter, had instructed that Formosa hold and do nothing for a while. It was her opinion that dropping the contract would only aggravate Formosa's relationship with the individual.

"That memo implied that Formosa was paying off a senator with a lucrative contract, and everybody knew it. Formosa knew it. New Jersey knew it. Susan Wang knew it."

Then he did something stupid. He took the memorandums and his report to Jack Wu's office and told him it was wrong, especially when they were paying for sloppy work, and much cheaper and more efficient work was available. He told Jack Wu he was going to expose the deal with the senator. Jack wanted to know how many copies of the documents he had, and Dale told him he had the one he saw there, plus another one at home.

"That's when Jack got mad and jumped up and slammed his fist on the desk. I thought he was gonna climb on the desk. Then Jack said, 'This plant is going to be built if you're dead or alive. And I can arrange your death!'"

Dale said, "I nearly cried. You ever got so scared that you *cried*?"

He said after that threat he left Jack's office immediately and drove to Port Lavaca, thinking he needed to talk to somebody in law enforcement. But there was Jack Wu, following him over the causeway. "I was scared shitless. I didn't know if Jack was coming after me then or what. Then when I got to the sheriff's office, I went in one door and Jack went in the other."

Dale said he talked with the sheriff's department, but he was told not to expose the deal with Formosa and the senator. The sheriff was real tight with Jack Wu, and besides, the sheriff's department wanted a computer system from Formosa.

Next he went to the district attorney's office and talked with some official there. It was pretty much the same thing. He was told the D.A.'s office was reluctant to do anything about Formosa. They had even been reluctant to press charges against Formosa when they had their big hydrochloric acid release earlier and shut down all the roads. The district attorney had given some bullcrap excuse to the public that it would cost the county too much money to prosecute, but the plain truth was, he was scared.

Dale said he knew his options were running out. Who else was there left to call except the Texas Rangers? He got the number of a Texas Ranger located in Victoria and called the man on his truck phone.

"The Texas Ranger said to call him again at his office 'cause he didn't want to talk on his car phone, but he was already starting to sound weird and strange when I started talking about Formosa and the senator. I figured he was wanting to have my call set up so he could tape me. . . . So I taped *him*. Now there's two of us with that phone conversation."

Dale smiled, but his lips hardly cleared his teeth. "You want to hear the tape? I got it out in the glove compartment, right next to my gun."

So we went outside and got into his truck with the padded upholstery and the thick dashboard. I patted the leather seat like it was a fat doe-eyed cow, and Dale laughed and reached over me and into the glove compartment. He removed his gun, then pulled out the tape. "I know," he said. "The money's good. That's what pulls everybody in."

I leaned forward while Dale shoved in the tape. It wasn't a long tape, and the ranger's voice didn't sound alarmed or even concerned. A state senator with a lucrative contract with a chemical company doing business and seeking permits from the state? Why, that was just good business sense. It might be unethical, but it probably wasn't illegal. And as for Jack Wu's threat—was that *really* what it was? It's just one man's word against the other's. If Dale didn't like the job, he should leave. Get over it or get gone.

The tape ran out and we sat, saying nothing. I had never heard a live Texas Ranger saying *anything* before, much less say what he had, so when Dale turned, it took a minute to focus on him and not the Texas Ranger still in the tape deck. But I don't think Dale saw me neither. He pointed causally to the gun that was laying on the seat between us and said, "This is the next thing left after you."

21

Kickbacks Paid;
Internal Memos Conveyed

I was a cedar pole stuck in the mud alongside a riverbank, measuring the rise and fall of the bizarre happenings in the county, and the security man was a high-water mark. He was like a bad B movie where you have twenty-four hours to save the planet and nobody believes a word you say. It was an old, old story about the planet going down.

Still, I had a skinny avenue to take my case before the governor's office. The union secretary in Texas City had a lawyer friend that had a favor owed him because of his campaign contributions to the governor, so after much haggling and letters going back and forth, five of us, armed with information, got an audience with Governor Ann Richards's office—only not with the governor.

The meeting didn't go well. The lawyer was aggravated he hadn't got his meeting with the governor, even though Formosa had earlier in the week. So the man told the governor's press secretary as much, and the press secretary just gave him one of her netherworld looks and said, Why, we aren't all that far off from the governor's office. Why, if she leaned back hard enough in her office chair and if the door was open, she could probably point it out.

I wasn't aggravated. I was just confused. I couldn't figure why the governor's representative didn't take notes while we talked with her. Because we talked. We were regular chatterboxes. First me, then the union men, then Dale. So in my confusion I turned in my chair and watched her watch Dale and the union fellas. I thought, *Maybe the reason she's turned her head sideways and doesn't talk and doesn't write nothing on her pad is because she's heard this stuff a hundred times. Maybe senators holding hands with industry is done every day of the week.*

Nothing happened in the governor's mansion. Nothing got wrote on the pad, and not a feature moved on the woman's face or a hair got out of place on her head. Apparently Dale could just keep his ole information. So he went back to Point Comfort and sat in his office at

Formosa, doing absolutely nothing because nothing was what Formosa wanted him to do—until they could figure out what to do with him. He was beginning to look like a whistle-blower, but Formosa wasn't sure. Senator Armbrister wasn't in the newspapers yet.

Then another worker pulled up to the fish house. He was fifty-three years old and his small contracting company had been destroyed by Formosa. Everything he had worked for in his life had been put in jeopardy. He had tried for months to get Formosa to deal with him fairly and honestly, and the last thing he had ever wanted was to get involved in a lengthy and expensive lawsuit. But he was involved. There was no getting around that.

Jack was just one of four hundred contractors comingling out at the plant site. He said his contract with Formosa had been straightforward. The contract called for Formosa to supply the material, while his company would supply excavation services, forms, and finishing labor. The work of building 300 foundations was supposed to be completed in 120 days. But the job took 260 days.

"This was due to the failure of Formosa to arrange deliveries of concrete and other supplies on time. It's a common complaint among the contractors. Heck, the contractors nearly worked on top of each other."

Then he discovered that work not included in the contract was expected of him, but Formosa officials assured him that the company would be responsible and provide compensation for the delays.

He said Formosa never acted less than extremely satisfied with his work, but it changed after he asked Formosa for what he thought was a conservative payment of 356,000 dollars for the delays. Formosa began finding fault and charged back 82 days of delay on his company. Now his company was no longer in business.

"I've talked with other contractors, and they talked about the countermeasures Formosa's officials were suppose to take against contractors who complained. If a contractor made a claim for extras, for demobilization or mobilization or whatever, they were never to authorize payment. Just get the contractor to do the work and if the contractor complained, then they were to notify him that the contractor was complaining. If the contractor kept it up, they were to take the contract from him and make sure that he lost his money if he argued about the claim."

So he got strung along. After he gave his estimate to Formosa for the delays, one man wrote that Formosa would pay 58,000 dollars on the claim. Then a month later, another man said Formosa would pay 104,000 dollars. Then two days later, still another man wrote a letter that Formosa would pay 50,000 dollars.

Jack was sitting on a blue shrimp box and his long legs spilled out into the room. He wore the kind of hard blue dungarees that men wore into fields, and a light blue windbreaker that wasn't buttoned, and ever' now and then he turned a button.

Jack said he had seen other contractors as messed up, and talked about a memo where Formosa discussed their strategy of good cop, bad cop.

"I've figured the only way I'm going to get a fair deal with Formosa is to fight for it. I even tried to get Ms. Wang to talk to me and listen to reason, but it didn't happen. My company's already destroyed, but I can still get some justice in the courtroom."

"Is it just the contractors getting the raw deal out there now? What about worker safety problems?" I said. I had talked with workers so much, I sometimes wondered if I didn't have my own perspective as skewered as tin by an old nail.

Jack shook his head and his chin barely cleared his chest. He said he thought that Formosa's practice of demanding that contractors cut their costs further and further was jeopardizing the well-being of a lot of workers. One worker died when the boom he and his coworkers were hanging from was hit by lightning. It killed him and jolted the rest from the scaffolding.

"Why were those workers out there in the middle of a lightning storm anyhow, if it wasn't to keep things moving? Making up for lost time."

Then a single mom was killed her first day on the job with heavy equipment. He didn't think she had the first hour of training for the job. The tractor she was operating rolled over on her. She left two little babies for somebody to raise. Another man fell thirty feet and died. But there was something else going on too. Kickbacks. Payoffs. Formosa's New Jersey office had hired a private detective to see how wide the talk about kickbacks was spreading among the contractors. Find out who knew what.

Jack said he'd give me the name of a contact who knew something about the kickbacks, but he wasn't sure the man would talk with me.

258   An Unreasonable Woman

"He's plenty leery at this point. Formosa's yanked him away from his original job with the contractors because he complained to New Jersey about the kickbacks, and now they have him in the sand pit. Maybe he'll talk and maybe he won't. He's a good guy, though. You can trust what he says."

After Jack left, I sat with that name and number written on a piece of paper. I glanced at the window and it was still wide open, so I went to the window and took out the stick and lowered it. The window fell hard, but wouldn't lock because the lock had rusted off long ago. Anybody that really wanted to could break into the fish house. I didn't know why I was even shutting the window. Then I went back to the desk and dialed the number.

A man answered and said I was lucky I caught him, because he was fixing to head to Louisiana the next morning. He was going home for a while. His job at Formosa was damn sure costing him a lot of commuting, and he wished he was at Formosa's Louisiana plant, but he wasn't, so that was that.

He didn't say why he wished he was gone to Louisiana, and I didn't say why I called. I just mentioned Jack and the man said, "Jack's a good, decent man." He wouldn't go any further in the conversation, so I blundered on and probably tripped every wire in the man's head. Finally he stopped me talking and said if Jack trusted me, then he imagined he could do the same; except he had a condition. He wouldn't talk anywhere in Calhoun or Victoria counties. There were too many people that knew him, and if they didn't know him, then he was damn sure they knew me. If we talked at all it was going to have to be a good ways from both counties.

I said, "How about Bay City? And tomorrow? Ain't that on your way?"

He said Bay City was some on his route, and since he was bringing his documents, I might, if I had any higher-level person around, just bring them along too. The stuff he had was worth seeing. Somebody could land in a lot of trouble for it, and he was tired of being the only one holding it.

High-level person? I wasn't acquainted with any, unless he was talking about a free lawyer like Blackburn. So even though it was late I called Blackburn at his house, and he said he wasn't doing nothing, just drying his clothes. He lived in an equal-opportunity house. It sounded like he did all right, because his voice was bumpy like he was sitting on the wash machine on the sling cycle. What was I doing at this hour of the night? Blackburn said. Wasn't I home yet?

I said, Nope, I wasn't home. I was trying to arrange a meeting, and his voice went Oh!, like it saw a cliff and went off. I told him I had talked to another worker, and Blackburn wanted to know if the man was meeting me in a decent place this time. Not out in the bushes or in the fields. I said, No, no, just Bay City in a courthouse parking lot.

"The man wants me to bring somebody important along. And you're about my limit," I said.

Blackburn said, Well, he appreciated the thought. And he probably could do it. Didn't know why he couldn't.

The next morning I got the girls off to school, then loaded up the two babies with sleep still in their eyes. For two reasons: first, so Baby wouldn't get no madder than he was (what could a woman do with two babies along?), and second, so the Louisiana man would talk and not clam up after coming that far (what man didn't trust a woman with two babies along?). So I drove the hour and a half it took to Bay City.

I was the only one in the parking lot, so I parked in the middle where I could see everything come and go. What was in back and what was in front and what was on either side of the courthouse. I waited like I'd done the night before, only now I had two kids wide awake and tearing up the van. By the time the Louisiana man showed up in his truck, the kids were filthy dirty from rolling on the metal floor, so I parked the van alongside his truck and went over to his window.

He rolled the window down and stuck his hand out. His name was Buddy Bodiureux and he looked my age, only carried it better, like a man does sometimes if he's part Cajun. Buddy wasn't a gushy talker, and he didn't move his hands off the steering wheel the whole time we talked. I stood at the window and kept an eye on the kids and on Buddy sitting in his truck with the windows rolled down.

He said he had worked for Formosa for two years, but before that he'd went to Louisiana State University and Delgado Junior College in New Orleans. To get away from the teaching environment he started his own construction company, which he had for about fifteen years until the economy in South Louisiana went bust. That's when he went to work for Formosa.

About that time Blackburn pulled up in a car with a woman. The woman was quiet and small in a dark blue wind jacket, and she sat in her corner and said nothing even when Blackburn pulled up to us. I figured she might be Blackburn's wife.

I don't remember what all Blackburn said, but he said a lot. More than normal. His eyes looked feverish and wild, and I started to ask him if he was sick, but I looked at his wife and decided I wouldn't. After a minute of indecision of where we were all gonna sit, the wife got out and pulled her wind jacket tight in front, then with her head down, she walked among the trees in the cement parking lot. Blackburn was left sitting behind the wheel and he blinked his eyes, then glanced at us and said, "She's all right. She's just gonna take a walk." So we all climbed into his wife's car, and Blackburn went in back and me and Buddy got in front, and ever' now and then I'd shove the door open with one foot and look over at the babies. Once Crockett peered through the window, with a hammer he'd found somewhere.

Buddy said his job was to be construction manager, and that was more or less what he did. He would go out into the field daily and visit with the contractors, or just walk by their areas to see what they were doing. To see if there were any obvious safety problems. There weren't too many safety personnel out at the time, and if he did see something that was unsafe, he'd holler at safety and have them go in and look at it. Then he coordinated the work within a unit to keep contractors from working on top of each other.

Blackburn leaned forward and said, "How does that contracting go? You know, the bidding or whatever it is they do."

"Ohhh, the low bids and all that? When I first started out in my own construction business there was very little bidding. You just went out and showed the man your costs and your labor and he would say, Well, it's either too high or it's fine, let's go to work, whatever. And there was some negotiating, but it was more on what should we do. Should we leave this out or shall we put it in? Should we make this bigger? Should we make it smaller? But the cost of doing these jobs was pretty much set.

"Now, at Formosa it's different. Generally what happens is bids are sent in for a particular job, and the low bid gets it. Then the low bidder enters this negotiating phase, where after the bids are received someone—the engineers or someone in New Jersey—negotiates a price with the bidder. Every contractor I've talked to said they got a letter that said they were going to be negotiating. And all the contractors pretty much said the same thing, and the letter to the bidder said something like 'Your bid is competitive, but it is 5 or 6 percent too high.' That sort of thing. I know Jack got a letter like that, and Formosa told him he was 6.5 percent higher than the next low bidder and Formosa's budget. And actually he was three hundred thousand dollars *lower* than the next low bid."

Blackburn said, "I'd think that'd constitute mail fraud if it went through the mail."

"Formosa's response was, 'We're in a free market where there's a willing seller and a willing buyer. The people who run companies are mature individuals and know what they can accept and not accept. . . . Everybody has to take responsibility for their actions.'"

Buddy said the negotiating-phase letter was some of his complaints. But then he got something worse.

"We had some contractors that were complaining that they had been asked to send or give funds to people so they could get paid for jobs or buy a contractor. It was a little kickback scheme going on. The primary person that was involved was James Morrison, who was the manager of contracts in New Jersey. His boss was J. N. Chen, who is the corporate vice president in charge of the company's contracts.

"I had contractors making statements that Mister Chen knew all about it. Now, does that mean that Formosa in New Jersey knew about the kickback scheme? Were they a part of it? I don't know. But I know that twice before my final finale I brought up the subject of kickbacks, and each time I was told not to talk to contractors. They didn't tell me why. My boss, Bill Holladay, would come to my desk and tell me not to talk to contractors anymore. I'd ask him where he was getting all this and he wouldn't say. But he has only one boss, and above him is J. N. Chen.

"I had a meeting with Jay Su and my boss in Point Comfort, and Jay Su thanked me for all the work I'd done and said I was being transferred to the maintenance area. He indicated that the move was requested by my boss because I was . . . 'too friendly to the contractors.' So even though I presented it to Formosa's corporate offices in

New Jersey, someone decided that I shouldn't be in the position that I was in, and therefore I was transferred to the maintenance area, and now I'm managing the sand-pit area."

"How much of a kickback scheme was really going on?" I said. "Was it *all* of the contractors?"

Buddy said, "Judge for yourself." He pulled out some papers and handed them back to Blackburn and handed more to me. The papers were copies of canceled checks and typewritten statements from contractors, and memorandums sent from Buddy to Alice Nightingale and Susan Wang, the Chairman's daughters, in New Jersey.

"The contractors said it was done pretty subtly. Morrison would ask for specific sums. Say he had certain expenses. His wife's birthday, or he and his boss, J. N. Chen, would sure enjoy being put up at an Atlantic City, New Jersey, hotel. Stuff like that. I think those checks are for around twenty thousand dollars. I don't know how many more is out there."

He didn't know how much Formosa was involved either. He was transferred into the sand pit before he found out much more than that contractors had paid thousands of dollars to Formosa's purchasing agent, James Morrison, who reported directly to J. N. Chen in Livingston, New Jersey. The payments ran from personal checks to cash to what looked like plane tickets. Those contractors who gave money to Morrison said he was just the "bag man" for his higher-ups.

Buddy said he had hated what happened to Jack. Jack was a good man and didn't deserve what happened to him. And he knew things were going bad. There were so many complaints out there on site. Long delays. Constant interference from Formosa officers. Then the nonpayment thing. He said he didn't know why some contractors were treated generously by Formosa and some flat weren't.

"In one of our meetings J. N. Chen told us to string the contractors out, string them along, and sooner or later the contractors will have to settle and then they'd settle out of court or whatever. I know this sounds like I'm beating the Taiwanese up. . . . But I'm not. There are some Taiwanese that are as straightlaced as what I hope I am. But there are others that believe beating a contractor down is legitimate and the proper way to do business. And *that* is why I am at the sand pit. I wouldn't put up with it."

Buddy said we could have the copies of the canceled checks and the

statements from the contractors and the memorandums from himself
to Alice Nightingale and Susan Wang. He didn't care what we did
with the information. He looked tired of the whole mess, and something on his face said, *If it goes to a reporter, then so be it.*

I grabbed everything he gave until I had ever' paper he had brought
into the car. I felt like a rat hauling off a shiny gold watch, with a free
and clear path to his hole. I didn't even tell Blackburn's wife good-bye;
I just hopped out of the car, slammed the door on Blackburn, and told
him I'd talk to him later.

I walked back to Buddy, who was finally hauling off to Louisiana. I
started to say what I'd do with the documents, but he just raised his
hand and said, "I don't want to know. They're yours now." Then he
gave a short wave and rolled up his window, and that was the last I
saw of Buddy.

It took me two days to figure what to do with the papers. One day to
know it'd be a reporter and another to find the reporter. I was all
washed out on talking to the governor or another senator (more than
likely working for Formosa anyhow) or another EPA investigator who
I was sure would tell me it wasn't his jurisdiction. I tried first one
paper, then another, but the woman who had written a couple of stories before on Formosa was out having a baby, so I called the reporter
in charge of special investigations.

I don't know what the reporter was doing before I called him, but
after I called him he was already moving here. He sounded like it
anyhow, saying, What, what, what, and yeah, yeah, yeah every time I
said something. He talked quick like a mouse in a rattlesnake cage,
then he'd start laughing and spoiled the whole image I had of him
looking like a mouse. He said he had to finish up the story he was
doing, but he'd be down tomorrow. Tomorrow.

Then it was tomorrow and there he was, moving fast like I imaged,
nearly as fast as he talked, dropping papers and notepads and stumbling over the whole mess, then asking the same question down what
he had asked while he was up. Oh, he was going to fool them. I could
see it already. His appearance and his walk and his laugh was going to
put them totally off guard, but his words were going to grab them sure
as God made little bunnies.

He had a name like Joe Blow. Mark Smith. Same thing. Lethal

man-stick of dynamite if I ever saw one. He drove down in a pale rented car with his stuff crammed in front and back, and when he asked me if I wanted to take a little ride with him, he shoved papers and reports and maps off onto the floorboard.

I gave him copies of everything I had, and every time he'd look at a copy of something he'd suddenly stop, look at me with his brown fire-cracker eyes, and say, "What do you suppose they'd say if I asked such and such?" Then he'd fall over laughing and say, "Oh, what the heck! Let's do it!"

Mark could have been a wrestler, winding and confusing every opponent, then winning hands-down because he had stumbled over his opponent's head and knocked him out cold. Instead he was a reporter, and irritated nearly everyone he interviewed.

He dogged everyone at Formosa and thought nothing of calling up Susan Wang or James Morrison or FBI agents and pestering them with questions, then hanging up and re-calling them because he had just thought up another question. Blackburn didn't like him, but I thought he was hilarious and brilliant enough to win the Pulitzer Prize. He was Casey coming up to bat in a Peter Sellers movie.

Eventually Blackburn called Susan Wang in New Jersey and asked her about the kickbacks, and she gave him the story that it had been an employee that was involved and they had no evidence of anyone higher up. Then she sent Blackburn a letter that an attorney at their New Jersey headquarters had sent to the FBI regarding their own in-house investigation.

The letter admitted that approximately twenty thousand dollars of bribes or kickbacks had been "secured" as hard evidence, and besides Morrison, "there may or may not have been" other officials involved. There was no evidence tying Chen or other top officials to the scheme.

The trail ended there. The FBI wasn't admitting to any investigation, and Chen wasn't talking. A company spokesman said Formosa's attorneys were advising Chen not to talk about the case.

I started wondering who did the private investigation for Formosa. And just how many private eyes are there in the state of Texas? Eventually I tracked down Formosa's private investigator and got friendly with the receptionist, 'cause the private eye wasn't saying nothing. She said the investigation was going real well and her boss was uncovering some interesting stuff, but Formosa called and ended the investigation. They had enough information and didn't want it to go any further.

Mark went through court documents and talked to builders and FBI agents (who refused to confirm or deny they had an investigation into the bidding practices), and eventually his story made headlines in the *Houston Chronicle*. Then Jack went to trial in Calhoun County and won an eleven-million-dollar judgment against Formosa because they breached their contract and defrauded Jack's company. Formosa appealed, and the last time I talked to Jack he said the Chairman told him that even Jack's grandchildren wouldn't see that money.

22

A Bay under Siege;
an Activist Born

It was a prelude to something and I should have seen it coming. After all, it was part of the same money-bucket theme as kickbacks and extortion. The prelude went this way: A school board president on his term out dropped off a copy of Formosa's tax abatement agreement at the fish house and said that Doug Lynch, the county's economic development director, had walked into his office, threw the agreement on his desk, and said, "You *are* going to sign this agreement! It *will* get done!"

That rancored the school board president enough to do the same thing the state inspectors in Corpus Christi had done. He told me, "See what you can do with it." Well, I called Froggie, who was a second-term school board trustee and in his younger days had briefly been hired by the same school district to teach high school football to a largely nonwinning team.

When I said Froggie's name, he said nothing. Then he sighed hard and said, "Diane, Diane, Diane." Then he hung up.

I looked at the phone for a minute, then I packed all the kids in the van and drove into town. "How come," I told my mother, "my own brother won't talk to me on the phone about a school board decision?"

"Oh, he won't talk to any woman. You should see how he treats me."

"I'm not askin' him to be my brother here. I just want something of what he was elected for."

"He's a man, don'tcha know! And you better be careful or he's gonna make you get outa that fish house. Forget it! Take those kids and go on home. Only thing he's gonna tell you is to mind your own business."

"This *is* my business! Who else knows more about Formosa?"

"Oh, who cares? Let it fall in the ocean and see who cares! He's just like your daddy; he's like all of 'em. They think, *Why don'tcha stay home, you stupid woman!*"

She gave me a hard, clear look that said, *Ain't you stopped yet?*

Didn't that do it? Then she turned and slammed the back screen door and grabbed a bent-up deck bucket left over from thirty years of washing decks. But I wasn't finished. I waited for Froggie again, and this time I didn't bother to call. I told myself I wasn't fixing to relearn that mistake of talking to my flesh and blood more than twice.

The school board met with Formosa behind closed doors, and I sat the whole while in the hallway, with two babies asleep on the bench. A little after midnight the door swung open and two Formosa men, swinging identical briefcases, walked out of the school board meeting, and I walked in dragging two babies. The board members were seated around a curved row of tables, and they looked up when I came in. I didn't wait on introductions or niceties. That had vanished about eleven o'clock in the hallway.

I said I didn't understand why the school district was giving away millions of good tax dollars to Formosa when the district had already shown they were in a budget crunch and needing to eliminate teachers. Girls' basketball coach. Special services. The papers had mentioned the elimination of as many as seventeen teachers. It didn't make sense! We didn't have a budget for teachers or classrooms, but we could hand a hundred and fifty million dollars to Formosa from the tax payroll. Didn't Formosa's history of environmental destruction in Texas and Taiwan and Delaware and Louisiana mean anything, or was there nothing that tempered their decision?

The school board members said nothing and asked no questions. There was no debate. Most of them (and certainly not my brother) didn't even look at me. They messed with papers Formosa had brought or pens they seemed to find. As I rose to leave, a silence stretched as tight as an army blanket on an army cot. That was when I knew that blue moons could come and go before that school board found a tax break it didn't like.

I left the documents I had brought on the table, took both babies by the hand, and left. Then I waited for Froggie outside in the dark parking lot. I knew it wouldn't be long. There was not going to be any agonized debate in that meeting room.

The school board meeting dissolved sometime after one o'clock. I sat in the van, resting my chin on the steering wheel, waiting on Froggie. When I saw him come out alone, I shut the door softly and walked out to him.

He saw me coming and stopped, saying, "Diane, uh . . . Diane."
Then he turned and groaned like he was going backwards and I was
somewhere in the road he was retreating on. Finally he stopped and
said, "Diane, uh . . . we're just gonna have to split the blanket on this
one. We're just gonna have to do it."

"Split what blanket?" I said. "Whadda you mean?"

"I mean you working for me. Being down there at the fish house.
This is getting too big a mess. I'm gonna find that fish house burned
down one day!"

"Burned down? What! Are you sayin' you're *firing* me? Because I'm
asking a couple of questions any parent with kids would ask?"

"You *ain't* no parent with a kid!"

"I've got *five*! Where've you been half my grown life?"

"I mean you ain't a *typical* parent with a kid. Look, Diane . . . uh,
Diane. Oh, hell. I'm not discussing this any further." Then he walked
backwards, shaking his head and retreating until he nearly backed
into his truck. Finally he turned and shoved himself in his truck and
drove off.

I told myself if Froggie got much more terrible, then I wasn't gonna
put BELOVED BROTHER on his tombstone. If it wasn't blood that kept
brother and sister together, then what did? What was he gonna do
with a fish house when he was just squirreling away in the ground,
with no beloved nothing and only a pile of sand over him?

But I was gutted too. It wasn't just one and not the other two or three.
I wasn't gonna count how many. All I knew was Formosa was turning
into as fine a precision tool as I would ever find; cutting off large chunks
of my life like it was hog ears lopped off in a field and thrown out
because it wasn't no good for hearing anymore. The hog was dead.

So Momma's dream fell apart and the fish-house job was dead. My
brother didn't come to tell me again, and I didn't call. I just went to
the fish house and pulled my files out of the drawers and left Donna
Sue a list of answers to give anyone who called. If I pulled any coup
at all, it was leaving Donna Sue in charge. She was forty-five years of
ready and showered holy hell over Seadrift's bastion of male fish-
house owners. For Froggie's shrimpers she became the Florence
Nightingale of fish houses, because for every nickel and dime raise she
wrestled from the fist of a shrimp buyer, Donna Sue wrestled the fish-
house owners again and gave it to the shrimpers. She gave the best

prices, kept the cleanest fish house, and had the only bathroom that didn't stink. Her only downside was that she, inevitably, launched a price war on shrimp and caused Froggie lots of grief in the huge overhead in bleach and Pine-O-Pine.

I took the *SeaBee* and went shrimping. I left the house in the dark, while the kids were still sleeping, then with a half-filled coffee cup on the dashboard and all the van windows rolled down, I drove all the way to the bay with old black night and the musty smell of mildew lulling my senses.

I worked the boat alone. Not out of any economics, but from the awful truth that I didn't like talking and I didn't like the racket of other people talking. And deckhands talked. They never shut up. They warted the fool out of captains with talk about the weather and the net they were dragging and where they were dragging and when they were gonna pick up, and if a captain accidentally dropped the mike on a VHF radio, a crowbar couldn't get the deckhand off.

I liked the ten or twelve hours alone where I never opened my mouth or had to push a deckhand aside because I had to stride in one intense rubber-booted motion from wheelhouse to winch to shrimp doors until I kicked a net off the stern and watched it fall into the deep black sea.

In hindsight, I could've used a deckhand that day out in the middle of San Antonio Bay when the squall came out of the west. In hindsight, I could've used a buddy shrimp boat following me and the *SeaBee* to our first morning drag. Maybe then I wouldn't have panicked so much while the *SeaBee* sank beneath me in the gale, and I would have found the wrench to tighten the stuffing box much quicker, and they could've loaned me their automatic water pump because mine was *sabotoged. Gone. Wires missing.*

But hindsight is flimsy when the only requirement is endurance. So I endured, I took the *SeaBee* home, tied her up, and went home to lick my wounds. I was recuperating when a five-times-removed relative of Pancho Villa showed up in my yard and sent in his wife, while he sat out in the truck with the kids. The state of Texas was suing him for fifty thousand dollars for an oyster sack of illegal redfish, and the state wasn't messing around—they wanted the money pronto, and every day he didn't pay, the interest was compounded.

The outlaw in the truck and I believed something was out of whack. There was definitely a difference in enforcement between fishermen and chemical plants. When was the last time Formosa or Alcoa or Union Carbide had six holstered officers come into their facility like they had at the fish house? Acting like they owned it. Or a uniformed officer come on Formosa's property and haul off the contents of their railcars loaded down with PVC pellets, because Formosa violated their air permit? And *fines*? Formosa's billion-dollar operation was fined twenty-five thousand dollars for a hundred-and-forty-eight-thousand-pound release of vinyl chloride that could abort babies in their mother's bellies, yet the state of Texas fined a poverty-level fisherman fifty thosand dollars for thirty-five redfish.

I called up Blackburn and told him I wanted to sue the dang state of Texas. Blackburn said he wasn't filing a lawsuit—but I did have a point. The National Marine Fisheries seemed willing to enforce the Endangered Species Act when it dealt with shrimpers and the turtles, but when it came to the agency backing up their earlier concerns on Formosa . . . well, it was a different story.

Blackburn said, "So if you want to gripe about selective enforcement, then bring up that little nugget."

I told Blackburn to bring it up himself. I would get a press conference together down at the docks in Port Lavaca, and he could just get his little self down there.

Maybe I was getting smart about these press things, but I didn't think any irony was getting lost on the fact that we were holding our press conference overlooking the very bay that had become a dumping ground for industry. Mercury mess by Alcoa and a little ethylene dichloride mess by Formosa—now in its fifth month of cleanup.

What had started as a "little twenty-four-gallon" leak of ethylene dichloride into a ditch had turned into a twenty-seven-hundred-gallon leak into the ditch and turning basin of Lavaca Bay. Now five months later, the EDC concentrations remained high, and a state report noted that either Formosa's estimate of the leak into the water was low or else there had been other unreported spills.

So three parties sat in a Catch 22. If Formosa did any further cleanup in the water basin, then the entire warehouse and pier was gonna be undermined and fall into the water. If that happened, then the Navigation District and a long, long line of ships and barges were gonna come to a screaming halt. Then to compound the problem, the state environmental agency said they wouldn't even touch Formosa's new permit for a tank farm until the cleanup was finished. It was damned if you do and damned if you don't. What to do? What to do?

I couldn't imagine a more fitting place for a press conference. A bay under siege. A bay outraged. My demonstration and press conference would be very timely.

That day it all fell into place. One domino hit another domino, *ping, ping, ping,* and it went down pinging on the little red checkered table in my head. I wasn't aware of moving down a planned path, so I didn't step aside and watch it or call it by name. I just knew I had one thing to do, and that was focus on Formosa. Then whatever I did poured from my gut and ran straight to my eyes and hands and feet and said, "Over yonder, over yonder." And so I went. Baby said I was obsessed and crazy, but I knew I *saw* something.

The day of the press conference was clear and hot. I had picked a corner of the docks that was next to the harbor water, and the shrimp boats were lined up one side and down another. I had tried for two days to get shrimpers to take their boats a little ways out into the bay and protest, but they took one look at redheaded Rick with his white button-down shirt collar, and another look at a Sierra Club representative with her typed press statement, and decided they saw a bunch of flaming environmentalists. These were the Somebodies who were ruining fishermen's lives and were probably part of a bigger Something that was hammering nails so loud in their coffins that they couldn't sleep good at night.

I was aggravated. "Don't you fellas know they're out here to help y'all, for God's sake? They're on y'all's side."

"For *now*," they said, "but what about *tomorrow?*"

It didn't do no good to tell them to take it one day at a time. Shrimpers figured it was *days* they were marking time on. It wasn't years. They didn't have that luxury.

Then Blackburn showed up at high noon with his pretty wife, walking like he was Doc Holliday, rehabilitated and on a stroll down a board sidewalk. He walked leisurely across the smashed oyster shells and the heat, and saw instantly that I was stressed.

I didn't mind him bringing along his wife, did I? he said, and I said, No, no. It was the shrimpers. The shrimpers weighed heavy on me.

Well, Blackburn said, he had dealt with students plenty of times.
And shrimpers couldn't be any worse than students, could they?
He'd go across the harbor and talk to them. Did I think they'd talk
with him?

Oh, hell, why not? I said, and pointed out some shrimpers.

Eventually I got through the day. I went from one end of it to the
other, and no part of it not painful. I gritted my teeth, tasted bile, and
could've puked. Smiling was hard. Talking was tough. Then too, there
were conference conflicts. The Sierra Club was worried about being in
the same press conference as Tee John Mialjevich, a shrimper from
Louisiana. Tee John was famous for protesting turtle excluding
devices (TEDs) and saying outrageous stuff, and the Sierra Club sure
didn't want to look like they were endorsing Tee John and not the
Ridley turtles.

No, no, I said. This is just about unequal enforcement. If the Coast
Guard wants to get on boats with shotguns and ammo to enforce
TEDs, then let's have a little equal opportunity here and have the
state inspectors go into the chemical facilities with the same type of
gumption. Line up a few of those plant managers against a wall and
put a B on their heads. No more of this double-standard mess!

Tee John didn't act up much (even though every environmentalist
there was watching him, nervous enough to puke) and said protection
of the estuaries of the Gulf should be the main focus of environmental
enforcement, since those bays and marshes were the major food and
nursery areas for marine life. He didn't say nothing about turtle soup
or burning nets, or advocate ramming Coast Guard boats or pitching
National Fisheries people overboard.

Next came a longtime activist from the attorney general's office in
Louisiana, and he was more famous than Tee John. Willy Fontenot
was eloquent and quiet-spoken, a Southern son of some long-gone
plantation owner (at least he looked like it) who once stood in the
same place as the wall-to-wall petrochemical plants and tanks and
asphalt that existed there now. It was Cancer Alley—a place as notorious as New Orleans. Willy was slowly going blind, so when his head
tilted and his soft brown hair fell on his shirt collar, his thick glasses
glinted like pearls in the sun.

Willy questioned the enforcement of TEDs when the government
of Mexico offered no such protection to the turtles' sensitive nesting

area. There were large areas of the Gulf exempt from the federal law enforcing TEDs, and Willy thought it was unfair that a little farther on down the coast the turtle excluders were unenforced, and those same shrimp caught in unenforced waters could be turned right around and shipped, free of export taxes, straight back into the United States.

A mile down I got my turn, and by then I was the best little hangee in the county. I would have marched right up to a rope and hung. No excuses, no complaints. A thing to be done, and so I did it. It was very liberating not caring a fig. And I wouldn't have cared even if nobody was there. I would have said my piece to the wind and the water, same as it was my flesh and blood. Two or three times in my life I have been in that peaceful place, and what would land me there was something in my head or the right word or my hand doing the right thing. Sometimes it was nothing but the moment, and I was there at that moment on that harbor. I could have been stone-cold silent and said no word, and yet it would have been all right. Just me and my intent was all I needed.

Then it was over, and those that came, went. Blackburn with his wife, the bit of press, one helicopter that flew over, hoping for a sky shot of shrimp boats protesting on the water. Tee John went back to Louisiana, and the Sierra Club breathed a sigh of relief. The shrimp boats that Blackburn had got to come out in the harbor were now tied up and the captains long gone.

Willy came over before he left and introduced me to some union people. He said to always keep the workers in mind and remember that being in Louisiana was like being in Texas, and us Cajun folks had to stick together. Then he laughed and his glasses flared like fire in the sky, and he climbed in a rented car with the union fellas and left. I watched the car until it hit the pavement.

Rick was the only one left. Usually he was the first to leave because he had at least six more projects somewhere and a dozen grassroots groups he worked with and saw to. Who knows what price he paid for being the only breathing, living, grassroots-oriented nonprofit group in Texas? He sure didn't have a girlfriend.

So seeing Rick still there was an indication of something, but I didn't know what. He didn't call me "Dianey," and that wasn't good. He said he wanted to give me a newspaper article. He knew I didn't get the Houston paper, and this article was something I needed to see. We sat in his car with the doors wide open and his stuff piled everywhere. The backseat was full of boxes and nearly finished protest signs. Rick wanted me to see the headlines in the Houston paper. EPA MAY GRANT EXEMPTION TO FORMOSA PLASTICS. The article said a draft document by the EPA had given a finding of "no significant environmental impact" to Formosa, and the finding would allow Formosa to skip an expensive and time-delaying environmental study. The decision had been made even though environmental groups opposed the permits, and the company had been cited for record fines, and U.S. Fish and Wildlife and National Marine Fisheries had formally asked the EPA to require a full-scale environmental impact statement.

Rick watched me read the article and said, "You know what this means, don'tcha? It means it's finished. It's over. It was a done deal anyhow. It's just finally in black and white so we can read it."

I was stunned. How could a billion-dollar chemical expansion be ignored so completely? We had the law, and the law was meaningless. You can't get a hearing date. You can't get spills and criminal acts investigated. Fraud? Kickbacks? My own boat sabotaged? It had all stopped like a big clock hand came out and stopped. But that big old green money wheel was moving. That thing just keep on moving, and what you thought was stopped was really only a couple of seconds on the wheel's turn. It was a moment's hesitation. I felt like a huge game was being played—on me, on ordinary, regular people! In this game there were ten thousand stupid rules, like dot all your *i*s, and send in your petition properly and timely, and file all your legal briefs with the proper and duly appointed judge, and follow the proper sequence in the Codified Federal Registers. As long as us regular, ordinary people kept busy playing the game and we believed we were doing everything right and it would make a difference and we could control our own lives and make things better and safer . . . well, then the game was working!

Then the Game Makers were happy. 'Cause really, now, were the Game Makers all that bad? The game made things maybe lukewarm, but so what? What's wrong with lukewarm? It's really us—the Game Makers!—who have all the risk and the worry. *We are the ones who carry you!* So if someone needs to be bellyaching, well, then it should be us. *You ordinary people are only in the belly of the thing. We are the Thing Itself!*

Well, I was pretty incensed.

"They're not gonna get it!" I said.

Rick was quiet and his eyes were pale as old paper nailed to a fence post. "This isn't the *beginning*, Diane. This is the *end*. You've got a little bit you can do, but you're gonna be trailing the parade from here on out. You've done some good. You cared. That's more than most."

I looked at Rick and tried to stop with a frown everything he was thinking, 'cause somewhere inside, it was exactly what I needed to stop for myself. So I said again, harder, "Formosa's not getting it, Rick. They're not getting the bay. They may have everything else, but they're not getting that."

"There isn't much you can do at this point."

"I can think of something! I'll think of something!"

"Oh yeah, what? We got a lawsuit, and what's it doing besides collecting dust in some federal building? Take another petition to Austin? Do another protest? We just did one, Diane. How much press and concern did you see? There is nothing, Diane. *Nada*. Between me and you and our little legal eagle, we've about covered the high spots."

A thought came out of the blue clear sky and hit me. "I can do a *hunger strike!*"

"A what?" Rick laughed, and shook his head. "Dianey, a hunger strike! Nobody, but nobody does hunger strikes in Texas!"

"Why not? Somebody named Mitch Snyder did one in Washington. I just read it!"

"Mitch Snyder's dead! The strike probably killed him!"

"Well, there's Cesar Chávez. You always talk about Cesar Chávez. How many was that man on?"

"That's California, for Chrissakes! That ain't *here*. It ain't Texas, by a long shot! Good Lord, people will think you're crazy as hell. South Texas is a world all its own, which I don't need to tell you. It's got its own little rules about what works and what don't, and a woman doing a hunger stike *sure* ain't one of them."

"It's something I can do, Rick. Why not? I don't need nobody else. Don't need no money. What do I need? Just me doing it!" I looked at Rick, and he looked back with his eyes not so pale-looking anymore.

"I mean it, Rick," I said.

"You can do a hunger strike? You think you can?"

"Sure, what's so difficult about it? A couple men already done it."

23

Hunger Strike

I had gone too far, unfurled a flag I now had to ride under. Question was, how long could I ride? A week? Two? I was getting to know the human condition so well I was even beginning to suspect my own, so after leaving Rick, I drove home, called the reporter from the *Victoria Advocate*, and said the thing I forgot to mention at the press conference was that I was going on a hunger strike to protest the EPA decision. A hunger strike! she said. When?

Tomorrow, I said. Tomorrow is when I do it.

Then the thing you do after you've told a reporter you'll do such a far-fetched idiotic action is: *You do it!* Otherwise you go soft. Then the next morning your compromised self looks up from the soft bed you lie in, and with undying gratitude you say to the ceiling above you, "Thank you, dearlordjesus, for keeping me safe from that crazy idea!"

It is the same reason why an Indian in a bad losing war will say, "It is a good day to die," and on the same day ride into battle. He sure doesn't sleep on it. Too much thinking can kill a vision. Our worst fears prance out, and those little dancers take knives to everything we hold dear.

So besides not sleeping on it, the other thing I didn't do was tell Baby. Baby saw no flag waving in the bay. It was too much like a lost cause for the fishermen, and "fishermen," Baby said, "don't deserve nothing." He had no more to give. He had lost it all, and nobody better never call him a fisherman. He would hit any man that called him that.

I told Donna Sue, and she said, "Who all is helping you on this one?" and I said, "Just you, honey."

"Well, what the hell is Rick doin', then?"

"Rick is handlin' the press, except he thinks it's gonna take a week of starvin' before folks believe it's serious."

"Well, ain't that peachy of Mister Rick? Let you wait a week. And I suppose you know a whole lot about hunger strikes?"

"I know you don't eat."

"Ohhh, you're in *good* shape, then! And I suppose you've talked to Blackburn about this. He thinks it's okay and he's gonna be *right* there behind you."

That wasn't how it went. Blackburn got quiet, and I knew exactly what he was doing in Houston. He had taken his black cowboy boots off the desk and removed the hard candy from his mouth and shoved his rolling leather chair hard against the desk.

"Wilson," he said, "do you have any idea how I feel when I see you do things like this? *All* these protests? This hunger strike? I feel like a *failure*! I feel like you don't have faith in me. The *only* place I see this action going is downhill. You'll get hurt and the cause is damaged, and nothing will change!"

"Blackburn! *Those chemical plants are not gettin' the water! No more.* We've got to draw the line somewhere. Besides, I ain't got time and the bay ain't got time for a fancy lawyer to put us on his schedule to save us. Jesus Christ wasn't no lawyer!"

Blackburn said, Well, I wasn't a Jesus Christ either, and don't expect any help from him. He would try to get our lawsuit against Formosa filed and get the judge to give us a hearing date, but otherwise I was on my own.

I thought, *Lawyers be damned*, but what I felt was something nearer terror. I had yanked my feet so high off the ground that there wasn't dirt beneath me. More than that, I knew exactly *nothing* about hunger strikes. How to stage them, *where* to stage them, and what happens in between. Rick said he would send me some papers on civil disobedience and maybe that would give me some ideas. It was all in the same ball park anyhow. Civil disobedience. Hunger strikes. Sit-ins. Heck, he remembered all that stuff. Well, I remembered too, only I read in the paper about it. I had never did any of it. But Rick didn't send the papers, and I didn't think nothing of it. Rick had fifty more groups just like mine. But I thought, *What is so difficult?* Mitch Snyder lay down outside a big vacant building in Washington and fought city government for the homeless, and Cesar Chávez got a tent and drove stakes down in the grape fields of California. I decided if they could stake out a territory for their cause, I could too. So I took my hunger strike to a shrimp boat on Lavaca Bay.

The day I left for the boat, I told Baby, and he said, "So you've finally gone mad?" And I didn't disagree. I flat didn't want an argument. Guilt had already staked out the veranda of my front shirt because I had decided not to tell the kids anything other than that I was going to the bay and they'd be staying with their daddy and grandma for a while. I was afraid they'd worry about dead things and dead cats and dead grandpas and dead mommas. I reasoned, if I didn't die, the kids had nothing to worry about. But if I did, then they'd have worry soon enough. That was my logic. So I said nothing. I just let Baby rain on me until I walked out the front door and he yelled after me, "I'll tell the kids when you die. Maybe they'll cry."

As I went out the screen door I strained to stay in a place I'd never been before. Maybe that was why I forgot everything and took nothing but a pair of jeans and a couple shirts and my white rubber boots. (I had never been to the bay without the boots, so they were an old habit and nothing else.) Donna Sue brought everything else. Blankets. Toothbrush. Used milk jugs full of water. A *National Fisherman* magazine. A couple newspapers. She had it all stuffed in the backseat of her car, and when I got in, I looked at it. You would have thought we were going camping. I shoved my spare clothes on the floorboard and put my hands in my lap and said nothing for the entire trip. I don't even remember the drive over to Lavaca Bay. I had already left, and my body didn't even pause. No wonder people in accidents don't remember the cars that hit them.

When we got to the bay Donna Sue wanted to know what boat I was staying on, and I said I didn't know. I hadn't asked yet. But that wasn't entirely true. I *had* asked—I just never got an answer. The old fish-house man I had asked didn't need to answer because he had nothing but no written all over his face. So I hadn't chased it any further. Now with Donna Sue and her blankets and her milk jugs full of water and my white boots and clothes filling her car, I saw I had to.

I asked the fish-house man, "What boat you figger is more than likely not goin' anywhere for a while?"

The old fish-house man looked at me, then he looked at Donna Sue with her look of impatience growing like a thunderhead fixing to clap, and he said, "Oh, hell. Take Jackie Wayne's over there. The *Ketcha*."

So that was how I borrowed the *Ketcha*. Got from a fish-house man who didn't own it, but knew somehow that the owner (who lived in Houston) wouldn't be around for a while. And he hadn't. The *Ketcha* had been sitting for so long that the rust stains draining from old, old bolts wouldn't wash off. Donna Sue stayed for an hour, ripping off old gray, damp blankets left on a bunk by some (she said) degenerate pothead-dopehead-deckhand for the clean ones she'd brought fresh from home. Then she went around and opened all the side doors on the wheelhouse and stuck a coffee can underneath a window that would open, and pried a screwdriver in another that wouldn't. The wind just sat there, immobile, not minding her a lick, and wouldn't even step over the foot-high doorjamb.

I trailed her into the cabin and shoved the captain's chair around so I could get a clear view of the harbor through the side cabin door. Then I sat down and propped one bare foot against the wheel and left the other on the cabin wall.

"So what are you gonna do?" Donna Sue said.

"I'm gonna sit right here," I said.

"All day?"

"Sure. Then I'll probably go out there and sit on the deck awhile. Sittin's gonna be about it, I guess."

"You want me to bring you any . . . " Then she stopped herself. "Oh yeah, you're not eatin'. How about coffee, then? That ain't eatin'."

"Nah," I said. "It's better if I keep it real simple. Nothing is nothing. You can't quibble over that. Maybe you can bring me some hot water. . . . I might *think* it's coffee."

Then she left and it got real quiet. That afternoon went backwards like birth in reverse. From chaos to stillness. I was suddenly unborn and back in a water world, and what I heard was the silence when a thousand demons quit jabbering.

No reporters showed. No baby cried. No phone rang and no letter to write. Every dish was done. The evening came and went and then the night came, and those were the only two things I allowed on the boat. I had water in the milk jug, but I didn't drink it. I sat shoeless, my feet flat on the deck, and watched the water late into the night. When I went to bed at midnight, I heard the cypress boards in the boat creaking like people walking.

I didn't mind the silence; it was an old friend. And I didn't mind not eating—too many years on a boat with nothing but coffee. So if there was anything to miss, it was the kids and the coffee and what to do with my hands. I hadn't been that idle since I was seven and lay over a hole in the wharf and watched the water until the shrimp boats came in and I had to move.

By the second day I knew my mistakes. First, I had no phone and no way to hook up a phone, so I had no idea what Rick was doing. The other mistake was when Donna Sue came down and brought a newspaper and a cup of hot water, and I sat on the back deck and pretended it was coffee. It *wasn't* coffee. It was plain hot water.

I was hungry that day and the next, but on the fourth day, it quit. I wasn't parched and gray and weathered neither. I felt like I could do a hunger strike for a hundred years. I felt *good*!

Donna Sue wasn't convinced. I was hungry. She damn sure knew I was. "You know," she said, "nobody's gonna know if you get a little something ever' now and then."

I told her my integrity was the only thing I had to my name. I didn't have a bunch of supporters. No money in the bank. For people like her and me, integrity was our best part and we don't need to go messin' around with it. We cash that one in, then we weren't no different from Formosa or those damn politicians. Besides, I didn't mind a little pain. I'd had too many babies and lived with a man too many years. Pain wasn't what bothered me.

I could have got thoughtful and fingered my skull and asked, What bothers me? but I didn't want to think that far. I didn't want the second hand of my brain racing that fast. Besides, more than I liked questions, I liked being right there on that boat with my bare feet square in front of me. That was about as complicated as I wanted to get.

The *Victoria Advocate* reporter showed up on the fifth day. She said she needed a story for the next morning's newspaper, and her editor told her to write something good about Formosa.

She said, "How do you write something good about the devil?" She was a pale, thin Yankee woman that I had talked on the phone with ever' now and then, and she wore a hat. I was intrigued by the hat and the pale blue ribbon it had around the crown for no apparent reason. It was the kinda hat a woman went sailing in, only this reporter wasn't going sailing. It was windy, though, so to keep the wind from whipping it off, the reporter kept her hand on it the whole time.

She said Formosa was possibly activating their plans to file a lawsuit against me and Texans United. Now, what did I have to say about that?

"Ohhh, I'd just dearly love to see that," I said. "A lot of things need to see the light of day. Just tell 'em to go right on ahead."

The reporter laughed and wrote what I said down on her pad. Then she looked up. "Personally, I don't think Formosa will. I think they're just talking. They send people down to the newspaper all the time to talk to the editors, because they think we're not tough enough on you or else they think the newspaper is too tough on them. The paper is hard put not to go along with it. How do you *not* go along with a billion dollars?"

Besides, the newspaper had already told her not to quote me. She thought it was because they saw me as some kind of freaky nut. They figured Jim Blackburn was the real person behind all the opposition anyhow. They didn't see how an uneducated fisherwoman was capable of generating that type of opposition. The newspaper's only question was, Why Mister Blackburn?

I started to say the newspaper wasn't the first one to think I was a felled fence on a dirt road nobody went down. But I didn't. I was starting to get convoluted thinking, and thought that saying nothing was eating nothing, and if I said something then I was eating something and *that* wasn't a hunger strike. My thinking was as crazy as that.

The reporter stood against the boat railing, then took a clean handkerchief out of her purse and wiped the railing clean and sat down. She wanted Blackburn's and Rick's phone numbers. "I can quote them," she said. Then she abruptly laughed and stood up again. She said she had to go see that devil of a company and get a comment from them. Before she left she got me to stand out on the bow of the boat, and took a couple of pictures. She stood on the docks, a white-looking flower dug up from a Kansas or Iowa field and wearing a hat I had never seen the like of. She raised her hand and said, "Don't stay on this too long. No sense in letting them kill you over it."

That was the only company I had the rest of the day. I went to the stern of the boat and lay flat on the deck. It was just me and the boat and the water and some silence so bred in desperation and anxiety and now so physical that I could have hired a midwife to squat over the quilt and direct the birth. Later a man came to the wharf and yelled. "Do you see them? Over there on the other side of the docks? They think you are plenty loco. *Mucho loco*, but I said I think I'll come anyhow. I am a man and you are a woman. You sit on the docks. A woman alone. I too am alone."

I tried to say something, explain the hunger strike he thought was so crazy. Maybe I could tell him how the sky over Formosa lit up from a dozen flares. What do you fight for? What do you believe in? Don't you see that fire over there?

He was a short, compact man whose neck was missing, and his head wouldn't reach my chin even if we stood together. He did not understand, so instead he stared with bold black eyes. I said nothing else. I laughed once, hard. I had been sleeping on the engine hatch on the back deck, and apparently that had drawn my shadow man, so I got up and took my quilt and moved to the cabin. He left and didn't return, and I was amazed how a man would—without warmth—romance even very large bones such as mine.

It took five hours for strangers to come again. I opened my eyes and there they were. And it wasn't just one stranger; it was seven, and all seven strangers wore black suits and white shirts, and when they came closer I saw one wasn't a stranger at all. It was Fred going nuts.

Fred didn't fool me. He was calm and confident now and his hand didn't shake and the gold chain that he wore around his wrist didn't rattle, but when he pulled out his pocketknife and cleaned his fingernails, his fingers trembled.

"Who's your buddies, Fred?" I was sitting up on the bunk with Donna Sue's quilt around me. All seven men crowded in the cabin.

"I'm not telling you," Fred said, and looked at me briefly, then down at his nails.

"Not sayin'?"

"Nope," said Fred. "Not saying. It doesn't concern you."

"Well, why did you bring 'em here?"

"Just to show them what you look like. Everybody wants to see the crazy fool on the shrimp boat. . . . So I thought I'd bring them on over. Let them have a look."

Then he turned suddenly, not moving his feet, just twisting his shoulders like he was bolted at the hips. He looked at the men and tossed a white hand towards me. "Well, here she is, fellas. Take a good look. And why don't you tell her what you just said, coming over here. Tell her what you said."

The men said nothing and they all turned and looked at Fred, then turned back to me.

"They're being modest," Fred said. "They wanted to know if you were some kind of kook. Are you some kind of kook, Miss Wilson? Do you think you're Gandhi or something? Don't you know you're just shooting yourself in the foot with this nonsense? Losing every bit of your credibility. I don't believe you had much, but you've *certainly* lost it now."

"Well, I guess I've got nothing to lose, then."

"You know, you really need to get off this hunger strike! Just get off of it! Maybe we can talk about some collaboration later on."

"Talkin's over with, Fred. . . . Unless y'all want to do an environmental impact study and stop the construction. Go tell your boss that."

"We are *not* stopping construction! And we are *not* doing an environmental impact study. The EPA has already told us we do not have to, and we're *certainly* not going to volunteer. I don't know *why* you keep insisting on something that is not going to happen."

"Well, we've got nothing to talk about, then, Fred, and y'all are just crowding up my boat. So why don't all y'all just vamoose on outa here?"

Fred made no outcry. He merely turned and took what faith he had left of that big church made of pipes and cement and cinder and climbed off the boat. Fred was still intact, though. Still sane. He wasn't murdered today. Not yet, he wasn't. His faith would maybe keep him until the end of the week. Then I didn't know what would keep that man from unraveling. I could almost hear the wire unwinding.

That was the first and last time Formosa came on the boat, and I wasn't even sure Formosa had sent Fred. Maybe it was Fred that had sent Fred, and it was the last brick he had and so he had to fling it no matter what. Maybe he believed like the fishermen did—that somehow he could be saved from ruin by doing all types of dopey things—and that morning, Fred was almost like a fisherman.

Rick came the next day, a full day ahead of the seven he said he'd wait on. So while I sat where I always sat in the morning and never bothered to get up, Rick hauled a camera crew on board the boat. He was very, very happy and called me Dianey half a dozen times. He said he had action by the horns and he was wrestling it to the ground.

"I guess it's just me and you, Dianey. Let Mister Blackburn hide out with his little Rice crowd. Tell him to stay where he is on the lawyer side, and we'll stay on our side. This is where things really get separated, isn't it? The men from the mice."

"Blackburn just thinks I'll hurt myself."

"Oh, now, Dianey, he isn't so worried. . . . But no need it get into that. We've got things to do."

So we captured our little captivating story and made a press release and a bold statement to hand out to the press. "But not in this county," Rick said. A press release in Calhoun County, where corporation and industry ruled, would go nowhere except the trash can. (One local editor suggested to Rick that they *might* cover the hunger strike if I got pitifully near death and went to the hospital.) Rick said he was taking the video and the press release to Houston, where we had a fighting chance.

"Now, how long did you think you can stay on the boat and not eat?"

"As long as it takes," I said.

Rick looked at me. "Why don't you take some juices? Lotsa people go on hunger strikes and drink juices. Nobody would say anything about you drinking fluids. You'd last a lot longer too."

"Nope. Don't want things to get real complicated. Just plain water."

"All right, Dianey. You're the boss. But you might try squeezing a little lemon juice in your water. That'll keep your electrolytes balanced."

"Sure. Might do it."

In the evening Rick and the crew left and they all turned once and waved, and the man with the video camera held it to his eye and filmed the wave good-bye.

That night I really missed the kids. Six days was the longest time I had been without them, and suddenly I didn't know when the hunger strike would end or if it would. Maybe it wouldn't. Maybe I'd never see the kids again. That possibility was suddenly real, and another one fell fast on its heels: being dead as a doornail. I felt like an addled gambler, drunk as a hoot owl and throwing dice for his life. Maybe that last memory of me walking out the door and Baby saying "Maybe they'll cry" would be my last. And I didn't even see Baby. The screen door had shut on him.

• • •

Whoever says a hunger strike don't make you nutty, don't know nothing. It was the middle of night and nobody was around, yet I was talking to myself out loud and asking questions. Is it simply life or life with meaning that matters? Which one? Which one? A fisherman drowning didn't have time to ask that kind of question, and when he *wasn't* drowning he was so busy scratching for dollar bills, he still didn't have time. Then a man working at a chemical plant was too tired or too sick to ask. And a woman with a dozen kids *never* had time, and when she did some baby came along needing a diaper change or another one needing a bottle. Something came along.

So I considered myself real lucky to be where I was; smack-dab by myself in the nuttiest thing I had ever done, and so got to ask the question nobody had the time or energy for: Was it more important to search for meaning and when you found it, be willing to die and bleed, or was it just better to breathe?

I was looking at the stars and maybe dreaming. Maybe Rick never came. Maybe Calhoun County didn't exist and Formosa wasn't burning. Maybe I was space-dreaming about sky and flight-dreaming about birds, and when I wasn't, then I became like a fish approaching land without lungs and a flyer approaching the sun without wings.

Donna Sue showed up the next morning and wanted to know what in the hell was the matter with me. I said nothing was the matter with me. The sun was up and I was getting cold, was all.

"Where's that Rick?" she said. "Where the hell is he?"

"Rick's come and gone," I said. "You missed him."

"Believe me, I don't miss Rick. There ain't a damn man that I miss. Not even Sanchez's sorry ass. I'm getting real fed up with him too."

Then she looked hard at me. "All right, all right," she said. "This ain't funny no more. You're *gonna* tell me when you're gettin' off this thing! Look! I'm gettin' my quilts. . . . We're ending this thing!"

I watched her jerk milk jugs and sling things around. Then she stopped and turned around. For once her face was red and not white.

"Do you know how angry I am? Do you know what I feel like doing when I see you looking like this?"

"Wally ain't here, so you can't do nothing."

"This ain't a bit funny."

"You're finally seeing me serious. That's what you're seeing. Maybe Formosa will too. Maybe the EPA. I'm not playing a game. I'm *saying* something, and I'm saying it in my own peculiar way. Maybe that's been the problem all along. People are so deaf that you've got to figure out new ways to reach their ears. Maybe I got to go through their soul."

"Oh, sure. Let's talk to Formosa's soul. I can't wait till you tell them that."

"Formosa's got a soul. They gotta. How else are they gonna change? It's easy to forget because they act so bad all the time, but really, it's just remembering our souls. Like a dream. We're the dreamer and we dream everything. It's you. It's me. It's Formosa."

"I think you're losing it. I think this hunger strike has shoved you right over the edge." Donna Sue stood, stiff and hard in her jeans, then she suddenly quit. She shook her head and showed a smile so tight her teeth showed through the skin.

"All right," she said. "So what did I expect? Hmmm? Right to the end! Let's go straight to the damn end of this thing so I can go just as crazy as you!"

"There you go."

24

I Strike at the Gates of Hell

The shrimper said we were a bunch of gotdang environmentalists and I had till sundown to get off his gotdang boat. And there I was, thinking there was only one donkey on that boat, and now I found it was two and he had just drove all the way from Houston. He said he was eating his supper and minding his own business, then he looked up (innocent enough and still minding his own business) as a reporter said "Port Lavaca" and he thought, *Ohhh, a man can't even eat his supper anymore, but has to look on the TV screen to see his own boat staring him straight in the eye.*

It was Jackie Wayne in the flesh. He drove all the way from Houston to see for sure if that gotdang environmentalist he had seen the first time on the TV set was the same gotdang environmentalist he was seeing now.

"I got things to do on this boat, woman! I gotta get ready for the Gulf run. I can't be spending time foolin' with all this bullshit!"

"This ain't bull. Besides, I'm a shrimper and I'm doin' this hunger strike partways for you shrimpers! We need clean bays don't we?"

"I saw it on the TV set. You're a gotdang environmentalist. Shoving turtle shooters down our throat! I know what you are!"

The rest of the conversation was like a ten-year-old on a box with a stick, trying to hit as far up a tree as he could so he could knock down a coon. Then the man finally quit hitting and got back on the docks. He turned and yelled, "You better be off this boat by tomorrow or I'm pitchin' you off. Won't need to die from any hunger strike, girl! You can drown."

So that was the only reason I said anything at all to Donna Sue about chains at Wal-Mart. But Donna Sue was quick, and she said, "What happened?"

I said, "Nothin'. I'm just fixin' to change things up a bit."

"Why? What's wrong with the boat?"

"I need the strike more in Formosa's face. So get some chains and a lock down there at Wal-Mart. Get some of that heavy, heavy stuff. None of that light porch-swing crap. What we use on the boat. Then get me a lock."

"What am I supposed to do with it?"

"Not *you*, honey . . . *me*! I'm gonna take the chain and lock myself to Formosa's front gate out there. Maybe the pillar. Which one do they got anyhow? A pillar or a front gate?"

Donna Sue looked at me and started swinging her head. Swinging and saying at the same time "Nope, nope, nope."

I felt real patient, almost like a momma explaining to her four-year-old baby-child why they were fixing to blow up the kitchen. "Now, look, Donna Sue. It's time to change things up a bit. Everybody does it. You think that Mitch fella just laid there and that was it? No. He was bound to have done something else. Then Cesar . . . hell, who *knows* what all that fella did. I just need to turn things up a notch."

"Ooh, sure. That notch of killin' yourself."

"No, that ain't it at all. All you gotta do is go to Wal-Mart. Drive over there and get that chain."

"I'm getting Baby! I'm telling him to come and get his wife! 'Cause *I* ain't gonna be here no longer. You do that chain bit all you want, but I will not help. That's where the line gets drawn, sistersue!"

"Allrightallrightallright. Simmer down. I won't do the chains."

"You promise?! You won't do it?"

"Now, how am I gonna chain myself if I don't have the chain? I just need to get off this boat for a while is all. How about taking me down to that little park beside Formosa? Just drop me off for a while. A couple of hours."

"What for?" she said.

"'Cause I need a little air."

"You've got plenty air here."

"Well, it's *different* air there."

Donna Sue watched me for a long minute, then she said, "You're not going nuts on me, are you?"

"No, honey," I said. "I just need a little outin' is all."

I walked around the boat and picked up my spare jeans that didn't fit and my shirts, and I put on my white boots, and folded up the blanket on the cot.

"Why are you bringin' the blanket?" she said.

"It needs washing," I said, and she said, "It don't need washin'," but I picked up the blanket anyhow, and climbed off the boat and walked down the docks to her car.

My legs felt heavy and disconnected and I was breathing hard, but my head felt like I'd just heard the screen door slam and a kitchen explode all at the same time.

It took ten minutes to get to the park, and when I got out I wasn't scared or wondering what to do anymore. I was grinning like a monkey in a tree and could barely keep from laughing. Over my shoulder, Formosa was a chain-link fence away and doing everything it normally did on a hot summer day, and just stinking up the whole sky.

Donna Sue was watching me like I was fixing to steal her purse, and her mouth was straight as a line on a chalkboard. "You're gonna be here and not someplace else when I get back?"

"You see me walkin' anyplace in these boots?"

"Nope, I don't," she said.

"Well, then," I said. "There you go."

So she left, and there was nobody but myself on that cement park bench. A trash can had a sign that screamed in big black letters: DON'T MESS WITH TEXAS. So I didn't. For fifteen minutes I didn't mess with a single solitary thing Texan. Then that "no messin'" feeling went away, and behind it came something fresh and green as a tornado howling over the water, and it brought air and rain and something to do with my feet.

My feet were still in the white rubber boots. I hadn't taken them off, even though having them on in that hot park made about as much sense as cement shoes. That's why it took so long. I had to drag the white boots every step of the way down the highway, and even when I got to the intersection where on one side was Alcoa and on the other was Formosa's front property line and behind *that* the one thousand miles of tubes and pipes and big-bellied tanks and high-looking towers and flares that was the booming business of Formosa, I didn't stop. I just kept on going.

That's not to say that I knew what I was doing or that there was a plan. Because there was no plan in the walking. There was just the walking. At some point on the road, I turned right. It was easier that way, and my white rubber boots were heavy and hot, and sometimes the sharp smell of shrimp on the back deck of a boat or the bay early in the morning mixed in with the boot's hot, rubbery smell and for a minute I'd forget where I was. Then I remembered, and I walked until I was in front of Formosa's old office and the old VCM plant. A big sign made of two-by-fours and plywood and hammered into dead gumbo dirt and fried carpet grass announced: FORMOSA PLASTICS CORPORATION, TEXAS. Behind the sign was a sterile line of redbrick offices with glass windows and venetian blinds, and one long sidewalk leading to all the air-conditioning going on. Nothing moved, not behind the venetian blinds and not in the parking lot. There was an employee gate on the side but nobody went through.

My walk felt like a leisurely Sunday evening drive through a chemical plant, and I had come to the part in the ride where the driver felt tired and pulled off to the side of road to rest his weary bones in the grass a bit. So I walked off the highway and down a ditch and up a ditch, then I walked across the grass until I got to the Formosa sign. It was nearly as tall as I was, with letters dark in the middle but fading slightly at the edges, and it had a big eye that symbolized something in Chinese. I didn't know what, but it didn't stop me from sitting down.

I wasn't trying to hide, but at the same time I wasn't looking for trouble. I was simply tired. I didn't know how it was possible for someone to start a morning on a shrimp boat and by high noon be sitting next to a sign on a chemical plant. But here I was. It wasn't mornings or high noons I'd ever seen in my life, but then life was getting stranger by the minute. Then life cracked open and spit out something, and I nearly laughed at what rolled across the grass and hit my foot.

Well, it didn't hit my foot first. *First* thing it did was come out of the main office door and stare at me. It was a chocolate-colored, short-sleeved security suit, and it carried a walkie-talkie and ever' now and then the suit would put the walkie-talkie to its mouth. Finally it quit that and walked down the sidewalk and out into the sun, and there it stopped. Both hands on its hips and its feet wide apart. I looked back and did nothing. I thought nothing. I was sitting cross-legged, with my hands on my knees, and now and then I'd feel the wind over my head and I'd look up and watch for a second, then I'd look back over to the security man and he'd still be staring.

Then he started moving across the grass, and I wondered what more of that cracked life in the afternoon I was gonna get, but then a second man came out. Then three. They stood in a huddle, not exactly looking at me, but not exactly *not* looking at me. Finally one of the men walked out on the sidewalk and onto the grass and he came straight to me.

"Let's go inside and talk," he said. "We've got an air-conditioned office. I can get you a cold drink or something. How'd you like that?"

"This is plenty good right here," I said.

"Aw, now. C'mon. You're not comfortable out here. The ground is hard and there's probably ants."

"Nope. No ants."

"Well, look. Let's just go in for a little bit and cool off. Then you can decide after you've cooled off whether you still want to come out or not. I won't stop you. Promise you, I won't."

"I think I just wanna sit here. Maybe a couple more days. I can use my boots as a pillow."

"All right, all right," he said. "I *guess* we can sit awhile."

Then he sat down with his brown shoes stuck out in front and his pant legs coming up to show off his new brown socks. He yanked the cuffs and whacked at the dirt, then he pulled his walkie-talkie off his belt and stuck it on the ground next to him. He turned his head sideways, and one minute he'd look at me and the next he'd look at the security men standing in the middle of the blazing hot yard.

"So what are you doing here?" he said. "What you got in mind?"

"Just sittin'," I said.

"Just sittin', hmmm?"

"Yep, just that."

"Not trying to do something else? Not trying to cause us some problems?"

"I'm on a hunger strike, but now I'm just sitting."

"You know what I see when I look through those windows over there? What those workers see when they drive past? Pretty stupid woman. That's what they see."

"You been talking to Fred?" I said.

"Noooh! I've got a lot better things to do than talk to Fred about you. You're no big concern of ours. It's just unfortunate. Cause you're obviously hurting yourself and no one else with this, this . . . well, I don't know what. I don't think anybody understands why you're doing this."

"Hunger strikes have a long history in this country for fighting injustice. Gandhi used it all the time."

"Gandhi isn't from Texas! And how *dare* you compare yourself to him! Is *that* what you're trying to do? Act like Gandhi? Be Gandhi?"

The man yanked his hand from his knee and nearly fell when he tried to get up. His new brown socks had disappeared, and now I had his knees staring me straight in the face.

"You saying ordinary people aren't capable of courageous stuff? I think they are. I think *everbody's* capable of it. We just forget it most the time."

"Oh, that's just great! That's just fine! Everybody's a hero. Oh, heck! Oh, piddle!" Then he whirled and his eyes went to a security man standing in the grass with his walkie-talkie at his mouth, and the security man, seeing the man suddenly standing, decided it was a sign to charge, so charge he did. The man with me frowned and raised one hand and sharply waved off the security man.

Then he sat down again. His legs were crossed at a crazy angle and his brown socks showed and so did his white skin. We didn't move. We just sat and talked about us being in the middle of the yard in the hot blazing sun. Then an hour went and trucks and cars starting lining up at the employee gate, and as they drove past, nearly everyone did something. They either honked their horns or yelled and gunned their motors or squealed tires and left burnt rubber marks from the road to the highway.

The man sitting never saw any of it. He sat with his back to the road and wouldn't turn even when someone yelled his name. They yelled two or three times. "Hey, McGee! Hey, hey!" Then somebody laughed from an open truck window, yelling "Mageeeeee!" and McGee's face went red, and I thought, *So that is his name. McGee.*

After all the employees left it got quiet, and there were only the security men in the road and a group of men in business suits standing at a glass door and letting out all the air-conditioning.

McGee turned to me. He was serious, he said. He was one serious *hombre.* "Let's just finish this inside. Then somebody can take you home."

"Nope, McGee. I'm spending the night here."

"You're *not* spending the night here! You *can't* spend the night here!"

"Sure I can. I can use my boots for a pillow."

"I didn't mean that you are not *physically* able. . . . Look, don't you know we could arrest you? This is trespassing! This is against the *law*!"

"Well, arrest away. Hop to it."

It was getting evening and there were shadows on the dead grass, one for him and one for me, and they were watery and long and dark and not one had eyes in its head. When I wasn't watching McGee trying to get me off the grass, I was watching the shadows and seeing if they were alive or dead.

I felt light- and airy-headed. Since I wasn't walking around with my heavy boots on, there wasn't a thing holding me down. I'd finally caught up with myself from wherever far back I'd been, and I was two foot in the air. But I certainly wasn't gonna tell McGee I was two foot up and that somebody just snapped on the lights at the old home place. It was real hard to think about jail time or the near-evening with all those home lights blazing.

Then Sanchez was there. Dark as the evening was and industrial strength as his steel-toed boots were, I still recognized him. He came down low to me and hissed, "Don't be a idiot! Look all who's around."

"Who's around?" I said.

"Half of Formosa, you moron. McGee's standing two steps over there with his ears cocked. So shut up!"

He said he was just a messenger. I had a grand slam waiting in Houston. What grand slam? I said, and he said it was some deal that my hippie friends in Houston were doing. Earth Day something-something. I didn't know it was Earth Day, I said, and Sanchez said, "Well, you keep this little starvation thing going and it's liable to be the first of a long line of things you forget. I've been in the military, little sister. I know this type of stuff, and it comes under the heading of *survival*. You ever heard of that? *Survival?*"

I smiled a long, slow smile in my head hearing Sanchez, because it wasn't Sanchez gone! Not *vamoosed*! Not *adios*! But *hellllo, ameeego*! It was flesh-and-blood Sanchez with his dollar-ten-cents hamburgers and his thermos of black coffee thick enough to make the rust quit on an iron nail.

"Where you been for so long?" I said.

And Sanchez looked at me and thundered, "Where the hell do you think I've been? Where all those damn hippies in Houston oughta be. Working! Working! Got me a job! Been getting lots of hundred-dollar bills from Formosa and stashing them in an old sock and burying them in the backyard."

He said, "That nut in Houston's got a deal for you. It's a whole lot better than this deal here . . . sitting on this hard ground. Hey, little sister, just think about it! Who knows how many thousand hippies you can stir up in Houston! So c'mon. Let's get outa here!"

Sanchez might have been a false hellbender, but he moved me. He was my brother, come to fetch me from Formosa's hell door. So he dropped me off in Donna Sue's yard and wouldn't come inside. He'd see us later. When his job was a little more secure. I didn't know whether Donna Sue heard him or not, but for a second she stood at the door under the harsh porch light, and a fierce tangle of emotions ran over her face. She looked at Sanchez leaving and me coming up the path and said, "Get in here before I kill you."

Then at six the next morning we left for Houston and drove blind to that unknown park in the middle of Houston. Donna Sue was in a Winchester mode; gunning first for Blackburn because she said she expected more out of him. (He was probably her substitute for Sanchez, saying Blackburn whenever she meant Sanchez.) I was half gone on the front seat, with a radio blaring out Willie on a country-western song. It was Pancho and Lefty being gunned down in some sorry shoot-out. *Federales* everywhere. Mexican soil and dust and blood everywhere. Then Lefty leaving for Ohio or someplace like it, with no money in his pockets. I was Pancho going facedown in the dust.

An hour later we stopped under a pile of trees, so I guessed we were there. I didn't remember Houston having trees. But there they were. A splendid little pile of trees with a name I couldn't remember. Then we walked and walked and covered what seemed to be four miles of woods at some country-western version of Woodstock. In a clearing was a half-open stage. The part that was open was where the twenty thousand people were hanging out and lounging and talking and drinking and eating sandwiches out of natural-colored wicker baskets. The part that was closed was for the speakers and the singers behind a curtain.

I was behind the curtain for a while, then I was onstage. I remember the roar of the trees that twenty thousand people stand under. I forgot what I said, but it didn't matter. I didn't care if I was seen or heard or if I walked or didn't walk. Later a woman came up to me and cried and wanted to hold my hands and I said, "I can walk it," but had no idea why I said it. I watched the trees over people's heads and saw how the light was heavy at times on the limbs, then how other times it made the leaves almost like spiderwebs—not leaves at all.

Then somebody got me a chair and a table for my petition, and I sat under the trees and listened some more. A woman with a feather pinned in her hair brought me a bottle of water and she sat it beside me, and then another woman came and asked how I was feeling and if I was taking any vitamins. I said, No, no vitamins, and she acted horrified and left, and when she came back she put two white bottles beside my hand. Nobody is ever going to know the difference, she said. You *need* vitamins.

Later Rick came and he looked tired and pleased about something and he was smiling. "Well, Dianey," he said. "How are you doing?"

"She's tired, is what she is," Donna Sue said. "She should have been out of here hours ago."

Rick squatted by my chair and put both hands on his knees. "Well, what about it, Dianey? What do *you* want to do?"

I said I was ready to take the hunger strike someplace. I didn't know where. Maybe the EPA.

"I think we can do that. Let's get ahold of a couple of my staff and do a little brainstorming. If you want to call the EPA you can do it from my office." Then Rick stood up (a strange redheaded man in a white cowboy hat who used to watch parades, but now created them), and we followed him out of the woods.

To the EPA secretary, who knew nothing, I was just another phone call. She said Mister So-and-So wasn't there, but she'd have him call me. I said, Looky here. I'm a woman shrimper with five little kids and I've been on a hunger strike two weeks now, and I wanna talk to somebody *today*.

The secretary said nothing for a second, then she said, Just a minute. She believed she just saw someone come through the door. Then a minute or so went past, and a man came on the line and he said he was the assistant to Mister So-and-So and how could he help me?

I said it again. A woman and a shrimper and a mother and I was on a hunger strike. Rick was listening at my elbow and saying real low and fast, Yeah, yeah, tell them you're a mother. Got kids.

"I want to talk to the regional administrator about Formosa."

The assistant said, "Well, for that type of a meeting you should send the request in writing to the regional administrator and address it to the Dallas EPA headquarters. Your letter will be answered in twelve working days, not including weekends or holidays. That is the standard policy for addressing requests for meetings and complaints before the regional administration."

Rick was at my side and his face twisted, "Oh, that's just the standard ole crap. Tell them you're comin' up there. Tell them you're bringing the hunger strike to their front door!"

So I did, parroting Rick. "I guess I'll just have to bring the hunger strike right to all y'all's door, then. Bring along my five little kids. Maybe a few supporters. A little press."

Then the man said, Oh, just a minute, just a second. Then he was gone longer than the first time, and when he came back it was another man. This other man said his name was Norm Thomas. Chief of Federal Affairs. What could he do to help me?

What had sprung out of spontaneity had now turned into a pretty good plan, so I repeated the brand-new plan. I wanted to talk to the regional administrator about Formosa's expansion, and I planned on staying on an already two-week-old hunger strike on their very doorstep until I did.

Ohhh, that's not necessary, he said. He'd come *down there* and talk to me. He didn't want to inconvenience me, and besides, he had to be in Port Lavaca in a couple of days anyhow, to talk to Formosa, so he could just as easily stop by and talk to me.

Naw, I said. I just needed to see that administrator. I'd come on up tomorrow. Me and my kids. I sure hoped they didn't mind the kids coming along.

Ma'am, ma'am! he said. He didn't believe I understood how important he was. He was *Chief* of Federal Affairs. He was not anybody's flunky. He held a very important job!

Norm was fixing to say more and I knew it, but I butted in anyhow, being the interloper that I had become. I said I believed he was just trying to keep me down in Port Lavaca and away from Dallas. Trying to put me off. Was that what he was doing? I was starting to know a whole lot about maneuvers like that, I told him.

He *definitely* was *not* trying to put me off. Most definitely *not*! And to show his sincerity, I could tell *him* where to meet. That way it was the EPA who would be out the expense. And I could bring along whomever I wanted. As many as I wanted. Now, not twenty or thirty, he said. That *wasn't* what he meant. But he would give his word it would be a serious meeting.

That was how Blackburn reentered a hunger strike he had wanted nothing to do with: I wanted Blackburn in the meeting. I told Rick and he looked hard at the ceiling and said nothing. Then he said "Well, all right . . . but we're having it in *my* office. Not his!"

The meeting was planned for Houston and in Rick's office and in two days' time, and it wasn't going to be none of this just-dropping-by-to-see-you-on-my-way-out-of-town-from-a-meeting-with-Formosa. We invited press and told Norm Thomas, and he said, "Please, just none in the room. It will discourage frankness." So we compromised (my first in a long line of holdouts) and Rick said, "Well, as long as we've got the press afterwards."

Blackburn didn't like it, and I said, "Now, what is it you don't like besides Rick," and Blackburn said it was Rick he didn't like. He thought Rick would ambush the EPA man, and then the EPA would feel cornered and get hostile, and Blackburn said we didn't need any more hostility from the EPA.

I said I didn't think Rick would ambush the EPA man, and Blackburn said, "Well, you better just make sure, Ms. Wilson, 'cause we want a happy EPA."

I was starting to feel like I had three husbands instead of one; three men to make happy, and not a one easy. I had a knot growing in my skinny stomach, and my teeth ached from where I ground them. Then Donna Sue left for Seadrift, and I stayed in Houston with friends of a friend, and on the scheduled day of the EPA meeting ten activists showed up in Rick's office.

Then the EPA man arrived. He was alone and unannounced, saying nothing to nobody, and I thought he was just another professional activist. Maybe a director of a national group. He made his way directly to me and talked friendly and low, and every now and then he'd lean over and laugh about something. He wore a gray suit that went with his gray hair, and if he had been a movie star and in the movies, he would have been the polished gangster. The right-hand man to Marlon Brando. It was only later I found out he was the EPA Chief of Federal Affairs.

That wasn't the end of the surprises. Maybe it has to do with unexpected things coming in a brisk lineup of threes—just like death. Maybe it was just that cracked-life thing and it couldn't help surprising. We went into another room. A houseful of environmentalists (falling short of the twenty he didn't want) and one lone EPA man. Norm was now not so friendly, and his movie star gangster role was in full swing. He listened and watched every speaker, carefully took notes, and talked like every word he said was being measured. And it was. I watched him as intense as I would a cranky triggerman.

Norm said he was very involved in Formosa's expansion and he wanted to assure us that the documents that had been leaked indicating a study would not be done on Formosa were premature and incorrect. No decision had yet been made.

"That decision is being studied very, very carefully," he said. Then he turned his head and looked at me. "*Very* carefully."

What went on between now and when the decision was made on Formosa would have a lot to do with people like us. It was good that there were people as committed as us, he said. He was very impressed. Then he thanked Mister Blackburn and Mister Abraham for arranging the meeting, and he especially wanted to thank me. Call him anytime, he said.

If a man can say something important without actually saying the words, but convince people that he had, that man was Norm Thomas. I felt he had come from Dallas to personally deliver me a message. Blackburn thought so too. He said it looked good. Real good. The meeting turned out better than he thought, and I could tell Rick that Blackburn said he could handle a meeting well if he wanted to.

I told Rick some of Blackburn's message, and Rick said he was pleased too. They were all surprised by Norm Thomas's words. Something had obviously changed within the bowels of the EPA and just maybe that environmental study would be delivered on Formosa's doorstep. We just needed to hold on a little longer to make sure. Then Rick called me Dianey two or three more times, but before I left he stopped and frowned and said, "You can tell your EPA man the next time you talk to him that Jim Blackburn had nothing to do with arranging that meeting. He was just a party invited, just like the rest of them."

25

Death Threats and Deals

The hunger strike continued, but there was a difference. We were a family now—brothers and sisters—and nights we stopped in Dallas or Austin were not nights at all, just noontime in the family's fight. Recruits came from all corners: local union members from Texas City; a white-haired aging Don Quixote from Croton-on-Hudson, New York, who, having pointed his considerable lance at Union Carbide for several decades, now was prepared to point it at Formosa; a documentary filmmaker/activist from Maryland; and a sister from Greenpeace. The sister lived in New Orleans and called on the phone and asked what could she do. Just tell her.

Now and again I'd call Blackburn from a motel room in Dallas or Greenpeace's tiny headquarters in Austin, which were next door to the Texas Chemical Council, and I'd say what I was doing and he'd say what he was doing. Our hearing request for the marine terminal had been granted by the Air Control Board, and he wished the dang thing would hurry up and get over with. We both *knew* what Formosa was doing: finagling so that the durn hearing wouldn't be done at all.

So politics was getting messy! Texas now had a Democratic woman governor who had been elected with the support of the environmentalists and saw herself as an environmentalist, but the only glitch was Governor Ann Richards was expected to recover Texas from the disastrous recession of the eighties. She had a balancing act to perform with economic development on one side and environmental protection on the other. She had already been taken to task by one Austin editorial writer, who said the environmental governor of Texas was approaching Formosa's pollution and expansion problem on the Gulf Coast like a stick of dynamite; she hadn't touched it! For a woman who wasn't known for shyness, it was real strange to see her silent on this one. The writer predicted Formosa would become Governor Richards's first key test.

Then a newly elected woman mayor of Port Lavaca wrote to Austin an outraged letter about Formosa's permit delays, saying that the propaganda being disseminated by Mister Blackburn's group did not represent the attitude of the county! Actually, she said, the people in Calhoun County were very sensitive to the environment. They had coexisted with the petrochemical plants for over forty years, so they knew what they were doing! The problem was the press releases and demonstrations and falsified petitions and inflammatory statements from Mister Blackburn's group. Possibly Mister Blackburn's group was trying to split the county on racial lines.

Rick was livid about the mayor's implications that our actions had been guided by Blackburn, and Blackburn was hot about the mayor calling the action racist, but I was twenty days into a hunger strike and wasn't getting riled about nothing. I was as centered as I was ever gonna get without being a rock on the equator.

Blackburn said he just wished our lawsuit was as fine and dandy as I felt. All that suit was doing was going nowhere fast, and Formosa's lawyers had filed a motion to have the case dismissed. Actually what was going on was what activists sometimes call "burying the lawyer." Formosa's lawyers were trying to bury him in paperwork. If they couldn't get us one way, then they'd try to get us another.

I was oblivious to it all. The hunger strike had struck an eternal chord in me, and if I hadn't known I was a momma with five kids, I'd have believed I was a show at a movie house that had been running for years. That was a short-lived fantasy 'cause the kid thing and the momma thing kept coming up, and since I was a momma of five it had a multiple factor of five. The Texas Chemical Council wondered publicly: Who is taking care of that hunger striker's kids? That woman starving herself to death certainly isn't!

I expect that if sore is something you can worm out of yourself when you're on a near month-old hunger strike, then I was sore. I wondered privately if the Texas Chemical Council had ever asked Cesar Chávez or other male activists about their kids' whereabouts. No, I didn't believe so. It was probably just women that got asked that question. Still, I missed seeing the kids, but Baby said hell would freeze over before he'd bring the kids to me. And don't think about coming home to see them neither, he said. Twenty-four days on a hunger strike and twenty-four days of not being home was too much for any man to take.

Eventually that changed and so did Baby's pale-water eyes. It happened one early Friday morning when a helicopter flew over the dusty oak trees in the front yard. The craft hovered, then shots were fired. Whether the shots came from a man let out on the ground or one who simply fired from the open door of the helicopter, it was never known. Baby's momma had went down the road to mail some letters, and the bullets whined past and hit the ground and sent up small dust clouds at her feet. The dog was shot twice, one bullet exiting his neck and the other lodging in his leg. The dog limped over to the trailer door of my momma-in-law and bled all over her front porch.

Baby called me in Austin and said, "Whatever you do, don't come home! Someone either wants to kill you or scare me, and they've done it all right!"

He said he called the Port Lavaca sheriff's department and waited an hour for the deputy to arrive, and then didn't know what aggravated him more: the deputy's attitude that he was a hallucinating Vietnam vet suffering from some post-'Nam craziness, or the helicopter shooting incident itself.

He said his momma asked the deputy what he thought might have provoked the attack, and the deputy wouldn't comment except to say that if that daughter-in-law of hers ever landed in a hospital, then he guaranteed that they were gonna lock her in a mental institution.

That pretty much cinched it for Baby. His eyes were opened. But that wasn't the end. Later that night a helicopter hovered over the house long enough to make Baby's skin crawl, so he walked over to his momma's trailer and said he needed a gun, 'cause the one he had wasn't gonna do it. He needed two guns even if one had bird shot. His momma said, get yore uncle's gun! So Baby drove into town, and a plastic Wal-Mart bag on the floorboard of the van flew up in an air current and caught around his shoulders and head, and right there on that black road somewhere outside of Seadrift, Baby believed his life was ending.

There was nothing I could do in Austin except make a lot of calls with no results. Greenpeace sent a female detective from California, but later had to turn around and use her themselves. I was stuck in Austin and twenty-five days into an action that was getting remarkable for the dissension and misfired personalities being dredged up. Everybody that was anybody had and gave an opinion on the hunger strike. Most knew of Gandhi and Cesar Chávez and Mitch Snyder.

They said, Yes, yes, yes, they knew all about it, and it was all very high-minded and good, but what of the others? What about the ten Irish men who went on fasts in the Belfast prisons? Dead, every one. And it wasn't pretty deaths. The organs wasted away and the intestines withered. Then their mental state before they died was no picnic. Fatigue. Confusion. Disorientation. It was pure suicide!

I said, The most famous Irish gunman of all time never used a gun. His name was Bobby Sands, and he died on a hunger strike.

Died, died? they yelled.

Then there was one who got quiet and looked me in the face and said, "It is not those who inflict the most, but those who endure the most who will conquer in the end." Then he said, "I don't like it, Diane. But I'll support you."

So I stayed on the hunger strike, and when we did our press conference near the capitol, more people showed than I'd ever seen. After the press conference, I found a dark room and lay down on a couch, and a few minutes later the shadow that leaves when we all leave came up from my belly and a furious electrical storm rose behind it. It burst from the room, and I was the head of a glorious comet streaking across the sky, trailing white fire and ice, and I knew at that moment what it was to be a mountain or a rock or a river or a comet.

I thought I died, but I didn't. I didn't die that day or the next. Then on the twenty-ninth day of the hunger strike, Blackburn called and said Chairman Wang and his daughter had showed up in his office. They wanted to know what it would take to end the strike and the fight.

I looked at the window in the Greenpeace office and it was a square window on a white wall, and I just looked at the window and said, "What?"

Blackburn said it again. Wang and his daughter wanted to negotiate. He had suggested a couple of things he knew I'd like: environmental audits of air emissions and wastewater discharge and solid-waste management. Independent safety performance audits.

"I told them we want to pick the contractors who will do the audits and be involved from the floor up."

He had other suggestions too: establish a corporate reward policy that would promote safety and environmental concerns to an equal standing with production at the facility. Then a community advisory committee.

Blackburn said, "Now, what else would you like to add to that list, Wilson? What else would make you happy?"

I thought a minute and said, "I want something for the worker."

"Okay. That one's added to the list."

So it was, and I thought nothing of it. The worker was just another player in the field we were fighting on. What could be more natural when you are negotiating a pact with a chemical plant than including workers? That's what I thought, and it was probably what Blackburn thought too. It was just everybody else who sensed the significance like wolves do when they smell a new cat in the night.

And it was different, all right. Worker issues in an environmental agreement? I had not forgotten about the demonstration earlier where workers had opposed us, but I brushed that one off as a case of mistaken identity. Hadn't I talked to the workers in the plant enough to know where their hearts really were?

I was unprepared and Blackburn was unprepared, but we didn't know it and showed up anyhow. I brought along two union men, and Gail from Greenpeace, and Rick (who Blackburn and Gail would have just as soon I had left out entirely). We met in Blackburn's office with Formosa's attorney, and all sat around a conference table in a room with glass on every side I cared to look. Gail was hunched over, in jeans and a corduroy shirt, and her hair tumbled down all around her shoulders, and said she was itching for a cigarette. Formosa's attorney, a thin woman with black hair who said just about whatever she wanted to say, said, What is a woman from Greenpeace doing smoking cigarettes? Then she proceeded to tell the rest of us seated around the table that *she* didn't smoke and *she* did yoga, and as far as she was concerned, Blackburn was the only one at the table worth a durn. That set off nearly everybody at the table (particularly Rick), but that's the way we started: nobody on one side liking anybody else on the other (expect maybe this skinny woman lawyer that liked Blackburn), and even people on the same side not liking each other.

Then we went in deeper water. We decided the worker issue would be the first thing discussed, since it would probably be the hardest for Formosa. And it was. But that issue was got over and agreed on, just like every last thing on our list. Eventually we had an agreement that intertwined environment and unions and community. On the worker side, Formosa agreed that all their present and future plants would be open to union organization, and during any organizing campaign Formosa was to remain neutral and not hand out antiunion propaganda or intimidate or exact reprisal from any employee who joined the union. Lastly, Formosa agreed to use union contractors and union workers on all future construction projects.

On the environmental side, we would be given unrestricted access to all sites where Formosa planned or was constructing plant facilities, and given unrestricted access to all information about the facilities and the construction. Audits were to be conducted two times a year for as long as the facility was operational, and we had the right to select the date and the representatives, and Formosa would foot the bill.

Then there was a provision for endangered species review and an agreement that the impact of Formosa's wastewater discharge into Lavaca Bay would not result in measurable degradation, and to that end Formosa would pay a consultant we chose to conduct a baseline survey of environmental quality within Lavaca Bay, and would also fund an analysis of the existing discharge point into Cox's Creek. If there was an area of contamination in Cox's Creek, Formosa was to undertake cleanup efforts.

Finally there were provisions where Formosa agreed to comprehensive air modeling of emissions from the existing and proposed facility, and in the event that they exceeded air standards, Formosa would engineer changes to bring the emissions into compliance.

There was a corporate policy and financial reward structure emphasizing environmental and safety considerations, and a provision set up to buy out homes of property owners in Point Comfort, and there would never be any plant facilities on acreage known as the Tejano Farms or on any land north of Karancua Bay or land adjacent to the river pouring into Karancua Bay.

For the agreement to work, I had to get off the hunger strike and give up my opposition to the marine terminal and tank-farm permit and to end the lawsuit in federal district court against Formosa and the EPA. I was also not to oppose the Corps of Engineers permit to allow expansion of the port facility, and not oppose the substitution of raw condensate and naptha as the fuel source for the facility.

The negotiations took four hours of talking and smoking cigarettes and coffee going back and forth, with arguments and issues and a few personal fights just because the personalities wouldn't mix. When everyone was satisfied that an agreement was reached and I was going off the hunger strike, we all shook hands, except Greenpeace, who wouldn't with Formosa's lawyer. Finally there was another hour in Blackburn's office where the notes of the agreement were typed out. And Donna Sue drove up from Seadrift and picked me up at Blackburn's office, and on the way home we ordered a pizza in Goliad.

I went home. Even though I had been gone a month, the doors of the house weren't locked and the kids were glad to see me. They fell around my legs and patted my skinny arms and wondered about my sunken eyes, and every room I went into, they followed. The kids had a ton of stories to tell: dogs being shot and blood on the porch and helicopters in the sky. Ramona showed me a picture Crockett had drew of a sky raining bullets. Slowly we all came around, and the kids got used to me and didn't follow me around so much, and I was only confused with long sentences and understanding what they meant. Donna Sue said I had fried some brain cells, and I figured she was right.

I believed we had won and I held the thought like a bird in the palm of my hand. The third night home, Andy Boy from the union hall in Texas City called. Formosa had reneged on the worker part of the agreement. The hunger strike had obviously been the only leverage that got the workers' right to organize in the agreement, but since the hunger strike was ended, the leverage had vanished. On top of that, Formosa's attorney had offered the union fifty thousand dollars if they would just go away.

"How do you like that? Offering us a freakin' fifty thousand dollars! We told them it was a violation of federal labor law! Shit! We couldn't take that money."

So here I thought an action was oh, so simple and was over and done with, but there it unraveled all over again. I was thinkin', *Stupidstupidstupid*, but it was too late for even that. I was off the hunger strike and I had no leverage. What was to keep Formosa from backpedaling until the whole agreement was trampled? Was there no honor left in the world? Can people sit and look one another in the eye and say words and give promises and then ditch the thing like it was a soiled napkin?

I called Blackburn and he said, "Yep, Formosa has backed out on the worker issue, but I'm still trying to keep the other parts intact."

"We have no other actions we can do? We can't *force* them to honor the agreement?"

"Now, how are we going to force them? Twist their pinkies?"

"Well, how long do you think those other parts will last? What's to keep them from going back on another? Or the whole damn thing? Is the agreement about what's convenient for Formosa? What they feel like doing?"

"We're just seeing the raw power of a corporation, Wilson. Corporations don't like handing power over to workers any more than they like handing it over to people like you and me. . . . And frankly, I think they hate handing it over to workers most of all. I see it now, but it's a little too late. We were lucky we got a discussion on the workers. I've had a lot of negotiations with industry over the years, and this is the first where a worker's right to organize was involved. There's nothing we can do about it, Wilson. Forget it. A lesson learned. We just have to trust Formosa to keep their word on the rest."

"Blackburn! They offered the union fifty thousand dollars to vanish! That's a damn bribe!"

But Blackburn laughed and said, "Oh, forget it! That's in-house lawyers squabbling. You don't tell all you know when you go into negotiations. If I didn't know better I'd say you've got a good case of sour grapes."

"*Sour grapes!* Because I went on a hunger strike for thirty of the hardest days of my life, then watch it all fall apart because Formosa doesn't feel like keeping their word? You call that sour grapes? If it had been *you* on a hunger strike, you'd have taken them to the Supreme Court and sued the britches off them!"

Blackburn laughed, and I could tell he was having a high ole time at my expense. I was just amusing as the dickens. He said he was just glad I was off that hunger strike. And another thing: As my lawyer, he'd advise me not to repeat all that money stuff to the press. Sometimes information like that had a way of flipping back and whacking you in the face.

But I didn't need lawyer's council to tell me where it hurt and why. So I called the reporter I had talked with on the shrimp boat and told her that the negotiations had fell apart and that the Oil, Chemical, and Atomic Workers's International union had been offered fifty thousand dollars by Formosa's attorney. I didn't know what to make of it, I said, but it was sure killing any trust I had in Formosa. I told her when it came to citizens negotiating with big corporations, there were land mines galore.

The next day, headlines in the newspaper lay peaceful with big black letters, and I thought to myself, *Well, what did you expect?* The headlines read: ACTIVIST, UNION PUSH ORGANIZATION AT FORMOSA. I thought nothing after that, only how bad for how long will it go, because further on down, the paper quoted Formosa's skinny attorney saying, "*First*, Ms. Wilson brings us environmental issues, *then* it's worker safety, and *then* she wants a union. We can't *force* a union down the throats of our workers. And as for that bribe, why, there was no bribe offered by Formosa. There was a discussion about bulletin boards. Now, there might have been a fifty-thousand-dollar cap on that."

Then it stopped for a day, but two days later the paper ran an editorial that said it appeared that Ms. Wilson's critics were right when they said she had a hidden agenda in her environmental chess game, and that agenda was to *organize* the Formosa workforce for the Oil, Chemical, and Atomic Workers's International union. So I wasn't a fisherman after all. After these thirty years on the bay, I was only a union organizer, even if Rick told me I couldn't organize chalk on a chalkboard.

"Oh, it isn't serious stuff," Blackburn said. "That paper just singed your hair a little bit. And what did you expect anyhow? A squadron of cheerleaders?"

Donna Sue said, "The hell with them! I didn't want you to sign with Formosa in the first place. Now, why did you have to do it?"

"I'm real tired of fighting," I said.

"Oh, that's just that hunger strike talking! You've got fried brain cells and your body's wore down. You ain't finished fighting by a long shot. I know you."

Maybe she was right. I called Blackburn back and said I didn't want to negotiate with Formosa anymore. I couldn't trust them not to axe and reinterpretate everything we had agreed on. Formosa wasn't getting my silence for a two-bit agreement that was getting miles and miles from what we had negotiated in his office.

Blackburn agreed. He sounded tired and wasted down to nothing. He was up to his eyeballs in crocodiles with the whole mess, he said. He'd call Formosa back and tell them the negotiations were off.

• • •

I figured it was done with. Thirty days of a hunger strike I didn't want to say was wasted because the EPA was slowly, slowly turning to demand an environmental impact study on both Formosa's Texas and Louisiana projects, but the strike certainly hadn't put on the flesh and bones of an agreement. It was more like a stick horse leaning against the barn.

Then I got a call from Blackburn—without tone or warmth. So I said, "Who is this?"

And he said, "It's Blackburn."

"What's the matter? What happened?"

"Nothing's the matter. Nothing's happened. I just think we ought to start negotiating with Formosa again."

"Why? I thought we decided we weren't working with them. We can't trust them. What's changed?"

"I was just tired that last time we talked, Wilson. I had a lot of work at the office piled up—the law practice isn't going—well, it just isn't going. It'll get better, though. So I've started talking with Formosa again. I just wanted you to know."

I said, "Are you sure you're all right, Blackburn? You don't *sound* all right. Something's wrong."

Blackburn said, No, no. He was fine. Fine. Then he said, "I'll talk to you later, Wilson," and he hung up, and I stood in the dark with the phone in my hand and tried to figure how a man could be two different men in one week's time and still say nothing was the matter.

I guessed the negotiations were on. The paper said so. The Victoria reporter had talked to Blackburn and he was quoted: "We're not bringing anything back to the negotiating table that we don't think can be agreed upon by Formosa or by my client."

Then Joe Wyatt, speaking for Formosa, said, "We have always been interested in continuing the negotiations. We never said we wanted to stop. Presently, we are setting a date for the next round of face-to-face negotiations between Wilson and ourselves."

So I waited for the call saying when we would sit down face-to-face and try to negotiate again. Maybe it would be Blackburn in his real voice, or maybe he'd have that lawyer tone like he hadn't seen or worked with me more than twice, and then it would be me wondering what happened to that time when Donna Sue and I had pulled shrimp boxes into his office and sat on his floor, barefoot and going through files, and he had laughed and we had laughed, and once he had even sang a Willie Nelson song.

Two weeks later Blackburn called from his car phone. He was on a long drive back to Houston. He had just met with Joe Wyatt and Jack Wu and Formosa's woman attorney in Corpus Christi. He had had a hard go of it, he said, but he believed he was getting somewhere with Formosa.

I was confused. "Getting somewhere on what?"

And Blackburn said, "With the negotiations! I think I'm holding my own with them, though."

I listened to his voice go on and on. Blackburn was happy. He was engaged in battle. Soon as he had the agreement in a legible form, he'd let me read it and see what I thought. Then I could sign it.

"I'd like to see what you got, Blackburn."

And he said, "Oh, sure, sure. Let me get back to the office and I'll fax you something."

Only he didn't fax and he didn't call, so I did some more waiting on a man and got a place sore in my belly where I was sticking all my thoughts. Memories had festered, crusted over, layer after layer after layer, until now they were thick enough that either I carted them out or they were going to bury me alive.

Finally Blackburn called and said he wanted me in Houston the next morning. When I got to his office I could look the agreement over, ask any questions I had, then sign the thing.

I don't know what happened next. Maybe that sore place erupted, but whatever it was I didn't recognize the voice coming out my mouth. I said, "I don't know about all this negotiating you're doin'."

Blackburn's voice stopped. Then it came back double the lawyer and icy cold.

"What?" he said. Blackburn was ready, and I knew it and he knew it, so he said it again like he was loading a shotgun for the second time that day. "What?"

"Blackburn . . . how come you didn't tell me a week ago when you went to Corpus to negotiate with Formosa? I thought I was the client and it was supposed to be a face-to-face meeting with me and Formosa."

Blackburn said nothing for a minute, then he said, "You're too emotional. It was better that I handled it. You'd have got upset."

"*Upset?* Upset is when you leave me out! And I have a right to be upset! This is *my* home! This is my bay! Where do you get the authority to do all the deciding and leaving us out of it? What are you—reading our minds now? A lawyer's so great and wonderful he don't even need his clients anymore?"

"Wilson! I *told* you I was talking again. Besides, I'm not just a lawyer here. I'm an activist too. I've as much right to be involved as you are."

"Well, dang it, Blackburn. I sure wish you'd tell me when you're the activist and when you're the lawyer. You're confusing me with all this switching around."

"*Listen!* I've been working my *fuckin' butt* off on this deal, so you can just get off your gotdam high horse!"

"And *I've* been working my butt off too, Blackburn! You haven't been the only one. . . . And I put in thirty damn days on a hunger strike you think was nothing!"

"I never said it was nothing! That's your own damn pity call. And if you don't come tomorrow and sign that agreement after all the arranging I've been doing, then you can just forget it. We can't work together. You're wearing me out. I'm tired of this shit!"

"Well, *adios*, Blackburn. It's been nice meeting you."

"*Adios*, yourself!"

We both hung up. I stared at the phone and couldn't believe it. I had yelled at him worse than I had ever done with Formosa. Still, I didn't know how I could have done anything different. The sitting and waiting and listening and not saying nothing would finally have driven the spot in my belly into my chest, and then I'd have quit breathing altogether. Talk about a sore loser!

But I couldn't believe it was entirely finished. That was just mad blistering talk. We still had a lawsuit in federal court. We had an air permit hearing that had to be finished. Then too, Blackburn had too much of an emotional investment in our work together on the bays, and while it wasn't me personally but more the bay, I knew I represented the water in some form to the lawyer in his Houston tower. Blackburn would call back. I didn't know what he'd do, but I *knew* he'd call back.

It was the earliest he had ever called. I couldn't even find the light switch, so I picked up the phone in the dark. Blackburn said, "Are you coming up to my office today?"

I said as gently as I could, "Blackburn, I'll drive up there and we can talk about this, but I'm not gonna sign that agreement. I wasn't any part of it, and I didn't negotiate it. Nobody negotiated but you. So I *can't*! I don't know what's on it, for crying out loud. We can talk about it, though. Maybe you can tell me what's going on."

"Look, do me a favor, Wilson. Either you come today and sign the damn thing or don't come at all. I don't want to talk. I'm tired of talking."

"Then I guess I won't come, Blackburn."

So that was the second time we split and left more unsaid things. It took two days before I could get the words to tell Donna Sue, and she stood in the door of the fish house and said, "That ain't gonna last. Blackburn likes us too much."

"Well, you go tell him and remind him, 'cause I don't think he remembers it. I don't know what's the matter. One minute he wants to quit, then the next he's knee-deep in meetings. I don't know who he's talking to, but it sure ain't you or me."

"Oh, Blackburn'll be back."

That's what I hoped. Any day, any hour now. Blackburn would be back with that lawyer's icy voice gone and him laughing and wishing he was down on San Antonio Bay, wearing white rubber boots just like me and Donna Sue. But he didn't, so I waited and hoped on nothing.

It took a month for him to call, and then he called in the evening because he was waiting for it to get as dark as it could be before he said what he had to say. "I want you to let me go, Wilson."

I was overjoyed with the sound of his voice. I laughed, "What? Let you go? Where to? I don't have a chain around your neck." It was as though the fight between us had vanished. What's a cuss fight between friends? Nothing. So Blackburn had talked without me. So what? What was the big deal? We were friends. We were comrades in a war. We were the Sonny and Cher of the environmental movement, for God's sake! Just you and me, babe.

"You know what I mean, Wilson. I want to resign. I don't want to be your attorney. I don't want to be a part of the lawsuit." Blackburn's voice was as dead as a rat in the water.

"What? I don't understand. I don't know . . ."

"*Wilson!* I'm signing my own agreement with Formosa. *I can't* be your attorney. I *have* to resign. I just want you to say you'll let me go. I *have* to hear you say that. Say it! Say the words."

"*No!* Blackburn, don't! No! Not that!"

"Wilson. Listen to me. I *have* to. My firm's in trouble. . . . I don't know. I may have to let someone go. This whole Formosa thing has gotten like a black pit. It's overwhelming! I can't keep this pace up. It's gotta stop."

"Blackburn! You *can't quit*! We've been fighting so long—nearly three years! This is everything we've worked for! I know it's overwhelming, but we'll make it. We've got the lawsuit! The hearing!"

"You can still do it. I'm not stopping you. I just *can't. Not anymore.* Get yourself another lawyer."

"Another lawyer!" I laughed at the idea. A lawyer besides Blackburn? "Who, Blackburn? Who?"

"I don't know. There's lawyers out there."

So that's how it came. Out of the dark, and it stayed in the dark even while I heard Blackburn talking in my ear, saying how he had to quit and how he thought he was doing the best thing and how it was hard for him too. I just stared out the window and watched the black night march across the sky and across the porch and into the room where I stood.

I thought it was a joke. It had to be a joke. Signing an agreement with Formosa? It had to be crazy. In five minutes he'll call back and laugh at how he'd fooled me for five whole minutes. But he didn't hang up. He just said it over again, "Let me go, Wilson. I want you to say the words. Say it's okay."

So I said, "Okay, Blackburn. Do what you want. This isn't no jail cell. I don't keep nobody that don't wanna be here."

26

Pain and Defeat

The difference between men and women is that we are planets apart. So when Rick said something crazy or Blackburn said something crazy or when Baby said nothing at all but just broke out more windows, I would look at them all like they'd just flew in on some foreign plane I'd never saw. I couldn't discuss it with anyone. Donna Sue didn't believe Blackburn's desertion anyhow. She said, What would he do without us? He needed us more than we needed him. He was a needy man, that one. I just knew I had a marine hearing to get through—without a lawyer—and now Baby was slipping off into the oak trees with his pearl-handled pistol that was no good for nothing but blowing heads off of rattlesnakes, only it wasn't rattlesnake season.

On the day of our air hearing against Formosa in Austin, I called Donna Sue to come and get me, and told her that when she got there not to blow the horn or make any noise. Just open the door and let me and the kids in. So that's what she did, only Baby heard, and he stood near the corner of the house, not moving forward, not moving back. He just stood with the gun.

I put the girls in first, then Crockett, and figured if there was going to be trouble, it'd be then. So I shut my eyes, waiting for the sound of something different. I didn't know how different—maybe it would be no sound at all, like how lightning strikes with no noise. At least that's what everyone says later: They never heard a thing.

Then I left Donna Sue at her house (she couldn't go to Austin—she was having trouble too) and drove with the five kids to a press conference in front of the capitol steps, and afterwards to a hearing before the Air Control Board where either the commissioners would say yes to Formosa or they'd say no. The capitol press and the television cameras had already arrived, and the union men from Texas City had even drug a labor-sympathizing legislator from the capitol halls to stand before the press and the microphones.

Crockett went wilder than he had gone in a long time and I didn't know whether it was what we had left at the house or the whole movement from house to car to the streets of a capitol that set him off like a roman candle. He climbed the bricks on the west wing of the capitol, using the quarter inch of mortar between bricks like most people used five inches on a ladder. Finally, to keep him still, I pulled him in front and put both arms around him like I was a coat he had on.

The press conference didn't take long. Hard statements in front of harder capitol steps, and all around the sun fell under its own weight. There was no wind to take anywhere, so it fell on us. Later they all left: the OCAW men to Texas City and the chemical plants, and the AFL-CIO fellas to their Austin offices, and Rick and Greenpeace to the half-dozen other events that filled up their days and their lives, and this one wasn't any different just because it had Formosa in it. I went to the Air Control Board hearing and already, on the outside of the building and waiting for me, were three buses: identical tin cans with gray swirly writing and smooth black windows to keep the air-conditioning in. They were empty. The riders were all inside the building and had been long before I arrived. They were mostly Formosa employees and contractors: men with neatly combed hair, in hard jeans and permanent-press shirts and wide belts with wider belt buckles. Some brought their wives and girlfriends, and they all sat in a crowded auditorium waiting. I sat next to them in the only seat available.

The crowding was a problem. Formosa's attorneys could tell there was a problem. Now, how on earth were the Air Control Board commissioners to know that the workers sitting next to the activist weren't with the activist, but instead with Formosa? Who was with who? So the skinny woman lawyer (who did yoga in the mornings, never lit up a cigarette in her entire life, and offered the union fifty thousand dollars to vamoose) stood up and said to the commissioners sitting behind a table and in chairs a little bit higher than the rest, that if it wouldn't be too great an intrusion, she'd like to present to the commissioners the entire support team of Formosa. Then the whole room stood up and looked around, benign as a soap commercial, and some smiled and some just kept their hands near their shiny belt buckles. And they all knew something I didn't know, and that was standing is enough when you've only got one fool sitting. The chairman of the Air Control Board stood up from the table and said because of the number of people present and the unreasonable length that the hearing would have to go on if everyone was allowed an unlimited time to speak, he was only allowing two minutes of testimony.

Then the skinny black-eyed lawyer stood up and said since there was *such* a crowd, she hoped it would not be too much of an inconvenience if the harried elected officials from the three counties being affected by the court's proceedings could present their testimony first. So the harried officials came one by one and presented a copy of their typewritten speech to every commissioner present, and one as evidence to be entered in the state's record to show that they were supporting Formosa.

Midway through the speeches and after about the twelfth time it had been told about the economic impact of Formosa's expansion and how many men had already been hired and how much was at stake if the permit wasn't granted and how much had been put at risk because of the bad press on Formosa, the chairman of the Air Control Board stood up. He was a young man and looked fierce. He said he was going to have to admonish Formosa's supporters if they spoke again of the plant's economic impact on the area and that Formosa's problems were due to a lot of bad press.

"Sirs," he said, "just because you spend five hundred million dollars on a project doesn't give you the right to pollute. The press isn't the problem; the problem is the pollution."

As the chairman spoke his voice floated out over the microphone and over our heads, and I was grateful for that one voice. There was no Blackburn in his black suit and white shirt who would ward off the men in their dark jeans like they were biting flies eating at my hands; nobody to keep the eyes of officials in flat brown shoes from eroding my soul. That hearing was the fullest I ever felt Blackburn's absence. I said somewhere, *You get through this one and you can get through them all. This one will fix you and it will break you.*

After the speeches ended and after some twenty employees and various contractors and every county judge and every mayor of three counties had stood, Formosa's lawyer took letters from Senator Armbrister of Victoria and Representatives Hunter and Dohlen from Corpus Christi and Goliad to the commissioners' table and said that the state officials couldn't be present, but still they wished to send their support for the permit.

Then the faces quit talking and the men quit getting up and

scooting between rows of chairs and dozens of boots, and the chairman moved only slightly in his chair when he looked to me and said without saying it out loud, but with his mouth, "Are you ready?" I nodded my head. This was my two minutes.

I got up, not recognizing my own feet or hands on the backs of the chairs as I went past. A dozen faces turned and a few words were said, but I didn't look and I didn't hear. I walked straight to the microphone. I didn't have handwritten pages or a typed speech, so I just spoke low into the microphone. I said I was opposing Formosa's permit because of their bad history of compliance and their disregard for the environment. I said they could not be trusted with our bays and our lives, and their pollution shouldn't be rewarded with a permit from the state. Then I glanced over to one of the women commissioners, and said that the Air Control Board member Mary Ann Wyatt should resign her position, because her husband, Joe Wyatt, was employed by Formosa and often acted as a spokesperson.

That was my last act, and nearly the board's, because the only thing left was the commissioners' vote. So everything went quiet until I sat down again, then the wife of Formosa's spokesperson got up and excused herself from the vote, then a man who said his personal opposition to Formosa would bias his vote, then another woman—the board's only physician—who said that she did not feel comfortable voting on Formosa's permit, and that the supporters might come back before this board thirty years from now because they had cancer.

I was ready to leave, already having heard many times before that a permitting agency was *going* to permit. That was it, plain and simple. Agencies were in the business of permitting. Still, I had a wild hope, but I didn't want to see it dead at my feet, so I got up to leave and in the leaving I heard the vote: 5-0 in favor.

Formosa's supporters rose cheering: their bodies and limbs moved instinctively and mingled like leaves shook from a tree. I didn't feel nothing until I got to Donna Sue's car, where a tired woman activist sat with my kids. The woman's eyes said plenty. She said nothing. She had been to permit hearings before. She knew what happened. She gave me a tight smile in a hot parking lot and scooted across the front seat, and turned her back while Formosa's employees piled on the parked buses.

I don't know what bothered me more: the excessiveness of every act of Formosa, so that if I had one man or one child, then they had to have ninety or a hundred men and every one of them wearing a corsage with blue ribbons and FORMOSA written in gold glitter down the side; or Blackburn's absence, which underscored everything, so if before he had been a buffer, now he was the river that led everything straight to me.

One day not long after the hearing, Blackburn's office sent an itemized bill for the hours he had spent representing me, and the balance owed was a hundred seventy-five thousand dollars. I stared at the paper a long time. Was I supposed to pay the bill? So I called Blackburn's office and talked with the secretary, and she talked with someone else and they said, No, no. The itemized bill was for my records.

What records? Why after all the pro bono work and no mention of money did I now know the cost of every phone call and every time Blackburn had sat down and talked with me, and if I wanted to know which meeting cost more, I could have gone to my itemized bill and found out?

When Rick called, I asked him, "Why do you think Blackburn sent me a bill for a hundred seventy-five thousand dollars that I'm not supposed to pay?"

Rick went crazy. "Why? Why? Whadda you think! I think Blackburn's been bought off. That hundred-seventy-five-thousand-dollar bill is it!"

"Blackburn's office said it was for my records."

"Records, my hind foot! It's his payoff. Maybe Formosa's going to reimburse him for all his legal work! We don't have to let him go, Diane! We can force him to stay. He's our lawyer! Hell, he's got to finish what he said he'd do."

"You can't make somebody stay who don't want to stay, Rick. It can't work that way."

"It's Blackburn's legal obligation. He's violating his professional obligation!"

"I can't do it. Blackburn worked without pay, and if he can't stay for whatever reasons—maybe it's his business, I don't know—then I'm letting him go just like he asked. I owe him that much."

"You don't owe Blackburn shit!"

"Yes, I do. What I owe, I pay back."

There was something wrong about the whole deal, but I shut the screen door on it and only now and then saw the top of its nagging, gripping head. At least I didn't hear the voice. Then Blackburn's office called and said Blackburn was formally resigning as my attorney, and it would be decided in Houston in front of a judge who would also rule on Formosa's motion to dismiss our federal lawsuit. Blackburn wanted me there.

Then Rick called and said, "You know what's happening, don't you?"

I knew. Blackburn was legally severing ties with us. I didn't know he would go down that channel, but he was, so I was going there.

"If it takes a federal judge, Rick, then I guess it takes a federal judge."

"He's going to kill our lawsuit," Rick said.

"Then he's gonna kill our lawsuit. I'm not keeping a man who doesn't want to belong. I ain't ever in that bad a shape, Rick."

There was four parties in that judge's office and none of us right with the others. Just a bunch of mismatched boxes somebody randomly tossed from a truck without looking, and nobody cared much except the boxes, if they had had tongues to say so. And some of us had tongues and some didn't, and I was one of those. I sat on an empty pew in a courtroom where all the parties were estranged. Even Blackburn, except every once in a while, he came back and sat beside me and said, "Is everything all right?" And I said, "It's all right." Then he'd leave, and Rick would come and sit down and fume so loud I could have heard his breath from outside the courthouse. Then before Rick left he leaned over and said, "I'm not letting that SOB go. This is a bunch of shit!" And I didn't say nothing except stare where the judge sat.

The judge explained himself and why he hadn't heard our case. He said he hadn't made a court date to hear our lawsuit against Formosa Plastics because both parties had asked for delays, and before I had time to act surprised or even turn to Blackburn and ask, "Is this *really* the reason?" the judge said that no matter what he did, somebody was going to be unhappy, so it would be in everyone's best interest if a compromise could be reached.

Then he allowed Blackburn to get up and talk to him, and never once did Blackburn turn to look at me or Rick. Blackburn said he had philosophical differences with his clients that could not be resolved and he had negotiated the best deal he could get from Formosa, but his clients rejected it. Then he said that over a two-year period he had provided legal services in excess of a hundred fifty thousand dollars, and he said he couldn't afford it anymore.

Some of the stuff Blackburn said was new, and I thought, *Oh, was that it? He was broke. He was tired and wore out, and I was a bad client because I wouldn't compromise with Formosa at all.* And it was just then in that courtroom that the insight entered my brain. Brand-new. And nobody else, because Rick had been thinking it all along and so the courtroom news was nothing new.

Next Rick got up and said that Blackburn had agreed to take the case without pay and he should be obligated to see the case through to a court decision. He said, "We gave Blackburn the case to litigate in court and not to be used for leverage to reach his own agreement with Formosa. Texans United doesn't have the money to hire another attorney of Blackburn's caliber, and his removal will finish the case. There will be irreparable harm done."

But the judge wasn't sympathetic and didn't look like he was crying about nothing Rick said. Then the judge looked over to me and asked if there was anything I wanted to say, and I said it was all right if Mister Blackburn wanted to resign. I knew that he did, and it was all right.

Then the judge shoved his face into his robed neck so it was mainly his eyes that the four parties saw even if it was his voice that we heard, and he said he was granting the request of Mister Blackburn to resign as legal counsel to Calhoun County Resource Watch and Texans United, based on the cost of litigation and the failure of his clients to negotiate.

I sat immobile. It was a treacherous game, and even though the judge said the case wasn't ruined, all four parties knew it was.

Wally certainly knew it, and rushed to the fish house when I finally drove back. He said, "We've won! We've won. You can quit now!" Wally didn't even mind Donna Sue's killer looks. It didn't matter what was on her face, because Wally believed Formosa had won and when they won, he won.

Except it didn't end. I believed it never would. The fight would go on and on—one act spurring another. And there was Rick and Blackburn's feud. Blackburn insisted *he* wasn't feuding; he was way above any petty ego-pissing contest with Rick. He was just defending

himself from Rick's constant attacks. And Rick had found the biggest
of all Blackburn's soft spots. His credibility. His reputation. Rick
turned Blackburn in to the Houston Bar Association, saying his action
of withdrawing as our attorney and signing his own agreement with a
company we were fighting constituted illegal behavior before the bar.

So Blackburn called again and asked if I would come to Houston
and sign some papers so he could fight Rick's accusations. There
comes a time when all is excess and overkill, and somebody looking
would ask, Doesn't your work mean anything to you? But that wasn't
it. The time to speak had gone past, and with it all the words to
explain what was happening. I was just trying to tie a knot in a thing
done. A demon thing finished. Only Rick didn't want it finished, and
Blackburn just wanted me to hurry up and tie the damn knot.

I was running out of blood. I knew I was getting low when I sat in
Blackburn's office in bright, bright morning light and read what he
wrote on my affidavit. I nearly said, "I believe it's all gone, Blackburn.
My blood is running white now." But I didn't. I signed my name on
papers I didn't write, and maybe they were lies and maybe it was somebody's perspective, just not my own. All I knew was I paid my debt.

I was full of pain and not worth any further harm, but still I couldn't
quit. I didn't know how to stop. So I went shrimping again, and one
evening I stood in the door of the fish house, when Donna Sue said,
"I'm glad it happened. I never wanted you to sign." Then she walked
over to the shrimp vat and stirred the shrimp I'd brought in and
shoved them up the ramp with her wide broom. Ever' thrust she made
with the broom, she said, "I'm glad. I'm glad!"

I didn't know why Donna Sue was glad, because her glad meant I
would have to fight again, and I didn't think I could ever fight again.
But Donna Sue figured different. She said Blackburn would be back.
He'd quit that Formosa, and when I got rested and when he came
back, then we could start fighting again. Just like before. Or nearly like
before.

That was the reason she told Blackburn I was still at the fish house. I
had tied up the *SeaBee* and had my hand on the van door when she
came outside the fish house and yelled across the harbor that Blackburn
wanted to talk on the phone. He was calling from Formosa, she said.
He's right across the county.

I didn't know why he had gone to Formosa and I didn't know why I crossed the harbor and picked up the phone, but I did. It was the same old Blackburn I remembered. The man who could sing country-western better than me, and who could wonder, while he twirled a pink-wrapped candy in his thumb and forefinger, why I never knew the correct names for the shorebirds I saw every day of my life.

Blackburn said he had had a long day with Formosa and gave no explanation. He didn't want to talk about Formosa anyhow. He said, "I miss working with you, Wilson. I might have a couple of minutes before I have to get back to Houston." So I said, "I'll be here on the docks, waiting."

I waited on Blackburn coming from a long day at Formosa, and Donna Sue left, but she turned once and said, "I *knew* he would be back." But I didn't say nothing. I didn't think he was coming back. I didn't know what he was doing.

The only cool spot in the whole harbor was the back of the fish house, so I took two shrimp boxes and set them on the back dock, facing the *SeaBee*. Then I made a fresh pot of coffee, and twenty minutes later that Blackburn showed.

He walked across the dead grass in his black suit with the coat gone, and now it was only his white shirt and black pants he was wearing.

I said, "You look tired, Blackburn."

And he said, "I am tired, Wilson. I am bone tired."

His voice was just a whisper at the corner of the fish house where he stood. Then he stepped down on the docks and, without saying anything, sat on the shrimp box and leaned his elbows on his knees. "This is what I like. This right here. It's perfect here. You're perfect here. That's why you fight so well here."

"Because I live here?" I said.

"You got a sense of place, Wilson. Most people don't have it and don't even know it exists. People are too uprooted. Too mobile. They never get to experience what you have right in this little town. And I don't know whether you know it or not—or even believe it or not—but that's an essential starting point for spirituality. You're a very spiritual person, Wilson. Anybody ever tell you that?"

"Nope, Blackburn. That ain't what they say."

"Well, it's true. That's why you and I have always had a bond in this fight. You get your spirit from San Antonio Bay and Lavaca Bay and Spirit Center Bay, and I get mine from Smith Point and Christmas Bay and Galveston Bay."

He said he wouldn't be alive now if he hadn't found that same sense of place in later life that I had had my whole life. He wouldn't be alive. Or if he was, it would be because the drinking hadn't killed him yet. But it was going to. It sure was going to.

That had been eleven years ago. He had finally went to an AA meeting and they had told him to find a higher power, and he said he saw no higher power in the Baptist God, so they told him a higher power didn't always have to be a Baptist god. It could be anything he deeply believed in or wanted to believe in. So that was when he decided Galveston Bay would be his higher power, and he went to the bay and sat with it and felt it and tried to understand and truly love the spartina marsh and its long-billed waders and the red-winged blackbirds, and the finger mullet schools and blue crabs gliding in the silt, and the flatfish and the flounders and the rays moving ethereally across the muck.

There was an odd peace between me and Blackburn, and it came from the old rotten wood underneath us and across the flat water, where the boats were tied and barely moved. We didn't talk about the agreement. I didn't want to hear something that was splitting us apart and how he had sat at Formosa's all day, designing an agreement and press statement that all the parties could live with and none of them would regret.

Blackburn didn't talk about regret except once. He said what he was doing was either the best thing he had ever done or it was the worst. He didn't know which it was, but it was hard. "It's harder than your fighting, Wilson. At least with fighting, you know it's fighting and nothing else but this. . . . This agreement, I don't know what it is sometimes. I'm making it up as I go."

I didn't have a shot-torn flag to wave as he left. If I had, it was lying on the ground at my feet while I was wondering if his car was gonna be the last of Blackburn. From there it wasn't long off before I wondered if my fighting *wasn't* too easy. Maybe it was the only thing I knew how to do. And it wasn't so much as the proper or the right thing to do as it was I didn't know another, and if another came along, would I know it? A passel of gray images blended with the horizon:

pollution and chemical plants and fishermen and the bays and environmentalists. The war was *very, very* complicated. Maybe the war was so complicated that it took different soldiers for different times, and now it called for a different kind of soldier. A peacemaker. A compromiser. A negotiator.

I rode home in the dark, and stumbled on the broken and missing boards on the porch, then went through the front screen door that slammed like a child's cough. The kitchen was lit from an old circling Sears fan with four fluted glass shades, and it went round and round above my head and the wind went round and round, and the babies come up to my knees and grabbed my jeans.

I looked at them and asked, "Ain't I fought enough? Ain't I done that?" And the babies patted my jeans and Santanna wanted to be held and Crockett didn't, so I held Santanna on my hip while I started supper. It was only later, as I lay quiet on the sun-harsh sheets, that I said to nobody in particular but only the chipped paint above my head that listened: *Tomorrow, I quit. When I wake up tomorrow, I will be done.*

27

A Woman Enters the Sea

I figured the bay wouldn't miss me for one hour, so instead of leaving the docks at five, I waited one hour, then climbed through the window at Froggie's fish house.

I said, "Blackburn? Are you up?"

Sure, he was up. He *had* to have been up. It was six o'clock in Seadrift and six o'clock in Houston, and what else do you do at six in Houston except get ready to go through all that traffic?

He said, "Wilson? Is that you?"

And I blurted out, "I want to sign that agreement with you. I'm fixin' to go shrimping, but I just wanted to tell you that before I went out."

"Are you sure you want to do this? I know I'm ready to lay down my sword, but are you ready to lay down yours? This isn't a game."

"I know it. But I'm tired of fighting. I think you're right about trying something different. Maybe we can do some good."

"Now, you know I'm not twisting your arm here. That talk yesterday was just talk; it wasn't about twisting your arm to get you to sign."

"I know it, Blackburn."

"And you're still willing? Not fixing to launch into another fight two weeks down the road?"

"No, Blackburn. I *told* you. I'm finished fighting."

"Well, all right, Wilson. I'll call Formosa when I get to my office and see if I can get them to go along with the idea. You know, they're real nervous about you. . . . Probably figure this is just another strategy like that hunger strike. 'Cause it can't be, Wilson. This has got to be a heartfelt attempt at compromise. If you don't believe in it, it won't work. It can't."

"No, no. I'm gonna work at it."

"Well, good, Wilson. It's *good* to have you aboard. I won't lie about that. You don't know how glad I am. It's real scary making a lone move like this."

After I hung up and climbed back on the *SeaBee*, I knew I was going somewhere other than the bay. The whole time I was shrimping, I thought this other thing and wondered where it was leading me. I didn't put a right or wrong to it. It was just someplace different than the fighting, because the fighting was making me wearier than the sun and water could make me weary. I wanted a place where there was some shade for a while, and who knows what else. Maybe it'd be all right. Maybe I could do it.

Which was the *wrong* thing to be thinking. You don't get married thinking *Maybe I can do it. Maybe I can.* Those words are a surefire indication that something bad is wrong somewhere, and *nobody* better be saying any marriage vows soon.

But I wasn't alarmed. I wasn't dragging my shot-torn flag. I believed the damn thing was soiled and dead on the ground. By the next day it didn't matter anyhow. The entire environmental movement in Texas knew about the deal, and Rick was the first to call. He said, "Don't you know this is a *sweetheart* deal!"

He was yelling over the phone, and I wasn't talking back and wasn't even thinking about talking back, but simply staring into the white wall of the fish-house office. Rick said Blackburn's agreement was a deal so the governor of Texas could congratulate Blackburn and Formosa on a very positive agreement that the state of Texas could live with, and now they could keep on permitting a bad but vastly improved industry. And everybody's happy!

"This way Ann's first real test on the environment as a governor is cleared! She has hurdled the whole mess! Now nobody can say she doesn't have the presidential potential to handle controversial issues when she has to. This is a political scam! A sweetheart deal! The entire Democratic Party in Texas has turned tail and run. If you sign this agreement you will be endorsing a policy of rubber-stamping permits and allowing more violations and unsafe practices than we've ever seen before. The entire coast will be ruined, and it will be your fault!"

Rick said he'd always known I couldn't refuse Blackburn nothing, and now my move to sign was just more proof. Whatever Blackburn said, I run and did.

"Look, Diane. If you can't tell Blackburn no, then just come to the press conference with us, and we'll do the blasting. All you've got to do is stand there and keep your mouth shut. We'll do the blasting for you."

• • •

Somewhere about the middle of the day, Blackburn called and said that I was supposed to meet him in the rotunda of the capitol and that we'd both walk over to the press conference next to the Senate chambers from there.

"There's *pleeenty* alligators out there, Wilson. We've gotta stick together and hang tight."

I didn't say nothing, but a sound came outa somewhere, maybe from deep inside my chest, and I didn't know whether the sound was loud or not, but however it sounded, it was digging a hole in a dam that was fixing to break. Somehow it was all connected, and when one link started going, the whole chain started rattling off the stern it was leaving. And when it was gone, when every last link was gone, I was finally calm. I didn't know just yet what I was going to do, but I knew what I couldn't do, and what I couldn't do was two things: surrender or fight. I was conflicted in my soul; a gulf as wide as night from day and wind from rain, and they all took up residence in me like a two-headed freak in a barn show.

I thought: *It isn't even past noon and I've already heard and done all this and come back full circle on the thing, and now I am swallowing the thing like a snake swallows its tail. But it has to go down. I can leave no end loose. I take it all with me. Not a crumb on the fish-house floor.*

I got up from the broken fish-house chair and looked at Donna Sue and said something, and she just turned and looked at me, saying something herself, but I was already gone to the door of the van. Then I drove the fifteen minutes to the country and the old house, and some of the girls were on the porch and some in the kitchen, and the babies were in the sand.

I said, "What is it y'all want to do today?" and the two oldest said they wanted to go to the mall in Victoria, and the little one said she wanted to ride the horses on the merry-go-round. The carousel? I said, and she said, The merry-go-round! So it took three hours. The going and the being there and the merry-go-round that was a Ferris wheel turned on its side, and the colored horses in gold and silver and burgundy and Christmas green. While I sat there on a metal chair with wooden sides and watched the girls go round and round on the horses (and their half-eaten hamburgers lying in stiff wrappers on the seat beside me), I didn't think a thought. I was empty of anything

besides simply being, while a Ferris wheel on its side would spin my
girls on wild burgundy horses.

Just before sundown I made it home and pulled into the yard and took
the girls and the babies to the porch, where Baby sat and said nothing
at all. I said, I have to go back to town and check the boat. I think I
forgot to tie a rope. And Baby said, You didn't even go shrimping
today. And I said, I know it. I still have to check the boat, though.

I didn't say good-bye to anybody. I turned once and looked. So this
is how it is when it is your last hour, and I drove down the road and
looked at a oak tree and said, This is how it is too. There wasn't a thing
I didn't pass that my mind didn't say, *This is it. This is it. This is it.*

None of it slowed me down. The whole commotion took no more
than fifteen minutes, and every minute was just another chain coming
off the deck, and I didn't even hear the noise when it hit the water. I
just knew it hit the water. It might have made a song after a while. I
don't know.

Then I was in the parking lot of the Pic-Pac grocery store, and I
went inside and walked down an aisle until I found the aspirins and the
sleeping pills and the Vicks Vapo-Rub in the hard blue glass. I took
two packages of sleeping pills and counted the pills, then I went over
to the ice-cooler windows with the Cokes and Dr Peppers and root
beers and wine coolers, and took two bottles of cheap strawberry wine.

Now the night was clear and it was quiet and no wind, and in the
windless night I drove the van to the bay, and took the *SeaBee* out into
the bay. It was on the way out that I formed an idea for the sleeping
pills and the wine and the boat and the water that rose all around me,
although it was still a windless night and I began to breathe hard just
thinking about it.

I was a woman leaving and on marked time, and whether I had thirty
years or thirty days or thirty seconds, the place was going to be the same
when I arrived. I moved in the night by instinct, not turning on the
depth meter or the running lights or the radio, and the only light was
the faint green smear from the compass going south with a little bit of
east in it. Then I had nowhere else to go. I had arrived. So I pulled down
the throttle and shut off the motor, and while the boat lay still and the
lapping water was a cat's mouth on the wooden hull, I stood in the cabin
and opened the wine bottle and the package of sleeping pills.

I took a handful of pills and thought nothing. I simply stared through the cabin door and out into the night and the black water. Then I took another handful of pills and a swallow of wine, then another, then with the half-filled bottle of wine I went to the side of the boat and threw it out across the water. I listened as the bottle hit the water, flat and final and simply something to listen to while my blood ran cold.

I don't remember putting the anchor over, but I did that too. I was going someplace, but the *SeaBee* wasn't. She wasn't going to drift halfway across the bay and be found the next morning, hard aground on the flats and salt marshes, while I wasn't going to be found at all. 'Cause I was going to disappear. Roll off in my sleep or my stupor into the sea from the stern of the *SeaBee*. The sea would be warm and the salt wouldn't even sting, but lay crystals in my hair and on my arms and legs, and I wouldn't be any different from a shrimp gliding in its ghost body through the water to some destination it didn't know but sensed same as the water sensed the wind and knew how to talk.

That was what I planned anyhow. So I went to the engine hatch where the wood was warm and lay down and told myself, *Now go to sleep. Now shut your eyes.* But my eyes wouldn't shut and I wouldn't go to sleep, so I turned and lay facedown and breathed on the wood, and the wood breathed back on my face and my chest. Then I got up and went to the stern and sat on the edge, but I didn't fall over there, so I got up again and went to the middle of the deck in the heart of San Antonio Bay and lay on my back and said, "Now quit breathing!"

Then I felt it. My breath slowed and quieted, and my chest wouldn't rise and move my shirt, and I put my hand to my face and felt it cool to the point where there would be nothing by midnight if it went that long. Only I was wide awake behind my lids and in my head, and I knew I'd be full awake when I smothered from the weight sitting on my chest.

It wasn't what I wanted. The order going backwards and not forwards. Not sleep, then death; but death, then sleep. So I shut my eyes and willed fast sleep and tried to draw the night to me like water on my tongue, only it got brighter and brighter, until finally I believed a tugboat had found me and directed its spotlight on me and the *SeaBee* in the middle of the black bay. Voices came off the tugboat and walked around, and I nearly felt them on my arm lying on the deck, and when they came close they got louder and louder, a man's voice and a young girl's voice, and I heard them talk about nothing at all, just commonplace things, like talk around a supper table with lights in the hall and in the kitchen windows.

Then my breath got tiny and quiet; a pearl that fought in a weed-choked field to come to me, and after it did I wondered if it would come again or if the voices would quit and the lights would go out.

So that was all. I thought it wasn't, but it was, and it was just the hours that made it different. I was there until three in the morning, and I'd seen early morning a hundred thousand times, so I sensed it more than I had a timepiece that said it. I finally found I could walk with my tiny breath. It wasn't going to kill me, and nothing on that cool, hard deck was going to kill me, because I wasn't going to die that day. I wanted to, but I wasn't going to die.

So begging for sleep, but refused somehow, I went to the bow and pulled on the rope until I pulled the anchor up, and then I walked to the cabin and started the engine. It was such a commonplace sound—the hard roll of a diesel engine.

I took the *SeaBee* back across the bay and to the harbor, and then I pulled up to the docks and threw one rope and tied it and then I walked off the boat and drove home. When I walked through the front screen door and climbed the stairs and went to bed, nothing was said. Not where I went or what I did, because somehow the news made it back to Baby (no boat leaves the harbor without six others knowing). He said nothing, and I slept through a day and through the next, and after that I wouldn't take any phone calls or any messages or answer any questions except to tell Donna Sue I was home. So it was only later I found out what had happened and what I had missed, and maybe it was for those reasons that Blackburn had called seven or eight times.

He had waited for me. He had waited a long time in the rotunda of the capitol, then finally walked alone to the press conference where he and Susan Wang were to announce his agreement with Formosa. At the press conference Blackburn said he believed his agreement was the first time a company had ever allowed an outside party to have some say and control over its environmental and safety audits. Then Formosa's woman attorney added that it was "unprecedented" and they'd like to see the agreement become a prototype for other partnership agreements, and Susan Wang said the agreement was "reversing the adverse relationship that is usually encountered between industry and environmentalists."

A spokeswoman for Governor Ann Richards was present and she said "it was a very good start," and restated what the governor had wrote in a letter to Jack Wu earlier: that if the agreement that had orginally been negotiated with Calhoun County Resource Watch and was now with Jim Blackburn was fully implemented, then "the agreement could lead to very positive improvements in Formosa's performance and public credibility."

Before the conference ended, though, three Greenpeace activists dressed as Blackburn and Formosa and Governor Ann Richards interrupted the conference and threw fake money at each other in a street-theater demonstration. Blackburn was shown as money grubbing, with Formosa dollars pasted all over him. A Greenpeace activist read a statement that said Formosa could not write an agreement that Greenpeace would sign, and Rick condemned the agreement in an open letter to Blackburn, where he wondered aloud if Blackburn was taking money and said the agreement was nothing more than a closed-door sweet-heart deal.

Later Donna Sue came to the house and brought me newspaper clippings of the event and its fallout. She leaned against the porch pillar and read in a flat voice an editorial from the *Victoria Advocate*. It was about the losers on Formosa's agreement. The writer found it impossible to understand why anyone would oppose the agreement that Formosa signed with Jim Blackburn. It was unprecedented in its scope, and remarkable and a testament both to Mister Blackburn's persistence and the company's increasing willingness to overcome its spotty environmental record and thereby earn the trust of its neighbors.

The editorial said the loser was the sad Seadrift shrimper who was cheated of her participation in a historic agreement, and Rick Abraham and his cohorts should be ashamed of themselves for pressuring her and thereby abusing her trust.

Because things mattered once, did they matter still? I didn't know. I looked. I searched about like it was a spot on my dress I was worrying over. I wasn't dead. I knew that. My breathing was fine, but it wasn't earth's air I was breathing. I didn't eat and I didn't dress more than my jeans required, and I wouldn't have combed my hair except the girls told me to, and when they did, I did because it mattered as little that I did as that I didn't.

PART THREE

PART THREE.

28

Island of Fire and Solidarity

Maybe the cyclone was winding down. It was late in the evening, and I stood at the stove frying cut flounder rolled in yellow corn-meal in a skillet of hot grease, and the kids at the table were eating red beans from a bowl. The dusty light that came through the window was hard on their heads, but at the stove I could hardly see my hands.

I remembered Chien's voice, so I didn't ask who it was or why he was calling. I imagined him sitting still in his office chair, not having changed clothes or even moved his engineered diagrams far from his hand, while the hard Houston light slid like surgeon's steel through the white venetian blinds. Chien never slowed as words worn smooth by familiarity rolled out of his mouth, and I didn't stop him. I just saw new possibilities leap from the phone. He wanted me to come to Taiwan in ten days' time. He said I would need a passport and visa quick, quick, because he wasn't sure if word hadn't already got far ahead of my trip. He was trying to get his own visa approved, but after twenty years in the States and his long history of dissidence, he was almost sure to be rejected by the Kuomintang government.

I heard the word *Kuomintang* like it was a spice I was taking off a rack and asked him why he wanted me in Taiwan. He said he was only the go-between for an environmental group that had been following my fight with Formosa through the Chinese press, and they wanted to sponsor my trip to Taiwan. A legislator, Ding-nan Chen, who had helped organize citizen action against Formosa in Taiwan, would be my personal guide on the trip. The group was illegal in the eyes of the Kuomintang government.

Chien said the ruling party, which had installed itself in Taiwan following its defeat in the civil war with China in 1948, had tried to buy legitimacy with high growth rates and rapid economic develop-ment among the native Taiwanese, and now the only thing that kept pace with the rapid economic growth was the speed of the island's environmental destruction. For every square mile on the island there were 270 cars and 3 factories blowing smoke. An island wrought with chemical plants and nuclear plants, but alongside of it an increasingly successful democratic and grassroots environmental movement challenging the island's elite. The grassroots groups were especially anxious over Formosa's latest project: a sixth naptha cracker and the 30,000 more downstream factories it would feed.

I jabbed a hard brown flounder with a fork while I listened to Chien talk of China's and Taiwan's destiny, with mine thrown in like a stick into an already burning pile of winter leaves. I said yes, I'd go. I didn't think there was anything else to say. It was another branch of a path already found, and it didn't occur to me to refuse. Then what was patched for a week between me and Baby was suddenly severed, and he said he knew all along I wouldn't quit. I had just rested for two seconds.

I went to Houston for the visa and the passport, and then I tracked down a widowed aunt that would keep the babies and the girls while Baby worked offshore, or help him if he didn't. On the day the first Gulf War was declared, I flew eighteen hours to Taiwan and a war zone. At least it looked like a war zone. There were two hundred soldiers in a drafty, cold airport, and none of them knew why I was there and not a one was glad to see me. I didn't know where my hosts were. I figured they were bound to know I missed every plane starting in Houston, with its torrents of rain and confusion over a declared war.

So it was midnight in a dirty, drafty airport with high, wide sides and bad lighting, and maybe half the island's military force packing big guns like the M-16 Baby carried in Vietnam. Eventually it dawned on me that I was never getting out of the airport unless one of the soldiers helped me. I watched the soldiers until I found the youngest one in the entire airport army, and I walked over to him with my phone list of professors and activists and legislators and journalists (all probably on the verge of being arrested by the same government that had given him his gun).

I shoved my paper at him and stuck my finger under one legislator's name. Ding-nan Chen. Then I took two quarters out of my purse and pointed with the same hand to the phone. "Ring-a-ding-ding!" I said. "Do you *comprende*?"

The soldier's eyes were like black olives in a glass bowl, and when he shoved his gun under his arm and cocked the end nearly at the airport ceiling, his face split into a grin and the olives disappeared. Ah, yes! he said, and took a coin from his own pocket. He phoned twice, then walked back, then another soldier came and talked with the first and those two drew the attention of the officer. The officer didn't smile as he walked to us and glanced at their guns leaning against a wall, then at me in passing. He snatched the list from the soldiers.

He was a no-nonsense soldier prepared for war (not in the Gulf, perhaps, but *somewhere*) and he *definitely* had a lot better things to do than babysit a big Western woman lost in an airport and doing nothing but causing his troops to lay down their arms. So he walked to the phone and called twice, then when he finished, he walked back and handed me the list and raised one hand.

Out of nowhere a wire-thin man arrived. He was short and wearing a white flowing shirt untucked over black pants. He was a human hurricane. A live dynamo. Infested with *pronto*! With no fanfare, he grabbed my big suitcase and started dragging it out the airport doors. I ran after him, alarmed at losing the only thing I had to my name. He blinked twice, then giggled. Not to worry, not to worry! he said.

I followed my suitcase into the night and to a waiting car that was so unremarkable I can't even remember the color. By the next morning the situation hadn't improved. No one had called for me, so I was worrying about everything. The YMCA. The suspicious desk clerk. I figured my Taiwan contacts were arrested. I figured I was lost for good. I'd wander the Taipei streets the rest of my Texas-born days. So I stuck a note on the lobby desk when there was no clerk around and went down the street, hunting the only thing that could possibly give me some cheap, fast comfort: hot coffee.

If I hadn't been so big and drawn stares, I would've cried. But where do you cry on a cold gray street when every cranny and alley seemed filled to the brim with ever' living soul in Taipei? When *did* these people sleep? In the predawn light, I hunted a café as furtively as coons hunt clams on the waterfront, and when I found one, I went in and sat down. It was a dusty café where the only light was the natural light pouring in from a giant window that overlooked the street I just walked down. I ordered coffee and what I thought was the cheapest thing on the menu, and made my second mistake beyond that first one about not changing American dollar bills. Coffee *wasn't* cheap. And it was loaded down with sugar and cream, and boiled over the top of the cup and spilled down the sides when I held it. I drank it anyhow.

On my second cup I discovered there were at least five distinct conversations going on at different tables, and none of them were in a language I'd ever heard. Lulled by the bad light and the faint incense that hung on everything and everyone, I turned and watched the picture show. It slid past jam-packed traffic. A million taxi drivers in a dawn race, with the exhaust from their million cars and the black sedans where dark windows cracked so very little. Then, taking up two lanes and in no hurry about nothing, were old, wrinkled men with funny hair and woven shirts and obviously from some century not far off where wooden carts were still pulled by huge blond-colored cows with long horns the same size you'd see on any given day of the week in a field in Texas.

And *everywhere* were the motor scooters. They were a plague. A swarm of bees that moved with a hundred different colors, and every one clutched from behind by a beautiful woman with flowing raven hair and dressed in scarlet or cobalt blue or white with long embroidered sleeves. The scooter drivers seemed to annoy everyone they came near; a dozen horns were blowing. The riders were fearless, though, dashing in their dark good looks. But around their faces and fastened with tight rubber bands were white surgical masks.

Surgery seemed to be the mask of choice. From the tiny mothers with their carefully combed children to the old elegant couples who walked sedately. Masks on beautiful people! *Oh!* What would I see next?

I put my hand to my chin and drank my sugared coffee and marveled at two women who dropped from out of nowhere. They were delighted to see me and cried, "Dieen, Dieen! The momma! The momma!" They drug up chairs and blocked aisles and flung their purses out into the middle of the table. They had been sent by Legislator Chen to hunt me down! They were members of the New Housewives Association, a group that was forging links between the emerging feminists and the environmental movement.

The woman named Linn was a professor in chemical engineering at Taipei University, and her thick hair was as even as chopped iceberg lettuce. "Our group has arisen like everything else. When the central government lifted martial law five years ago, the direct mass action went from a hundred and seventy incidents to well over a thousand." She seemed proud of the number, and whirled her hair to whatever opposition lurked in the café.

Then she pointed to the men on scooters and women with children wearing white masks. "See! It is the same in the Taiwan Elementary School in southern Taiwan. These students and teachers wear surgical masks to filter out the pollution from the factories. Here in Taipei the air is so contaminated with sulphur dioxide and nitrogen oxides that it is harmful seventeen percent of the year. And *that* is according to our lenient Taiwanese standards. Your standards consider one hundred forty or one hundred fifty dangerous and warn people to stay indoors, but in Taiwan? Readings of two hundred or three hundred are very common. A reading must be well over four hundred before it rates as anything near hazardous."

She said what else can you expect with their hundred thousand registered manufacturers and probably an equal number of unregistered ones, then two million cars, then double or three times that of motor scooters, then twenty million people? She expected any day to walk down the streets of Taipei and see people wearing the gas masks the soldiers wear!

She shook her head and sighed. "Until the government does something different, the poor people will just have to get used to living with headaches and vomiting from breathing contaminated air."

Linn said, "Ah, yes, it is bad, but it was worse then." In the sixties the ruling Kuomintang party had the profound and *truthful* revelation that the masses of industries couldn't continue to congregate unchecked in the few urban areas of Taiwan. So Taiwan's planners launched an aggressive policy of encouraging manufacturers to set up in the countryside. The result? A substantial number of the island's ninety thousand firms located in the rice fields and along the waterways and beside residential areas.

Another disaster! So to check *this* helter-skelter pattern of economic development that was erupting, the government enacted zoning— token, you can believe—legislation barring firms from setting up in agriculture fields. But as expected, that legislation remained largely unenforced, so by the mid-eighties over 40 percent of the new firms were located in the wrong zone. As these industrial and residential developments moved onto the rich, fertile rice fields, the government compounded the mistake *still* further by encouraging the clearing of forested land for the *agriculture* that had been evicted by *industry*.

Linn was wearing a starched white cotton shirt, and when she turned the white of her shirt was pale as her skin. "You look at Taiwan today and you must think it has always looked like this. *Ugh! So ugly!* All these cars and pollution and millions of people and those thin, ugly little trees down the street. But once it was so different. It is the truth! My grandmother tells me so. So beautiful. She said when the first Portuguese sailors saw Taiwan they called it *Ilha Formoa. Beautiful Island.* But now! With all of the development and the mismanagement and lack of insight from the government, it is no longer so. The forests that once covered the entire eastern coast are almost completely destroyed, and the second-growth broadleaf which has replaced them have been reduced by over twenty percent.

"Now what exists is a vast network of industrial roads that have opened up the forests to logging and agriculture and development. And with the predictable results: serious soil erosion. Half of the island slopes like baggage falling off a donkey's back. Some say as much as forty percent! It is a wonder anything is left on the mountain. . . . And, in fact, it probably isn't. Some villagers have reported whole slopes of bare soil and mud sliding away."

The other woman spoke. She had kept silent for more than an hour, watching with her mouth open a little, like a mother watching a favorite child recite a poem. But before she spoke she laughed a hard sound. Two men from a near table turned and looked at the woman, said something briefly to themselves, then turned back to their talk. The woman glared and said to their turned backs, "Ah, the men! I hope they choke on their cigar smoke!"

Then she turned back to me. "These environmental problems always deliver us women issues. It is so predictable. It isn't only the trees and the rivers and the mountains that are endangered on this island. The aboriginal people's traditional economies and culture has been undermined by the goverment's policies. Everyone and everything is sacrificed at its altar!

"For a while the aboriginal people had a chance to survive. But now, with this new reserve policy of the government's that allows private development companies to come in and buy tribal land so they can 'more fully utilize the land's potential'? Well, things have changed for the worse. Crop yields have declined. There are few game animals. The fish have disappeared. But the *most* serious is the people's cultural mores. All their sacred things have been violated, and what has not been violated has been ransacked! A few years back one of our own county governments gave the go-ahead for the construction of a hotel within the Bunan Tribal Reservation, and no one even bothered to obtain the permission of the tribal people. Naturally the developers never knew the hotel was sited right on top of a tribal cemetery. Then they started digging up bodies! Oh, what a mess!

"*But* the government says there is no space for sacred burial grounds! Think of the development that would be lost! Now that the people's economic base has eroded and their cultural values thrown over in the process, a great exodus of young aborigines have left for the coastal cities. It is *tragic! Tragic!* Many of the young aborigine girls have been herded into prostitution. It is everywhere, this prostitution! In Taipei or any major city you care to look! Our sources say as many as one-third of all the young aborigine women have worked as prostitutes. The trafficking in girls is very profitable. The girls can sell for as much as five thousand dollars. Even ones as young as thirteen. It doesn't matter to their buyers if their young bodies are immature. The girls can be given breast implants. And hormone shots. Then to prevent the girls from escaping, their buyers tell them if they try to leave, their sisters will be kidnapped to replace them."

The woman suddenly stopped, as though she had strolled past one of the dozens of booths outside the window and spotted a pretty scarf and offered to buy me one. Then her head turned, and as it did, the cigar smoke from the room wound a scarf across her face and floated for a moment in my own eyes, and I blinked hard and could think of nothing to say.

She seemed bitter, and twisted her words like they were lemons on a tree. The dull ozone-laden light sprawled catlike on the table and coated our hands with artifical gold. Natural light didn't operate in this conversation; only sunlight laced with ozone and the stench of young aborigine bones. Talk of children seemed to have quieted the one woman, and she sat in the last dregs of light and drank her coffee. But the first woman, with her cotton collar, was as carefree as any young Houston housewife planning her day at the mall. She leaned over the table and sketched on the café's paper napkin. When she finished, she shoved the napkin to me. It was a drawing of me with a head full of curls, and underneath it she had wrote, *We Love You!*

On the third day with a very cold morning, I stuck my foot into the Formosa Straits. I had tromped from city side to countryside, from the north end to the sound end, and from east coast to west coast. I had been carried by car and by bus to the environmental fight. There were dozens of people. Crews of reporters. Underground TV stations. Professors and students. Activists from the Environmental Protection Union, and the Taiwan Association for Human Rights, and the Homeowners Association, and an Earth Day group.

Always, always there was another river they wanted me to see. And always it was more damaged than I could imagine. The Keelung River was little more than a flowing cesspool, devoid of fish and almost completely dead, and the Er-Jen River was no longer scenic. There were carcasses of pigs instead of fish, and black oily water and yellow, foul-smelling smoke rising from the stream.

Legislator Ding-nan Chen, who had arrived in the middle of the first day and who was still there three days later even though he nursed a bad cold brought on by giving speeches he was probably on the verge of being arrested for, seemed determined to be my personal guide. He was involved in all aspects of my trip. He cleared the way for rooms and meals and made sure I got my sugared coffee in the morning. Then when we sat in meetings with EPA heads and directors of the Ministry of Economic Affairs, and even once in a long, dark chamber where reporters and TV cameramen asked questions and took pictures and behind us on the wall a huge four-by-four black-and-white picture of Chiang Kai-shek hung, it was Chen who stood quietly attentive, his white hands motionless against his black suit.

What did I do to warrant this attention? I was astonished to think that I had something I could give or teach them. My trip felt thoroughly undeserved. For the moment though, Legislator Chen explained the problems with the Er-Jen River. It was contaminated with mercury and copper. And the Houchin River! That one was devoid of life. The fisherfolk could catch no fish and local farmers in the area were *forced*—what else are they to do?—to use that thick black water to irrigate their rice fields. As a result, tons of rice produced was laden with carcinogens. And *still* it was sold throughout Taiwan.

"The east is all we have left of this island. It is the last natural, unpolluted place. The west coast is a depressing scene of hopelessness and destruction and contamination. All of the forests are gone. There is less agriculture and less fishing. Industry rules supreme. That is why we *must* fight so hard. And it is *not* that I am opposed to development. I have said before, and I only hope others will not distort or smear my position. I am opposed to *pollution*. Not industry or prosperity. So we fight to keep out the worst development such as Wang Yung-Ching's number six cracker."

Chen said, "I will tell you this. We will oppose Wang's plant to the very end. There will be no compromise in Yilan's opposition to the number six naptha cracking plant. If the central government and Formosa persist in their unholy alliance to flout the law and build the number six plant in Li Tse, then the four hundred fifty thousand residents of Yilan will form a human chain to fight a protracted war. We will resist this plant with whatever means is necessary!"

I tried to envision a chain of people, from the shop owner to the street sweeper to the farmer in his field to the fishermen in his boat, all forming a wall fencing Formosa out! I was amazed of that kind of commitment that colored out of lines and talked out of turn.

"So how do you manage to get that? That kind of commitment?" I said. "y'all sure different."

Chen laughed, and two red patches of fever stuck posts in his face. "No," he said. "We are the same. How else would we have heard of you? It is simply that we have been so long and so hard under seige. And it *is* a seige. . . . Perhaps an *economic seige*, but I'd like to see a battleground that has done less damage. Even the casualties are the same. That is why our anti–number six banners against Formosa's tycoon say: STOP NUMBER SIX OR DIE! What have we to lose? Perhaps we will save our lives."

He looked at me, and his mouth softened and the lines on his forehead messed up like an eraser messed up a sentence.

Chen said they had fought a long, protracted battle with Wang Yung-Ching. In 1988 the tycoon had bought acres of land in Ilan County in North Taiwan to build the number 6 Ching naptha cracker. But the Ilan residents had protested it strongly.

Then Wang threatened to take his business to China. That was a standard strategy that naturally threatened a government so insecure that it was worried about losing its most wealthy industrialists to the mainland, so the government panicked. They promised to find some-place else for number 6. Gwan In, in Tao Yuan, West Taiwan. But number 6 met more protests there. Then Wang Yung-Ching decided to take his many-parceled plastic plant to Texas.

Still, even though he went to Texas, the idea was not finished. Wang said he wanted to build at least one and probably two naptha pro-cessing plants and an oil refinery. He would submit formal proposals to the Taiwan government the next month. Then the same old tactics started that were used to shove the number 5 cracker through. Since 1987 local residents and environmental groups had tried to halt number 5 because of the severe toxic waste and public health and safety risks, not to mention the economic inviability. But the three years of intense direct action and public hearings were of no avail, and in September 1990, construction began and twelve thousand riot police troops stood poised.

"All of Taiwan's TV stations, major newspapers and magazines, and radio stations are controlled by the government, so naturally we had those headlines: NUMBER FIVE PROTESTERS ARE CRAZY RADICALS WHO WANT TO DESTROY THE ECONOMY, or GREEDY CONSPIRATORS HOPING TO PROFIT FROM COMPENSATION. Or IF WE DON'T HAVE NUMBER FIVE CHING, WE WON'T HAVE ECONOMIC GROWTH, AND IF WE DON'T HAVE ECONOMIC GROWTH WE WILL DIE. IT IS ABSOLUTELY VITAL FOR THE ECONOMY."

I laughed at Chen. "Oh, I've heard those kind of headlines myself!"

"See," he said. "There is a great deal we have in common."

The next day we went to Houchin, where the factory's noise and the roar of 150 chimneys that flared smoke and ash and God knows what chemical made the villagers' windows and doors rattle. It was per-petual morning, for it never got dark and nobody slept, and when it rained, Houchin's rain was yellow acid rain. One event recorded said a westerly wind blew a cloud of vapor containing yellow oil over Houchin, and when it cooled it immediately formed little pools of oil that dropped on farms and even on the local villagers who were out-side at the time.

Five days into our trip Chen said it was to be his last for a while. We were inside a high, rusted chain-link fence that separated a

schoolyard from one of Formosa's factories. Chen thought with
my children and experience as a mother, I would truly understand
the extra burden that unrestrained development brought to the
children in Taiwan. I understood, all right. It was a hard yard to
stand in. No grass and no birds, only the bad consistency of a dead
and troubled chicken pen. Behind us the schoolhouse had been
permanently discolored by the constant flame and smoke bel-
lowing from the factory.

Chen said I would have to forgive him for leaving, but perhaps he
would be forgiven because he had brought a much finer replacement. A
fellow activist. Dr. Shin-min Shih. A professor of chemical engineering
at the National Taiwan University and part of the executive committee
of the Taiwan Environmental Protection Union. Chen said Shih was a
very serious man and a noted ecologist known all over Taiwan.

I was dumbfounded to be put into such learned company. Actually
it was pretty funny, because a hundred times I had been told the
reason they had brought me to Taiwan was so they could learn something from us talented Americans. The women with their blunt hair-
cuts said it, and I heard it on the buses and in the cars we traveled and
every time we had a meeting with a roomful of activists in some little
cubbyhole that was obviously underground. We Americans had something to teach them. *Teach? What could I possibly teach them that they
hadn't known twenty years before I'd even heard the words?*

It was Shih, standing tall and thin with his belly set somewhere
back inside his rib cage, that told of the ins and outs and jailings and
near-jailings of activists in Taiwan. I knew that environmental and
social activism in Taiwan was mainly illegal. Martial law was lifted in
1987, and since that time more and more environmental protests had
erupted all over Taiwan. The environmental group Shih was a part of
had started in 1987, and it had been their hope that it would be a cat-
alyst to unite citizens from all walks of life and all parts of Taiwan.

"Yes," he said, "we are the environmental thugs and bad elements
that our government-owned newspapers say threaten public security.
That is partly the reason why my wife lost her teaching job. And such
a bad element she is! The evil, wretched woman is working to build
schools for autistic children where none have existed before, because
the government has been much, much too busy spending money on
other things. Perhaps she will be arrested for that evil enterprise! The

Public Security Bureau of the Police Headquarters says it is just a guise what we do anyway. We are only using the environmental and labor and agriculture concerns to provoke senseless violence and engage in extortion and profiteering. Profiteering! It is such a huge laugh! We will all be punished under the racketeering laws."

One young man had grown so tired of Formosa's lies and their plans to build yet another polluting factory that he climbed one of their chemical tanks and tied a banner to the rigging that read STOP NO. 6 OR DIE! He had been sentenced to two years for his act.

"We in Taiwan feel it is our solemn duty to warn the Third World countries of the horror story behind our economic miracle. Sometimes we feel it is an impossible battle, that it is too late for Taiwan, much less to try to reach any other country with our story. Look there now! See! There goes one of Formosa's trucks, dumping right this very minute."

I turned where he pointed to a dump truck with the Formosa diamond logo printed on its side. The truck drove out onto a sandbar, stopped, unloaded, then as suddenly drove off. It left behind a five-foot heap on the river sand.

Three years ago, Shih said, Wang had promised them that his plants would be so clean that goldfish could be raised in the wastewater from his Yilan plants. Wang Yung-Ching said he wanted the wastewater from his plants safe enough to drink. But what have been the results? The Lung De plant in Taipei has received the most fines ever by the government. Every worker in Yilan knows that Formosa emits illegal air pollution in the night and that it shuts off its wastewater pipes before inspection by the Public Health Agency. So they could not trust them to deliver what they promise.

"You too should not believe them," Shih said. "If the wastewater from the plant in Texas is to be safe for your bays, then you will have to be the one to demand that something happens. Don't wait on Formosa. It will never happen that way."

My life was corrupted by a radical germ. I spent the rest of that week in an agitated state, barely keeping my arms and legs inside my shirt and shoes. I wanted to flail out, get home. Strike my arms in a swimmer's pose and head for some recognized Gulf shore. I could barely keep my tongue from lashing everything to death in my rush to

get there. Near the end of my last day in Taiwan, we were in the far-
thest corner of some mountain town, miles out into the countryside
and in the pouring rain. The rain was a solid sheet that covered fields
and bushy black trees and tiny but now rain-swollen roads, and a
thousand people stood under umbrellas and heavy coats with heads
hidden and faces obliterated, and in the brief black minutes when the
lightning streaked, they looked like worn pilings stuck indiscrimi-
nately in a wet field.

There was no sound except the montonous roar of rain. I sat on the
front stage and watched it all. I was one of five speakers and posi-
tioned to speak before a man who was circled by four men. It was the
second time I had seen that particular circling. The first had been in
a video of the demonstration in front of Formosa's building in Taipei.
Thirty women, hands held, formed a circle around some speaker.

The mayor sitting next to me explained. He said that the circle of
people protected the man, and if an assassin's bullet ripped through
the night, then the people in the circle were to stop the bullet with
their own bodies. It was a great honor to be part of the circle.

Times like that, I doubted I was real or if I existed at all. Maybe it
was a dream. A dream where the rain hit the lights more than it
missed and the vapor hissed and sputtered and threw a million tinier
lights showering into the night. At my feet a steady string of water fell
and grew fat and blackened one entire end of the stage.

When the activist with the four men circling stood up to speak,
another larger group approached from out of the rain and held hands
and faced outward—towards the rain and the fields and assassins'
guns. The mayor said the speaker was very highly regarded. Many
considered him the spritual father of the democratic movement in
Taiwan not only for his great courage, for he had been imprisoned
many, many times for his outspoken criticism of the government, but
also for the high price he had paid and great suffering he had endured
for all Taiwan. And it was truly the greatest price of all, the mayor
said. His family. Because while the man was in prison, a group of men
kidnapped his mother and small twin daughters and took them to the
basement and stabbed them with knives. Only one daughter survived.

"Now, for his daughter's safety and for his own, he lives outside of
the island. But he knew the importance of this meeting tonight and
how urgent it is to keep hope alive among the people. He says they

must not forget. They must not get so comfortable with their posses-
sions or so fearful for their lives and jobs that they forget what we all
cry for. That is why he has smuggled himself back into Taiwan."

I barely saw the man hidden behind the dozens of people. He was
medium height and thin, and his face was worn. He wasn't someone
I would remember a month later, but his words and the slow roar that
came from the fields as he spoke that night, I took back on the plane
and kept months later for the dry, dry days in Texas.

The man spoke, leaning into the crowd and the rain and the black
mountains all around; he spoke words that caused sudden cheers and
erupting cries to come from nowhere and deposit again and again,
heavy and hard, on a stage at my feet. I was shivering.

The mayor said, "He says, 'What is it you are afraid of? Is it death?
Is that the thing that stops you? I have seen death, and it is far better
than living forever on our knees.'"

I tried to look at the speaker and see what set him apart and made
him able to say the words that he said. Was it in his eyes or the way
he held his shoulders or the way he stood on stage that said, *Here is a
man that is a hero and is able to bear all. Here is a Gandhi or a Pancho
Villa or a Mitch Snyder. Here is someone the heavens have chosen, just like
Jehovah picked Moses and the Alamo picked Davy Crockett.*

Well, I didn't see it. He was a smallish man that could have vanished
in a crowd in ten seconds flat, kicked off a bronc before the bell.
Matter of fact, the man was flat unremarkable and the most unspec-
tacular human I had ever seen, yet that was why I was so excited. He
was nobody and everybody, and in the process could be *any one of us.
Why, he could even be me!*

29

A Radicalized Woman

Where the sun rose in my head and the stars, east and west, came up in my eyes, I was a new, radicalized woman. I certainly knew and sensed my coming. Nobody had to shock me with a wire. Nobody had to send me back to Taiwan and to the mountains and the rain and a worker's house for me to know there comes a time when the home needs protecting and the line needs drawing, and anybody that dares cross it acts at their own peril.

Baby saw it next when I came back from Taiwan, and he went out on the front porch swing and shot bullets into the ground with his pearl-handled pistol. That was his life for a while.

My life, on the other hand, was playing all-fired catch-up. When I came back from Taiwan, I found that a lot of water had gushed under the bridge and some of it was good spring water and about what I expected, and then some was nothing but pure ditch-water poison. On the good side, I knew that the EPA was making Formosa do an environmental impact statement. It wasn't publicly known, but it was known by those in the know. I had found out the day before I'd left for Taiwan, when Norm Thomas in the EPA had called and told me my little wish was finally coming true. I could go to Taiwan knowing that when I got back, Formosa would be dealt the hard fact of an environmental impact study.

So when I got back home two weeks later, I wasn't surprised. I wasn't surprised either when two days before the EPA decision was announced, Formosa came springing like a greyhound outa the gate and said they were *volunteering to do an EIS*.

Naturally I kicked stuff, and when the newspapers called and asked what was my thinking on Formosa's change of heart, I said something about leopards not changing their spots and rats leaving a sinking ship. I wasn't very gracious.

There was other stuff I hadn't expected. Formosa's Louisiana project was sent clean back to the closet. It was a sad day for Formosa. Not only did the Texas plant get earmarked for an EIS, but their proposed five-hundred-million-dollar rayon plant in Louisiana would be studied too. For the Texas project (where a billion and a half dollars had already been spent and the plant was almost totally built, with workers hired) the EIS couldn't do much damage. What judge or jury or EPA official on the face of the earth was going to kill or even change a screw on a two-billion-dollar deal already done in hard concrete, even if it did violate half a dozen federal environmental laws? Nobody. That's what a judge said. "Who's gonna tear down something already built? Nobody in their right mind."

But in Louisaina the plant wasn't built and a dime hadn't been spent, except for the politician that was indicted for accepting payola connected with the deal. So the delay of an EIS sent shock waves out into the production world. The EIS became a coffin-sealing blow, and Formosa started rethinking the rayon plant.

In Texas, besides the EIS being a galling experience, the study wasn't doing nothing but costing Formosa less money than what one of their new production units would produce in a couple of weeks. Besides, the forty-two-inch wastewater pipe was already lying in the bay with the diffuser at the end so it could spray the waste far and wide, so it wouldn't be a single, concentrated toxic stream that violated every rule and regulation in Texas's code book. And it was already hooked up, and the federal government and its permit was the only thing stopping them.

Then the earth cracked open and from her fiery bowels two men came roaring *zero discharge*! Actually only one man come roaring (the other man came later), and it was more like he was cussing, because what he said over the telephone was something like: Why the hell are you after Formosa's damn wastewater permit? Make the sunuvubitches do zero discharge!

Then he calmed down and said he'd read in the Houston papers that I was fighting Formosa's permit—their wastewater permit. Wasn't that so?

I said, Yeah, that's what I was doing, all right, and he said, So why don't you just get them to do zero discharge? That'll solve all your problems. And I said, I didn't know such a thing existed, and he said,

Oh, shit on that. He worked for a company in Houston, and that was what they were selling right that very minute. What kind of zero-discharge technique did I want? Reverse osmosis? Side-stream softening? Brine concentrators? There were so many companies in the country using zero-discharge techniques that he couldn't even count them. He'd have to sit and think awhile before he could count them.

"You *know* how it's done? You've actually seen it?"

"Hey, honey! We install the things! We do the whole ball of wax, from the feasibility studies to pilot testing to process engineering. You name it and we do it. We even train the operators to run the damn thing if you want us to. Startup. Service assistance. Whatever."

"Well, how come I haven't heard of y'all?"

Hell! he didn't know. The *companies* knew about them, that was for damn sure. They may not use their services, but it wasn't because they didn't know they were around. They just *chose not* to.

"Do you figure Formosa knows about y'all?"

"They'd have to be brain-dead if they didn't. Plain brain-dead. *Every* company knows about us. We don't make a big secret of it. . . . My God! Whadda you think we're in the business for?"

He said he imagined that Formosa's people had already sat down with them at one time or another. He wouldn't doubt it. There were plenty of pluses for installing zero-discharge technology: the desire for clean water, environmental concerns such as mine. Then there was the ever-rising cost for pretreatment and discharge.

"It's where the twenty-first century is gonna take us. It's the logical next step," he said.

In the meantime, the company he worked for was moving out of the Gulf Coast area because nobody was buying! And that was why he called. He figured, hell, what did he have to lose? If he couldn't get the companies interested, maybe he could get the companies' critics interested.Was he on to something or what? Maybe it was activists like me his company should have been talking to.

The fella's name was Brian and he didn't have any silent moments. His company, Resource Conservation, specialized in process design of water-separation systems. It was the leading designer and supplier of evaporation and crystallization systems in the world. Then he talked and talked and eventually said something about hanging up and things to do. He said he was sending me some information in the mail.

In two days' time the short post office lady dropped a huge packet on the post office desk. I drug it home, and the kids piled around and pulled one slick pamphlet after another from the box. What had arrived was the salesman part of zero discharge. The pamplets said the technique was over twenty years old and virtually *any* plant could go zero discharge. It illustrated in blazing color a dozen diagrams where tubes went everywhere; sometimes to big fluted tanks and squares, and sometimes to cylinders like huge spinning tops. Crystallizers and centrifuge systems and brine concentrators and distillate pumps. It was a whole new valley of words.

Then Brian called again and asked did I get the material, and said maybe I should be speaking to the governor about it. He would be willing to go to the governor's office and give his two cents' worth, because the truth was (and a piece of rotten luck that was), his company wasn't selling, and if that didn't change soon his job was gonna be gone, gone, gone.

"Actually the technology isn't selling anywhere on the Gulf Coast," he said. "It *should* be. It's *the Gulf Coast* that is right there on top of the list of the Toxic Release Inventory."

"I know that list," I said. "I can count the hours in my fight from there."

So I called Blackburn up and said since you're talking to Formosa these days, why don't you tell them to go zero discharge? and Blackburn said, They aren't going to go for that and you know it, and I said, Ask anyhow.

Zero discharge? What's that? they said. We've never heard of it. It's not possible for a chemical plant to go zero discharge. What are you, crazy? Tell us where you've ever heard of a chemical plant in the United States—the United States!—going zero discharge!

I told Blackburn I'd find out. I was researching everything else anyhow. I had a different file in my room now, and it went along with the other hundred files and the battered phone with its mile-long cord that Crockett kept working on, and the typewriter with the ribbons that fouled because Crockett had worked on that too, and the fax machine and the copier and the box of half a million sheets that was all that I had left from the million given to me by a supporter out of Houston.

Also, and this I didn't tell Blackburn, I was collecting legal briefs and lawsuits and anything filed on behalf of the Clean Water Act and

National Environmental Policy Act and the Endangered Species Act. I had a cardboard box of old cases where judges spouted opinions on everything from injunctions to recycling. In one case a judge said that the failure of the EPA even to consider recycling was "arbitrary and capricious." *Arbitrary and capricious!* I fell in love with those two words and wrote them on the wall so I wouldn't forget them.

Then I dug out and reread all of Blackburn's old briefs and researched the federal acts he'd mentioned and the cases he'd quoted and read those too. I read everything I could get my hands on: the Federal Register's Council on Environmental Quality, Executive Office of the President; forty most-asked questions on National Environmental Policy Act Regulations; the Clean Water Act and the Endangered Species Act; and the federal CFRs outlining the permit proceedings for the National Pollutant Discharge Elimination System. I read everything from U.S. Fish and Wildlife Service studies, to the Status and Trends Program of the National Oceanic and Atmospheric Administration, to the University of Amsterdam's exploratory data analysis of measurements in sediments from industralized areas in the Netherlands. I knew of the accumulation and release of petroleum-derived aromatic hydrocarbons by four species of marine animals, and the density, diversity, and incidence of deformities of benthic invertebrates near a vinyl chloride discharge point source in the Niagara River watershed. And if there was stuff that I didn't understand, I knew how to call an expert on it. I had a seven-hundred-dollar long-distance phone bill, and I kept the phone from being shut off by paying only the local service and not the long-distance, *then* switching the long-distance companies. I had switched so often I didn't know *who* was carrying me anymore.

Then I made a calculated move for Formosa's federal wastewater permit, and Blackburn called a week later. It was late in the evening and I was standing at the window with Santanna on my hip and watching the sandhill cranes come out of one part of the sky and land in a big bush near the house. Everytime a crane landed it yelled and squawked, then another one would alight and it'd do the same thing all over again.

Blackburn sounded low and whupped and said he was still at his office. It was late. He got quiet and said nothing for a minute. Finally he said all kinds of alligators were circling around his eyeballs. He was depressed and worn out and he missed talking with me.

"So what are you doing now, Wilson?" he said, and I said I was watching the birds, and I was going after Formosa's federal permit.

Yeah, he'd heard that, he said. "But, you know, Wilson . . . the shrimpers aren't going to help you, and Formosa doesn't even need your cousin Wally to stop them anymore. All those sportsmen clubs and Texas Parks and Wildlife are going after the shrimpers so fierce they're gonna be busy enough just watching their own backsides without worrying about you."

"Maybe so," I said.

"It's not a *maybe*, Wilson. A few shrimpers called and want me to represent them at a Parks and Wildlife commission hearing. . . . And the environmental groups think you're some kind of a nut. That last hunger strike probably did it. I told you it wasn't going do any good. Look what's happened. We're split up. Everything's in a mess. About the only good thing that's happened is my agreement with Formosa."

"Hmmph," I said.

"All right, little Miss Holier Than Thou, *who's* gonna help you? Who? There aren't a hundred lawyers out there, you know, wandering around just looking for some radical to help. . . ."

But I wasn't looking for a lawyer. I was too busy typing up a brief to the EPA administrator, objecting to his decision denying my request for a wastewater hearing. The administrator said he didn't believe there was any new information I could add to a hearing, but I had thirty days to appeal the decision to the EPA Environmental Appeals Board in Washington if I wanted to.

Well, I figured I had a whole lot of new stuff! I had twenty boxes of information, didn't I? I knew I was probably being naïve and stupid about the whole hearing, but I didn't care. I figured there were times when ignorance was a good thing. Then you don't realize all the fine bone china you are trampling over, and you figure the only reason there is a forty-two-inch discharge pipe already in the bay is because somebody didn't yell long and hard enough for zero discharge. I was remembering Shih's words very well.

I barreled back into the process and filed an appeal to Washington at the last minute, and the outraged wails that came from Formosa and all their attorneys in their Dallas high-rise office were like asteroids blasting out into the night air.

I wrote the Appeals Board and told them that I believed bias had entered the decision-making ability of the EPA in Region 6, and it had produced an overall pattern that was deplorable and inexcusable under any reasonable interpretation of federal law. I wrote over thirty pages and cited reasons why I believed the EPA had acted in an arbitrary and capricious manner and exibited bias not in accordance with the law regarding Formosa's wastewater permit. I called them everything under the sun. I cited a million instances of mumbo jumbo. Once I even referred to Formosa's lawyers as hired gunslingers. They hadn't studied dioxin contamination. They hadn't studied zero discharge. I wanted a hearing! I said. *Give me a hearing!*

I had no notion what the Appeals Board in Washington would do, and I never had a dream that night. It only mattered that I focus with a Taiwan-born intensity on zero discharge. I was excited, so naturally I called Blackburn.

"Maybe next I can go after Alcoa's discharge. Then after that Carbide. Who knows how far we could spread this zero-discharge thing?"

"The gospel according to Ms. Wilson!"

"Hey, Blackburn. I wasn't the one that wrote the Clean Water Act. They said zero discharge by 1985, and I'm just lettin' 'em know they're *waaay* overdue. That's all."

"Well, just go on and dream your little dream, but I'm not going to be a part of it. Matter of fact, Wilson, you're giving me a real headache. I thought we could still work together somewhow and you'd see that *this* Formosa package was *finished*! I've tied a damn bow on the top. But no . . . I can see we can't talk anymore. If you need to talk to me about something anymore, Wilson, you can call Jack Matson. Jack's a friend and an engineer. You can trust him to answer your questions. Let him be the go-between, if we've got to have one."

Ten seconds before Blackburn hung up for what I figured was the last time, he said, "You'll remember Jack. He was a member on the Air Control Board and had to excuse himself that time the Air Control Board voted on Formosa's permit. He secretly roots for you."

"You think in all his engineering expertise, he might know something about zero discharge?" I said.

And Blackburn said, "The man's got a doctorate, Wilson. He knows everything! He probably had a patent on the damn thing before you were born."

• • •

So I got Jack. Jack by way of Blackburn and Jack by way of Penn State University, where he was a full-time professor of chemistry, and when he wasn't doing that he was a full-time director for the Leonard Center for Engineering Excellence. I called him up after Blackburn hung up on me, and when I told Jack what I was figuring on doing, he said, "Way to go! Go for it! I'll back you up any way I can."

Jack had a long history with zero discharge. Back in the 1970s, he had worked with a couple of chemical companies on achieving zero discharge. One was on the Houston Ship Channel and the other one was in California. In those days he believed zero discharge was an idea whose time was right around the corner. The world had bright, bright people looking for new solutions. Peace. That whole thing. But it wasn't to be.

"And why not?" I said.

"Money, Diane. Money. The regulations and the agencies didn't push the concept, and when it's cheaper and *legal* to pollute . . . well, why do something different? So the companies don't. It's as simple as a money issue."

"So any company can go zero discharge. . . . But it'll just cost some money? Is that what you're saying?"

"Sure. Going zero would add about fifty percent to waste-treatment costs. . . . Which means if a plant spends about two percent of their capital on waste treatment—which, by the way, most plants do—zero-discharge implementation would boost that amount to three percent. It's not out of the ball park like companies would like you to think. Some *states* have actually demanded it. They have some pretty countryside and they don't want it ruined by the facility, so they say, 'Zero discharge. Do it or don't come at all.'"

"What would it cost a chemical plant like Formosa to go zero discharge? You know, a ball-park figure?"

Jack said. "Fifty million. Somewhere around there."

"That pipeline out there already cost them seventeen or eighteen million," I said.

Jack laughed. "Well, then, for a few ten million more, they could've had the entire stream recycled and who knows how much water saved. Millions and millions of gallons a day, probably. And who knows what they could do with the salvaged material? Probably make money on it. Then think how much salt they could keep from going into the bay."

Salt? I never even figured on salt. I was worrying too much about the other stuff. I knew, though, that some of the mess in Cox's Creek was because of the salt. The state said Formosa's discharge had increased the salt content twenty times over and changed the entire ecosystem. What was fresh was now salty.

"I would imagine there's eighty to a hundred tons of salt a day in Formosa's waste stream. Imagine that going into the bay. You know how tricky salinity is out there with the shrimp and the fish. A little too much either way and you got a disaster on your hands. Shrimp don't live and the fish can't survive."

A hundred tons of salt a day barreling out of a plastics factory and down two thousand feet of PVC pipe, then out into a twelve-foot-deep man-made basin that was dug into Lavaca Bay's mud and oyster-shell reefs, just so a diffuser that sprayed benzene and chloroform and EDC and phenol and copper and chromium could be thrown like dishwater from a pail into a bay less than four feet deep on the average.

So 160,000 pounds of salt and hundreds and hundreds of pounds *per day* of weird chemicals went to a wild, watery cradle woven with cane from marshland and sea grasses and saltwater flats and ancient oyster reefs. Did the bay know and sense the violation? Did it smell the coming, when before it knew only the relentless ebb and flow of a tide and the sound of gray heron feeding and the great wind at its breast and the hundreds and hundreds of years it had been silent and slept beneath the benign stars?

30

The Vietnamese Connection

The man in the monkey suit said, "I am fired! Fired! What do you think of that?" And I didn't think nothing, so nothing was what I said. But that wasn't the beginning. The beginning was when the monkey-suit man sent me a page out of an engineering magazine with no name, so I didn't *know* it was the monkey-suit man that had sent it. Matter of fact, I didn't know *who* had sent it. Then a week later he sent me a typed letter with information he said I ought to know about. That was when he signed his name at the bottom: Fred Olneck. Regulatory affairs man, formerly of Formosa.

I'm sure all the items on Fred's list were important, but one in particular caught my attention, so I called him and asked him about it. Fred wasn't surprised that I called; I suspect he wanted me to. But he was nervous and his voice shook and rose up and down like a kid fiddling with the volume on a radio. I didn't know if he was gonna get loud or get low or vanish entirely.

That's when he said the stuff about being fired. Oh, he had been fired from his job, all right, but not before he had caught, late one night, the *new* plant manager (the one I had dealt with had unexpectedly left, and this "new" plant manager had been a plant manager before—a recurring role) and an aide changing the shipping-monitoring reports on contaminated PVC powder being shipped out of the plant on railway cars.

To verify what he had seen that night, Fred got some of his crew to discreetly remove PVC samples from the railcars to test for vinyl chloride levels, and when the samples came back from the lab with the majority of them significantly above the maximum limit, he took it to the plant manager.

"The plant manager just smiled. How do you like that? No surprise. Anyhow, it wasn't long after that episode that I was fired."

Fred said he didn't know what he was going to do without a job. He felt like he was teetering on the brink of something. It'd been hard on his family. One minute he had a job and was supporting his family, and the next minute he wasn't. Then they had to move. He was in Richmond now, a little place outside of Houston. Spent all his time looking for a job. He had filed a discrimination suit against Formosa with the Equal Opportunity Commission, but he didn't know how that would go. Who was going to believe him when he said the discrimination went the other way and that it was a white man that was being discriminated against this time? What kind of sympathy would that get him?

But it was the truth! Before he had been fired it had come down the corporate grapevine that *somebody* was going to take the fall for the mistakes that were being made at the Point Comfort plant, and the word was out: A white boy's gonna take the fall.

"Well, that white boy was me! I was the sunuvubitch—excuse my French, but that's the way it was. I was the sacrificed lamb."

Fred said he suspected something was going on. Things that could have been done at the plant weren't. Then it got so peculiar that he and Larry Peyton decided to take pictures and send them directly to New Jersey. They felt it was possible that someone, or a group of someones, had deliberately stopped recommendations from reaching New Jersey.

"So did the pictures change anything?" I said.

"Someone in the company sent out an order that *we* weren't to be allowed inside the units! How do you like that? Larry was the plant manager and I was regulatory affairs, and we couldn't go into the units! I don't know where that order came from. Maybe it was the Taiwanese supervisors from the plant. . . . There *definitely* seems to be two different levels operating that plant. One that *appears* to be running it, then the *actual* level where things are really ran. Who knows what it is? We sure couldn't figure it out."

There comes a time when you've heard too much and been told too much, and somewhere in that conversation with Fred, reality went off into the stratosphere. I was wandering around in the ether with my eyes bugged out from an overdose of reality. A hundred times at meetings I'd have someone stand up in the rear of the room and go on and on about me minding my own business and letting the plants alone. Quit picking on those plants! Don't I know that these companies know what they are doing? There are agencies out there that take care of this kind of thing!

But did the agencies know about this? I sure couldn't believe I was the only one privy to this kind of information. So did the agencies know but just weren't telling, or were the agencies just as ignorant as us? I didn't know which one was worse.

I didn't know what to tell Fred. I was even having slim pickings talking to the media. The local newspaper and TV station might cover Fred if I'd oblige them first by getting ran over by a train. I suspected the media was getting sick and tired of my horror stories about the very people they felt were making our little county great. Besides, I was getting tired of it myself—dragging out my story a hundred times and trying to explain the unexplainable. I did it with *60 Minutes* and went nowhere fast. The man wasn't impressed. Every time I laid a document on the table about a worker getting sick or the risks they took at their jobs or the map showing where they had buried something with backhoes, the TV scout would look at me and twist his nose a little out of joint.

"We've done *that*!" he said. "We've done worker stories. The public's tired of hearing it, and politicians being bought is old news. Maybe if you got the goods on some congressman on camera, but this stuff . . . hmmm. Don't you have any videos? We've got people who can get us investigative videos. . . . The real down-and-dirty stuff. We get the cream of the crop, girl. People are begging to be on our program!"

The only thing I could tell Fred was that I was still fighting. I hadn't given up. I was going after Formosa's federal wastewater permit and was trying to get them to recycle their waste stream. Go zero discharge. There was a company in Houston that specialized in the technology; I had heard a little bit about it.

Fred said, "Formosa looked into that one right in the beginning and decided it was too expensive."

"Formosa had a meeting with that zero-discharge company?"

"Sure. I guess it's the same one. How many are there in Texas? Anyhow, Formosa said no go. Too expensive."

Somehow in my little psychic world, I'd known all along that Fred in his monkey suit would be way more than Fred in his monkey suit appeared to be. How I knew that, I can't say. Maybe right along with those dreams coming true, there are times when you know people are a whole lot more capable than they're showing at the moment. You just have to wait around to watch it happen.

• • •

So Fred got me addicted to out-of-the-ordinary contacts and out-of-
the-ordinary behavior, and I figured then that the Vietnamese were
the next order of things. Why not? I had wore out my welcome a hundred times over with the local shrimpers, so even my uncles and
cousins and brothers would groan when they saw me. They'd duck
behind a net or climb into their truck and pretend they never saw me.
Didn't I see they were wore out and wanting to forget? They didn't
hope. They were just men marking time on the water and waiting for
that axe to fall.

I went to Joe. Joe was a net man like me and had come into it the
same way, which was tutelege from a cranky old net man who'd
learned it the hard way and expected everybody else to do the same,
and also from doing a hundred net-patching jobs exactly like the first.
Joe's net patching had started in Palacios, where an old net man found
young Joe on the docks. Joe came in on the first wave of war refugees
that had poured in from Vietnam after Saigon fell, and there was
something in that baby face that the old man liked. Maybe it was the
idea that Joe had come over the water young and alone, or maybe it
was Joe's general liveliness. Whatever it was, it made enough of an
impression that the old man made room for Joe in his net shop and
he let the kid fill net needles for a nickle a shot.

When the net man died, Joe had a business, and the fact that Joe
remained congenial and unchanged throughout it all made him about
as much an abnormality on the docks as I was as a woman. Joe was
Vietnamese in a part of the country where wars were remembered
fondly, and the Vietnam war hadn't been that long ago and what vets
had returned were still living and a little bit screwed up, and I knew
because I married one.

So misunderstandings and hard feelings were as bountiful as the
morning glories that ran the ditches, and it didn't matter that three-
quarters and probably *all* the Vietnamese that located in Seadrift had
ran from the communists—because nobody bothered to introduce
anybody to anybody. The Vietnamese might as well have been communists. Stranger things had happened in Seadrift.

The Vietnamese lived outside of town in a pasture called
Vietnamese Village or Trailer City, named so for all the old trailers
and lean-to shacks. Then there was the crab plant that came from

nowhere and the Yankee carpetbagging businessman that brought it and brought the Vietnamese, and so they cinched their place on the townspeople's list of things they didn't like, in case the Vietnam War hadn't done it.

The crab plant was a profitable eyesore: a big old tin building filled with blue crabs caught from the bay, and looking like a barn from the outside, but on the inside a burgeoning enterprise. It had long wooden tables with stainless steel inlays where the Vietnamese women stood from daylight to dark, only taking breaks long enough to feed the kids or the old grandmas and the old grandpas, and it was there on those wooden tables that the dull blue crabs brought straight from the fish-house ice vault were dumped and re-sorted and dumped and re-sorted again. Most of the crabs that went through there were either shipped out live on refrigerator trucks to San Antonio and Corpus Christi airports or boiled and their meat handpicked by the women.

The Vietnamese men were the crabbers and went into crabbing big time. They got five and six hundred brand-new crab pots and brand-new boats and motors and trailers, and every day that more and more boats and more and more traps went into the water, there came with them a little more trouble. This trouble was a two-headed lady who didn't much care whether it was reluctance or flat unwillingness of the parties involved to communicate traditional rules for fishing, or the circumstances and psychology of a people fleeing a hostile and warring country. Lady Trouble didn't care. So a number of charges and personal insults were hurled back and forth, and it wasn't long before some of the local fishermen were calling the Vietnamese the same names the soldiers had called them in Vietnam. I heard them called "slopes" and "gooks" forty times a day, and it didn't help none that fresh fears were sown about the bays being overfished, and it only intensified the day a Vietnamese crabber was accused of setting his string of crab pots too close to a local crabber.

The local crabber was Billy Joe Aplin, a mainly congenial crabber with a nice wife and nice kids and a mown yard and a string of red canna lilies that ran down one side of his house. Billy Joe had went crabbing with his family on the day that the Vietnamese crabber had placed pots next to him. Billy Joe yelled and words were exchanged and Billy Joe and his family thought the Vietnamese man and his brother made threatening gestures, so Billy pressed charges and two men were arrested. Later Billy changed his mind, so the Vietnamese men were released and Billy Joe decided he needed to get out of crabbing and sell his skiff and start shrimping. One hot day in August, Billy Joe passed two of the men he believed had harrassed him, and some witnesses said Billy Joe got out of his truck and approached one of the men and beat him ruthlessly, and others say he struck the man only once. Whatever it was, the Vietnamese man and his brother jumped in their car and went home and got a gun. When they returned to the bluffs, Billy Joe was shot five times and died.

With that shot a town ignited. Within twenty-four hours a Vietnamese home was firebombed and young local boys who had no inclination whatsoever for guns and violence suddenly started driving around town with shotguns and .22s in the trunks of their cars or on the floorboards of their pickups. One night a man I went to grade school with swam the harbor and burned several crab boats docked at the wharf.

The majority of the Vietnamese recognized the seriousness of the situation and packed their bags and left town. Then the media came. They descended in droves, and helicopters hovered like mud wasps on a mud hole. "It is a powder keg," they hollered home, "just waiting to blow! Maybe it'll blow this week!" A dozen reporters drove into town and hunted a story and sought out the worst of the worst. The worst mouths and worst drunks in town were quoted, and a three-year-old child was photographed holding a rifle on his shoulder.

Next the Ku Klux Klan entered the town and offered to sponsor a protest on the streets of Seadrift and burn a representation of a Vietnamese boat. The town got angry and said the Klansmen were nothing but opportunistic outsiders and wanted nothing to do with them, but the media thought different. Seadrift was a town with 1,200 racists and was portrayed as such in most of the major coverage. ABC's *20/20* devoted a segment of its weekly program to a report on the circumstances surrounding Billy Joe's death, and papers throughout Texas detailed the killing, boat burnings, and subsequent trial and aquittal of the two defendants. Then a French director made a Hollywood picture based on the events and called it *Alamo Bay* and portrayed local fishermen as racists and ignorant bullies, and it was probably for that reason that the movie was shot in Rockport, a coastal town about fifty miles away, and not in Seadrift.

The town was devastated. The task force that had been created by the governor had disbanded, and all the recommendations that had been devised didn't come about because there were no funds to implement them. Eventually the Vietnamese crabbers came back and bought homes that weren't just around Trailer City, and the women in the crab plant went on strike and demanded higher wages for themselves and for the crabs that their husbands and fathers and sons sold to the plant. They won. Then in a few more years Vietnamese crabbers started running the fish houses for themselves.

There wasn't a pact made. Time just went on, and some of it was good times and some of it wasn't. A good time was when a Vietnamese crabber disappeared in a squall and the local shrimping fleet went out and hunted for his body. A bad time was when a shrimper got mad at all his bad luck and took it out on all the Vietnamese crab pots filling the bay by going out and cutting every buoy on every crab pot he could find.

It was complicated with me talking to Joe, and I used the excuse I was buying some net webbing.

"Number nine. Inch an' five-eights. About two hundred meshes," I said.

"That's a lot of webbing for patching a hole," Joe said, and I didn't disagree, but I needed Joe standing still for a minute and counting meshes while I snuck up with my idea. For several minutes I listened to Joe's low counting and the slow dropping of webbing onto the cement floor. Now and then Joe would stop counting and he'd look up and grin and tell me another rumor he'd heard that morning. In the net shop Joe heard every rumor that ever surfaced on the bay, and he smiled and laughed at every one like a shrimper in America was the funniest man alive.

After I'd heard one or two of his best and my webbing was tied in a bundle with a piece of twine, I leaned on the counter and delivered my proposition. "Joe, whadda you think are my chances of getting some support from the Vietnamese shrimpers?"

Joe wrote out my bill carefully and looked up. "Support on what?" he said.

"Zero discharge? You know, keeping the bay clean."

"Whall, I'd theenk they'd be for it. They know they need a clean bay.

They don't theenk too much of Formosa. Theenk you're all right . . . hah hah, for a wamon. Any wamon who shrimps and fixes nets. They theenk she is probably all right. So . . . probably so."

"Do you think they'd demonstrate?"

"Bee a heppie?"

"Sure, something like that. With me, somewhere in Port Lavaca. Out near the water."

"Whall, maybe. When they're not shrimping. They are funny fellows, sometimes. Maybe they will, maybe they won't. I will see."

So one evening Joe called and said he was bringing three Vietnamese representatives to the fish house. I realized then how badly I needed these men. All four men walked in the office. They were all friendly, and not a one didn't smile that I couldn't see a mess of teeth everytime. Joe's uncle was the oldest and looked a bit like Joe and had a net shop in Palacios. The youngest was the newly appointed representative of the Vietnamese community, handsome as all get-out and enamored of his new wife. The last man was TV Tran, who was about as rowdy a redneck as ever I was gonna see coming out of the Vietnamese. The men said that getting Vietnamese support amounted to soliciting the first round of talk from the elders (which more or less was who they were), then getting the second round at four in the morning when all the Vietnamese shrimpers were on their boats and still in the harbor and tuned into the same VHF radio channel that ever' other shrimper was, so Catholic prayers could be delivered over the watery waves of a radio transmitter. My plea for support could be manuvered somewhere behind the benediction.

I didn't expect what I eventually got: two hundred willing and ready demonstrators just needing to know the time and the place and just how far did I want them to go anyhow? I said I didn't want them to go so far as get arrested. This was just a peaceful demonstration and our gripe was Formosa's wastewater permit, plus we were demanding that they go zero discharge on their wastewater.

"You people make a living on the bay. You have a right to demand how things are gonna be done. No need to be bashful about nothing."

And they weren't a drop. They had a hippie zeal, and the mommas and the poppas—some in pointed straw hats and flip-flops and black loose pants, and some in T-shirts and jeans and white rubber boots, and over half with their own signs shoved high above their heads as they chanted and held hands and went in a circle in the middle of a cement parking lot in front of Lavaca Bay—had an exuberant way beyond any protestors I had ever had. The demonstrators were a mix of Vietnamese crabbers from Seadrift and shrimpers from Palacios, and a mixture of women and children from both.

Then there was Formosa's corporate officers. They stood in suits and heavy silence in the hot sun, made even hotter by the cement parking lot, and they stared at the Asian part of a triangle that was unexpectedly developing on the Texas Gulf Coast. It was a mess, sure enough. And so in angry confusion Formosa's officers directed video cameras at the Vietnamese. The Vietnamese protesters didn't care. They were wired on the pure energy of their newly born Texas dream, and they were better believers then anybody else around. Nothing, but nobody, was going to stop *their parade.* A week later Formosa paid a little house call to the Vietnamese community. They were concerned that the Vietnamese people had not heard that there was no such thing as zero discharge. Why, any idiot should know that. Just allow us one visit! One! That's all it will take to prove the idiocy of zero discharge.

Joe came to the fish house and was in my face with *earnest* scrawled over every inch of his own. Could you *prove* the techniques existed? Did you know the names of the chemical companies where zero discharge was done?

Whyyy, sure! I told Joe I would bring the information if he'd just give me the place to deliver it, and Joe said when Formosa got to the part in their speech at the Vietnamese community center where they said zero dicharge didn't exist, he'd wave his hand and I was to get up and declare them liars! Which, basically, I did, and it was better than most things I never prepared for. A week before the meeting Father Joe, a Vietnamese priest and a natural activist, arranged another meeting in the Catholic church in Palacios. In front of old church pews and white plaster statues, I explained Formosa's wastewater permit and how it affected the bays where the shrimpers pulled their nets. Zero discharge was their future. It would guarantee, as no other thing could, a future for their children on the Texas bays. Had they come all the way from the shores of Vietnam just to be shoved out off Texas's?

So some folks were put in charge of a press release and some folks were told to get other people and their kids to the meeting, then Father Joe, who wasn't a bit concerned about overkill, got the neighborhood women to make about ninety signs that they Scotch-taped to the walls of the community center. On the evening of the meeting, two helicopters flew in from Houston (one from an English-speaking television station and another from a Vietnamese newspaper), and the television and newspaper reporters took turns pulling representatives from the community and Formosa outside for interviews.

Inside, every folding chair was filled and every wall held signs. A Vietnamese man in the back doled out cans of cold soda water. I sat about midways in the room and I'd brought along both my babies, which only added to the pure pandemonium of thirty other babies loose in the auditorium and drunk on sweet soda water. A harried Vietnamese man ran after the babies and threatened to tan every hide that didn't sit still.

I knew Formosa hadn't expected such an attentive crowd, nor the press with it's unexpected Asian flavor and interviews that seemingly came out of the blue. For two seconds I felt sorry for Formosa. They were sitting ducks and never even suspected it.

Jack Wu from Formosa was the first speaker. He said that for ten years Formosa had had no bad experiences with the Vietnamese shrimpers. You have always been a very quiet, hardworking people, he said, and you have seen us the same way. Then suddenly, two weeks ago, you showed up so unexpectedly. We called Palacios and said we need to sit down with your group and talk. Answer your concerns. Now, we know that your shrimpers are concerned that our discharge permit will cause the closing of Matagorda Bay.

Joe Wyatt got up next, and his voice had the ring of authority because who (especially the Vietnamese, sitting in their folding chairs) had ever seen the inside of a chemical plant, much less a utilities unit where millions of gallons of wastewater delivered that liquefied muck that was stamped APPROVED by the great state of Texas? Who? Why, these two men with their suits and their briefcases. They were experts who knew the ins and outs of technology and what process was the cheapest and best all-around moneymaking scheme for a company. They knew what was best for everybody around.

The Vietnamese watched and listened, not missing any part of what the first one or the second one said, just waiting and listening and watching until Joe Wyatt got to the part that was gonna cook their goose. Joe Wyatt said zero discharge didn't exist and whoever said so didn't know squat about squat.

Joe Wyatt said, "Someone is misleading you. Go back and ask them for documentation. There is nothing worse than someone trying to mislead folks about what goes on in this state. And we know there is this woman in Calhoun County—Diane Wilson—who claims there is a method of treating water with zero-discharge technology. I am here to tell you there is *no such system!*"

So Joe the net man stood in the front row, where he had been waiting, and he said, "All right! Okay!" to the men he had never seen before. Men who had never walked the docks or the boats or dealt in the webbing his life was fashioned from. It was only right he should stop them. When the net man raised a flat hand to their surprised faces and beckoned to me with the other, Jack Wu leaped to his feet and seemed ready to start some wrestling match right there on the Vietnamese Community Center floor. As it was, he only got to pound a briefcase to death with his tiny fists.

I was ready as a new-laid egg. A wide audience lay like a road before me, and on it were people descending, as eager to reach me as I was them. So I told my version of zero discharge, and Formosa yelled, Lies, lies!—throughout the night. There was no pretense of cordiality. In fact, the meeting never settled down and nobody ever shut up entirely.

31

The Sinking of the SeaBee

I couldn't have invented the final insult. It came because the EPA confused my name. I said my name was Diane and that I was calling to check on Formosa's discharge. I didn't say I was a woman fisherman or that for the last three months I had demanded an evidentiary hearing that the EPA administrator had emphatically denied, and I had appealed that denial in Washington. Something distracted the EPA attorney. Either she was having a bad day or I was one of a dozen calls she could barely remember. So the EPA attorney mistook my voice and mistook my name and believed she was talking to Diana Dutton, the newest and brightest lawyer on Formosa's team. She spent several uninterrupted minutes discussing Formosa's ongoing discharge into Lavaca Bay.

I was facing the bedroom window and out across the pasture were trees and across the trees were dusty lanes where wild deer walked, and beyond that and among the waist-high grasses, a wild tangle of morning glories wove freely up grass stalks. It was a common sight in an uncommon conversation. I waited for it to get real. I waited for the attorney to explain herself or correct her mistake, saying she was talking about some other plant's new discharge and not Formosa's. Eventually I stopped her.

I said, "You're talking to the wrong Diane. I'm not Formosa's attorney."

"You're not Diana Dutton? You're not Formosa's attorney?"

"No, ma'am. I'm the Diane on the other side."

The rest wasn't hard to arrive at. It was actually pretty easy. The realization that Formosa was discharging without a permit and the EPA knew it and the state knew it and none of them bothered to tell the third party because she didn't know she shouldn't believe in federal law. Well, that was the engine that drove me fast to what I'd been waiting for since I first heard of outrage.

It was my point of departure. And I *had* to depart, because anything less would have made me a liar in my human body and destined me for spiritual mediocrity and early death by drowning. Then too, the outrage was compounded because the EPA wasn't going to do anything about Formosa's illegal discharge. Yes, they admitted it was illegal, but enforcement was at the EPA's discretion. The workers were hired! The plant was built! Environmental laws were waaay behind the political truth that agencies were in the business of permitting, and just about as handy as a nose rag when you need a nose rag. It took me three days. The first to vomit my supper over the rails, the second to see the *SeaBee* as a solution, and the third to vomit my supper over the rails. Sink the *SeaBee* on Formosa's illegal discharge pipe! It was outrageous even for me. But it was the only act I believed capable of jarring the jaded souls from the hard places they sat entrenched. Because words weren't heard, petitions went into trash cans, lawsuits gathered dust in judges' offices, and briefs discussing the nation's rivers and oceans were as cheap as the paper they were faxed in on.

The drowning, not the sinking, concerned Donna Sue. "So what are you gonna do? Go down with the boat or get off first?"

"Sink or swim? Swim or drown?"

"This ain't a bit funny."

"Well, Donna Sue, that wrench opening the stuffin' box only turns from inside the boat."

"Well, how 'bout a life jacket, then? You don't swim, so how 'bout that jacket?"

"Nah, don't see hanging on to any safety net. Besides, this is a symbolic act! That's why I'm painting the *SeaBee* white! Just like a little virgin bride."

"Oh, hell," she said. "Just drown then. Formosa's gonna be tickled to death."

My next potential convert and cohort was Deputy Dawg, so between my paintbrush and Donna Sue's paintbrush and the gallon of white epoxy paint, I talked urgent instructions into Deputy Dawg's ear: First, remove the *SeaBee*'s diesel engine so I won't be a dang polluter when I sink her, then second, haul me across the bay to Formosa's discharge pipe!

Nah, nah, nah, he said. He wasn't gettin' a hundred FBI fellas all

over him. No, sir! He was out! But he would take the diesel engine.
So every time Deputy Dawg dismantled something on the diesel
motor and swung around to grab a wrench, he got my white paint
instead. Finally I left him at the docks, still pulling off gears and bolts,
and went to Donna Sue's house to get her phone book. I was looking
for a shrimper to pull me to Formosa's discharge. One shrimper's
name popped up. He was a former constable and known for strange
trips to Mesquite Bay, so I called him and he said, Nope. And I said,
Well, what about your brother? And he said, Nope on him too.

Next I figured I would offer money. Shrimpers always needed
money. One shrimper in particular had a bad shrimp season, then a
heart attack, then his net and shrimp doors were lost overboard and
he was so bogged down in debt that he couldn't see straight. So I
called and said, How 'bout towing me around to Formosa for five
hundred dollars? And he said he wasn't towing anybody all the way
from Seadrift for no amount of money, and besides, didn't I see there
was a dang norther out there?

I said, "How 'bout five hundred dollars just to tow me halfway?"

"Oh, it ain't worth it."

"A thousand dollars."

"Well, maybe a thousand dollars."

Donna Sue looked at me hard when I hung up the phone. "Now,
where in blue blazes are you gonna get a thousand dollars? Just pray
tell!"

"I don't know. I'll get the thousand somewhere. . . . Everything in its
own time. The dollar in the dollar's time. It's just that other shrimper
to tow me the first half that I'm looking for next!"

And I was. Like cheese calling the moon home, it was Sanchez ever'
which way I turned. Sanchez with his misdeed done. Sanchez clam-
oring for attention and dancing like a banshee on the eye of a needle.
I was thrilled with the serendipidy of it all! Formosa's trek to destruction, and it began in their own air-conditioned offices! I called
Formosa's receptionist at the switchboard and told her some bull, and
she put me on the line with Sanchez.

"What are you doin'?" he said.

"Lookin' for you, Sanchez. I need you for a little job. Won't take
long. I need your boat, too."

"Whadda you want my boat for?"

"To haul me out into the bay! I'm sinkin' the *SeaBee* on top of Formosa's discharge pipe!"

"Oh, hell! You're a-lyin'!"

"Nope, I ain't."

"The Coast Guard's gonna hang you out to dry!"

"Nope, they ain't. They gotta catch us first! I need you to tow me out there, so c'mon. And just to the Port O'Connor docks."

"You think I'm slap-dab crazy? You want me sent to jail?"

"Ohhh, nobody's gonna get sent anywhere. Besides, you wanna do it. This is just your type of thing. We head out after dark. Take a little trip down the intercoastal."

"You better shut up! Jack Wu's probably got his ear pasted to this phone!"

"I'll shut up after you say yes!"

"Don't talk anymore. I'll see you at the docks in twenty minutes."

So I knew I had Sanchez. He had disappeared down my road. And I had done the same. But I figgered there had to have been a molecule of vanishing bone somewhere in Sanchez all along. My asking just spotlighted the gristle and popped him down like a rabbit in a rabbit hole.

Now, this sorry business which has drug on for three years is fixing to end in a heartbeat. I intend to take the *SeaBee* down quick. I don't know how quick, but I'm thinking *quick-quick*. No need to piddle around when you've got a shrimp boat sinking.

Donna Sue wasn't happy. She stood on the docks with Captain Deputy Dawg, who had my boat motor in his pickup truck, and she wouldn't wave and she wouldn't leave. She was as into contradiction as she was into menopause.

Me, I have this feeling of leaving, but mainly I am satisfied. It's the first time in my life I have ever had a plan, and the first time I've ever been this far down an illegal road. Actually it's a little more than illegal. Sanchez says it's a federal crime.

Ten minutes farther in the bay and I quit seeing the docks and I quit seeing Deputy Dawg's truck. It's just rain now and the great open bay and a whole lot of mad-looking water. I can't see Sanchez's boat up ahead, towing me, but once or twice I imagine a Coast Guard cutter's found me and the men in the cutter stick out ten different smoking guns from their port-side window. I tell myself to not get lily-bellied. They're just Coast Guard. Put on their britches one leg at a time, just like the rest of us.

I got some time on my hands, so I figure what on the boat will and won't float. My thermos of cold coffee will go straight down. My rubber boots will sink. The deck bucket will go. So will the shrimp doors, and there goes five hundred bucks. That little red package of barbecued corn nuts Donna Sue threw on the catch-all will probably float forever—bob like an effervescent Coke can and shine on the water until a dolphin comes along and gobbles it up.

I've got another hitch in my plans. A norther's howled from nowhere and sits frumpy and mean, chawing on the whole Gulf Coast like fire ants on a dead frog. Or so says the NOAA weather channel—front going nowhere, just sitting to be sitting. So I've got cold rain and gale winds along with the reefs, and along with the Coast Guard, who want me behind bars if I do what they think I'm fixing to do. And the shrimpers? The shrimpers are gonna do what the shrimpers are gonna do, and more than likely it's getting sore and cranky about the federal thing.

Sinking the *SeaBee* is not a simple act. Not just a maneuver by a shrimper-turned-activist-turned-desperado. I had to unhinge myself just to *think* about sinking the *SeaBee*. But getting to the doing part? That required a down-home burying blues song that lamented the mildewed walls and the fiberglassed deck and years on a boat where water and wind knew your name.

And the poor *SeaBee* boat? What's her thoughts? She just floats in the harbor like a trooper while I'm the General Patton in the streets. Just a boat's lowly concerns is all she has: my rubber boots on her deck. And the minute I do come aboard, she talks like I've been gone a hundred years. *And where were you?* she says, and I say, *Just bed and back to bed, and in-between the you and the me and the water.* Privately I think I'll die when I finish her off.

The wind is aggravated. A wind no weather station mentioned until too late, and she tears me to bits, then picks up the pieces and pitches them back to see me flinch. I begin to worry about other things besides the Coast Guard. Submerged reefs. Towlines. I pull on my old torn rain slicker and go out on the bow and check the rope dragging us. I don't see Sanchez ahead steering his boat. Then I do. He comes out on the back deck and hollers something, and I shake my head. *Can't hear you.* Then I go back inside the cabin and camp out on my dry thoughts.

Baby is plenty mad at me. He will probably give me a divorce over the whole thing 'cause (and he didn't say this; I just got it for free from his eyes) it ain't every day a woman takes out her boat and sinks it, and the same day she does is the same day a divorce is called for. I am in rare territory and divorce material, and I don't know what to think so I pray, Dearlordjesus, please forgive me everything it takes to get to the burying hole of the *SeaBee* and divorcing Baby. I am praying an awful lot. An old habit that totally contradicts all the swearing I've done and all the divorcing I'm fixing to do.

Baby said he sure wouldn't do it. (I'm talking about the sinking and not the praying.) Hell could freeze over before he'd sink the *SeaBee.* That was marine plywood on that boat! Didn't I know nothing? A hundred dollars a sheet for marine plywood! So I left Baby on the front porch swing and he didn't say another word past that marine plywood remark. We had a talk of sorts earlier, and while it was pretty clear that Baby would get the house and I would get the boat I was forever sinking, we never said the word *divorce.* He just said, "If you wanna sink the damn boat, well, have at it. Jus' have at it."

I guess I'm having at it. I sit in the cabin and figure I have three hours left. If the rope breaks, then I have longer, but I don't want to think that way. Negativity is definitely not an option for this so-called federal crime, so I say three or four more prayers and quote scripture from memory to further along my criminal career.

The dead are in deep anguish, those beneath the water and all that live in them. Death is naked before God; destruction lies uncovered. He spreads out the northern skies over empty space and he suspends the earth over nothing.

In their rush to leave unhallowed ground, the prayers pour like juice from my quart-jar heart. I pray the Coast Guard doesn't find me! Pray the damn norther lets up! Pray the *SeaBee* sinks gotdarn fast! Then I get so tired of looking for God holes in that norther sky that I quit and just hope the whole enchilada isn't in trouble.

Twice I think Sanchez's towrope's broke, but it was just the waves and the current and the rudder doing whatever it wants to do. Otherwise I know what a sailboat sounds like; exactly how a shrimp boat sounds without her diesel motor. What eighty years ago was a common thing in Seadrift: fishing boats and oyster skiffs and wooden oars and schooners with white sails and fishermen with no eyes because the man with the camera on shore couldn't catch the fishermen's soul. Couldn't catch the light in their eyes.

I am feeling knee-deep in crazy. Sinking the *SeaBee* is as nuts as I've gone in a while, but it is late and I'm out of coffee. Time has slipped up on me while I think about sinking my boat and sinking my marriage. So I focus on nothing but the last part of the plan—the place where everything leads. Wasn't that what Grandpa used to say? Everything leads to the end?

Nah! he says. It was everything *leading to the water!* (I am arguing with Grandpa, talking like one crazy woman to a crazy man, and our sea clothes are blue and exactly the same.) Grandpa says that he faced water in the morning and he faced water in the dead of night. His whole life was one blind tilt to the water. Well, heck, you know the story, he says.

That is for sure. All those tilts in the deadest of night and now they are *mine*. I have never did so many deliberate acts in my entire life to get me to the place I am. Yesirree. I am working my way to the sea's boneyard, and I'm not particular about staying alive.

Grandpa agrees, but privately he doesn't understand my detachment, and privately I don't understand why he has come back. Maybe it's not him. I could be hallucinating. I've had enough coffee. Or it could be the howling black norther and the boat so crazy in the water, moving in leaps and jerks and going through troughs of waves, then hitting the rope with a jerk. Grandpa is a ragtag old tale anyhow. Been dead years. I remember when he died and misunderstood somehow that he had taken his old suitcase and left town. No dying and throwing dirt all around while he lay in a casket in a new shirt and pants; Grandpa just left town. Now he sits on the catch-all of the *SeaBee* with his wounded leg still wounded and his runny sea eyes like yesterday's scrambled eggs and he talks to me.

So what's it gonna be? he says. Go down with the boat or get off?
Sink or swim. Swim or drown. Make up yore mind, woman!

32

Sanchez Comes Home

Sanchez is on the back deck, hollering into the wind, so I get out of my captain's chair and lean out the cabin window.

"What?" I yell back.

He hollers again, so I go out into the rain and edge up, half crouched, against the bulwarks. The wind is howling like a train gaining speed and loaded down with nothing. The towrope is tight over the bow and I look past it to Sanchez standing upright on the stern, completely covered in a gray slicker except for his bare head and feet. He seems unconcerned with the rolling waves.

We throw words out, but the wind fractures them like cat bones. Finally Sanchez throws his arms up and goes back inside the cabin and jerks the boat in neutral. The boat stalls on a wave's peak and Sanchez comes back out and jerks on the slack towing rope. When the two boats are close, Sanchez stretches out his arm and yells, "Get on aboard!"

I hesitate a second, then leap off the bow and land flat on Sanchez's boat. As I glance back, the *SeaBee* lunges in a wave, and Sanchez waves me towards the cabin. "She's okay," Sanchez says, and lets the towing rope slide through his hand. I watch until the *SeaBee* stops rolling, then I go into the cabin.

Sanchez's cabin is big and customized with cheap wood paneling over marine plywood, and going into his cabin is like entering a cabin in the woods. A half-dozen windows are barred to keep the wind out. In every corner is an electronic gadget, and they are all running and their red eyes are sore from hatching out information. On the catch-all, where everything from twine to spare engine parts are tossed, is a two-burner butane stove with a pot of coffee that has boiled over. I pull off my slicker and hang it on a nail, and Sanchez comes in and shoves the throttle forward. Then he sits down in a chair and grabs a bag of almond M&M's and offers me some. Naw, I say, I just want

coffee, and I grab a denim shirt off his bunk and use it to handle his
boiled-over coffeepot.

Then I sit on the edge of the bunk with the coffee between my
hands, and Sanchez sits *not* like he is expecting to be shot, but more
like he is fixing to be the shooter, and all the while one bare foot holds
the steering south with a little east in it.

"Well, whadda you thinking?" I say.

"Thinkin' you better thank your lucky stars I'm your brother, 'cause
only a big brother would do this for you. And nobody else!"

I don't know how to answer that truth, so I laugh. I'm happy I have
Sanchez. So we talk with the effortless ease of winged flight, only we
aren't that high; we're lower, more on a level of the intercoastal canal
and submerged marsh, and even that doesn't matter because it is night
and black as all get-out and we have just took the final turn at Turn
Stake and headed north to Formosa.

Sometime after eleven we pass Wally's fish house and the sportsmen's
camp and the place, more than once, I had picked up Sanchez's shrimp
in a truck. I think about the other shrimpers and wonder if they have
heard of the action.

Sanchez has his doubts about the shrimpers and doesn't believe a
frazzling soul will show up for support.

"What about the Vietnamese shrimpers?" I say. "They ain't
Anglicized yet."

"Well, you never know about the Vietnamese. I won't call that one.
. . . But that bay gets plenty durn *rough*, baby sister. Pleeenty durn
rough! A shrimper can lose a boat out there real easy-like. I'm just
thinkin' you're lucky you got me. *Figure* from there! You're gettin' your
boat out where you want it, ain'tcha?"

"I'm gettin' it partways. If my thousand-dollar man don't show, I'm
gonna be hell out of luck."

"What does it matter if you don't got anybody else? *You got your
brother!* Hell, most people would be jumping up and down to get that
much! Especially as crazy a thing as we're doin'. So family is *it*!
Nothing else! Kiss that other crap good-bye!"

Sanchez turns in his chair like he is drunk from a bottle I ain't seen
yet. His bare feet are ever' which way over the wheel and the catch-
all, and times I wonder who is steering the boat. The second

Sanchez turns on the cabin light to hunt some spilled M&M's, I see he is drunk on the same old thing that made him outrun a game warden's boat three years before, and now it is a second time he is outrunning something with *authority* in the title. Probably the Coast Guard. He looks young in his drunkenness, a fool maybe, but a young fool, and ten or fifteen years of despair has dropped from his life like old pants off an old man. Don't tell me people don't like getting shot at, especially near misses. I can see it plain as the light on the cabin ceiling that Sanchez is reveling in it. He is whooped up as any drunk in a kitchen, drinking vanilla extract.

One hour later Sanchez gets his exact wish. I see it first through the back cabin door so I turn and say, "There they are!"

And Sanchez says, "Holy shit! The Coast Guard? The Coast Guard?"

"More than likely. Shore ain't the Bobbsey twins at the seashore. They've got flashin' lights too! Three boats, I believe."

"Oh, hell! Turn off that cabin light!"

I do, but it is only a cabin light and not lead bullets, so it don't do any good. The Coast Guard boats are still coming for five confusing minutes, and it is hard to tell which boat is coming first: two large cutters or the smaller roustabout. Finally the smaller boat takes a run at our stern and Sanchez runs outside and yells, "Watch my railings, you idiot!"

A uniformed man is standing outside the cabin yelling into a loud speaker, "*Is Miz Wilson aboard? Do you have a Miz Wilson aboard?*" It is a disembodied sound, like a voice coming over a school loudspeaker, and every word is flat and empty and suited for the banality of children's halls, but not the midnight waterway going from Brownsville to Mississippi. I feel mad about something I can't name, so I walk out on the back deck of Sanchez's boat and see the black, tearing night and the waves that rush, and the only thing that is solid is a uniformed man standing and, above him, the flashing lights of a Coast Guard boat.

Sanchez pays attention to none of it. The Coast Guard boat might as well have been a log floating in the current, coming into sight, then gone to Louisiana. Sanchez makes a couple of maneuvers with his boat, sharp turns this way and that, and the Coast Guard boat makes the same maneuvers, and lost in between is the *SeaBee* that is floundering in the rough seas. Finally the Coast Guard boat clears. It is a

short boat, mostly cabin with radar and antennae and barely enough
room on the back deck to swing a cat good. I count four men, three in
a port window and one standing outside. As the boat comes closer, a
Coast Guard officer moves to board our boat, and Sanchez shoves the
boat into neutral and runs out on the back deck and shouts off the
stern, "Your tearing up my boat, you moron! Keep your damn boat off!"

The officer waves him away and keeps coming. "We are boarding
your boat, sir. Request permission to board your boat."

He is young and panting hard, and once aboard he doesn't let a word
come between any of us until he is directly in my face. "Are you Miz
Wilson?" he says. "Ma'am, are you Miz Wilson?"

I say, "I don't recall."

"You don't recall? You don't know if your name is Miz Wilson?"

"I don't recall that. I sure don't."

He looks at me hard, then throws his hands up and walks to the
cabin after Sanchez. "Sir," he says, "sir, you're going to have to bring
this boat alongside. We have reason to believe you are carrying Miz
Wilson, who we believe has terrorist intentions. Please, sir, to that
dock over there. Otherwise you are an accomplice. So please, sir. That
is an order. Bring this boat alongside."

"Hey! Hey, do I look like an idiot! I can't maneuver while your damn
boat is up my rear end. I'll ram a hole in both of us!"

"We can move off, sir."

"Well, move off, then! Get outa my way!"

The Coast Guard man moves from Sanchez to the bulwarks but not
off the boat, and I tell Sanchez to back up and let me back on the
SeaBee. Even if I have plans to sink her, I don't intend for her to be
knocked between the pilings and the Coast Guard like she is an old
bucket.

So for ten minutes, me and Sanchez haul ropes and boats, and the
Coast Guard youth just stands there watching it all. I shove the bow
of the *SeaBee* off Sanchez's boat, and the Coast Guard roustabout
won't get out of the way because they're naturally thinking every move
we make is a subversive one, and so they move counterways, and that
only succeeds in corralling all three boats (and one without a motor
and a captain) into a corner only big enough for one.

Finally I grab the rigging on the *SeaBee* and heave myself over the
side, then frantically run to shove Sanchez's stern off the Coast

Guard's stern and mine off of both of them, and at the same time try to put the *SeaBee* in a position so I can toss a rope to a piling on the dock. It's a now-or-never place; a conjuction of docks and Gulf shrimp houses and Gulf shrimp boats and twisted and rotting pilings and old wrecks of old riggings and the last structure before the intercoastal canal widens from a narrow path to a broad mass of more conflicting currents: the rock-strewn jetties of the open Gulf waters, and the deep beginnings of Matagorda Bay.

The Coast Guard seem to think I am escaping without a motor, and they yell from whatever corner and boat they're on. Once from a boat and two or three times from the docks they holler, "*Miz Wilson! Return to the docks! That is a direct order! Miz Wilson! Miz Wilson!*"

I hear cursing, then a laugh. It is Sanchez. He tries to yell over the Coast Guard to tell me something, but in an instant the channel opens and a path clears and I ignore Sanchez and throw a coiled rope and miss. I yank in the wet rope and bundle it again and then lunge out for a piling. This time the rope hits heavy against a piling, but the *SeaBee*'s drifting weight yanks it off and the rope drags down the docks like a blind and beaten dog. An ensign sees the rope and starts in a chase after it, and seconds before it is yanked from the docks and into the water, he grabs the loop and flicks it over a piling like a child tossing a rattlesnake into a waiting gunnysack. For a second he forgets he is Coast Guard; he is a boy winning a thing for the first time, and I hear his laugh clear from the *SeaBee*. I smile, amused at the boy and amused at this night that is like no other night, where such dissimilar parts can be such blood brothers in their conspiracy to ruin one another. I tie off the rope and wait to be pulled in.

There is no hope, so I don't try explaining. I just wait while the clipboards and official documents start on Sanchez at the far end of the docks and, finally, end with me where I am tied up. I know what is in store. For Sanchez, a full-scale two-hour no-bullcrap Coast Guard inspection (which, without a doubt, Sanchez will pass with flying colors). I will get an interrogation. They won't even bother with an inspection. They can easily see I won't pass. I don't even have a motor.

I ain't arrested, they say, but I need to know this is serious business, little lady. Serious! I face terrorism charges with eighteen years' imprisonment and half a million dollars in fines. And the *SeaBee* is being confiscated. That boat is not to leave the docks! Do I understand that? Not until I receive further instructions is that boat to leave the docks.

So I ain't just an organizer and I ain't just a fisherman. No, I am a terrorist on the high seas! I can't help smiling, and the young ensign wants to know why I am doing all that smiling. Now, why is that? Did I think the situation was funny? Did I think *he* was funny?

"No, honey, I don't think you're a bit funny."

This boils on about two hours, with the Coast Guard running back and forth with information and clipboards and what one is saying and what the other is saying and what really is the truth in the matter, until finally the officer says they are finished with me, but my boat stays where she is. I am free to leave the docks. Sanchez walks barefoot on the dock, and his slicker top is gone and his shirt is wet and alongside his mouth a little something keeps rising like a moth's wings right before it takes flight with its new body.

"Whadda you want to do?" he says. "They're pretty suspicious of me right now. Told me I better take my boat and get along. So you gonna ride back with me or sit around here for something else?"

"Oh, just sit around, I guess. I've got that other connection a little later on."

"Yeah, I know what you got, but that other connection ain't liable to show if you got half the Coast Guard station sleeping on your boat."

"I'll figure somethin' out."

"Well, you better figure *good*, because those fellas got a burr in their saddle about you sinkin' that boat."

I hear what Sanchez says, but something else is coming from his face besides the words. *He is glad!* Tired and wet and drug through God knows what kind of inspection, Sanchez's perilous thinking from that very first spontaneous act three years ago hadn't stopped. It didn't stop when he quit the bay to join Formosa, and it didn't stop when six Coast Guard officers stepped on his boat and opened up their clipboards.

"Maybe I should just get outa this rain and quit gettin' soaked," he says, and I say, "Yeah, maybe you should." I hear what he *really* says all the same.

Sanchez and I leave about the same time. He throws a rope and takes off down the channel, and I go around Clark's fish house and take off looking for a phone booth. I walk north and hit every small motel I knew of. The rain hasn't quit, and high up and next to the light poles the air throbs like a wrist pulse. Smoke from a barbecue joint filters from somewhere. I forget how many motels I walk past. Some are boozy-pink and half-lit and one is painted with a Hawaiian scene, but none has a working phone. Finally one does, so I call Donna Sue.

Donna Sue wants to know who all is there. Just myself, I say. But it'll be different at daybreak. That thousand-dollar-bill might pull in one.

Donna Sue says she doubts it. She hasn't been asleep and nobody's called, so whadda's that tell you? Deputy Dawg wasn't coming neither. He was dead alseep. Even a thousand dollars won't pry that man out.

I don't touch it anymore. But still I look down the wet streets and look at every trailer and every lit window, and wonder if maybe that truck tire stirring on some shell isn't one of my shrimpers. Who else would be galavanting out this late at night?

Donna Sue meets me down the Port O'Connor highway, and I don't need to listen to a thing she has to say 'cause nothing is what she has to say. I oughta be thankful for Sanchez is what she doesn't say but thinks, and I know it by how little she says, like the truth is done inside out. A mirror message you read backwards. So maybe the reason I won't get any more shrimpers to help is because it is blood like Sanchez says it is. How many brothers do I have working for Formosa and capable of the convoluted mythic rebirth Sanchez is capable of? Maybe *all* the shrimpers are capable of it. Which leads me back to my starting place again, and I realize I am tired. I am tired and thinking in circles.

We don't talk, but when we get in the door and before the coffee's made, my thousand-dollar shrimper calls.

"It's three right now. I'll meet yah at the fish house at daylight. Be there, woman."

So we turn around and do everything in reverse. Go back to the Port O'Connor highway and back through town and down the four blocks that will land us at the docks on the intercoastal waterway where the *SeaBee* is tied. There is a charged note in Donna Sue's voice, a quality something like a child seeing her momma's face right before the executioner throws the switch.

"You know, you don't *have* to do this," she says, and I'm thinking, *Well, this is a first.* Donna Sue advocating *not to fight*! But I don't turn to see; I just sling myself out onto the shell road and don't stop walking until I am at the docks. I walk down the wet dock where the *SeaBee* is tied, and when I step on the boat three things happen simultaneously. Two truck doors slam and a man's voice says, "Miz Wilson, *what* are you doin'?" It is five uniformed Coast Guard, and every one from a single truck and every one blinking back the night.

"I ain't doin' a single solitary thang," I say, "so why don't you fellas just climb on back in that truck and go on home?"

"Ma'am. You know we can't do that, and I believe you know why."

"Fellas, all I'm gonna do is climb on that boat and go to bed."

"Well, ma'am, if you don't mind, we'll be here just makin' sure."

"Well, just hop to it," I say.

I leave them on the docks and go into the cabin and climb below. I get an oily life jacket off a nail, then double it for a pillow and lie on the cabin floor. It is three thirty. Underneath, the diesel fumes and old shrimp smells float up, so I shove the cabin door open with one boot and from the floor I watch the wind take an old tin-covered light wired to a piling and whip it to death. Thirty minutes go, then an hour, then a Coast Guard youth sticks his head in the cabin door and says, "Miz Wilson? Can we get you a pillow?" And I hear him, but I am in some long-confused dream where boats sink and rise, so I say, startled, and without even knowing what I refuse, No, no, no.

At last the rain quits, but still daylight won't come. A flashlight moves across a wet deck. I get up hard and pull my slicker tight around me and stare out the door. The coming is exactly like I'd planned. My thousand-dollar shrimper with a towing rope at dawn. Only he doesn't carry a rope. He comes empty-handed and carries exactly nothing, and the three Coast Guard men behind him carry nothing too.

The shrimper doesn't move into the cabin, but stands at the door. "Diane," he says, "I can't tow yah. These Coast Guard fellas here tell me they'll take my boat. I can't have that. You know I can't have that. So I'm sorry, but I can't do what I said. You know, that thang . . . "

The shrimper's hard hand is clutched near the latch where I sometimes bolt the door from the inside. He acts like he wants to leave and his eyes go sideways to the docks, then to the Coast Guard officer that stands almost at his elbow.

"You understand?" he says.

382 An Unreasonable Woman

And I say, "Sure, sure. I understand."

Then before he turns and leaves, he says, "'Nother thing, Diane. I would never have took that money. I know I said I would, but I wouldn't. I'd done it for nothing. You know that, don'tcha?"

"Sure," I say. "I know."

"Yeah, well, just wanted you to know. I'd have done it 'cause . . . you know, about all that crap you talk about."

I watch him walk away and after him the Coast Guard, and when they are both gone, I walk out on the deck and stand under a gray sky getting grayer by the minute. Two more government trucks have pulled up next to the first, and now a dozen Coast Guard men mill around and do nothing but watch me and a morning sky get muddier by the minute.

Maybe fate did it. Finally I get irritated with all the looking and shout from the deck, "Ain't y'all tired just sittin' around, waitin' on me for somethin'? Ain't y'all got nothing better to do?"

One officer looks very thoughtful and pulls his clipboard down so it is almost at his regulation belt buckle. He says, "Just making sure you don't go anywhere, Miz Wilson. That's all."

"Y'all see me standing here with another boat? Where am I goin'?"

"Just doing our job, ma'am."

Oh, fine! Formosa can be out there discharging tens of thousands of gallons of wastewater illegally and sending benzene and chloroform and metals and cancer-causing, baby-aborting chemicals snorkling everywhere under the sun, but have a woman loose with a boat and a wrench, why, then they have to call out the government trucks and militia and have men lined up on docks to watch her every move. What illegal bones in my old body disturbed them?

Even with Formosa an hour and nearly a bay away and the *SeaBee* tied with more ropes than she'd ever been tied and an ensign posted fore and aft and my dismissed thousand-bucks shrimper a clear indication of my failing support with the shrimpers, they still think me capable of impossible feats and so, in a perverted fashion, I believe too. There is nothing like the roundabout way an enemy's eye can send fresh inspiration when you need it most. I sit at the dragon's threshold without any men, yet I know that when the final Coast Guard cutter sails off, I won't. I won't leave. I will howl and the rain and the wind will howl in matching octaves above my own and nobody will hear, but we will make a stand. It doesn't take a continent. It doesn't even take a county. Sometimes all it takes is just one unreasonable woman and nature in alliance.

Forty years late, but I have returned. Forty years late, but I am back. I am not so silent now. I am on the water and with it and trying like hell to get lower. I don't watch the Coast Guard any longer. I don't care. Let 'em start a fire and make camp. I turn on my white rubber heels and walk across the deck to the starboard side and prepare to wait.

It's funny when you let go, how it all returns. A shrimp boat comes alongside just like we are two lone shrimp boats tied together in Mesquite Bay for the night. I have only to pull out my iron skillet for the fried shrimp to make it more real. But the captain on his boat isn't tied in Mesquite Bay. He raises one arm through the port window and shoves it high as he passes me. He is the cavalry leading the charge into Lavaca Bay, because another boat has started its engine and it backs from the harbor until the stern is level with mine. The captain walks out on the deck and raises one arm like the first has done. It is my thousand-bucks shrimper who was so sorry he couldn't help, and I am frozen to the guy wires of the *SeaBee* and I don't hear what he says. I stand with my boots immobile and I hold myself tight against the *SeaBee*'s wires.

I smell the shrimpers coming. Their diesel fumes leap from silver exhaust arms and their long, languid nets from tethered blocks billow out like women's dresses. Five boats jam the channel, and their wheel washes mingle in a vortex of white water. Then, as though collaborative, the boats roar off and hit the churning open waters of Matagorda Bay. I stare for a long time at their masts and the white crest of the waves that stays like a permanent artist's stroke against the dark sides of the boats.

In all there are ten boats, and more if I want to count the Vietnamese boats coming from Palacios. Then before it ends entirely, there is Sanchez. He has returned, the unreturning man, from the channel where he was leaving, and he steers past the Coast Guard and past the watching and dumbfounded looks, and he shouts once in a half-mad dance from the stern of his boat and he joins the fleet in the rolling southern sea.

33

Victory, Redemption, and Loss

In this dream I didn't move. I pressed against the SeaBee's bulwarks while the shrimpers on their God-almighty boats steered straight into madness. The Coast Guard stood book bound, their manuals clamped tight to their chests. Then, alarmed and in hot pursuit, the Coast Guard launched their boats back into the sea. What else could they do? There seemed to be a mass blockade in the making, an act of terrorism fixing to be performed somewhere, somehow, upon navigation and production and industry and progress! The Coast Guard had their orders! It was in their manuals!

So they chased and boarded boats and gave citations, but still the shrimpers wouldn't leave. Then the press arrived. A single helicopter landed on the bluff before the very incident that would eventually hit the Houston newspapers and the wire services and eventually the local papers. Formosa became the laughingstock of the petrochemical world; the carnival antics of shrimp boat blockades and boat sinkings and Coast Guard running every which way both shocked and thrilled their competitors. Some industry folks scented enough blood in the airing that they sent professional spies to haunt my house for files and information.

It wasn't long before those who watch these types of things made a judgment call, and that call was that Formosa's permits seemed unstable, and with instability houses tumble. So before long Blackburn called and said, "Wilson, I believe now is the time to dust off that zero-discharge concept and bring it on home. Formosa is sick and tired of your antics."

So my unreasonableness and Jack Matson's engineering brilliance and Blackburn's diplomacy was brought to the conference table in Formosa's new administration building, and there the concept of zero discharge was dumped onto Formosa's plastic heart.

If I had a plan, I never knew it. And if I found a plan had been there all along, it wasn't until the end that I found it. I think, *So much for plans. Vision and dreaming is enough.* How else to explain it?

That's exactly what the chemical plants wanted to know. Especially Alcoa, next door to Formosa. Jack Matson and I paid them a visit later and asked them to go zero discharge, and they looked in a worried northerly direction at Formosa for exactly ten minutes, then the plant manager said rather quickly, "Why, I believe that's doable."

Zero discharge is doable. So that's what I say to every nonbelieving chemical plant, and what I haven't gained in sophistication or professional etiquette, I make up for in unreasonable behavior. I am not so well behaved anymore.

Other things changed too. My boat is gone. The *SeaBee* was never the same after her engine was gone. It was like I removed her heart, and when I never had enough money to replace the engine or afford the harbor space any longer, Baby towed her to a reef. Now every time I run my trotlines and pass that reef, I see the *SeaBee* breaking up. Another board gone. Every norther takes her a little farther down.

Most of the men are gone. Dead, every one. Started burying one, and they all fell like flies. My daddy died first from all the cigarettes, and Momma said he was lucky he died fast, because Billy Bones was a proud man and what hurt him worse than the cancer was the indignity of dying. I had to lift him out of the bathtub a dozen times and give him his coffee with a straw.

Sanchez died two months later, after leaving the fish house. Nobody suspected nothing and he still worked at Formosa (but planned on leaving) and had on his icebox, anchored with a magnet, a long list of things he'd do once he quit work at the plant and started back shrimping. Sanchez was eating angel food cake, just like Grandpa did right before he took off twenty years before, only cake wasn't what killed Sanchez and it wasn't what killed Grandpa, but it sure was coincidental as hell.

Wally hunted me down after Sanchez died and grieved so bad his hands shook. So I cried for Wally and not for Sanchez, then a year later, Wally was dead. I didn't know what killed him but figgered after he left the bay that he was a dead man walking.

Blackburn signed two more agreements with Formosa, but never was far from the sight of Rick, who tormented him in the background and spurred activists to know just what he thought of the arrangements. In a publication paid for by Formosa, Blackburn explained everything he had accomplished with his agreements. The publication, with its diagrams and data on worker safety, looked good, and the state thought so and so did twenty other bureaus and groups who Blackburn had presented them to. But a presentation before Formosa's hourly workers, who did all the grunt work in the plant, brought laughs. They were sitting on different sides of the tracks, the workers said. And that ain't how things really go in the plant. Maybe you should've been talking to the workers.

As for me, I sit in another house now. It is quiet and I am close enough to the bay that I hear her heartbeat. Sometimes I am so content that I believe that I am dead too, just like Wally and Sanchez. Or at least I am in a high, high dream, and I lie down and the tide and water is the dream, and I dream the livelong night.

This house can't fail in its quietness. Because I am quit of every man save Crockett—who is the *ultimate* quiet man and makes no sound at all. His daddy still lives in the old house, in the salt grass, miles from the intercoastal, with a half-dozen boats that rot in the sun. I see him now and then. We never talk of our marriage. It is an old, old hurt and still sore, and neither one of us will go near it. He uses the gun for snakes still.

It is only my girls and Crockett that remain. The girls make mud pies along the water's tide line and help me hang clothes to dry in the wind. Then this little man sits in the window and draws lines in the screens, and as I pass and look at another torn screen, I say, "Who tore this screen, Crockett? Who did it?" And Crockett turns and his eyes are brown as river stones and he says, "The Formosa kid."

Epilogue

I dreamed about the harbor. Went down to the bay and nobody was there. No fishermen, no trucks, no boats. Maybe it's coming true. Froggie sold the fish house and only a white slab of cement remains as a marker. The fish house next door is gone too. Western Auto, the fishermen's store? Another casualty. The Vietnamese got hit hard with a crab die-off and half of them went north. The shrimp season failed again and again, and now you'll see more FOR SALE signs on the shrimp boats than captains.

My little brother John Boy bought a boat, then sold it, then got a job at Union Carbide walking the steel pipes. Froggie quit selling his shrimp for eating and instead sold his shrimp for baiting the damn-sportsfishermen's hooks, and in Port O'Connor he made a killing and Wally is turning over in his grave somewhere.

My second zero-discharge agreement with Formosa Plastics (the first one, in 1994, forced the plant to recycle 33 percent of its waste stream) tangled with worker's safety issues and stories of management manipulating wastewater-monitoring reports. In 1999, in the middle of a big showdown between FBI and EPA criminal investigators and plant managers caving in, I pulled out of the agreement in protest. They weren't keeping me silent with a phony agreement. Instead I took my vision of zero discharge before the Seadrift City Council and the Calhoun County Commissioner's Court and, as plant managers perched on chairs and wagged furious fingers at the commissioners, warning of dire consequences if they signed, we walked away with resolutions supporting zero discharge for the entire county.

Next I took zero discharge to Union Carbide and to DuPont. Neither even bothered to hide that they weren't budging past their crossed arms. Lucky for me DuPont had just submitted a wastewater permit to the state of Texas, so I demanded a hearing and subsequently went on another hunger strike. This strike lasted thirty-one days; half of that time I traveled to DuPont facilities across the country and the other half I sat on a hard metal chair across the street from DuPont's Wilmington, Delaware, headquarters. DuPont's response was that I was an ecoterrorist and probably eating apples on the sly, and quite frankly they didn't care how long I stayed on a strike or whether I starved myself to death.

Needless to say that hunger strike didn't produce an agreement, but it had an interesting side effect: in the following six months requests by chemical producers for information on zero-discharge technology quadrupled, and that highlighted the larger question of why industry's oft-trumpeted push for "pollution prevention" had rarely if ever included zero-discharge solutions.

I didn't fight all the time. I went out on my little skiff in the mornings and contemplated the birds and the fish and the elusive porpoises. Then the corporations messed with my mind where it hurt even more: Seismograph boats hunting for oil and gas appeared on the bays! They strung dynamite charges hither and yonder and proceeded to blow up the bay, and when a few fish blew out of the water, more knowledgeable heads than theirs decided that they needed *airboats* (the equivalent of jet planes on the water) to chase the fish away from the dynamite. So five zipping airboats met me every morning with their racket, and there went our fish. The fish didn't return to the bays for a year; the oil and gas exploration in the bays resumed and goes on to this day. It was within this window of opportunity that the idea for *An Unreasonable Woman* was born. What else to do but write and starve—a starving writer. I didn't invent it.

While I wrote, the work with the chemical plants continued. In 2002 I began a thirty-day hunger strike in solidarity with the people of Bhopal, India. Three to eight thousand of them died and half a million more were injured when Union Carbide's Bhopal plant leaked a huge quantity of toxic chemicals in December 1984. By 2004 it was estimated that another twenty thousand had died; thousands more still suffer, yet have not been adequately compensated. Every morning I sat in my truck at the front gates of the Union Carbide (now Dow Chemical) plant in Seadrift and passed out information about Bhopal to the workers. Nearly four days after the strike, I climbed Dow's fence and up a seventy-foot tower. There, on a tiny perch with my hands chained to the top railing of the tower, I threw over a huge banner: JUSTICE FOR BHOPAL.

Then a hilarious thing happened. Within hours of plant personnel spotting me, rumors flew fast and loose that I was chained to *every* chemical plant's tower throughout the county. I was everywhere! Eventually, I was drug from the tower by a four-man SWAT team in a steel basket hanging from a two-hundred-foot crane, and I was sentenced to four months in the county jail. In sentencing, the DA said I was a "dangerous woman."

Prison doesn't greatly bother me. I once saw a poster of the enormously grinning Catholic priest, Daniel Berrigan, the Vietnam War era peace activist, being handcuffed and led by two FBI men to jail. Overhead was the caption: "Who is the More Free?" I've been arrested about thirteen times and in and out of prisons.

Risking one's life can be strangely liberating. That's what the sea counsels me. She still talks even though she's got a mercury Superfund on her left breast and vinyl chloride and phthalates on her right breast. She's a forgiving grandmother. Not unduly angry about the mix-ups and mess-ups and the confounding fact of healing taking so long. She knows it is complicated. My intent will keep her, she says.

Seadrift, Texas
May 2005

Acknowledgments

An Unreasonable Woman is my first book, and lord knows what would have become of it if Molly Bang hadn't read it and encouraged me to write more and Wayne Lore hadn't provided the space for my typewriter and my kids and Kenny Ausubel hadn't labored long and hard to find the book's home—Chelsea Green Publishing. To them, the book owes much.

I am also especially grateful to my publisher Margo Baldwin and my editor John Barstow and all of the members of the Chelsea Green staff who gave me invaluable advice and guided me through the editing and publishing process and made it a delight.

I am deeply indebted to Nina Reznick for her expert legal advice on clauses and contracts and everything that scares the holy bejesus out of me.

For those Unreasonable Women (especially Nina Simons who birthed the dream) who inspired me and made me strong and a part of their gathering I am forever grateful. With love: Rachel Bagby, Jeanine Canty, Anna Marie Carter, Caroline (Wild Woman) Casey, Claire Hope Cummings, Susanna Dakin, Malaika Edwards, Susan Griffin, Carolyn Raffensperger, Belvie Rooks, Kristin Rothballer, Nancy Schaub, Tara Sterling, Terri Swearingen, Barbara Whitestone, Catherine Porter, Medea Benjamin, Jodie Evans, Nina Reznick, Nina Utne, Anna Lappe, Lauren Klein, Pramila Jayapal, Toby Herzlich, Alissa Hauser, Diane Haug, Theresa Marquez, Ginny McGinn, Melissa Nelson, and Mayumi Oda.

I would like to express my deep gratitude to the many people who gave me their help and support during the years I worked on this book. It is impossible for me to mention them all by name. But some I do. I am especially grateful to:

Dr. Jack Matson for his long-time support and advice and for being one of the first advocates for zero discharge

Medea Benjamin and Jodie Evans for taking Code Pink and making her what she is today

Peter Warshall for his thoughtful consideration of my work and instigation of a long run of synchronistic happenings at Bioneers

Donna Sue Williams for being exactly who you are and believing in me when nobody else did

Kathy Yarborough for being the dream interpreter and taking all those pictures

Paul Hawken for his sage and helpful advice on my book and sitting at the table with me that time when I wouldn't dance

Kinnu Khrisnaveni for being a help and a natural administrator (which I'm not) and a sounding board for my crazy ideas

Robert Greenwald, Kenny Ausubel, and Alys Shanti for believing in my story and creating another medium for it

Michael Berryhill for being a friend and loaning out his blue house on the bay to every Tom Dick and Harry activist in the country

Patricia Callahan, the Jennifer Altman Foundation, and a special Unreasonable Woman for their generous financial support of my work and the zero discharge campaign. Without them the phone would be yanked and the truck hauled off.

Willy Fontenot for being a legendary environmental hero of the South and a constant friend

Gary Cohen for paying my lawyer and keeping me out of jail

Blackburn for being a friend and my lawyer even after I fired him

Bioneers for being a beacon in a storm. I aspire to your vision.

And finally to my kids, Ramona, Sarah, Goldie, David "Crockett," and Santanna. Without them I would have taken off for the moon a long time ago. Love and sweet dreams.